D1446929

Nazism in Central Germany

Monographs in German History

Volume 1

Osthandel and Ostpolitik: German Foreign Trade Policies in Eastern Europe from Bismarck to Adenauer
Robert Mark Spaulding

Volume 2

A Question of Priorities: Democratic Reform and Economic Recovery in Postwar Germany
Rebecca Boehling

Volume 3

From Recovery to Catastrophe: Municipal Stabilization and Political Crisis in Weimar Germany
Ben Lieberman

Volume 4

Nazism in Central Germany: The Brownshirts in 'Red' Saxony
Claus-Christian W. Szejnmann

Volume 5

The Church in the Second German Dictat
John Moses

Nazism in Central Germany: The Brownshirts in 'Red' Saxony

Claus-Christian W. Szejnmann

Berghahn Books
NEW YORK · OXFORD

First published in 1999 by

Berghahn Books

Editorial offices:
55 John Street, 3rd Floor, New York, NY 10038 USA
3, NewTec Place, Magdalen Road, Oxford OX4 1RE UK

Library of Congress Cataloging-in-Publication Data

Szejnmann, Claus-Christian W., 1965-
Nazism in central Germany : the brownshirts in 'red' Saxony / Claus-Christian W. Szejnmann.
p. cm.
Includes bibliographical references and index.
ISBN 1-57181-942-8 (alk. paper)
1. Saxony (Germany)—History—20th century. 2. National socialism—Germany—Saxony. 3. Communists—Germany—Saxony. 4. Fascism—Germany—Saxony. 5. Right and left (Political science)—Germany—Saxony. I. Title.
DD801.S352S94 1998
943'.21—dc21 98-49764
CIP

British Library Cataloguing in Publication Data
A catalogue record for this book is available from the British Library

Printed in the United States on acid-free paper

To Kate-Alice, with love

Contents

List of Tables and Figures

Tables

Figures

Acknowledgements

It would not have been possible to write this book without numerous helpful people. I would like to thank all my former teachers at Royal Holloway College who shaped my mind and contributed indirectly when I embarked on such a project, and discovered the joy of the academic profession. I am also grateful to all those who assisted me in the various archives and libraries I consulted. Several friends in Saxony helped me in some way or another and made several long research stays bearable: Kerstin and Wolfgang Kühne, Robert Beachy, Sabine Quednau, Evi Diendorf, Astrid Tschipke, Birgit Schöppe, Peggy Bachmann, and Familie Radespiel in Breitenhagen. Thanks also to the HH-gang Mutze, Stefan, Romeo and Jonathan, and Jürgina Binzen. Vanessa Cobb, Spencer Dalgliesh, Stuart Woodbridge, and particularly Pauline Brikci-Nigassa, kindly read through some parts or all of the manuscript (Robert Ojok helped with the map) and made valuable suggestions on the language front.

Thanks to my students and colleagues at Middlesex University, in particular to Cathie Carmichael, who has given me indispensable support and closely followed the various stages of this book. Mehmet Dikerdem and Martine Morris's friendship has made my work environment so much more enjoyable. I am also grateful to all the fellow 'Germanists' at the Modern German History seminar at the Institute of Historical Research in London, and also to Richard Bessel, Elizabeth Harvey, Helen Graham, Werner Bramke, Karl Heinrich Pohl, Simone Lässig, Jeremy Noakes, Oded Heilbronner, Michael Rudloff, Thomas Adam, Dirk Hänisch, Frank Snowden, Hans Mommsen and Richard Evans. In one way or another they have all helped me with this book. Jürgen Falter was extremely generous in sharing his Saxon NSDAP membership data for an evaluation in this book (with the consent of William Brustein). Conan Fischer and Detlef Mühlberger were both extremely considerate in their general support, practical help and encouragement over the years. In the final stages of this book I benefited greatly from the thoughtful and constructive advice of James Retallack and the efficient work of Barbara Newson (new editorial manager of Berghahn Books). Richard Overy, my former PhD supervisor, gave me confidence and inspiration, showed great interest in my work, and has been extremely helpful in every aspect.

I am also indebted to my parents, who gave me a great deal of love, faith and trust, and without whom my 'England experience' would not have been possible. Lastly, thank you Kate-Alice and Max Gabriel for brightening up my life and being so incredibly patient and understanding with my work.

Abbreviations and Glossary

ADGB	*Allgemeiner Deutscher Gewerkschaftsbund* (socialist federation of trade unions)
AH	*Amtshauptmannschaft* (administrative unit in Saxony)
ASP	*Alte Sozialdemokratische Partei* (Old Social Democratic Party)
ATSB	*Allgemeiner Turn- und Sportbund* (Workers' Gymnastic and Sports Union)
BA	Bundesarchiv Koblenz
BA DH	Bundesarchiv, Zwischenstelle, Dahlwitz-Hoppegarten
BDC	Berlin Document Center
ChVSt	*Chemnitzer Volksstimme*
CSVD	*Christlich sozialer Volksdient* (Christian Social People's Service)
DAF	*Deutsche Arbeitsfront* (German Labour Front)
DDP	*Deutsche Demokratische Partei* (German Democratic Party)
DNVP	*Deutschnationale Volkspartei* (German National People's Party)
DVFP	*Deutschvölkische Freiheitspartei* (German *Völkisch* Freedom Party)
DVP	*Deutsche Volkspartei* (German People's Party)
DVSTB	*Deutschvölkischer Schutz- und Trutzbund*
DVZ	*Dresdner Volkszeitung*
EK	Erich Kunz (personal file in BA DH)
ENAV	*Evangelisch-nationale Arbeitervereinigung* (Protestant Nationalist Workers' Association)
FK	*Der Freiheitskampf* (official NSDAP newspaper of *Gau* Saxony; first published on 1 August 1930)

Gau	Administrative region of the Nazi Party organisation
Gestapo	*Geheime Staatspolizei* (Secret State Police)
HJ	*Hitlerjugend* (Hitler Youth)
KdF	*Kraf durch Freude* (Strength through Joy)
KH	*Kreishauptmannschaft* (largest administrative unit in Saxony)
KPD	*Kommunistische Partei Deutschlands* (German Communist Party)
Landtag	State parliament
LVZ	*Leipziger Volkszeitung*
MdI	*Ministerium des Innern* (Ministry of the Interior)
MSPD	*Mehrheits-Sozialdemokratische Partei Deutschlands* (Majority Social Democratic Party)
NSBO	*Nationalsozialistische Betriebszellenorganisation* (National Socialist Factory Cell Organisation)
NSDAP	*Nationalsozialistische Deutsche Arbeiterpartei* (National Socialist German Workers' Party)
NSFB	*Nationalsozialistische Freiheitsbewegung* (National Socialist Freedom Movement)
NSfS	*Der Nationale Sozialist für Sachsen* (The National Socialist for Saxony; official Nazi newspaper for Saxony between the end of 1926 [in print since March 1926] and December 1928; published by Straßer's *'Kampf-Verlag'* in Berlin; predecessor of the SB)
OPG	Oberstes Parteigericht (highest party court)
Reichstag	National parliament in Berlin
RPW-II	Second ballots of the elections for the Reich President
SA	*Sturmabteilung* (Stormtroopers)
SAP	Sozialistische Arbeiter Partei (Socialist Workers' Party)
SäStKa	*Sächsische Staatskanzlei* (Saxon state chancellery)
SB	*Der Sächsische Beobachter* (successor of the *NSfS* and official NSDAP newspaper in Saxony between January 1929 and June 1930. Published by Straßer's *'Kampf-Verlag'*)
SED	*Sozialistische Einheitspartei Deutschlands* (Socialist Unity Party)
SI	*Sächsische Industrie* (weekly newspaper of the VSI)
SlSch	Sammlung Schumacher (collection in the BA)
SLV	*Sächsisches Landvolk* (Saxon Landvolk; successor of the *Sächsischer Landbund* [Saxon Rural League] –

	which was affiliated with the DNVP – in 1928; officially independent)
Sopade	*Deutschland-Bericht der Sozialdemokratischen Partei Deutschlands.* 1934–1940 (Report about Germany by the German Social Democratic Party, 1934–1940
SPD	*Sozialdemokratische Partei Deutschlands* (Social Democratic Party of Germany)
SS	*Schutzstaffeln* (elite Nazi organisation)
STA D	Staatsarchiv Dresden
STA L	Staatsarchiv Leipzig
StA L	Stadtarchiv Leipzig
StDR	*Statistik des Deutschen Reichs*
StJbDR	*Statistisches Jahrbuch des Deutschen Reichs*
StJbSa	*Statistisches Jahrbuch für den Freistaat Sachsen*
SVB	*Sächsisches Volksblatt*
SVBl	*Sächsisches Verwaltungsblatt* (Saxon administrative publication)
USPD	*Unabhängige Sozialdemokratische Partei Deutschlands* (Independent Social Democratic Party of Germany)
VB	*Völkischer Beobachter* (official NSDAP newspaper)
VdSL	*Verhandlungen des Sächsischen Landtages* (minutes of the Saxon state parliament)
VNR	*Volksnationale Reichsvereinigung* (Reich Nationalist Alliance)
VRP	*Reichspartei für Volksrecht und Aufwertung* (Reich Party for People's Rights and Reevaluation)
VSI	*Verband Sächsischer Industrieller* (Association of the Saxon Industrialists)
WP	*Wirtschaftspartei* (Business Party)
Wp	*Wahlperiode* (period between elections)
ZAS	Zeitungsausschnittsammlung (newspaper clippings collection)
ZSäStLA	*Zeitschrift des Sächsischen Statistischen Landesamtes*

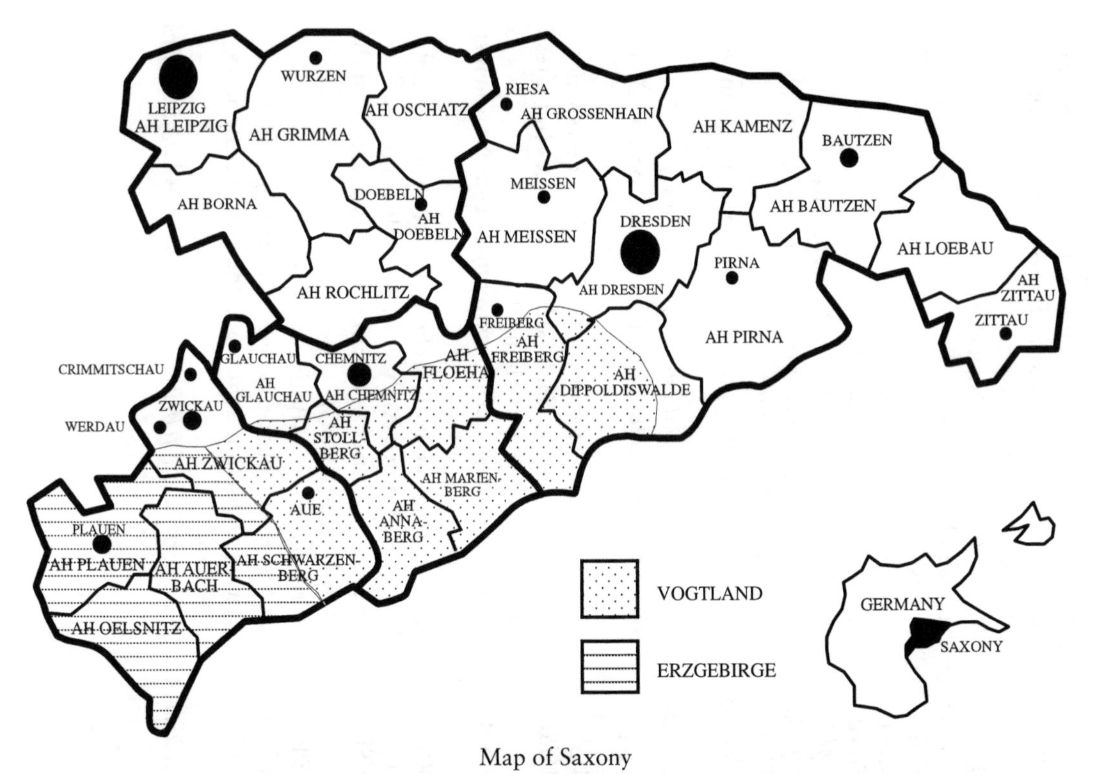

Map of Saxony

Introduction

The Fall of the Berlin Wall and its Link with Nazism

> ... The standpoint of the government in Bonn – that World War II has not yet ended – is tantamount to a call for a licence for militaristic provocation and civil war measures. Such imperialistic policy disguised as anti-communism represents a continuation of the aggressive goals of fascist German imperialism at the time of the Third Reich ...
>
> (Part of the Resolution of the GDR Council of Ministers, 12 August 1961, which explained the building of the wall in Berlin)

> Mauer ins Museum!
>
> (Put the Wall into the Museum! Slogan during a demonstration in the GDR in 1989)

The existence and legitimacy of the GDR was based on its claim of being an anti-fascist state. Nazism was specifically ignored in the local and regional history of the GDR, as contradictory day-to-day aspects of conformity, partial loyalty and resistance would have challenged and damaged the dogmatic Marxist interpretation of fascism and the 'glorious' anti-fascist activities of the Communists. The fall of the Berlin Wall in November 1989 interrupted the totalitarian control over the access and interpretation of sources.

Generations of historians have tried to explain how the collapse of republican government and Hitler's rise to power was possible, and how the Nazis managed to become a mass movement in nearly every region, town and even tiny village in western Germany.[1] This book claims to be different on several accounts. It fills one of the enormous gaps that remain in our historical knowledge about central and eastern Germany.[2] Little research had been conducted on Nazism in Saxony before 1989, and thereafter this has changed only slowly.[3] This is regrettable because Saxony was not only the Nazi *Gau* with by far the highest population, and most NSDAP members, but also one of the earliest strongholds of the movement. Thus it was crucial for the rise of the Nazi party on the national level. Furthermore, Saxony's background as the most industrialised and urbanised region in Germany and as the cradle of the labour movement makes the development of the brownshirts in 'red' Saxony a particularly interesting case study. By contrast, nearly all regional studies of Nazism have focused on agricultural or semi-industrialised rural areas and emphasised Nazism's middle-class constituency. The only comprehensive study about the heavily industrialised Ruhr region in western Germany is in many respects out of date.[4] However, the fact that the Nazis did particularly well in Saxony in recruiting members and gaining votes in elections, did not necessarily mean that they gained overproportional support from workers.

Unlike most conventional studies about Nazism, this study does not focus predominantly on the Nazi party, but deals instead with the complex relationship between Saxon society and Nazism. It traces contacts and similarities, but also conflicts and differences between both. It raises questions as to how Saxon society shaped Nazism and was itself shaped by Nazism; and it tries to comprehend why Nazism thrived and was able to mobilise a powerful mass constituency in some areas, while this was not the case in other settings. The investigation covers a time-span – roughly between the end of the nineteenth century to the period immediately after the Second World War – that bridges several distinct periods of modern German history, allowing us to analyse important issues concerning continuity and breaks with the past. The development of distinct mentalities and modes of behaviour by individuals, groups, clubs and parties – and their relationship with Nazism – are observed in a changing environment, providing a synthesis of the phenomenon of Nazism in the context of social, cultural, economic and political developments.

To explain Nazism, this book also provides a portrait of Saxon society in the first half of the twentieth century. The over-emphasis of the hegemony of Prussia has led to a narrowing of our understanding of the course of German history and the neglect of important regions like Saxony. However, Saxony underwent its own experiences and developments which were often linked with the Reich – and Prussia – but frequently it also took alternative routes in the social, economic and political spheres. Furthermore, Gerhard A. Ritter has argued that Saxon history provides a special kind of mirror (*Brennspiegel*) that highlights central problems of German historiography in new ways.[5]

Saxony provides a particularly fascinating case study as it entered the twentieth century with a striking imbalance between a long tradition of economic modernisation and a strong working-class movement, and a particularly reactionary political system. This social landscape was marked by extraordinary tensions and polarisations which created two time bombs that exploded after the First World War. Saxony was hit harder by the economic depression in the interwar period – in particular in 1923 and then from 1929 onwards – than any other region in Germany, because it had failed to modernise its economic structure in the decades before 1914. In the political sphere, a poisonous legacy from before the war continued to permeate Saxon society after 1918. The revolution catapulted the organised working class to power and the Social Democrats carried out a remarkable programme of democratic reforms against the vehement opposition of the majority of the bourgeoisie in the first five years of the Republic. Two completely different visions of how society should look confronted each other in a Republic which allowed enormous scope for development.

A survey that covers such a long period and is restricted in size cannot attempt to cover all aspects of society. Nevertheless, this study tries to capture some of the major tendencies, beliefs and views in Saxon society and explain how Nazism grew and operated in this environment. To do this the author has used a variety of conceptual and methodological approaches. As to the structure of this book, we highlight important features and developments by looking through several 'windows' at Saxon society, rather than following a convential chronological approach. The first chapter introduces Saxony and its people, and the main social, economic and political features and developments in the state. The economic survey accounts for Saxony's early industrialisation, its failure to modernise its traditional industries at the end of the nineteenth century, the devastating effects of the First World War, hyperinflation and the slump, and the development of its economy during the Nazi dictatorship. The overview of the social and political development in Saxony highlights the strong tensions and divisions that existed between organised labour and large parts of the bourgeoisie within the state. A survey of the origins and development of the Nazi movement in the region rounds up the introductory chapter.

The following three chapters look at the relationship between the Saxon population and Nazism from different angles. All deal with the divisions, contradictions and problems which Saxon society was facing due to the uneven process of modernisation and how this produced opportunities and constraints for the Nazis.[6] Chapter 2 focuses on the role of Nazi propaganda and the economic crisis for the rise and success of Nazism. It is surprising how little both of these crucial factors have been scrutinised at regional and local level and to what extent many historians have taken their significance for granted. This section attempts to convey the atmosphere at the time, explores how people reacted during a period of increasing hardship, uncertainty and anxiety, and observes how the political players responded to the crisis and to what extent they captured the imagination of the various groups in Saxon society.

Chapters 3 and 4 stress the division of Saxon society into two milieus and embark on a new approach in understanding the course of modern German history. Today most experts agree that the NSDAP managed to attract voters and members from all groups in society. Although middle-class groups played the most prominent role, Nazism also attracted a substantial stratum of workers.[7] These findings challenge the traditional view presented by Theodor Geiger and Seymor Martin Lipset that the Nazi movement was a 'middle class' phenomenon.[8] By focusing on the class divisions of German society, generations of experts restricted the Nazi constituency to the middle classes and became ignorant about the existence and motivation of other Nazi supporters.

The concept of milieu offers a wider conceptual framework than class analysis (or other factors such as religion, urban or rural residence, age and professional status) and allows new insights in areas class-analysis failed to grasp: to explain why so many Germans, who were divided by so many other things, united to support Nazism; and to explain why the brownshirts were successful in working-class Saxony.

Several decades ago Mario Rainer Lepsius explained the remarkable stability of the German party system from the beginning of the German Empire to the late 1920s by drawing attention to the deep roots parties had struck in various social structures, which he called 'milieus'.[9] Yet, whereas Lepsius identified four different milieus (conservative, liberal, Social Democratic and Catholic), more recently Karl Rohe has identified three even wider camps (*Lager:* conservative-liberal, Catholic and socialist) which fragmented the German party system.[10] This survey uses the term milieu to describe a strong centralisation of a specific culture in the form of mentalities and ways of life, which were linked to political orientation (also see chapter 3 (i)). A milieu is part of society. Hence it is not a constant entity but subject to change, and emerges and disappears. Extending Lepsius's basic thesis, it is possible to argue that there were numerous milieus which differed in size and often overlapped.

Chapters 3 and 4 focus on the two basic milieus in Saxony: the socialist milieu (mainly based on organised labour) and the nationalist milieu. Both milieus can be broken down into further sub-milieus: for instance, the Social Democratic milieu and the Communist milieu within the former; the anti-Semitic milieu and the conservative-elite milieu within the latter. Overall, it appears that mentalities were more important for the nationalist milieu, while ways of life were more significant for the socialist milieu. The division of Saxon society into the socialist and nationalist milieus is possibly due to the special polarisation between left and right and the predominance of Protestantism in the state (hence there existed no strong Catholic milieu). Whereas this model helps to explain the political behaviour of Saxons in the first half of the twentieth century, we are not suggesting that static and clear-cut divisions within Saxon society existed. Indeed, both milieus were dynamic and changed over time. For example, within both milieus one could observe a moderation or radicalisation of aims and activities, and an increasing or decreasing number of followers. There were also crucial overlaps and interchanges between both.

The discussion about the rise of the Nazis in the socialist milieu looks at the NSDAP's ability to become a mass party in an area with an exceptionally large industrial work force and a powerful workers' movement. The chapter about the rise of the Nazis in the nationalist milieu investigates the nationalist and right-wing culture – its clubs, organisations, celebrations, attitudes towards education and religion, press and parties, which were normally dominated by the bourgeoisie – its relationship with the Nazi movement, and its increasing shift to the right in the final years of the Republic. Both chapters also look at what happened to these milieus during the dictatorship.

Chapter 5 provides a sociological profile of the Saxon Nazi movement: its leaders, members (by Detlef Mühlberger) and voters (by Dirk Hänisch). Two leading experts in their field present sophisticated computer-based analyses to round off the broad synthesis of the book. The final conclusion summarises specific features of Nazism in Saxony, but also comes to wider conclusions and reassesses the relationship between German society and Nazism. Finally, twenty-three documents round up the study. They reflect on some of the major themes of the book in more detail, and will enable the reader to follow the argument at first hand and from a different angle.

The broad conceptual framework of the book made it impossible to include every aspect which would have been of interest. Some readers might also be surprised that the Nazis' racial policies – and in particular anti-Semitism – do not assume centre stage in this study. Recently it has been convincingly argued that the central feature of the Third Reich was that the Nazis were 'bent on creating a barbaric, racially-based utopia',[11] and the role of 'ordinary Germans' in the Holocaust has become the focus of attention. However, the main thrust of this study deals with the background and rise of Nazism, i.e., why did anyone from a comparatively modern society support such a radical and brutal movement? and, beyond that, how did Nazism gain mass support?[12] Building upon this, the book analyses a number of crucial factors in the relationship between Saxon society and Nazism in terms of continuity and change that help to explain the overall stability of the dictatorship. Although the Nazis' racial objectives and extreme anti-Semitism were crucial for some individuals and groups, neither aspects played a decisive role in securing mass support for the Nazis in Saxony before 1933 and during the dictatorship.[13] The final point the reader should note at this point, is that although there are frequent comparisons between the situation in Saxony and that in other regions in Germany, this study cannot claim to be of a comparative nature. The lack of space and the shortage of similar studies of this kind in other regions has not made this feasible. However, Saxony itself was far from being a monolithic entity. Although the state constituted a comparatively defined region with a long history, it possessed a variety of distinct smaller rural and urban regions, which made the constant awareness of regional differences and similarities within the state one of the most challenging and exciting tasks of this analysis.

Notes

1. E.g., see G. Nestler and H. Ziegler, eds., *Die Pfalz Unterm Hakenkreuz. Eine Deutsche Provinz während der nationalsozialistischen Terrorherrschaft*, Landau, 1993; G. Paul, *Die NSDAP des Saargebietes 1920–1935. Der Verspätete Aufstieg der NSDAP in der katholisch-proletarischen Provinz*, Saarbrücken, 1987; W.S. Allen, *The Nazi Seizure of Power*, London 2nd ed., 1984; G. Pridham, *Hitler's Rise to Power. The Nazi Movement in Bavaria*, London, 1973; J. Noakes, *The Nazi Party in Lower Saxony 1921–1933*, London, 1971.
2. See C.-C. W. Szejnmann, 'Review Article: The Missing Pieces are "Coming Home". Nazism in Central Germany', *German History*, 15 (3) (1997), 395–410.
3. One significant exception is B. Lapp, *Revolution from the Right. Politics, Class, and the Rise of Nazism in Saxony, 1919–1933*, New Jersey, 1997. Also see R. Pommerin, ed., *Dresden unterm Hakenkreuz*, Cologne, 1998.
4. See W. Böhnke, *Die NSDAP im Ruhrgebiet, 1920–1933*, Bonn, 1974.
5. G.A. Ritter, 'Wahlen und Wahlpolitik im Königreich Sachsen 1867–1914', in S. Lässig and K.H. Pohl, eds., *Sachsen im Kaiserreich. Politik, Wirtschaft und Gesellschaft im Umbruch*, Weimar, 1997, 29.
6. In this survey the term modernisation is used to describe 'a recognisable process of capital-driven social, economic, political, and cultural change occurring at differential rates over the past 200 years across Europe.' See H. Graham and J. Labanyi, eds., *Spanish Cultural Studies. An Introduction. The Struggle for Modernity*, Oxford, 1995. 10f.
7. See especially C.J. Fischer, ed., *The Rise of National Socialism and the Working Classes in Weimar Germany*, Oxford, 1996
8. T. Geiger, 'Panik im Mittelstand', *Die Arbeit*, 7 (1930), 643–52; S.M. Lipset, ' "Fascism" – Left, Right, and Center', in idem, ed., *Political Man. The Social Bases of Politics*, New York, 1960, 127–79.
9. M.R. Lepsius, 'Parteiensystem und Sozialstruktur: Zum Problem der Demokratisierung der deutschen Gesellschaft', in G.A. Ritter, ed., *Die deutschen Parteien vor 1918*, Cologne, 1973, 56–80.
10. See K. Rohe, 'German Elections and Party Systems in Historical and Regional Perspective: An Introduction', in idem, ed., *Elections, Parties and Political Traditions. Social Foundations of German Parties and Party Systems, 1867–1987*, Oxford, 1990, 1–25.
11. M. Burleigh and W. Wippermann, *The Racial State, Germany 1933–1945*, Cambridge, 2nd. repr., 1992, Foreword.
12. The book is a substantially revised and expanded version of my Ph.D 'The Rise of the Nazis in Saxony between 1921 and 1933', London University, 1994.

13. Our knowledge of Saxony during the Nazi dictatorship is still extremely limited, not least due to the destruction of many primary sources during the Second World War (see Bibliography). This survey only attempts to cover some of the many white spots that remain.

Chapter 1

From 'Red' Kingdom to Brown Dictatorship: Saxony from *Kaiserreich* to Nazism

> It is true that Saxony is only a small state, and its population only just surpasses that of the city of Greater-Berlin. Nevertheless, it was destined to play an important role for Germany and for the proletariat through its location at the heart of Germany, through the sharp confrontations between the economic and political contrasts within the population, and through the particular schooling of its working class.
>
> (W. Fabian, *Klassenkampf um Sachsen*, Löbau, 1930, 7)

(i) The Land and Its People

The origins of Saxony and its people go back to when the land was conquered by the German King Heinrich I in 929. The merging of Germans and Slavs over the next centuries led to the emergence of a new Germanic tribe, the Saxons. It was crucial for the further development of the Saxons that one dynasty – the Wettins (Wettiner) – ruled the region for more than eight hundred years. As Saxony was one of the heartlands of the Reformation, the predominant religion was Protestantism.[1] The large state of Saxony (*Kursachsen*) that had dominated the middle German region during the fifteenth century was smashed at the Congress of Vienna in 1815, which reduced Saxony to a secondary political power. The Wettins' alliance with Napoleon cost Saxony dearly and only a little more than a third of its former territory and two-thirds of its people remained as the Kingdom of Saxony, whilst the rest went to Prussia. Whereas the boundaries of Saxony have hardly changed since 1815, the political framework has changed several times. After Saxony picked the losing side in a decisive war again – this time in its alliance with the Habsburg Empire against Prussia in 1866 – the Kingdom of Saxony was incorporated into the Prussian-led North German Confederation and soon after into the German Empire. Henceforth, Saxony's sovereignty was heavily compromised by Prussian influence. The November Revolution in 1918 swept away the Wettin dynasty, and the Kingdom became the Free State of Saxony (*Freistaat Sachsen*) during the Weimar Republic.[2] After 1933 the state was brought into line with the centralised Nazi dictatorship. After the Second World War Saxony first became part of the Soviet occupation zone, and from 1949 on it was incorporated into another totalitarian project, the communist East German Republic (GDR). In 1952 the Saxon state was dissolved due to the creation of districts, but recently – after the re-unification of East and West Germany in 1990 – Saxony emerged as a new state within the Federal Republic of Germany.

During the Weimar Republic, the period with which we are predominantly concerned, Saxony was located in central Germany and was its fifth largest state (for the following see the map on page XVI). The Erzgebirge, a mountain region and the backbone of Saxony, stretches along the south and provides a natural border with Czechoslovakia. Leaving the Erzgebirge the landscape becomes gradually less hilly until it flattens into the plains in the north. Saxony's capital, Dresden (619,157 inhabitants), was the seat of parliament and administration. Other sizeable cities included Leipzig (679,159 inhabitants), Chemnitz (333,851), Plauen (111,436), Zwickau (80,358), and Bautzen (40,335). Saxony was divided into five administrative regions, the *Kreishauptmannschaften* (KH). Each KH itself was further divided into smaller units: twenty-eight districts called *Amtshauptmannschaften* (AH), and twenty-one free towns.[3] Excluding the city states, Saxony was by far the most densely populated German state. Its five million people comprised 8 percent of the German population, although its territory only covered 3.2 percent of the Republic. Whereas on average 134.2 people inhabited a square kilometre in Germany, the figure in Saxony was 333.[4] Saxony was also the most urbanised province in Germany: 34.9 percent of the population lived in cities of more than 100,000 inhabitants and only 23.9 percent in communities of less than 2,000 people (the corresponding figures for the Reich were 26.8 percent and 35.6 percent).[5] Industrial and agricultural regions were often intermixed and led to the development of many industrial villages.

Whereas Saxony's political influence in Germany had been declining since the late Middle Ages, its economic development continued to have an important impact on other German regions. Saxony had a long history of economic traditions and skills, frequently exported outside the region by diligent Saxons. After silver mining started in Freiberg in the twelfth century, the mining of other ores – including coal – slowly spread over the whole Erzgebirge. This led to an early development of metal production and spread advanced fiscal methods. Profit fluctuations in mining made people expand their horizons and look for alternative forms of income – e.g., wood making, flax spinning, wool and cotton spinning and weaving, knitting, lace making, glass blowing, watch making and the production of musical instruments – which started to spread throughout the region. The region's economic development was greatly assisted by Saxony's favourable economic location at the heart of Europe, and the long tradition of a free peasantry who frequently made additional income from cottage industries and mining. It is no wonder then that although the textile industry was Saxony's most prominent sector at the time of our investigation, the state possessed an extremely mixed and evenly developed economic landscape.

(ii) The Economy: The Burden of Early Industrialisation and Traditional Industries

Saxony was the first region to industrialise in Germany and one of the earliest industrialised regions in continental Europe.[6] Like Belgium, the region followed immediately in the steps of the British industrial revolution and completed this process by 1840, a time when Prussia had only just begun to industrialise in earnest. As in England, Saxony's industrial revolution was based on the textile industry. At the beginning of the nineteenth century Saxony was Germany's centre of the first mechanised cotton mills, whose machinery was imported from England, and later the town of Chemnitz assumed a pioneering role in machine building. Whereas Chemnitz gained the nickname of the 'Saxon

Manchester', Saxony itself – analogous to the reputation of England as the 'workshop of the world' – was called the 'workshop of the German Empire'.

Hubert Kiesewetter links the region's early and speedy industrialisation with the loss of fertile land to Prussia in 1815, which made Saxony dependent on food imports and forced it to increase industrial production in order to finance this.[7] A rapid population growth after 1815 continued to foster industrialisation. In turn, industrialisation led to the creation of one of the most dense railway networks in Europe, and the rapid growth of a whole number of large and medium-sized industrial towns. Nevertheless, in the mid-nineteenth century Saxony lost its position as the leading industrial region to the Ruhr region, which emerged as the industrial powerhouse of Germany. Saxony's lack of large coal fields made all the difference and became an increasing handicap to its economic development. Early industrialisation also brought several disadvantages in the long run. Saxony's old economic structure and traditions tended to make its industries less flexible and responsive to new trends or towards building up new industrial sectors. Additionally, Saxony's export-orientated industries reacted sensitively to world market fluctuations. When Saxony was hit particularly hard by the depression at the turn of the twentieth century, it was clear that the problems associated with the 'early start' were becoming more serious.

The First World War and its outcome dramatically accelerated these tendencies and added new problems for Saxony's economic development.[8] Its economy was hit particularly hard by the restrictions on trade during and after the war. In the 1920s Saxony managed to make good most of the lost markets in the East by exporting more to the West; however, these new markets were increasingly closed due to protectionism after 1929. Competition in foreign markets was growing too and the 'industrialising countries' were catching up, especially in the consumer goods industries, the backbone of Saxony's economy. Due to the loss of German territory and the creation of new sovereign states in Central Europe, Saxony suddenly also found itself at the periphery of Germany, bordering onto Poland and Czechoslovakia. Cut off from the Silesian coal mines and dependent on expensive Ruhr coal (and high transport costs), it faced a great economic burden. Its small and medium-sized industries found it more and more difficult to compete against economies of scale that were emerging elsewhere.

Saxony came out of the war facing a deep-seated structural crisis as an early industrialiser that was struggling to keep up with the continuing demands for rationalisation and efficiency. This was most evident in Saxony's textile industry. Generally speaking, the textile industry was an old staple industry that had slowly lost its importance during the industrialisation process. An investigation in the 1890s had also found technically backward and small-scale Saxon cotton mills that were clinging on to cheap labour and water energy and had missed the transition to a modern, large-scale, English-type machine-system.[9] Saxony itself was financially too weak to carry out fundamental changes in its economic framework, and financial resources at the Reich level were too limited. The consequences were disastrous for the region. The state followed the lurching economic course of the Reich after the war, but was normally hit earlier, harder and longer by economic downturns.

During the 1920s Saxony was divided into several economic regions. Southwestern Saxony (Chemnitz, Erzgebirge, Vogtland) was the most industrialised part of the state and possessed numerous industrial villages.[10] Its urban centres – in particular Chemnitz, Zwickau and Plauen – produced textiles, machinery and vehicles, but also a variety of other products. Most of the large-scale factories in Saxony were in the northwest – in and around Leipzig – the most significant industrial town in the state. Leipzig possessed a versatile industry, was a centre of the publishing industry, and held the largest commercial fair in Germany. Another industrial region centred around Dresden and the valley of the Elbe. Besides being Saxony's administrative centre, it consisted mainly of the machine, metal, tobacco and textile industries. Leipzig and Dresden were also seats of the graphic trade, fine-mechanical and semi-luxuries of national significance. Finally, in the east there were the plains of the northern Oberlausitz, Saxony's largest agricultural region; but there was also a prominent textile industry in the hilly Niederlausitz.

If we measure the level of industrialisation by comparing the percentage of the working population employed in industry and handicraft to the percentage working in agriculture, Saxony was the most industrialised state in Weimar Germany. Saxon workers comprised 54.1 percent of the working population compared to 36.9 percent in the Reich. The widespread textile industry explained the high proportion of female industrial workers in the state: one-third of all women were employed in industry compared to one-fifth in the Reich.[11]

Saxony's industrial structure was dominated by small-scale and medium-scale industry, while large-scale industry was comparatively unimportant. This also accounts for the great variety of products that were exported from Saxony. Looking at the most important industrial sectors in Saxony, the number of old and traditional industries is apparent. For instance, nearly 92,000 Saxons still worked in the cottage industry in the late 1920s. With the exception of the vehicle industry, Saxony was not well represented in new industries such as the chemical or electrical industries. The textile industry – Saxony's biggest industrial sector – employed 13.9 percent of the whole working population (3,024,969).[12] The state was the centre of Germany's textile industry and employed more than one-third of all Germans in this sector. The other major local industries were the machine, apparatus, and vehicle industry (employing 6.2 percent of the workforce), clothing industry (5.5 percent), building industry (5.1 percent), food industry, production of iron and metal goods, and paper and publication. The consumer goods industry clearly dominated over the producer goods industry. Basically, Saxony imported raw materials from which it produced manufactured goods which were then exported to other regions in Germany and the whole world. Consequently, more than any region in Germany, Saxony depended on exports and the world market.

Saxony never really experienced a sustained and deep-rooted period of economic stability after the First World War. Most importantly, in 1923 it was hit particularly hard during the hyperinflation, and in 1929 its economy entered a crisis more severe than in any other region in Germany (also see document 15 and chapter 2).[13] What made Saxony's economic crisis so particular was the enormous speed with which it unfolded and the scale of its impact. Saxony's rate of unemployment illustrates this better than any other individual statistic. The Saxon metal industry had one of the lowest unemployment rates in Germany in 1928, but from mid-1929 it suddenly shot up far above all other states.[14] Developments in the textile industry and building trade were very similar. Generally speaking, whereas Saxony had one of the lowest unemployment rates in Germany between 1927 and 1928, it exceeded all other regions by the middle of 1929 and remained the highest until September 1937.[15] There were about 690,000 registered unemployed in Saxony in the middle of 1932. These were roughly 23 percent of the total workforce. The 'real' figures, including the unemployed who were not registered, were substantially higher. Chemnitz, Plauen, Dresden and Leipzig had some of the highest unemployment rates amongst German cities.[16] Saxony's dependence on the import of raw materials and the export of manufactured goods proved disastrous and made the region a 'storm-centre of the trade cycle' (*Wetterwinkel der Konjunktur*). Between 1929 and 1932 its textile exports to the U.S.A. dropped by 56.1 percent and that of textile machines by 83 percent.[17] The severity of the crisis and its repercussions for the Saxons became evident from other statistics too: the number of bankruptcies per capita in Saxony was far above the Reich average between 1926 and 1932.[18] In 1929 Saxony had fewer live births than any other state, and the second highest male suicide rate in the country.[19] Saxony was also the only large state where fewer people married in 1931 than in 1913.[20]

During the Nazi dictatorship the economic situation continued to be worse in Saxony than in the rest of Germany at least until 1936. The hope of Saxony's industrialists for an investment boost from the Reich did not materialise. Saxony's border location with Czechoslovakia – a potential enemy of Germany – and the backward structure of the local industry prevented the Nazis from making big investments in the region.[21] The economic turning-point came in 1936 when Saxony became fully integrated in the Nazis' Four-Year-Plan. Rearmament encouraged a modernisation and change in the structure of the local economy, and led to a rapid decline in unemployment. There was a trend towards large-scale companies, and a relative decline in production and employment in the consumer goods industry – especially textiles – in favour of new industrial sectors. The employment in machine, steel and vehicle production rose from 75,049 to 231,408 and that in electrical engineering from 19,226 to 53,985 between 1933 and 1939.[22] These developments also enhanced the differences between the various economic regions and sectors. For instance, the region of Leipzig with its chemical industry and machine building thrived due to rearmament, while the old textile region of Crimmitschau and Meerane fell behind because it depended on export and was not integrated into the armaments boom.

The changes in Saxony's industrial structure accelerated further during the Second World War. The state became one of the most important centres of armaments production in Germany after 1942, because the restructuring of its economy released considerable reserves and its remote location seemed a natural protection against Allied bombing raids.[23] Werner Bramke and Ulrich Heß argued that the economic changes during Nazi rule laid the foundation for Saxony's economic lead in the GDR.[24] Certain developments in economic 'modernisation' during the Third Reich, however, were more than offset by the destructive results of Nazi rule: around 20 percent of the total industrial capacity of what became the Soviet zone of occupation was destroyed during the war.[25] The railway network was torn apart, and Leipzig, Chemnitz, Plauen – and of course Dresden – suffered great destruction and high numbers of human casualties. Furthermore, Saxony was hit particularly hard by Soviet dismantlement: 801 Saxon companies – nearly half of all dismantled companies in the Soviet zone of occupation – were dismantled by May 1946.[26]

The collapse of the Third Reich sparked off a whole range of new developments in Saxony, including significant changes in the population structure. Whereas the overall population remained around 5.5 million before and after the war, by October 1947 this included nearly one million displaced Germans from the East – mainly from Silesia and Bohemia – who had settled in the state.[27] Most of the new arrivals were integrated into the local economy, but many also rebuilt their traditional trade, which led to a change in Saxony's economic structure. There were changes in gender relations too. The SED's attempts to integrate as many women as possible into the economy slowly improved the situation of working women[28] and was a major break with the Nazis' reactionary policies towards the female sex. Additionally, the social composition of the industrial elite changed due to the nationalisation of industries, demilitarisation and denazification. The previous owners – who often spanned several generations of family business – were quickly replaced by working-class cadres who were then replaced by university cadres from the mid-1950s.[29] By that time, Saxon society had changed dramatically, when compared with that of the early 1930s.

(iii) Politics and Society: Hatreds and Divisions

The most striking phenomenon in Saxon society between the 'dual revolutions' in the late eighteenth century (French political revolution and British industrial revolution) and the end of the First World War was the contradiction between economic progress and political stagnation. Economic modernisation led to negative side-effects – particularly for the masses – and political backwardness caused a growing frustration among those who were excluded from the decision-making process. The revolution in Paris in July 1830 triggered off an entire year of unrest in Saxony, which was fuelled by unemployment and the reactionary political system.[30] Only under enormous pressure did the Saxon government introduce wide-ranging reforms, including a constitution and a modern and central administration, whose main characteristics remained intact until 1918.[31] However, frequent destruction of machinery continued, and small producers and craftsmen began to form a democratic movement as a result of the competition they suffered from a modern manufacturing sector. During the 1848/49 revolution Saxony gained the reputation of a stronghold of radicalism, and an emerging working-class movement allied with bourgeois radicalism. Their mutual hatred of authoritarian Prussia led to a long-lasting alliance until Saxony was incorporated into the Prussian-led North German Confederation in 1867.[32]

Prussian domination was an important turning-point for Saxony because it restricted further development of its society along the lines of its mighty northern neighbour. Although initially it led to some political reforms – most notably the introduction of general manhood suffrage for the elections to the North German Confederation – the long-term influence was not progressive. Prussia's traditions of militarism and a strong monarchy started to make an impact on Saxon society. Berlin also put pressure on Dresden to take a tough stance against any opposition to the state, particularly that coming from the workers' movement. However, Prussia worked hand in hand with like-minded Saxon governments who often pressed for even more reactionary policies than Berlin.[33] For half a century the Saxon government hampered the development of the labour movement on the basis of its restrictive Law for Associations and Assembly from 1850. The SPD (Social Democratic Party of Germany) also faced great disadvantages in the elections to the Saxon Landtag. Whereas the elections to the Reichstag were based on general manhood suffrage, the state elections excluded half of those who were eligible to vote in Reichstag elections and favoured rural constituencies.[34]

Despite all these handicaps the Saxon Social Democrats resiliently continued to grow more dynamic than in any other state and used the general manhood suffrage during Reichstag elections to mobilise voters. Indeed, the Saxon SPD managed to become the largest party in a German state for the first time when it polled 35.5 percent of the vote in the 1874 Reichstag elections, and continued to win the highest percentage of votes for its national party in every election to the German parliament before 1912. The local Social Democrats were thriving on the widespread problems caused by industrialisation. For instance, machine looms pushed more than 40,000 workers out of cotton weaving in the textile towns of Glauchau and Meerane between 1863 and 1880.[35] Both towns developed into some of the first bastions of the German workers' movement.

The SPD's success in turn rallied all other political forces. The electoral law for the state elections from 1868 fostered a sharp political polarisation between the 'parties of order' and the 'party of subversion' (SPD) because there were no run-off elections. The former included traditional agrarian elites and the new industrial forces, and stretched from the Conservatives over National Liberals to left-wing liberal groups. They all tended to unite behind one candidate to prevent the victory of a Social Democrat in electoral districts where the SPD was expected to do well. This political polarisation led to a gradual disappearance of a left-wing liberalism in the middle, and was further enhanced due to the negligible role of the Catholic Centre Party, which played a crucial moderating function in other German states.

When the Social Democrats still managed to increase the number of their seats in the Upper House of the Landtag, the traditional elites and bourgeoisie joined forces to introduce a three-class voting system in 1896, which was even more repressive than its Prussian model. The Saxon king conceded that the socialist movement had the advantage of uniting the bourgeois forces and rallying it behind the government.[36] In no other German state had the electoral law been restricted to this extent during the German Empire and the Saxon Social Democrats described their state as a 'playground of reaction' (*Probierland der Reaktion*): whilst their colleagues started to take up seats in other state parliaments, they went on to lose all of their seats again by 1901.[37] Two years later – during the 1903 Reichstag election – the anachronism of Saxony's reactionary electoral law became blatantly clear when the local SPD won its greatest ever election victory with 58.8 percent of the vote and twenty-two of the twenty-three mandates. This gained Saxony the reputation of the 'red Kingdom'.

The emergence of mass politics crystallised the tensions caused by modernisation and the backward political system. The strike of the textile workers in Crimmitschau (AH Zwickau) in 1903/4 developed into a symbolic conflict between workers and employers throughout Germany, and in 1905/6 there were mass demonstrations for electoral reform. There were other signs of social strain, too: at the turn of the century Saxony had an over proportional number of suicides, a high number of emigrants, and one of the highest number of illegitimate births in Germany.[38] Chemnitz and Plauen had the greatest housing shortage of all large towns in Germany, and in textile towns such as Werdau more than one-third of all infants died in their first year (see also document 1).[39]

Meanwhile the elite failed to come up with adequate answers to the 'social question'. When in mid-nineteenth century Saxony some bourgeois reformers emphasised the positive effects of industrialisation, seeing new factories as providing the proletariat with more stable employment, they overlooked the disastrous consequences of unemployment and atrocious working and living conditions. It was not surprising that they failed to attract the proletariat politically. The Protestant Church also remained passive and regarded social inequalities as a natural condition. The Social Democrats moved into a vacuum when they addressed the concerns of the common people and offered a solution to their misery: socialism. The pulling power of socialism and its exclusion of a reconciliation between labour and the rest of the society frightened the Saxon elites. Whereas they embraced Bismarck's carefully drafted social policy to appease the masses, they fought the SPD with every means and took its socialist rhetoric at face value. Karl Biedermann, an influential Saxon liberal, argued in 1900 that the middle class should mobilise to fight 'a battle of life and death' with socialism in which 'the price of victory is of inestimable value ...: social peace.'[40]

The elite's reaction to the labour movement seemed to be based on panic rather than realistic assessment. Before they hastily introduced the three-class voting system in 1896, the success of the SPD in the state elections was comparatively moderate and did not threaten the dominance of the traditional parties (the SPD only had fourteen of eighty-two seats in the Lower House in 1893).[41] Many who worried about the organised working class failed to understand that the vote for the SPD was often a protest against the social situation and not necessarily a support of socialist ideals. It also became increasingly evident that one needed to distinguish between the SPD's socialist rhetoric and its more practical day-to-day work: in the Landtag the Social Democrats normally pursued a realistic and constructive line and showed a willingness to compromise, particularly after 1909.

Similar to elsewhere in the Reich, the Saxon bourgeoisie had made a compromise with the traditional elite: they had refrained from politics in exchange for comparative freedom in the economic sphere and the suppression of the socialist threat. This worked well until an economic crisis shook the Saxon industry at the beginning of the twentieth century. It became clear that the Conservatives' agrarian interests of protectionism diverged increasingly from the export interests of the industrial bourgeoisie. Suddenly the uncompromising stance of the traditional elite towards any political modernisation, and their monopoly over the political sphere, became a thorn in the side of the bourgeoisie who had no political muscle to support their own interests.[42] The young Gustav Stresemann became the driving force in setting up a pressure group for the local small and medium-sized industrialists in 1902 – the Association of Saxon Industrialists (VSI) – which took hold of the National Liberal Party as a political platform. Henceforth they slowly distanced themselves from the alliance with the traditional elite and forced an electoral reform. However, the new electoral law from 1909 was still discriminatory and excluded a quarter of the electorate that was eligible to vote in Reichstag elections. It strengthened the National Liberals in the Lower House as compared to the Conservatives, without allowing the SPD to become too strong. However, the preservation of the Upper House allowed the Conservatives and the government to block any laws they did not like, and this remained the case until change came through revolution in November 1918.

The electoral reform in 1909 has recently led several historians to emphasise certain tendencies towards a modernisation in Saxony's political system before 1914.[43] Although this is certainly true in comparison with Prussia, it is still fair to say that the bourgeoisie missed a crucial chance to close the gap between themselves and the labour movement. Basically, their motivation was selfish, and they did too little, too late, to prepare the ground for a democratic system. After 1909 their priority was to stem the rise of the SPD and they were prepared to use undemocratic means. On this vital issue, they continued to join forces – despite many differences in interest and ideology – with the even more reactionary Conservatives who stayed in power until the end of the war.

In contrast to the south German states, where the Social Democrats had the possibility of finding alliances in parliament or during election campaigns, the SPD was more or less isolated in the Saxon party system before the First World War. This seems odd, as

Karsten Rudolph has convincingly argued, that despite the old reputation of the 'red Kingdom', the Saxon SPD was not revolutionary and radical, but moderate and unconfrontational.[44] It was typical that the Saxon SPD publicly rejected a mass strike after a wave of spontaneous street demonstrations and strikes had swept the country in late 1905. Indeed, other Social Democratic leaders – Fillipo Turati, Jean Jaurès and even Eduard Bernstein – criticised their Saxon comrades for a lack of radical resistance against the reactionary electoral laws and a loyalty towards an authoritarian state. Paradoxically, the dramatic success of the Saxon Social Democrats in recruiting voters and members and building up an impressive organisational network around the party, led to their comparatively moderate stance because they were frightened to lose what the rest of Germany envied them for.

The pronounced divisions in Saxon society did not prevent all groups from joining the war effort in August 1914 (see also document 2). For the SPD, the call to 'defend' the country, the hope of gaining concessions for participating in a united front, and popular pressure, proved stronger than their ideology of class struggle and the international fraternisation of workers. The behaviour of the Social Democrats also proved that they were committed to work within the framework of the existing society. But, as elsewhere in Europe, this 'social consensus' did not last long. From spring 1915 onwards there were strikes and disturbances against food shortages and bad working conditions, and the government hardened its censorship and meeting bans for fear of political agitation. When the war aims became increasingly strident in their imperialistic tone, the left wing in the SPD finally broke ranks with the united war effort, and in early 1917 the strong SPD district of Leipzig joined the newly formed USPD (Independent Social Democrats). Despite growing social unrest – in April 1917 the Social Democrats and the metal union mobilised 30,000 workers in Leipzig in the first political mass strike in Saxony[45] – the Saxon elite stayed in control and prevented reforms with coercion and delaying tactics until November 1918.

After the war a cooperation between organised labour and the bourgeoisie along the lines of a Weimar Coalition in the Reich did not materialise due to two factors. There were the legacies of the past: the deep-rooted hatred and mistrust, but also different values and ideologies, did not disappear overnight. Furthermore, economic, political and social developments in the postwar years never allowed for a period of tranquillity, but radicalised

Saxon society and enhanced the division into a socialist and nationalist bloc.

The first political phase – lasting from the end of 1918 until the end of 1923 and dominated by the Social Democrats – was crucial for the further development of Saxon society: it engraved the traditional polarisation between the labour movement and the bourgeoisie into the Republican environment and made any future collaboration between both sides unlikely. The revolutionary government of Majority Social Democrats (MSPD) and Independent Social Democrats (USPD) collapsed because the former followed a Republican course along the lines of Berlin, whilst the latter insisted on the continuation of the council system and a special path for Saxony.[46] The bourgeois parties were desperate to keep the radical USPD away from power and supported the formation of an MSPD minority government after the elections to the 'people's chamber' in February 1919. Eventually this led to a coalition government between MSPD and the Democrats (DDP) from October onwards. The USPD and all other bourgeois parties were in opposition.

Over the course of the next two years several developments changed this political constellation in Saxony. The most radical members of the USPD left the party, bringing it automatically closer to the MSPD, until their eventual reunion in September 1922. Within the MSPD the left wing became more and more influential due to a growing number of party activists' unease about certain developments and what they regarded as the careless behaviour of their right-wing colleagues in the government: army atrocities against workers, the assertive behaviour of the anti-Republican right (especially the Kapp-Putsch in March 1920), and the apparent inability of the SPD-DDP coalition government to carry out decisive reforms. The emerging political polarisation between left and right also led to a rapprochement between Social Democrats and Communists.

The state elections in November 1920 proved to be a turning-point: MSPD and USPD together gained 42.2 percent of the vote (plus 2.9 percent for the left-wing USPD), whilst the DDP slumped to 7.7 percent and the KPD (German Communist Party) gained 5.7 percent.[47] The choice of a workers' government had become a viable option in Saxony. Henceforth the MSPD was led by the left-wing of the party who regarded a Great Coalition with the DVP (German People's Party) as unacceptable as long as there was a possibility of cooperation with the KPD. From December 1920 onwards this led to several Social Democratic minority governments because the Communists were indeed prepared to support them. Meanwhile the Saxon DVP was also rock-solid in its commitment to a bourgeois government and rejected any alliances with the labour movement. Additionally, after the November elections the DDP started to pursue a militant anti-government stance to reverse the massive desertion of voters caused by their previous coalition with the Social Democrats. The political landscape of Saxony had divided into two opposing blocks.

This polarisation increased during the course of the next three years. The united front on the left enabled the Social Democrats to introduce a major programme of progressive reforms which caused enormous resentment amongst the centre and the right:[48] there was an active and modern employment policy; reforms in the economy and finances; attempts to democratise the civil service, police and judiciary; reforms in the municipal code, education, and the relationship between church and state; and finally, active measures to combat activities of the far right.

According to Rudolph, this 'left-wing republican project' opened up the possibility of creating a modern and democratic state and society. The powerful bourgeoisie and traditional elite, however, had a different vision of the society they wished to see in the new political framework. For instance, Saxon industrialists protested against the state's involvement in employment policy and insisted on a completely deregulated approach. They also opposed the revitalisation of state industries because of their concern about the additional competition for the private sector. Meanwhile the Conservatives and the Church vehemently resisted reforms that aimed to republicanise the civil service, foster democratic values and introduce a secular education.

The bourgeoisie's talk of a 'bolshevisation' of Saxony reflected how traumatic it perceived the reforms to be. This was not, however, what actually happened. The revolution had been bloodless and for outsiders rather undramatic. The Social Democrats had not nationalised the economy nor introduced a council system. In fact, the bourgeoisie continued to occupy the great majority of posts in higher and middle administration.[49] The reforms were left-wing democratic, but not revolutionary socialist. The Social Democratic governments stood firmly on Republican grounds and did their best to maintain social stability in the midst of a rapidly deteriorating national economic crisis which peaked in the painful experience of hyperinflation in 1923. Neither did the Social

Democrats make any concessions to the Communists which would have undermined the democratic system. On the contrary, they attempted to moderate the Saxon KPD to counter increasing pressure from Moscow and the party's ultra-left to start a socialist uprising.

The state elections in November 1922 – which widened the gap between the socialist and bourgeois camps in favour of the former (SPD and KPD gained 52.3 percent of the vote) – signalled an overall support for the reform policies of the socialist minority government. The bourgeoisie, however, insisted that there was a 'Bolshevist' rule in Dresden which threatened to destroy the foundations of Saxon society. When the left-wing Erich Zeigner became Prime Minister in March 1923 and the impact of hyperinflation led to rising unemployment and a hunger crisis with widespread looting and disturbances, the bourgeoisie turned its heavy criticism of the labour governments into an unprecedented barrage of attacks.

The *Reichswehr* (army) and the national government also were increasingly losing their patience with the situation in Saxony. Zeigner openly criticised the policy of passive resistance against the Ruhr occupation – in his view this was the main cause of the economic crisis – and suggested a solution through negotiations. Furthermore, the setting up of Proletarian Hundreds in Saxony – these were unarmed contingents which were manned by SPD and KPD activists and were formed to defend Republican institutions against counter-revolutionary activities from the far right[50] – also caused irritation amongst various groups, including the *Reichswehr*, the far right and the Saxon bourgeoisie. More generally, the left-wing Republican project was a thorn in the side of Berlin because it offered a left-wing alternative to the political compromises that were carried out at Reich level during and after the November Revolution. In late September Chancellor Stresemann (DVP) and President Friedrich Ebert (SPD) put the army in control by declaring a state of emergency. In this situation the KPD offered to join the government in Dresden in order to prepare the long-planned armed uprising. The Social Democrats accepted the proposal in the hope that they could counter Communist plans by forcing them to accept the democratic constitution and bind them into political responsibility.

The SPD-KPD coalition came to an abrupt end when the army – applauded by the Saxon bourgeoisie – removed the government from office in the famous *Reichsexekution* on 29 October 1923,[51] and established its authority in a violent manner which caused many casualties – even amongst peaceful bystanders (see document 3b). Stresemann and Ebert sacrificed the democratically formed Saxon government – and the one in neighbouring Thuringia – to appease the military and the Bavarian anti-democratic right, whose activities had been fuelled by their determination to get rid of the left-wing rule in central Germany. Further political developments in Saxony were overshadowed by this bloody legacy: labour and bourgeoisie had become bitter enemies and the united front on the left was in tatters. The SPD split over how to pick up the pieces after the coup: its majority was determined to continue the reform project with a workers' government, whilst an influential minority saw cooperation with the bourgeoisie as the only chance. The failure of a planned uprising brought the KPD into the control of the ultra left, who abandoned the policy of cooperation with the SPD in favour of outright confrontation.

The second political phase lasted from late 1923 until early 1930. An SPD minority government under Alfred Fellisch – tolerated by the DDP – only lasted until mid-December because it lacked the full backing of its own party organisation, and the DDP eventually insisted on forming a Great Coalition which included the DVP. In early January the majority of Social Democrats in the Landtag decided to form a coalition government against the wishes of the majority of the Saxon SPD. Although the 'rebel' Social Democrat Max Heldt became Prime Minister, the DVP was the real driving force of the coalition (it had strong support amongst the higher civil servants, industrialists and middle-class organisations). As a result, a large number of Social Democrats were removed from their positions in the higher civil service, and the new municipal code was revised (see chapter 4 [ii-iii]). The Saxon SPD bitterly opposed the new coalition government. After a long and bitter dispute within the party, the twenty-three 'rebels' were forced out of the SPD and regrouped as the Old Social Democratic Party (ASP) in June 1926. The genuinely democratic government ended when the state elections in October 1926 decimated its majority – most importantly, the ASP only gained four seats – and led to the creation of a broader government coalition which included the right-wing and anti-Republican DNVP (German National People's Party) from mid-1927 onwards. The elections also initiated the electoral decline of the traditional bourgeois parties (DDP, DVP, DNVP) at the expense of the dramatic appearance of special interest parties.[52] Whereas the WP (Business Party) scored its first major triumph in Germany (scoring 10.1 percent of the vote), another splinter party – the VRP (Reich Party for People's Rights and Reevaluation) – emerged during the elections (gaining 4.2 percent of the vote). Henceforth, the government – although it continued to be headed by Heldt – increasingly drifted to the right and continued the process of replacing the Social Democratic reforms with conservative and regressive legislation.

When the Saxon NSDAP participated for the first time in state elections in 1926, Hellmuth von Mücke and Fritz Tittmann gained the first seats in a German state parliament for their party.[53] Both consented to the reelection of Heldt as Prime Minister in early 1927 by handing in blank ballot papers. Their parliamentary activities over the next few years were contradictory: whilst they attacked the bourgeois government verbally, in practice they did not engage in serious parliamentary obstruction and even voted against several SPD-KPD motions of no confidence.[54]

The limited influence the Nazis were able to exert in parliament was transformed into a decisive one in the May 1929 state elections. Although the Nazis only won a modest 5 percent of the vote (their vote, however, nearly doubled from 74,343 votes in May 1928 to 133,958 votes), the acquisition of five seats suddenly gave them the key position in Saxony's parliament between the left's (SPD and KPD) forty-five seats and the bourgeois parties' forty-six seats (six months later the local elections produced very similar results for the composition of local councils). The situation created perplexity and two attempts to elect a Prime Minister failed. The confusion only ended when the Nazis indicated on 20 June that they would support a 'Marxist-free government' under Wilhelm Bünger, member of the DVP.[55]

Once more the Nazis contradicted their previous agitation against the parliamentary system. Hitler, who had participated in the election campaign, masterminded the negotiations with Bünger and played with the idea of asking for the Ministry of the Interior for Wilhelm Frick (see document 8). However, the parliamentary position of the Saxon Nazis was not strong enough to make that a viable proposition and Hitler settled for tolerating a 'Marxist-free' Bünger government. Bünger complied with all Nazi demands: he left the DDP and ASP out of the cabinet, and appointed two 'neutral' civil servants as Minister of the Interior and Minister of Justice.[56] The *Leipziger Volkszeitung* commented: 'Never in the history of the Saxon parliament stood a government on such shaky feet than that of Herrn Bünger who is totally dependent on the Swastika party.'[57] Shortly after the government was formed, however, Bünger seemed eager to prove his independence. He reappointed Georg Elsner, a member of the ASP and previous Minister of Employment and Welfare, to his post. This move left Bünger exposed to Nazi attacks.

The Nazis' decision to opt for comparatively constructive parliamentary cooperation in Saxony in June 1929 was an important watershed for the NSDAP. Hitler published a long article in the *Völkischer Beobachter* to appease those party members who categorically resented a cooperation with 'bourgeois parliamentarianism'.[58] The developments exposed the dilemma of those party members – in particular Otto Straßer and his *Kampfverlag* in Berlin – who followed a radical revolutionary strategy of disruption and noncooperation and who regarded Saxony as belonging to their sphere of influence. Politically, this meant complete isolation because they had only vague and unrealistic ideas about cooperating with the Marxist parties. In contrast to this, Hitler had learned the lesson of the failed Munich coup in 1923 and stuck to his revised strategy to overthrow the system through largely parliamentary means. To him, tactical cooperation with the bourgeois government in Saxony opened up the chance for the Nazis to gain the Ministry of the Interior, which was a crucial step toward power in Berlin. This strategy also appeased bourgeois voters with regard to Nazism. In that sense developments in Saxony from June 1929 onward laid the foundation for Wilhelm Frick's participation in the government in Thuringia in early 1930. But the same developments led to the expulsion of Otto Straßer and his followers when they bitterly opposed negotiations for a NSDAP coalition government with the bourgeoisie after the Saxon state election in June 1930.

The Nazis' deal with Bünger in mid-1929 reflected their cynical political tactics: they could drop him whenever it suited them. Henceforth, while the Nazis tolerated the government, they constantly threatened to bring it down when their demands were not met. Eventually, when Bünger supported the ratification of the Young Plan,[59] the Nazis forced his resignation: their motion of no-confidence was supported by a Landtag majority in February 1930.[60]

The fall of Bünger's government initiated the third political phase in interwar Saxony and lasted until the Nazi seizure of power in March 1933. From February to July 1930 Saxony was in a state of political limbo: the SPD's offer to enter a 'great coalition' was rejected by the DVP, and later in May the Nazis withdrew their previous promise to tolerate Wilhelm Schieck's (DVP) 'neutral cabinet of experts'. This was the second time that the Nazis had deserted the bourgeoisie. They supported a motion by the SPD and KPD to dissolve the Landtag and helped to force new elections. All three parties hoped to gain from the June 1930 state elections, but the KPD only acquired one new seat, while the SPD even lost one seat. At first it looked as if the calculation had paid off for the Nazis, who achieved their greatest electoral breakthrough in an important German state: they nearly tripled their electorate and became by far the largest non-Marxist party with 14.4 percent of the vote.

The Nazis benefited mainly from the dramatic decline of the DVP and DNVP – the disintegration of the bourgeois parties was in full swing – and by mobilising former nonvoters (see chapters 4 [v] and 5 [iii]). Another factor contributing to their strong showing was that their Munich headquarters had concentrated its efforts on Saxony for several months. Indeed, the Saxon election was Joseph Goebbels' first 'masterstroke' as newly appointed head of propaganda. However, the Nazi strategy to create a central German block of National Socialist domination, together with neighbouring Thuringia, did not pay off. The Saxon Nazis failed to obtain the post of the Minister of the Interior for Gregor Straßer due to the resistance of the DDP and VNR (Reich Nationalist Alliance). Hitler's publication of comparatively moderate demands in the *Völkischer Beobachter* and his personal participation in the coalition negotiations in Dresden made no difference.[61] As no agreement for a new government was reached, Schieck's 'cabinet of civil servants' continued to govern Saxony until its dissolution by the Nazis in March 1933.

Earlier and more openly than in other German states, genuine parliamentary democracy came to an end in Saxony in mid-1930. Like their party colleagues in the Reichstag, the Saxon Social Democrats grasped the nettle and tolerated Schieck's right-wing bourgeois government in order to keep the Nazis out of power. The increasing radicalisation also opened up opportunistic alliances between the anti-parliamentary parties: numerous attempts by the NSDAP, DNVP, SLV (Saxon Landvolk) and KPD to bring down the government were unsuccessful. The Nazis had every right to feel frustrated: their movement was growing at a breathtaking rate, but they continued to be excluded from power. The July 1932

Reichstag elections showed that the NSDAP had become by far the largest party in the state with 41.2 percent of the vote. However, although they were the direct beneficiaries of the dramatic collapse of the bourgeois parties (to a mere 10.5 percent of the total vote), the latter remained in power in Dresden.

Hitler's appointment as Chancellor in January 1933 made the Saxon government comply with Nazi wishes ever more frequently. From 27 February onwards the Saxon government initiated the persecution of the Communists who were quickly driven into illegality.[62] SPD newspapers were banned several days before the last semi-free Reichstag elections on 5 March 1933. While the NSDAP's share of the vote in Saxony rose to 45 percent of the votes (national average: 43.9 percent), the Marxist parties defended their position exceptionally well and still gained 42.7 percent of the vote (12.1 percent more than in the Reich). Saxony, as in the November election, was the greatest bastion for the Marxist parties at the end of the Republic. The state seemed more polarised than ever: the electoral districts of Leipzig and Dresden-Bautzen were the SPD's two strongest electoral districts in the Reich, and the electoral district of Chemnitz-Erzgebirge was the fourth best for the KPD, but also eighth best for the NSDAP. Additionally, the local elections on 13 November 1932 had led to alliances between the bourgeois parties and the NSDAP and had secured their candidates the leading positions in many places, while in some places the SPD and KPD had formed a long-awaited 'united front' to establish Marxist councils.[63]

As in the rest of the Reich, the Nazis exploited the momentum created by the March election and seized power with great speed. The fourth distinct political period in Saxony started: the racial dictatorship. On 7 March Frick authorised Manfred von Killinger to take control in Saxony.[64] Three days later Killinger forced Schieck and his government to resign and formed a provisional government.[65] Meanwhile the SA (Stormtroopers) and SS (elite Nazi organisation) ransacked and confiscated Marxist buildings and possessions, occupied town halls where they hoisted swastika flags, and started a wave of arrests. Much of this was done spontaneously and with violence. Contrary to widespread belief, the Nazis encountered some resistance. For instance, the mayors of Dresden and Crimmitschau refused to order the hoisting of the swastika flag at their town halls, and after sustained Marxist activities in the district of Annaberg, the Nazis were forced to carry out a second purge in the area.[66] All Democratic or Social

Democratic paramilitary organisations were banned on 13 March.[67] Meanwhile thousands of Saxons accomodated themselves with the new regime and flocked into the Nazi party. For instance, in the small town of Markranstädt the membership rose from 75 to 500 between 30 January and 1 May.[68]

A counter-intelligence service to combat 'bolshevist activities' – the predecessor of the Gestapo (Secret State Police) – and the first 'special court' were set up at the end of the month.[69] On 4 April Killinger issued a decree for the new formation of the Landtag, which stated that parties were able to send delegates according to their result in the last Reichstag election. This enabled the NSDAP to win an absolute majority in the parliament because the KPD and SAP (Socialist Workers' Party) were already illegal. The local councils and district councils were formed according to the same principle. On 5 May the *Gauleiter* Martin Mutschmann was appointed *Reichstatthalter* (Reich Governor) of Saxony and Killinger introduced his new cabinet.[70] Meanwhile parliamentary work was made impossible for the Social Democrats. Leaders of the SPD and trade unions were arrested, and tortured and murdered in concentration camps (see document 23). The Saxon SPD was officially banned on 23 June 1933.[71] When the SA paraded in front of Hitler at the *Gau* meeting in Leipzig in mid-July 1933, the Nazis' seizure of power in Saxony was long completed.

The year 1933 brought fundamental changes, but also some continuity for Saxon society. The SA and SS committed many atrocities, but Killinger also attempted to follow Hitler's orders to 'make sure that the revolution does not get out of hand, and that everything goes along orderly lines.'[72] On 10 March 1933 Killinger announced an official ban on further spontaneous action of any kind.[73] It makes sense that Hitler trusted Killinger, and not the more radical and brutal Mutschmann, with the 'delicate' task of seizing power without alienating the traditional elite too much. Killinger had good links with nationalist circles and as a high-ranking SA leader he seemed to be in a position to control the revolutionary aspirations of the Stormtroopers. At this stage the violence was directed primarily against working-class activists and Jews, whereas the Nazis attempted to accommodate the rest of society. The persecution of Marxists was particularly ruthless in Saxony: more than one-sixth of all concentration camps in the Reich were on Saxon soil in 1933.[74] The administration was purged and on 1 August Mutschmann boasted that he had dismissed 2,000 people from the state service.[75] Nine out of twenty mayors also left their posts in Saxon towns with more than 20,000 citizens by the end of 1933.[76] Whereas about 1,600 of 15,800 town employees in Leipzig were thrown out between January and September 1933 because of their party affiliation with the KPD, only around 250 people of a total of 18,700 employed in the judiciary were dismissed in Saxony[77] (this seems to suggest something about the political orientation of this profession). Largely successful attempts to wipe out the small but determined Marxist resistance movement continued into the mid-1930s.[78] Communist activists faced particularly barbaric treatment on the hands of the Gestapo. The brutal 'questioning under torture', but also the work of informers, led to an astounding number of confessions.[79]

The number of people affected by the Nazi seizure of power widened gradually. In 1935 a secret report claimed that the bourgeoisie was appalled at how the Nazis had placed their people in key offices; this process included the appointment of Nazi mayors.[80] There were, however, also numerous examples of continuity, particularly from smaller towns. In Raschau/Erzgebirge, several leaders of the local bourgeoisie with no long party affiliation or beliefs in National Socialist ideals, headed the new NSDAP leadership, and a well-known Communist continued his job as local teacher after a short imprisonment. The former branch leader and his wife, both loyal Nazis who did not want to cooperate with these circles, were thrown out of the party.[81] Former Social Democrats continued to occupy most seats on the management board of the largest consumer cooperative in Leipzig until 1935.[82] Until 1937 not a single top-flight member of the Gestapo in Leipzig had been a member of the NSDAP or the SS before 1933.[83]

Although the Nazis were able to seize power extremely swiftly, it took them longer to distribute the spoils. There was a fierce power struggle between *Reichstatthalter* Mutschmann, head of the NSDAP machinery, and President Killinger, head of the administration, that also involved deep-seated personal and ideological differences. Eventually, Mutschmann came out on top and was officially asked to take over the political leadership in Saxony in March 1935. Killinger had fallen victim to the SA purge on 1 July and had been suspended from all his posts a few days later.[84] Step-by-step the Nazis tightened their control and stamped their ideology onto society. Indeed, the Nazis racial policies brought the most dramatic changes to Saxon society. From March 1933 onwards, 23,000 Saxon Jews were subject to increasing isolation, dehumanisation and eventual deportation and murder (see also document 22; and chapters 3 [vi] and 4 [vi]). For instance, during the seizure of power in Chemnitz the SA forced all Jews in custody to clean the walls and buildings in the town of Marxist slogans,[85] in mid-1935 Stormtroopers assaulted a Jewish businessman in his shop in the centre of Dresden and smashed the interior to pieces,[86] and in mid-1938 a Jewish shop-owner in Annaberg/Erzgebirge committed suicide because his son had been forbidden to use the local bath (which had been built with the help of the generous donation from his grandfather) and was banned from attending the local school.[87] Saxony's long tradition surrounding issues such as health, race and hygiene were followed up by active measures in 'racial hygiene' (see chapter 4 [vi]). These included the first 'introductory courses for racial anthropology and racial care' in October 1933, and the creation of the 'state academy for racial and health care' in Dresden in 1934. These racial initiatives eventually ended in the Nazi killing of the mentally ill and sick. Around 15,000 people were murdered in a gas chamber in Sonnenstein sanatorium in Pirna, and more than 3,000 people were murdered with drugs and starvation in the sanatorium in Großschweidnitz during the Second World War.[88] In 1935 the Nazis started a rigorous policy of Germanisation of the Slav Sorbs in the Niederlausitz region.[89] Representatives of the Protestant Church who resisted the nazification policies were oppressed.

The attitude of the Saxon population towards the Nazi regime will be discussed elsewhere (also see documents 20 to 22).[90] It seems that – as in the rest of the Reich – the relationship between Nazism and the Saxon population was complex, multilayered and often contradictory.[91] There are numerous examples of widespread support for the Nazis, but also many forms of nonconformity towards the regime – particularly verbal incidents – which increased at the end of the war.[92]

During the Second World War, Saxons experienced increasing centralisation and rationalisation to improve efficiency. Meanwhile the terror and racial killing intensified. In the Zeithain camp for prisoners of war (near Riesa) between 33,000 and 40,000 Soviet citizens died of starvation, illness, exhaustion, or were murdered from mid-1941 onwards.[93] Even among Germans complaining or infringements of regulations frequently led to capital punishment, and there were a growing number of executions by order of court martial. The Gestapo in Leipzig executed fifty-two prisoners with shots in the back of the neck, only days before the arrival of American troops in 1945. Not far away SS troops and members of the Home Guard (*Volkssturm*) brutally shot and burned to death around 100 concentration camp prisoners.[94] A great lethargy was spreading amongst the population at the end of the war. During the 457 days and nights before 11 April 1945 the citizens of Leipzig had to rush into air-raid shelters 226 times.[95] Whereas Saxon society had changed markedly between 1933 and 1939 and this development had accelerated during the first war years, the most dramatic changes came during the years of 'total war' and with the new developments after 1945, when the destruction of Nazism led to the recreation of central and eastern Europe and the establishment of Communist dictatorships.

(iv) The Nazi Movement: Development and Organisation

The beginning of the Nazi movement in Saxony was similar to that in other parts of Germany. The first Nazi followers were radical anti-Semites and extreme nationalists who became activated by their disappointment with the outcome of the First World War and their rejection of the newly-created Republic. Most of them were members of other *völkisch* groups or paramilitary formations, particularly the *Deutschvölkischer Schutz- und Trutzbund* (DVSTB) (see document 4). In the course of the 1920s many *völkisch* followers joined the NSDAP because of its radicalism, and the disintegration of other groups over the years, or – from 1925 onwards – due to its activity as a political party.

Anti-Semitism was a widespread and established phenomenon in the region at the end of the nineteenth century. James Retallack called Saxony the 'cradle' of 'political anti-Semitism' in Germany, and the Pan-German League – which spread a more deep-seated and ideological anti-Semitism – had its most active and strongest branches in the region.[96] Additionally, Leipzig was the home of the Germanic (Thule) Order, and Theodor Fritsch's anti-Semitic *Hammer* publishing house and *Hammer* League.[97] Indeed, Saxony proved ground for many of the most influential politicians and publicists within the German anti-Semitic movement.[98] Anti-Semitism was also one of the most distinctive aspects of Saxon Nazism. It was no coincidence that Hermann Esser, a notorious anti-Semite, was the first prominent Nazi speaker who attempted to rally support for the movement in Saxony in the early 1920s. Nazis in eastern Saxony canvassed for a referendum to expel all

Jews who had arrived in the state after the outbreak of the First World War.[99] The emphasis on radical anti-Semitism was either enthusiastically greeted by newly recruited members or audiences in meetings, or it quickly drove them away again.

The ideas of the Nazi movement and stories of the orator Hitler and his Stormtroopers were brought to Saxony through a handful of members of the *Freikorps* or army, students, salesmen and others who had come into contact with the Nazis in Munich. As in other regions in Germany, the driving force of a few devoted followers was responsible for spreading Nazi ideology and founding local party branches. Fritz Tittmann, a locksmith from Zwickau, was the most important Nazi activist in Saxony during this period. Tittmann attended a Hitler rally in Munich in mid-1921,[100] joined the party, and founded the first Saxon Nazi party branch in Zwickau on 11 October 1921.[101] From Zwickau the Nazi movement quickly spread to other districts of Saxony, particularly the southwest (see document 4).

Apart from several earlier meetings in Zwickau, the Saxon Nazis appeared for the first time in public in a series of meetings of their various branches at the end of 1922. Tittmann spoke at each of them and displayed a striking aggressiveness and hatred of the Republican system. He blamed three groups for the misery of the German people: the Social Democrats were accused for most of the misfortune as they were held responsible for the lost war. Capitalists and profiteers exploited the German people, and the Jews were condemned as the driving force behind world capitalism and a conspiracy against Germany.[102] The Nazis portrayed themselves as looking after the betrayed and exploited masses. One follower explained during a police questioning: 'We fight for justice and order to protect the citizens.'[103] To them only radical and brutal measures could change the situation. Esser claimed in a speech in Zwickau: 'Until there are gallows in the streets at which racketeers and profiteers are hanged, one should not expect any improvements.'[104] He then appealed to all Germans to free themselves from the stiff traditional parties and to unite behind the desire for justice and pride for the German nation: 'The NSDAP does not want theory, nor a party programme, nor a party dogma, but the unification of all working classes ... to one big National Socialist Party'.[105]

When Walter Rathenau, the Jewish German Foreign Minister, was assassinated by right-wing fanatics in June 1922, the NSDAP was prohibited in almost every state in Germany. In Saxony all

Nazi meetings and parades were banned at the end of the year, after the local police had blamed increasing Nazi activities for the 'uneasy political atmosphere'.[106] The Nazis simply ignored the ban and continued to meet. The defiance of official laws, which in their eyes suppressed their idealistic beliefs and activities, and comradeship kept them involved and bound them together.[107] The Nazis regarded it as treason and a sign of weakness to give in to police pressure and obey the law. Even when the continuous Nazi activities led to a complete ban of the NSDAP in Saxony in March 1923,[108] it did not decisively curtail their activities. In any case, officials were frequently lenient towards Nazi offenders. This ranged from 'soft' sentences in courts, to 'special' treatment by the police. The Nazis in Markneukirchen attested: 'The police showed a lot of sympathy for the *völkisch* movement. They arranged house-searches in a way that it was possible to get documents and membership cards into a safe place beforehand.'[109] Additionally, as in other parts of Germany, the Saxon Nazis were extremely flexible in continuing their activities in an endless number of clubs they founded – in Markneukirchen they continued to meet in the rambling club 'Harmonia'[110] – making it difficult for the police to intervene. Nevertheless, one should not play down the impact of police surveillance and the reality of house searches and imprisonment. Six Nazis were imprisoned after a field exercise of the SA in the Erzgebirge in May 1923.[111] The Nazis also faced persistent pressure from the workers' movement who searched suspects for weapons and disrupted or broke up Nazi meetings. In the town of Werdau 'Communists forced their way' into a Nazi meeting and 'beat up the National Socialists with clubs and sticks'.[112] All this strengthened the Nazis' hatred of the Republican system and increased the internal cohesion (see also document 6).

In 1923 the Saxon Nazi movement was still extremely small and did not possess a central, efficient party organisation. This was a common feature of the movement outside Bavaria. There were only ten NSDAP party branches and sixteen bases scattered across western Saxony, with a total of only several hundred members.[113] Followers seemed to have met not more than once a week in pubs, like the Nazis in Plauen who gathered every Wednesday at half past six in the evening in a local pub.[114] As in other parts in Germany, Saxon Nazism was still mainly an urban phenomenon in these early years. Although members came from all social classes, including workers, middle-class men were overproportionally represented (see chapter 5 [ii]). They were part of a wider *völkisch* milieu that met frequently for celebrations and commemorations. Because the Nazi leadership in Munich was largely occupied with national developments and putsch plans against the government in Berlin, it did not pay great attention to the development of the movement outside Bavaria. Several factors explained the spread of Nazism in the 1920s. Heinrich Bennecke – a former SA leader in Saxony – emphasised the presence of a devoted leader:

> The development of National Socialist branches did not take place according to a plan before 1930, but depended on local conditions. If there were no suitable people for the development of the organisation, the areas were not sufficiently worked on or even completely neglected.[115]

Social, cultural, and economic conditions determined whether devoted local leaders were more or less likely to emerge and whether or not they would be able to build up a stable network of followers. In the Vogtland and the Erzgebirge, which became two of the greatest Nazi strongholds in Germany, the Nazis were a natural successor to the Pan-German League and the anti-Semitic parties. Both groups had flourished in these districts before the First World War, due to social and ethnic tensions caused by immigration of cheap Czech labour from across the border. Other contributing factors included Saxony's role as a transit station for emigrants from the east, including Jews, and popular disillusionment with the inability of the traditional parties to respond to economic crisis.[116] In the 1890s 'the anti-Semites appeared young and vital, willing to go further than the middle-class parties or the Conservatives ... which had been unresponsive to the needs of the *Mittelstand*.'[117]

The Nazis' aggressive anti-Marxism and anti-Semitism tapped into these traditions and had a natural appeal. These were also environments where political upheaval after the war had created strong tensions – the remarkable polarisation of local society was captured in the popular saying: 'There are only Communists and German Nationalists in the Vogtland'[118] – and where a large number of people were affected by a long-term economic decline. The Nazis' youthfulness, liveliness and vision of a nationalist revival seemed for some to be the only hope in desperate times and contrasted sharply with the traditional parties who appeared passive and out of touch with the needs of the masses. The proximity to Bavaria and Munich also fostered contacts between

Nazis across the border. For the extreme right, Bavaria became a 'safe haven' from restrictive laws and harassment from the Saxon labour movement. The Nazis were also able to move into a political 'vacuum' in the area: whilst the *völkisch* movement was extremely active, political parties of the far-right, particularly the DVFP (German *Völkisch* Freedom Party), did not have a strong presence.

The Nazis made little headway in eastern Saxony up until the early 1930s. This area was furthest away from the Vogtland and the Erzgebirge and centred around the towns of Kamenz, Bautzen, Löbau and Zittau. Several distinct groups proved largely immune to Nazism: a strong Catholic minority who supported the Centre Party;[119] a liberal-bourgeois milieu in and around Zittau (see also chapter 4 [iv]); and a strong working-class movement. The Nazis also admitted that they were not liked by the Sorbs – a Slav ethnic group of around 28,000 people who lived in eastern Saxony. Finally, they also found it difficult to expand their movement in a region that was dominated by tiny villages.[120] Although a few Nazis started to become active in northwestern and central Saxony in late 1922, here too the Nazi movement did not find favourable conditions for growth or local influence until the late 1920s. They were often hampered by personal rivalries. They also faced fierce competition from other *völkisch* parties and opposition from a particularly strong working-class movement.

Nazi activists in Saxony and other states were only loosely integrated into Hitler's plans for the attempted coup in Munich. After the party ban in March 1923 Tittmann had increasingly concentrated on the military training of local followers so that they would be able to support his Bavarian associates during a possible coup.[121] In September he moved the headquarters of Saxony and Thuringia to nearby Hof in Bavaria.[122] The plan for the remaining Stormtroopers was to wait at home or at local meeting places for the orders to travel to Hof, and then go forward together to assist Hitler in Munich. The sudden failure of the putsch prevented the plan from materialising, and a number of Saxon Nazis who had stayed in Hof were imprisoned by the Saxon police on their return.[123] Overall, there were only a few Saxon activists, probably less than 150, involved in all of these developments.

When Hitler was imprisoned and the Nazis were banned throughout Germany, the NSDAP organisation itself disintegrated. Only a small number of hard-core Saxon activists continued to spread Nazi ideas or, as in Freiberg, went for walks and simply socialised.[124] Throughout Germany the *völkisch* movement was split into many different groups and organisations which often overlapped, but also competed against each other. In Saxony there were four different *völkisch* political parties in the summer of 1924 alone.[125] Some of them only united in fragile alliances during election campaigns. The Saxon Nazis joined the *Völkisch* Socialist Bloc during the May 1924 Reichstag election, and the National Socialist Freedom Movement (NSFB) during the December 1924 Reichstag election. In contrast to many other areas of Germany, the Nazis dominated these alliances. The *völkisch* alliances in Saxony did not do particularly well in either election; but they achieved some striking results in the Vogtland, the southwestern corner of the state.[126] A significant event was the appointment of the textile manufacturer Martin Mutschmann as state leader (*Landesleiter*) of the *völkisch* alliance in Saxony during the NSDAP meeting in Weimar in August 1924 (for more on Mutschmann see chapter 5 [i]). Mutschmann's appointment signalled his rise as undisputed leader in the state and the simultaneous emergence of Plauen as the Nazi headquarters in Saxony. From there Mutschmann rebuilt the organisation in the region after Hitler was released from Landsberg prison.

The importance of the period between 1925 and 1928 was the slow transformation of the NSDAP into a more efficient and centralised organisation which was geared towards seizing power through electoral means. This was also when the Nazis demonstrated their ability to attract a hardcore of devoted activists. Both developments enabled the Nazis to exploit the economic crisis that hit Germany in the late 1920s. The main feature of the Saxon Nazis continued to be their radicalism and anti-Semitism: they openly warned their opponents – particularly the Communists with whom they had continuous brawls – that they would 'take revenge' one day; they molested and ambushed Jews, and hung up placards with texts such as: 'Death to the Jews' (also see documents 5 and 19).[127]

Hitler's official replacement of putschism with legality brought significant changes to the party in order to win mass support. The Saxon NSDAP created ancillary organisations such as a scientific association, a group for salaried employees, a Nazi women's group, and various other organisations to target all groups in society. Of national significance was that Kurt Gruber built up the Nazi youth organisation in Plauen and became the first leader of the Hitler Youth (HJ) in 1926. Wilhelm Tempel founded the

National Socialist Student Association in Leipzig in the same year.[128] The Nazis also introduced a weekly *Gau* newspaper, *Der Nationale Sozialist für Sachsen* (The National Socialist for Saxony; *NSfS*), which was published by the Straßer's *Kampfverlag* in Berlin from March 1926 onwards.[129] The SA slowly expanded, pursued propaganda and engaged in brawls with the workers' movement. It was, however, still a small force. Bennecke estimates that the SA in the KHs Leipzig and Dresden only had about 600 members each by 1929.[130] The Nazis made up for their lack of numbers with activism. In a typical report the Saxon police noted in spring 1926: 'The NSDAP was publicly the most active among all the parties on the right' and one of the busiest parties of all.'[131]

The growing number of districts – the NSDAP had five districts after the reorganisation in 1925,[132] eight in 1928, nine in 1929, eighteen in late 1930, twenty–one in 1931 and finally one district for each *Amtshauptmannschaft*[133] – reflected the growth of the movement in the state (also see document 17). Active party branches spread the movement into rural areas, particularly in the Vogtland/Erzgebirge. Although Saxony was only a medium-size *Gau*, it had by far the largest population of all Nazi *Gaue* and had one of the largest number of party branches and bases before 1933.[134] Mutschmann's hunger for power, and ability to spread his control slowly from the Vogtland to other areas, was openly praised by Hitler.[135] Furthermore, in contrast to the Nazis in northern and western Germany who resisted the centralising tendencies from Munich in the years after the refoundation, the Saxon movement was very loyal to the Bavarian headquarters.

Before early 1929, however, the Saxon Nazi party was still only an extremely small political force, its influence remained limited to western Saxony (also see document 6), and it frequently resembled a chaotic party that lacked central leadership and efficiency. For instance, Mutschmann had great difficulties in establishing his authority in eastern Saxony where Hellmuth von Mücke had tried to establish his own *Gau* in 1927.[136] The police in Leipzig reported on its local NSDAP branch that it was 'very disrupted due to personal friction and the existence of a large financial debt'.[137] The *Gau* headquarters in Plauen frequently complained that not all party branches were responding to circulars, and because of a lack of motorisation SA men had to painstakingly walk or cycle to remote villages to carry out propaganda.[138] Many NSDAP branches – such as the one in Leipzig where Walter Dönicke was 're-elected as leader' in 1928[139] – functioned like normal clubs where only a few members showed up to meetings and did not resemble a dynamic movement built up around a leadership principle. The NSDAP's affiliated organisations were still extremely small – there were only five HJ branches in the KH Leipzig in early 1927[140] – and the NSDAP continued to face strong competition from the radical right: the Nazis in Dresden only managed to outpace their immediate competitors in 1928. Nazi efforts were often not rewarded, as the frustrated comment from Nazis near the town of Döbeln showed: 'It is incredibly difficult to make any progress in this area … the population is indifferent.'[141] Not surprisingly then, the Saxon Nazis continued to face serious electoral limits and only gained 1.6 percent of the vote in the 1926 state elections, and 2.7 percent in the 1928 Reichstag elections.

In 1929 the Nazis achieved many local and regional breakthroughs that prepared the way for their 'take off' nationally in 1930.[142] After years of slow growth – sometimes even stagnation or decline – the increasing momentum of the Saxon Nazi movement was evident in the growth of party membership, number of party branches, and propaganda activities. Nazi gains in Saxony's Landtag elections of 1929 gave them the key position in the middle of the parliament in Dresden.

During 1930 the Saxon NSDAP became a mass party. Between 1929 and 1930 the Nazis more than tripled their party membership (from 4,609 to 20,180 between January 1929 and December 1930)[143] and electorate (from 133,958 in May 1929 to 561,371 in September 1930), and roughly doubled their propaganda efforts (see also document 13). The increase in public meetings in and around Leipzig from thirty-two in 1929 to sixty-two in 1930 was typical of the trend.[144] After 1930 the NSDAP mushroomed at an unprecedented speed. Between late 1930 and early 1933 its membership grew from 20,180 to 87,079, and the number of party branches and bastions increased from 132 to 783 (see document 17). The NSDAP branch in Dresden alone had thirty-two sections in 1931.[145] The number of Nazi meetings continued to double every year. Politicisation brought a massive increase of visitors to Nazi meetings: prominent party leaders like Goebbels and Gregor Straßer were regularly able to attract 5,000–15,000 people even outside election campaigns. There was also a dramatic increase in violent incidents: there were 351 reported clashes and verbal abuses in Leipzig alone between 1 August and 20 November 1932.[146] At the end of the Weimar Republic the NSDAP had become by far the largest party in Saxony and possessed a heterogeneous membership and electorate. On both fronts, however, the middle classes were over-represented and the working-classes under-represented (see chapter 5 [ii]–[iii]).

Whereas the NSDAP's affiliated organisations that had been around for a while – most notably the SA, HJ and National Socialist Women's Organisation[147] – expanded rapidly, the Nazis continued to set up more specialist interest groups for farmers, teachers, doctors, lawyers, stenographers, children, musicians, and many more.[148] Simultaneously, the Nazis made great efforts to infiltrate bourgeois organisations such as the Chemnitz Home Owner Association.[149] To increase their support the Nazis shed some of their radicalism – for example abandoning their section 'The State and the Jews' in *Der Freiheitskampf* in spring 1931[150] – and became more engaged in nonpolitical issues like regional traditions. At the heart of the expanding Nazi movement stood *Gauleiter* Mutschmann whose increasing hold over the party prevented his *Gau* – as happened in several other cases – from being divided into smaller *Gaue*.[151] The Nazis also benefited from the disintegration of the far right: three DNVP members of the town council in Freiberg and three-quarters of the dissolved paramilitary organisation *Reichsflagge* in Zwickau, joined the NSDAP.[152] There was a growing cooperation of the nationalist milieu with the Nazis, particularly during and after the anti-Young campaign. The town council in Zwickau supported an NSDAP motion to make the *Sächsischer Beobachter* the official newspaper of the municipal services in early 1930.[153]

Still, the Saxon Nazis continued to be hampered by severe limits before they seized power in March 1933. Despite their enormous electoral gains they remained excluded from power in the Landtag, and even in cooperation with the other anti-Republican parties, repeatedly failed to bring down the government. The Nazis were only slowly able to spread their success in the southwest to other areas in Saxony. A report about a propaganda tour through the 'completely unworked eastern Saxony' in September 1930 revealed: 'There were villages in which the people had not heard about Hitler.'[154] Although the Saxon SA grew rapidly, for a long time it remained a small force compared with the Republican *Reichsbanner*: whereas the Stormtroopers rallied about 4,000 men at their *Gau* meeting in May 1931, the *Reichsbanner* was able to mobilise about 10,000 activists at a district meeting in western Saxony one month later.[155] Although the Nazis had become the most active political force, compared with the mighty SPD apparatus it was still lagging behind in terms of members and party branches at the end of 1932 (see document 17). The Nazis, however, were catching up with enormous speed and overtook the Social Democrats in many areas, particularly in the southwest.

In the months before Hitler's appointment as Chancellor in January 1933, the Saxon NSDAP – as in other regions – was facing decline, internal problems and disputes. Its vote in elections had dropped from 41.3 percent to 36.6 percent between the July and November 1932 Reichstag elections, and another 9 percent during the local elections on 13 November. The dismal outlook changed only when Hitler came to office and new elections were announced for 5 March. Henceforth everything happened very quickly. The Nazis used the momentum to mobilise all energies for the election campaign and increased their share of the vote to 45 percent. Immediately after the elections they seized power. Killinger took over control of the government and state machinery, whilst the SA and SS seized power at the local level. Much of this was done spontaneously and with great brutality; in Chemnitz, for example, an SA leader shot a Jewish lawyer dead and drowned three young Communists in a pond.[156] Once Mutschmann managed to concentrate all power in his person by July 1934, he kept tight control over his *Gau* until the liberation by Russian and American troops in May 1945.

Notes

1. In 1925 only 3.6 percent of Saxons were Catholic. See *Statistisches Jahrbuch für den Freistaat Sachsen* (*StJbSa*), (1924/1926), 48f. If not otherwise mentioned, all figures are taken from the 1925 census.
2. The most important aspects of Saxony's constitution from 1919 had been stipulated by the Reich constitution. Saxony retained significant powers over police, education, religion and internal administration, while the Republic had power over foreign affairs, jurisprudence, the post, finances and the military.
3. KH Bautzen (461,115 inhabitants), KH Chemnitz (976,079), KH Dresden (1,393,026), KH Leipzig (1,307,312), KH Zwickau (854,784). In autumn 1931 an emergency decree joined the KHs Bautzen and Dresden, and dissolved the AHs Dippoldiswalde, Oelsnitz and Werdau.
4. *Statistisches Jahrbuch des Deutschen Reichs* (*StJbDR*), (1931).

5. F. Burkhardt, 'Die Sonderstellung Sachsens im Deutschen Reich und die wirtschaftliche Depression der Gegenwart', *Zeitschrift des Sächsischen Statistischen Landesamtes* (*ZSäStLA*), (1931), 72.
6. For the following see R. Forberger, 'Sachsen als Pionierland der Industriellen Revolution in Deutschland im Spiegel der Fachliteratur', *Jahrbuch für Regionalgeschichte*, 14 (1987), 243–53; R. Dietrich, 'Zur industriellen Produktion, technischen Entwicklung und zum Unternehmertum in Mitteldeutschland, speziell in Sachsen im Zeitalter der Industrialisierung', *Jahrbuch für die Geschichte Mittel- und Ostdeutschlands*, 28 (1979), 221–72.
7. H. Kiesewetter, *Industrialisierung und Landwirtschaft. Sachsens Stellung im regionalen Industrialisierungsprozeß Deutschlands im 19. Jahrhundert,* Cologne, 1988.
8. For the following see esp. P. Bramstedt, *Die Krisis der sächsischen Industriewirtschaft. Veröffentlichung des Verbandes Sächsischer Industrieller*, 67 (1932).
9. Forberger, 'Pionierland', 250.
10. Working population employed in industry: KH Chemnitz: 65.6 percent, KH Zwickau: 62.6 percent.
11. Burkhardt, 'Sonderstellung', 74.
12. For this discussion see *StJbSa*, (1924/26), 11–12; *StJbDR*, (1929), 19–22.
13. See G. Feldman, 'Saxony, the Reich and the Problem of Unemployment in the German Inflation', *Archiv für Sozialgeschichte*, 27 (1987), 103–44; K. Werner, *Die deutschen Wirtschaftsgebiete in der Krise. Statistische Studie zur regional vergleichenden Konjunkturbetrachtung*, Jena, 1932, 28f.
14. For this discussion see Bramstedt, *Krisis*, 52, 58.
15. Bramstedt, *Krisis*, 7; W. Bramke, 'Vom Freistaat zum Gau. Sachsen unter der faschistischen Diktatur 1933 bis 1939', *Zeitschrift für Geschichtswissenschaft*, 31 (1983), 1077.
16. *StJbDR*, (1932), 303.
17. H. Schwarzbach, 'Die Differenzen zwischen dem Verband Sächsischer Industrieller und dem Reichsverband der Deutschen Industrie 1931', *Jahrbuch für Wirtschaftsgeschichte*, 12 (3) (1971), 81.
18. See H. Adler, 'Die Wirtschaftskrise im Spiegel der sächsischen Konkursstatistik', *ZSäStLA*, (1932/33), 310.
19. *StJbDR*, (1931).
20. F. Burkhardt, 'Die bevölkerungspolitische Lage in Sachsen Ende 1932', *ZSäStLA*, (1932/33), 301.
21. For the following see W. Bramke, 'Die Industrieregion Sachsen. Ihre Herausbildung und Entwicklung bis zum Ende des Zweiten Weltkrieges', in R. Schulze, ed., *Industrieregion im Umbruch. Historische Voraussetzungen und Verlaufsmuster des regionalen Strukturwandels im europäischen Vergleich*, Essen, 1993, 291–317; U. Heß, 'Rüstungs- und Kriegswirtschaft in Sachsen (1935–1945)', in W. Bramke and U.

Heß, eds., *Sachsen und Mitteldeutschland. Politische, wirtschaftliche und soziale Wandlungen im 20. Jahrhundert*, Weimar, 1995, 73–91.

22. *Sachsen im Spiegel der Statistik nach 10 Jahren nationalsozialistischer Führung. Zum 30. Januar 1943 herausgegeben vom Statistischen Landesamt Dresden N6*, 8.
23. W. Bramke, 'Einleitung', in Bramke, *Mitteldeutschland*, 19; W. Bramke, 'Unter der faschistischen Diktatur', in K. Czok, ed., *Geschichte Sachsens*, Weimar, 1989, 507.
24. Bramke, 'Industrieregion Sachsen', 313; Heß, 'Rüstungswirtschaft', 91.
25. W. Matschke, *Die industrielle Entwicklung in der Sowjetischen Besatzungszone Deutschlands (SBZ) von 1945 bis 1948*, Berlin, 1988, 64.
26. Ibid., 195; Heß, 'Rüstungswirtschaft', 91.
27. M. Jahn, 'Veränderungen wirtschaftlicher und sozialer Strukturen in Sachsen 1945 bis 1947 bei der Ansiedlung Vertriebener', in Bramke, *Mitteldeutschland*, 305.
28. D. Weber, 'Erwerbstätigkeit von Frauen in der SBZ (1945–1949). Befunde aus Erfurt und Leipzig', in Bramke, *Mitteldeutschland*, 305.
29. F. Schulz, 'Elitenwandel in der Leipziger Wirtschaftsregion 1945–1948. Von den Leipziger "sächsichen Industriefamilien" zu Kadern aus dem Leipziger Arbeitermilieu', *Comparativ*, 5 (4) (1995), 112–23.
30. For this see R.J. Bazillion, 'Liberalism, Modernization, and the Social Question in the Kingdom of Saxony, 1830–90', in K.H. Jarausch and L.E. Jones, eds., *In Search of a Liberal Germany: Studies in the History of German Liberalism from 1789 to the Present*, Oxford, 1990, 87–110.
31. K. Blaschke, 'Das Königreich Sachsen 1815–1918', in K. Schwabe, ed., *Die Regierungen der deutschen Mittel- und Kleinstaaten 1815–1933*, Boppard, 1983, 83.
32. K. Rudolph, *Die sächsische Sozialdemokratie vom Kaiserreich zur Republik 1871–1923*, Weimar, 1995, 43.
33. Blaschke, 'Königreich', 97.
34. For this see W. Schröder, ' "... zu Grunde richten wird man uns nicht mehr." Sozialdemokratie und Wahlen im Königreich Sachsen 1867–1877', *Beiträge zur Geschichte der Arbeiterbewegung*, 17 (4) (1994), 3–18.
35. F. Heidenreich, *Arbeiterkulturbewegung und Sozialdemokratie in Sachsen vor 1933*, Weimar, 1995, 23.
36. J. Retallack, 'Antisocialism and Electoral Politics in Regional Perspective: The Kingdom of Saxony', in L.E. Jones and J. Retallack, eds., *Elections, Mass Politics, and Social Change in Modern Germany*, Cambridge, 1992, 88.
37. Rudolph, *Sächsische Sozialdemokratie*, 54.

38. R. Kötzschke and H. Kretzschmar, *Sächsische Geschichte*, 2 vols., Dresden, 1935, repr. Frankfurt, 1977, 373.
39. Heidenreich, *Arbeiterkulturbewegung*, 25.
40. Bazillion, 'Liberalism', 107.
41. For this see M. Rudloff, 'Die Sozialdemokratie in den Landtagen des Königreiches Sachsen (1877–1918)', in M. Schmeitzner and M. Rudloff, *Geschichte der Sozialdemokratie im Sächsischen Landtag. Darstellung und Dokumentation 1877–1997*, Dresden, 1997, 11–55.
42. K.H. Pohl, 'Wirtschaft und Wirtschaftsbürgertum im Königreich Sachsen im frühen 20. Jahrhundert', in Bramke, *Mitteldeutschland*, 325ff.
43. Most recently see Lässig, *Sachsen im Kaiserreich*.
44. For the following see Rudolph, *Sächsische Sozialdemokratie*, 55–71.
45. Heidenreich, *Arbeiterkulturbewegung*, 135.
46. For the following see M. Schmeitzner, 'Die sozialdemokratischen Landtagsfraktionen im Freistaat Sachsen (1919–1933)', in Schmeitzner, *Geschichte*, 56–121; K. Rudolph, 'Das Scheitern des Kommunismus im deutschen Oktober 1923', *Internationale Wissenschaftliche Korrespondenz zur Geschichte der Deutschen Arbeiterbewegung*, 32 (4) (1996), 484–519; Lapp, *Revolution*. Also see chapter 3 (i).
47. If not otherwise stated, all election results are calculated from *ZSäStLA, StJbSa*, and *StDR*.
48. For the following see Rudolph, *Sächsische Sozialdemokratie*, chaps 5–6.
49. SPD Sachsen, Vier *Jahre Sächsische Politik*, 1926, 12f.
50. Proletarian Hundreds were set up by various state governments. While they quickly expanded in Saxony after the SPD and KPD had come to an agreement in March 1923, they were outlawed in Prussia in mid-May. See H.A. Winkler, *Von der Revolution zur Stabilisierung. Arbeiter und Arbeiterbewegung in der Weimarer Republik 1918 bis 1924*, Berlin, 1985, 620f, 650. Also see chapter 4 (ii).
51. D.B. Pryce, 'The Reich Government versus Saxony, 1923: The Decision to Intervene', *Central European History*, 10 (2) (1977), 112–47.
52. For a detailed discussion of this see L.E. Jones, 'Saxony, 1924–1930: A Study in the Dissolution of the Bourgeois Party System in Weimar Germany', in J. Retallack, ed., *Memory, Democracy, and the Mediated Nation. Political Cultures and Regional Identities in Germany, 1848–1998*, Conference Reader, Toronto, 1998.
53. See A. Tyrell, *Führer befiehl ... Selbstzeugniss aus der 'Kampfzeit' der NSDAP*, repr. Leipzig, 1991, 382.

54. *Verhandlungen des Sächsischen Landtages* (*VdSL*), 3. Wahlperiode (Wp), 7. Sitzung, 11.1.1927, 143; ibid., 9. Sitzung, 20.1.1927, 169; ibid., 76. Sitzung, 19.4.1928, 2736f; ibid., 106. Sitzung, 19.2.1929, 3955.
55. *Crimmitschauer Anzeiger und Tageblatt*, Nr. 143, 22/23.6.1929.
56. *VdSL*, 4. Wp, 5. Sitzung, 4. Juli 1929, 88ff.
57. *Leipziger Volkszeitung* (*LVZ*), Nr. 58, 10.7.1929.
58. *Völkischer Beobachter* (*VB*), 9.7.1929.
59. New regulations of German reparations payments agreed in 1929. Financially they were far more realistic than the provisions of the Dawes Plan (1924).
60. For the following see Staatsarchiv Dresden (STA D), MdI, Nr. 11126/4, Januar-März 1930.
61. Hitler's demands were: (1) financial revitalisation; (2) protection of the national economy; (3) protection of the states from centralisation; (4) fostering of a nationalistic sentiment among the Germans; (5) maintaining the Christian-German culture. See *VB*, Nr. 149, 25.6.1930. Hitler stayed in Dresden between 14 and 15 July. See *LVZ*, Nr. 167, 21.7.1930.
62. Bramke, 'Freistaat', 1068. The KPD newspaper *Der Kämpfer* was already banned from 16 February onwards. See Heidenreich, *Arbeiterkulturbewegung*, 413.
63. *Sozialdemokratisches Gemeindeblatt. Mitteilungen für die Gemeindevertreter des Bezirkes Chemnitz-Erzgebirge*, 8 (3), 1.2.1933, 54ff; *LVZ*, Nr. 3, 5.1.1933.
64. Killinger was a prominent Saxon NSDAP leader and former member of the Freikorps Brigade Erhardt, the terroristic Organisation Consul (where he was involved in the assassination of Erzberger and Rathenau), and a leading member of the *völkisch* Wehrwolf and Wikingbund before he joined the NSDAP in 1928. In March 1933 he was appointed *Reichskommissar*. See STA D, Druckerei des NS-Gauverlages Sachsen. Zeitungstext- und Bildarchiv, Killinger.
65. *FK*, Nr. 60, 11/12.3.1933.
66. Ibid., Nr. 58, 9.3.1933; E.L. Lang, 'Kampf und Sieg der Nationalsozialistischen Bewegung im Grenzlandkreis Annaberg/Obererzgebirge', in *Vom silbernen Erzgebirge. Kreis Annaberg* vol. 1, 231f.
67. *Sächsisches Verwaltungsblatt* (*SVB*l), Nr. 21, 13.3.1933.
68. Bundesarchiv Koblenz (BA), NS 22, Nr. 271.
69. For the following see Bramke, 'Freistaat', 1070.
70. *FK*, Nr. 105, 6/7.5.1933.
71. Staatsarchiv Leipzig (STA L), PP-St, Nr. 19.
72. Berlin Document Center (BDC), Killinger, Oberstes Parteigericht (OPG), Killinger, December 1936/January 1937, 3.
73. Bramke, 'Freistaat', 1069.

74. The largest ones were Colditz, Dresden, Hainichen, Königstein, castle Oberstein, Sachsenburg and Hohenstein. See T. Mai, 'Der faschistische Gauleiter Martin Mutschmann. Die Entwicklung des Gaues Sachsen unter der NSDAP', Diplomarbeit, University of Jena, 1984, 130.
75. Ibid., 114.
76. H. Matzerath, *Nationalsozialismus und kommunale Selbstverwaltung*, Stuttgart, 1970, 80.
77. Bramke, 'Freistaat', 1071; M. Habicht, 'Verfolgung und Widerstand nichtproletarischer Kräfte im Raum Leipzig-Westsachsen 1933–1945', Ph.D. diss., University of Leipzig, 1990, 52.
78. Bramke, 'Freistaat', 1073ff; Habicht, 'Verfolgung'.
79. H.-D. Schmid, *Gestapo Leipzig. Politische Abteilung des Polizeipräsidiums und Staatspolizeistelle Leipzig 1933–1945*, Leipzig, 1997, 29–40.
80. *Deutschland-Berichte der Sozialdemokratischen Partei Deutschlands (Sopade) 1934–1940*, 7th repr., Nördlingen, 1989, Januar 1935, 70f; ibid., Juni 1935, 731.
81. BDC, OPG, Pillmayer, 'Geschichte der Ortsgruppe der NSDAP zu Raschau', 8f.
82. T. Adam, 'Arbeitermilieu und sozialdemokratisch orientierte Arbeiterbewegung in einer Großstadt – Das Beispiel Leipzig', Ph.D. diss., University of Leipzig, 1997, 206.
83. Schmid, *Gestapo Leipzig*, 23
84. S. Lässig, 'Nationalsozialistische "Judenpolitik" und jüdische Selbstbehauptung vor dem Novemberprogrom. Das Beispiel der Dresdner Bankiersfamilie Arnhold', in Pommerin, *Dresden*, 153. For the numerous disputes between Mutschmann and Killinger see the personal files in the BDC.
85. *FK*, Nr. 67, 20.3.1933.
86. *Sopade*, August 1935, 929.
87. Ibid., Juli 1938, 763.
88. See Kuratorium Gedenkstätte Sonnenstein e. V. und Sächsische Landeszentrale für politische Bildung, eds., *Nationalsozialistische Euthanasie-Verbrechen in Sachsen. Beiträge zu ihrer Aufarbeitung*, 2nd. ed., Dresden, 1996.
89. *Meldungen aus dem Reich. Die geheimen Lageberichte des Sicherheitsdienstes der SS 1938–1945*, eds. Heinz Boberach, 17 vols., Herrsching, 1984, 30.5.1940, 1195f.
90. See chapters 2 (vi), 3 (vi), 4 (vi), and the conclusion.
91. See esp. D. Crew, ed., *Nazism and German Society 1933–1945*, London, 1994.
92. M. Unger, 'Die Leipziger Sondergerichtsakten 1940–1945 und der Volkswiderstand in Westsachsen', in H.-D. Schmid, ed., *Zwei Städte*

unter dem Hakenkreuz. Widerstand und Verweigerung in Hannover und Leipzig 1933–1945, Leipzig, 1994, 192f.

93. J. Osterloh, Ein ganz normales *Lager. Das Kriegsgefangenen-Mannschaftsstammlager 304 (IV H) Zeithain bei Riesa/Sa. 1941 bis 1945*, 2nd. edn., Leipzig, 1997, 184.
94. Schmid, *Gestapo Leipzig*, 55–66. For the increased terror during the war also see Stiftung Sächsische Gedenkstätten zur Erinnerung an die Opfer politischer Gewaltherrschaft, ed., *Spuren Suchen und Erinnern. Gedenkstätten für die Opfer politischer Gewaltherrschaft in Sachsen*, Leipzig, 1996.
95. D. Kürschner, 'Leipzig im Frühling des Jahres 1945', *Sächsische Heimatblätter*, (4) (1995), 206.
96. Retallack, 'Antisocialism', 50; R. Chickering, *We Men Who Feel Most German. A Cultural Study of the Pan-German League, 1886–1914*, London, 1984, 144.
97. K.D. Bracher, *The German Dictatorship, Middlesex*, 1985, 109.
98. J. Retallack, 'Society and Politics in Saxony, 1763–1990. Reflections on Recent Research', *Archiv für Sozialgeschichte*, 38 (1998) (in print).
99. STA D, Sächsische Staatskanzlei (SäStKa), Nr. 134, Bezirk Zittau, 4.8.1924.
100. H. Stoschek, 'Die Entwicklung der militaristisch-faschistischen Bewegung in Sachsen in den Jahren 1919 bis 1925 unter besonderer Berücksichtigung der NSDAP', Diplomarbeit, Potsdam, 1967, 224f.
101. Zwickau was the fourth Nazi Party branch outside Bavaria. See Böhnke, *Ruhrgebiet*, 40f.
102. Bundesarchiv Dahlwitz-Hoppegarten (BA DH), Z/C 17411, Chemnitz, 29.11.1922.
103. BA DH, ZA VI 2029, Polizei Verhör, 23.12.1923.
104. BA DH, Z/C 17411, LPV (the full name of this newspaper is not known), Nr. 175, 19.12.1921.
105. Ibid.
106. BA DH, Z/A VI 2029, Dresden, 9.12.1922.
107. E.g. see the account by a former SA leader: BA, Kleine Erwerbungen Nr. 569: H. Bennecke, 'Die SA in Sachsen vor der "Machtübernahme"', 22.
108. BA DH, Z/C 17411, 'Bericht über die nationalsozialistische Bewegung im Freistaat Sachsen', 6.
109. *Fünfzehn Jahre NSDAP in Markneukirchen* (*1922–1937*), 17.
110. Ibid.
111. STA D, AH Glauchau, Nr. 24, 15.
112. Ibid., Werdau, 6.4.1923.
113. The NSDAP branches were: Zwickau, Chemnitz, Markneukirchen, Plauen, Dresden, Leipzig, Meißen, Freiberg, Aue, Werdau and Weida in Thuringia. There were bases in Mittweida, Radebeul, Adorf,

Eibenstock, Klingenthal, Falkenstein, Schneeberg, Schwarzenberg, Schandau, Gottleuba, Hohenstein-Ernstthal, Niederschlema, Neumark, Wilkau, Lößnitz, and Zwönitz. See BA DH, Z/C 17411, Zwickau, 23.3.1923.

114. BA DH, Z/A VI 2029, Dresden, 9.12.1922.
115. Bennecke, 'SA in Sachsen', 14.
116. Chickering, *Pan-German League*, 144f.
117. R.S. Levy, *The Downfall of the Anti-Semitic Political Parties in Imperial Germany*, London 1975, 95–7.
118. Quoted from Stoschek, 'Entwicklung', 241.
119. In the KH Bautzen 9.3 percent of the population were Catholics compared to 3.6 percent in the rest of Saxony.
120. *FK*, Nr. 55, 3.10.1930.
121. BA DH, Z/C 17411, Dresden, 11.5.1923.
122. *Fünfzehn Jahre NSDAP in Zwickau* (*1922–37*), 12.
123. *Fünfzehn Jahre NSDAP Freiberg, 1939, 6; Fünfzehn Jahre NSDAP Chemnitz* (*1922–1937*), 19.
124. *NSDAP Freiberg*, 14.
125. *Meißner Tageblatt*, Nr. 160, 10.7.1924.
126. Voting percentage for the *Völkisch* Socialist Bloc in the May 1924 Reichstag elections (percentage for the NSFB in the December elections in brackets): Plauen: 19.0 (13.2) percent, AH Oelsnitz: 17.6 (11.6) percent, AH Plauen: 16.8 (10.2) percent, Saxony: 6.6 (2.3) percent, Reich: 6.5 (3.0) percent.
127. STA D, MdI, Nr. 11126/6, Oktober 1926; *NSfS*, Nr. 25, 24.6.1928.
128. See P.D. Stachura, *Nazi Youth in the Weimar Republic*, Oxford, 1975.
129. The *NSfS* was replaced by the *Sächsischer Beobachter* (Saxon Observer; *SB*) in January 1929. Eventually the Saxon Nazis founded their own newspaper, *Der Freiheitskampf* (The Liberation Struggle; *FK*), in August 1930.
130. Bennecke, 'SA in Sachsen', 24.
131. STA D, MdI, Nr. 11126/6, April 1926. Also see chapter 2.
132. The five districts were each headed by a *Gauleiter* and had a total of about 3,000 members and thirty-five party branches in autumn 1925. See STA D, MdI, Nr. 11126/6, Oktober 1925.
133. *NSfS*, Nr. 25, 24.6.1928; *Der Gau Sachsen*, 1938, XVII.
134. *Partei-Statistik, Stand 1. Januar 1935*, ed Der Reichsorganisationsleiter der NSDAP, 3 vols., Munich, no date.
135. *VB*, 26.5.1926.
136. *SB*, Nr. 34, 25.8.1929.
137. STA D, MdI, Nr. 11126/6, Oktober 1926.
138. *NSfS*, Nr. 42, 16.10.1927; ibid., Nr. 41, 9.10.1927.
139. Ibid., Nr. 29, 22.8.1928.
140. Ibid., Nr. 7, 13.2.1927.
141. Ibid., Nr. 23, 5.6.1927.

142. E.g. see Böhnke, *Ruhrgebiet*, 122f; D.R. Tracey, 'The Development of the National Socialist Party in Thuringia, 1924–1930', *Central European History*, 8 (1) (1975), 40.
143. BA, NS 22, Nr. 1067.
144. *FK*, Nr. 18, 22.1.1931.
145. Ibid., Nr. 180, 5.8.1931.
146. STA L, PP-St, Nr. 92.
147. The Saxon NSDAP had attracted hardly any female members before 1923, however, and only had a small percentage of female members between 1925 and 1933. See chapter 5 (ii).
148. Szejnmann, 'Nazis in Saxony', 105, 137f.
149. *FK*, Nr. 57, 9.4.1931.
150. Ibid., Nr. 90, 18.4.1931.
151. For example *Gau* Ruhr was divided into three *Gaue* in October 1928. See Tyrell, *Führer*, 373–76.
152. *SB*, Nr. 44, 3.11.1929; STA D, MdI, Nr. 11126/4, November 1931.
153. *SB*, 3.3.1930.
154. *FK*, Nr. 30, 4.9.1930.
155. STA D, MdI, Nr. 11126/4 Mai 1931; ibid., Juni 1931.
156. BDC, Mutschmann, OPG, 4.12.1936.

Chapter 2

'Only a National Socialist Government Can Create Healthy and Orderly Conditions.' Economic Crisis, Propaganda and Popular Politics

> If the German *Volk* rises again one day, ... there will be a devastating revenge ... .
>
> (Hitler in Plauen, 1 June 1930)

> We are fed up with elections! We have had one election after another for fourteen years ... Help Hitler to achieve his great aims! His aims are freedom and respect for the German nation in the world, social justice for everyone who belongs to the German *Volk*.
>
> (*Der Freiheitskampf*, Nr. 53, 3.3.1933)

This chapter aims to highlight the period when the disintegration of democracy and the Nazi breakthrough took place. The main purpose is to capture the atmosphere of that time and with it the feelings, needs, desires and anxieties of contemporary Saxons. As the story unfolds and a growing number of people were turning away from the Republic and joining the Nazi bandwagon, the chapter pays particular attention to two other aspects. Although it is widely accepted that the economic depression and the collapse of the Weimar Republic stood in close relation to each other,[1] it is surprising how little attention most local and regional studies of Nazism have paid to the exact linkages between the slump and growing support for the NSDAP.[2] This chapter will scrutinise closely the effects of the slump, and the particular problems Saxony faced as a border region.

Of further interest will be the impact of Nazi propaganda, how it was organised and how other parties reacted to it. How successful were the various political parties in capturing the Saxon population? Until recently, historians have agreed that Nazi propaganda was essential in explaining the dramatic rise of the NSDAP's vote from around 800,000 to nearly 14 million between 1928 and 1932. From 1925 onwards Hitler's main objective was to mobilise as many voters as possible in order to come to power through the ballot box. This strategy led the Nazis to build up a tight organisational network all over Germany, through which the party developed a sophisticated mass mobilisation machine which became more and more centrally controlled and efficient. In his classic study about the Nazi party, Dietrich Orlow expressed the commonly accepted view that the twin basis of the Nazis' political success was skilful propaganda and effective organisation.[3] Since then, a number of historians have questioned the overall impact of Nazi propaganda and have argued that its success depended on the existence of a nationalist environment that broadly shared Nazi values. According to this view, the Nazis were only able to mobilise people who were already converted. Gerhard Paul concluded recently: 'A large part of the NSDAP electorate ... voted for Hitler's party independent of its propagandistic self-projection as they longed for a saviour and projected their own desires into the NSDAP.'[4]

Even in this regional study it is impossible to capture the variety of experiences of Saxons who lived in distinct regions and communities, who followed different professions, and were of different ages and genders. It makes sense to look closely at a smaller area while still keeping an eye on the rest of the state. The district of Schwarzenberg provides excellent conditions for a case study, due to the unique survival of secret monthly reports – with only a few gaps – about the social, political and economic situation between 1925 and 1940.[5] The district of Schwarzenberg covered a typically densely populated and industrialised area in the Erzgebirge and, like ten other Saxon districts, bordered Czechoslovakia (see map).[6] Around 70 percent of its population were employed in industry and less than 10 percent in agriculture. Its 132,000 citizens lived in fifty-one small towns and villages and produced various goods including machines, metal, enamel, men's wear, embroidery, paper, brushes, chemicals, paint and wood carving. The district of Schwarzenberg was in an area which became a major stronghold of the Saxon Nazi movement and one of the NSDAP's greatest bastions in the Reich.

(i) The Myth of the 'Golden Twenties'

After the war years had led to increasing hardships among the population, many Saxons continued to experience miserable living conditions during the first years of the Republic. Food shortages and unemployment were widespread and frequently responsible for looting and disturbances. Southwestern Saxony in particular, with its concentration of textile industries, faced an enormous crisis. In September 1919 the military commander of Plauen warned that the severe unemployment in the area could lead to 'unpleasant scenes' and that the people would feel abandoned by the government in Dresden.[7] Detailed investigations in several Saxon towns established a shocking picture of the condition of children. A doctor found that around one-third of all pupils in Plauen between the age of six and sixteen were wearing inadequate clothes (they had not worn underwear for years and wore ragged clothes and shoes) and that nearly two-thirds of all pupils were either severely undernourished or not sufficiently fed.[8]

Traditionally, historians have argued that the period of postwar instability peaked in 1923 with the Ruhr occupation and the devastating hyperinflation, but that the following year 'ushered in a period of economic recovery and stabilisation.'[9] However, recent research claims that the subsequent four years were not as tranquil as often suggested.[10] The situation in Saxony supports this reassessment: officials in the northwest described 1926 as an economic 'crisis year',[11] and a report from central and eastern Saxony highlighted how the modernisation of the economy led to devastating side-effects for workers and middle-class people alike:

> A growing circle of the population is affected by the decline and is burdening the funds for unemployment benefit or the welfare benefits. In particular, a large number of small businesses have ground to a halt. Many small businessmen and artisans will hardly be able to revive their

> trade due to the sharp struggle of competition. The current rationalisation of the large companies often takes place at the expense of the small ones; on these occasions the companies are cleared of the so-called disagreeable elements, wages and salaries are cut and the working conditions worsen.[12]

The district of Schwarzenberg, too, experienced a year of economic recession in which some factories had to shut down and many others introduced a shorter working week and cuts in salaries. Officials observed: 'The unemployment has devastating effects on workers. One can see worry in all the faces. Everyone asks himself where this is going to lead if it continues like this.'[13]

The political situation in Saxony was tense due to the referendum for the '*Fürstenenteignung*' (referendum concerning the expropriation of the former German princes) in June and the state election in late October. Whilst the SPD and KPD campaigned independently, most parties and organisations on the right formed an anti-Marxist front. In the district of Schwarzenberg, as in the rest of Saxony, the two Marxist parties completely outpaced their political opponents regarding public appearances. The bourgeois parties only canvassed shortly before the state election and largely depended on the support of the local press. The Nazis – who had established the district's first party branches in the towns of Aue and Schwarzenberg in early 1924[14] – were by far the busiest group on the right during the campaign. Together with the Communists, they were the only political activists who agitated throughout the year.

The Nazis made some remarkable electoral gains in several small towns in the district of Schwarzenberg in 1926. At a time when their movement was still comparatively small and unknown, one public meeting could make all the difference: in places where the Nazis had held at least one meeting in the year before the election, they gained an average of 7.4 percent of the vote. Where this was not the case, the figure averaged only 2.7 percent. Most significantly, the Nazis won 23.8 percent of the votes in Sosa and 17.8 percent in Zschorlau, where they had held three meetings respectively. The most striking feature of the Nazis' campaign was the great influence of the Munich headquarters. Hitler had ordered all party speakers to participate in the Saxon elections,[15] which explains the fact that the prominent Nazis Gregor Straßer, Heinrich Himmler and Joseph Dietrich spoke at two rallies each in the district of Schwarzenberg. Munich also checked and approved the leaflets that were designed by the Saxon Nazis for the campaign.[16]

Between 1927 and 1928 the economy and the mood of the population improved in most parts of Saxony, including the district of Schwarzenberg. Politically, the atmosphere was calm too. The campaign for the May 1928 Reichstag election was short and – with a few exceptions – peaceful. The SPD and KPD, but also the NSDAP, were noted for their busy campaigning. The Nazis in particular gained a lot of publicity because Hitler spoke at rallies in the major Saxon towns (also see document 9).[17] Compared with this, the bourgeois parties were quiet. In the district of Schwarzenberg they only organised three badly attended public meetings, one of which had to be cancelled because only eight people turned up.[18]

Underneath the surface of tranquillity, however, several problems accumulated. Throughout Saxony some sectors of industry continued to face recession – ninety-two factories were shut down in the state in April 1928 alone, the lace and embroidery industry in the Vogtland/Erzgebirge faced a severe crisis and the downturn affected a growing number of people.[19] In the district of Schwarzenberg, a number of factories were temporarily forced to close, innkeepers complained about a lack of customers, while farmers grumbled about their tax burden. In the fall officials stated: 'Industry is in the middle of a crisis which will affect all thriving industrial sectors in the end.'[20] Furthermore, the anti-Republican NSDAP had become the most active political party besides the KPD and covered the district with nine branches in early 1928.[21]

The strong link between the Nazis' appearance in public meetings and their local poll results continued in the May 1928 election. In villages and towns where the Nazis organised at least one meeting since the October 1926 election, they received an average of 8.9 percent of the votes, while only 4 percent of voters supported them where they had not been active. The small towns where the Nazis organised most meetings in the district continued to account for their greatest share of votes. The local Nazis – as on the national level – mouthed slogans against the November system and Marxism and, above all, tried to appeal to workers. Their main target was the SPD. From 1927 onwards their newspaper's (*NSfS*'s) column 'Letter from Sosa' reported on the Marxist stronghold and its SPD mayor Hille, and vilified it as the epitome of Marxist corruption. The Nazis, who nicknamed the mayor

'Isidor',[22] accused him of 'mismanagement', 'corruption', 'building a luxury home', 'neglecting the unemployed' and called on all workers to join the NSDAP.[23] In local affairs the Nazis frequently allied with Communists to attack Social Democratic maladministration or to underline their support for the unemployed. It is not surprising that the bourgeoisie in Raschau regarded the NSDAP as a radical workers' party.[24]

While the Nazis were wooing workers, they never neglected the middle classes: in early February 1928 they organised the meeting 'The new department store in Schwarzenberg – the ruin of small business and craftsmen'.[25] The Nazis' extreme anti-Marxism and their strong emphasis on nationalism had the potential to appeal to many middle-class people. A Nazi activist was appointed to lead the bureau of a local newspaper in Schwarzenberg because of his 'nationalistic attitude'.[26] When the Nazis' share of votes began to increase, more and more bourgeois parties – like the WP in Aue who offered the Nazis an electoral alliance before the 1928 election[27] – looked for cooperation with the newcomers.

(ii) Exploiting Crisis: Nazism and the Slump

In 1929 the economy continued to deteriorate throughout Saxony. Officials in the northwest assessed that the number of closures and unemployed showed a 'catastrophic economic situation' which 'came close to the inflationary year of 1923'.[28] Although the situation of the various economic sectors varied considerably, the visible impact of the crisis spread. Reports from the district of Schwarzenberg painted a picture of persistent unemployment, a depressed atmosphere among the population and the miserable situation of those who depended on social benefits. One indication of the worsening state of the economy was that a growing number of Saxons used the proximity to Czechoslovakia to buy cheap goods and services from across the border.[29] This had a devastating impact on the local economy. Tailors and shoemakers complained that people used their Czech competitors because of their inexpensive material and working costs. Farmers lamented that door-to-door-salesmen sold low-cost Czech food, such as eggs, in the region. Tobacco traders complained that people did not buy loose cigarettes any more but rather bought whole packets (which were comparatively cheaper) in Czechoslovakia. And finally, local people went to Czech pubs and restaurants to enjoy cheap drinks and food.[30] A representative of the Saxon government painted a gloomy picture:

> A particularly unfavourable situation exists in the regions which border with Czechoslovakia. The predominant industries, like musical instruments, embroidery, timber, and the toy industry, go beyond the border of the Reich. The competition in the immediate vicinity is able to substantially undercut its Saxon neighbours due to more favourable conditions of production in Czechoslovakia ... This attracts particularly skilled workers and increasingly causes Saxon employers to close Saxon factories to re-build them on the other side of the border. Craft and retail trade have been almost totally wiped out because the population keeps itself well stocked from the Czech border towns ... The Saxon border region is becoming more and more deserted.[31]

The 'Association of Saxon Industrialists' frequently attempted to make the Berlin government aware of Saxony's particular problems – calling one initiative 'Saxony's misery – Borderland misery' – and complained that the Czech shoe producer Batas exported millions of shoes to Germany, mainly to Saxony.[32] Even though legislation aimed to ease the problems for local industries, citizens continued to be able to buy goods across the border – albeit with some limits – until the end of the Weimar era.[33] Furthermore, there was an increase in the smuggling of items like shoes, leather goods, laces, gloves and tobacco products from Czechoslovakia to Saxony, which was difficult to control.

The Saxon Nazis responded to the growing economic crisis by initiating a propaganda campaign and – with the close cooperation of their Munich headquarters – held eighty-four public meetings throughout the state (five of those in the district of Schwarzenberg) in early March 1929.[34] Their basic message was to blame the Republic for the fact that German people had been living in 'slavery' for the previous ten years. To them, the acceptance of the Versailles Peace Treaty was at the heart of the problem (see document 10). Plauen coordinated the schedule for all speakers and designed and printed some of the leaflets.[35] Heinrich Himmler – who was in charge of Nazi propaganda in Munich – allocated the national party speakers, supplied the *Gau* with leaflets, and had the final say about the content of the leaflets. The campaign took exactly one-and-a-half months to organise and brought an immediate success: there were demands for new membership application forms from all areas of the state.[36]

Soon after the March campaign new state elections were called for 12 May.[37] The Nazis immediately organised a massive election campaign with national and local speakers, and Gregor Straßer announced: 'This election will be regarded as a barometer of the atmosphere among the population far beyond the borders of Saxony.'[38] The Nazis hoped that an electoral increase would make them the decisive force between left and right in the Saxon parliament. The allocation of speakers was decided at a special meeting which was headed by Gregor Straßer in Plauen in early April. Each national party speaker was assigned to speak at a specific number of meetings. Local party branches, even small ones, seemed to be able to bid for their favourite speakers on the list. The *Gau* informed the speakers where and roughly when to speak.[39] For example, Heinrich Himmler had ten assignments – including small villages – during the campaign. Once the allocations were fixed, the local branches contacted the speakers directly and negotiated the exact details. Speakers were able to choose the topic of the meeting and, if a meeting place had not already been hired for a specific day, even the date.

The Social Democrats and Communists, but in particular the Nazis (Hitler spoke in Annaberg, Glauchau, Leipzig and Zittau), were by far the busiest activists in the campaign. Even the SPD admitted that the previously 'insignificant' Nazis 'displayed great activity in meetings'.[40] All other parties, according to the police, 'kept a very low profile regarding agitation' and 'organised only a few election meetings'.[41] In the three-and-a-half weeks before the election the Nazis staged thirty-five public meetings in the district of Schwarzenberg alone, twenty of them with speakers from outside Saxony. On one day the Nazis also toured the district with several lorries full of Stormtroopers, mainly from Zwickau, and handed out leaflets while followers gave short speeches in the middle of market squares.

As usual, the Nazis fought their campaign not on issues specific to the state, but argued that there was no remedy for the misery in Saxony and that only a fundamental change in the whole system could bring an improvement. They claimed that left and right had sold out Germany and had divided the country, and that the NSDAP was the only force that would fight for all people and a united country (also see document 9). They preached to 'fight against pacifist Marxism' and 'international capitalism', and proclaimed an 'unremitting, relentless, uncompromising' struggle for 'national freedom and social justice'.[42] Several reasons explain the Nazis' broad campaign slogans. The first concerns practicality: most of the speakers who came from outside Saxony were not in a position to discuss local affairs in any detail. There were also the party's limited resources and its aim to create a centrally run and hierarchically structured machinery in order to win power in Berlin. The leaflets were nationally used NSDAP leaflets; some of them had a note about the state elections at the bottom.[43] Six months earlier Himmler had advised a Saxon activist that it was impossible for the party's propaganda headquarters to consider specific regional features.[44] Furthermore, the Nazis' broad themes let them off the hook of having to explain in detail how to solve the grave local problems. Instead of inevitably alienating various social groups in the course of such a discussion, they used broad ideas to appeal to nearly everyone.

The combination of the worsening economic crisis and skilful propaganda paid off for the Saxon Nazis, who suddenly gained the key position between the left and right in the Saxon parliament. In the district of Schwarzenberg the NSDAP doubled its share of the vote from 5.9 percent in 1928 to 11.4 percent in 1929, and continued to gain the best results in villages where it had campaigned most. The other parties had not paid attention to the Nazis – the SPD's official campaign guidelines had material against all other parties, except the NSDAP[45] – and were surprised at their gains. Success in the first half of 1929 was the 'take off' for the Saxon Nazis. The campaign for the referendum against the Young Plan from September onwards and the local elections in November provided them with a golden opportunity to accelerate their momentum and to assert their leading role within the nationalist milieu. The NSDAP, except for one DNVP meeting, was the only party which campaigned for the referendum and organised twenty-three meetings in the district. The activities were followed with particular interest by the population, and officials in Schwarzenberg noted: 'Even among the working classes voices were heard that Germany cannot fulfil the payment plan for such a long time.'[46] Roughly one-fifth of the local population went to the polling station to support the campaign. Again, it is striking that the Nazis did well in villages and towns where they had held most public meetings. Henceforth they determined the agenda in the public sphere and outpaced their political opponents in terms of agitation in most areas of Saxony. In the district of Schwarzenberg, month by month the Nazis organised more political meetings and attracted more participants than all other parties combined, until they seized power in 1933 (see document 13).

'Nineteen-hundred-and-thirty', to use the words of officials in northwestern Saxony, 'was the year of the strongest economic deterioration so far, and at the same time a year with a rapid increase in political radicalism.'[47] The number of unemployed roughly doubled in the state. In the district of Schwarzenberg the first serious clashes between the police and unemployed demonstrators took place. Additionally, innkeepers, small businessmen, craftsmen and hawkers complained about bad business, and gloomy reports about depressed industries piled up. To name but a few, in Schneeberg the toy and embroidery industry had completely collapsed because of lack of orders, in Eibenstock the production of beadwork and embroidery nearly ceased, and the people in Bernsbach expected a total breakdown of the economy.[48]

The confidence of the Saxon Nazis and their challenging behaviour in public grew steadily due to their success and the momentum they had gained. This again provoked their opponents, particularly the Communists, who were determined to resist the spread of Nazism into working-class areas. Violent clashes seemed inevitable (see document 14). Election campaigns in particular heightened existing tensions and uncertainties. Before the state election in June 1930 officials in the district of Schwarzenberg commented: 'Because of the confusing state of the economy, the majority of the population has its doubts which party they should follow.'[49] As usual, campaigning was primarily an affair of the SPD, KPD and NSDAP, who were all able to muster prominent national leaders for their meetings in the state. Officials noted that the Nazis were thriving in these conditions: 'The NSDAP's membership number is rising ... Particularly active were the National Socialists whose uniformed members appeared in considerable numbers in the villages. They gave speeches in public in which they praised their party as the one which will restore their fatherland again.'[50]

Whereas the Nazis attracted a growing number of people to their meetings and benefited from a politicisation of the masses, the bourgeois parties could not even attract reasonable crowds for their few election rallies. The June state election was a great success for the Saxon Nazis. In the district of Schwarzenberg they won 20.3 percent of the vote. It is striking that in the five out of a total of nine villages in the district where the NSDAP support remained below its state average (14.4 percent), it had not organised a single public meeting since November 1925. The places in which the

Nazis had held most public meetings in the previous twelve months brought them exceptional results: they gained 27.8 percent of the vote in Eibenstock where they had organised ten meetings, and 27.6 percent in Niederschlema with nine meetings.

It was crucial that the local Nazis were able to attract thirty-seven prominent national party leaders from outside Saxony – among them were Gottfried Feder, Heinrich Himmler, Gregor Straßer, and pastor Münchmeyer[51] – to speak in seventy-five of the total 242 meetings in their district between 1926 and June 1930. Well-known Nazis helped to lay the foundations for the spread of their movement and pulled in the crowds by attracting an average of 168 people to their meetings – a striking example was a Münchmeyer meeting in Eibenstock with 750 visitors in early 1930 – leaving their Saxon party colleagues' average of 97 people far behind. But all this would not have been possible without the relentless support on the ground of a few local activists. Erich Kunz from Zwickau was the driving force behind the success of Nazism in the district of Schwarzenberg and spoke at thirty-one meetings during the four years before mid-1930 (for more on Kunz see chapter 5 [i]). The sudden increase of Nazi meetings from 1929 onwards was brought about by Kunz, a handful of extremely active local speakers – nine of them spoke at more than one-third of a total of 765 public meetings between 1926 and July 1932 – a few prominent Saxon Nazis, and the national Nazi speakers. After distinguished Nazi speakers had toured the district in all major campaigns until June 1930, the local Nazis were able to continue the momentum on their own.

The Reichstag election in September 1930 was a propagandistic watershed in Saxony: henceforth there was a relentless all-year campaigning of Social Democrats, Communists and Nazis. SPD followers in particular adopted a more active style due to the dramatic growth of Nazism. Political mobilisation frequently exploded into violence, especially between Nazis and Communists. In late September 1930 there was a typical clash between both sides in Eibenstock: a local Nazi leader had called on his followers to demonstrate against Communist terror. When the 150 Nazis who had turned up met an even larger group of Communists who came marching down the street, a brutal fight developed with stones and picket fences. In the end, there were many injured and a few seriously wounded.[52]

Throughout Saxony the economic situation became desperate at the end of the year and employers frequently managed to push through substantial wage cuts in the face of a weakened trade union movement.[53] The general prediction was that 'a catastrophe was imminent in the Erzgebirge.'[54] Officials in the district of Schwarzenberg reported a 'very depressed mood' among the population and elaborated:

> The number of unemployed just grows more and more. The amount of long-term unemployment increased and caused the impoverishment of many families who can only barely dress themselves and are in debt. The acquisition of firewood, potatoes and clothes for the coming winter causes particular difficulties.[55]

The Nazis benefited from rumours and fears of severe political disturbances that the police would not be able to cope with. Officials commented: 'The atmosphere among the population regarding politics is tense and strained. Many people mention that only a National Socialist government can create healthy and orderly conditions.'[56]

(iii) Collapse and Despair: The Nazis Triumph

The year 1931 was one with no major elections in Saxony. However, internal reports of the Saxon government described a continuous radicalisation and political mobilisation:

> [The second Reich emergency decree] caused an enormous increase in meetings not only of the political parties, but also of the trade unions, civil servants and employees organisations, the war invalid association and the unemployed. The KPD, NSDAP and the *Reichsbanner* were competing against each other regarding party publicity and propaganda activities. Fighting parades, red days, propaganda rallies, *Gau* meetings, propaganda trips on lorries, parades and training marches followed one another ... hardly a single Sunday passed by on which a column either on foot or on lorry from one or another party did not come through the small towns or villages with the usual propagandistic presentation of music, flags and posters ... Minor incidents often led to clashes ... and the employment of strong police forces. One understands that peaceful groups among the population were increasingly voicing their dislike about these continuous disturbances.[57]

Physical clashes seemed imminent in the district of Schwarzenberg: small troops of party followers patrolled the streets, and there was a lock-out in a factory in Johanngeorgenstadt. A local report stated early that year: 'The hostility between the different parties has reached a point which will inevitably lead to a civil war in Germany.'[58] Meanwhile, the slump hit more and more economic sectors and individuals (see also document 15). As in the rest of Saxony, the atmosphere among small businessmen, shopkeepers, civil servants, workers, pensioners, teachers and unemployed was 'very tense' and 'embittered' due to the austerity measures from Berlin. Furthermore, the long-term unemployed had no firewood to heat their flats, farmers described their situation as a 'catastrophe', workers were appalled that they had to pay high church taxes while rich landowners only paid a small amount or nothing, innkeepers spoke about the need to close their premises if business worsened, and employers feared immediate 'industrial collapse' and complained about the reparation payments. Officials recorded widespread resignation and hopelessness at the end of 1931: 'An improvement of the economic situation is not expected, it is rather feared that the economy will collapse completely.'[59] The desperate situation drove 'large parts of the working population into the hands of the radical parties.'[60]

The Nazis continued to be the main beneficiaries: new recruits flocked into the party, new party branches and SA units were formed, zealous party branches flooded the district leadership with requests for prominent speakers, and a growing number of followers were seeking to acquire the speaker certificate.[61] Furthermore, the NSDAP received invaluable support from the bourgeois press. Party followers in Aue described their local newspaper as an 'incorruptible fighter for national and *völkisch* concerns' which helped to spread the ideas of Hitler.[62] The Nazis flooded the district with up to twenty-seven meetings each month in which they highlighted the suffering of various social groups. They organised more public meetings and attracted more people to their meetings than all other parties combined (see document 13). The other political parties were not able to match the Nazis' dynamism, let alone seriously challenge their steady rise. The bourgeois parties' seven meetings between October 1930 and December 1931 – none of which were directed against the NSDAP – contrasted sharply with the Nazis' 247 meetings. What made Nazi propaganda so effective was not that they introduced new methods – most of their style was copied from the Marxists, while the bulk of their slogans were a mixture of nationalist and socialist ideas – but that a political group of the nationalist milieu had built up a widespread network to campaign against the political system on the streets and in meeting halls. Previously this had been the domain of the left.

The local Social Democrats concentrated their main efforts in fighting Nazism and targeted the NSDAP in twenty-three of their overall thirty-nine meetings until the end of 1931. In quantitative terms these were pitiful efforts by a disintegrating SPD organisation against a well-oiled Nazi propaganda machine. For a long time the SPD had behaved similarly to traditional bourgeois parties of local dignitaries (*Honoratioren*). A Social Democratic leader recalled: 'In small and medium-sized villages and towns, and also in large towns, one only spoke before elections or on May the First. Normally the gatherings were for a limited circle only.'[63] These occasions seemed more of a restricted ritual than a powerful mass event. To be fair, the SPD's mobilisation ability in short election campaigns or for specific events was miles ahead of any other Saxon party throughout the 1920s. From then onwards, however, the Social Democrats were unable to respond sufficiently to the Nazis' relentless propaganda style in many areas. Furthermore, as government party and main creator of the system, they were clearly driven onto the defensive once the crisis unfolded. The Nazis in Aue predicted this well at the time of the SPD's last electoral success in May 1928:

> The SPD is visibly rejoicing its election victory. We congratulate them, after all they have to take responsibility for domestic and for foreign affairs in the future. And they will thoroughly fail again, which will open up the eyes of many German workers ... it was only a 'Pyrrhic victory'. It is true that the SPD still has a comparatively large electorate behind it, however, this is only a dead mass, which is only kept together by the party organ. Opposite this is the strengthened NSDAP. We have a fighting spirit, because we have the deep belief that we will seize victory in the final battle.[64]

After September 1930 the KPD in the district of Schwarzenberg began to take the fight against the Nazis more seriously and organised nineteen of its 123 meetings against the latter until the end of 1931. The Communists, however, were more keen on exploiting the crisis for their own purpose than throwing all their energies against Nazism. They gave eighteen talks about the apparently exemplary situation in the Soviet Union, organised at least seven meetings for the unemployed, concentrated five talks on the treacherous SPD, and held meetings on various other topics to attract specific groups in society. Whereas the bourgeois parties and the SPD were disintegrating and unable to respond adequately to the challenges, the only two dynamic parties left, the Nazi party and KPD, aimed at overthrowing the system (see document 11).

In the face of government helplessness and inactivity towards the growing crisis, people longed for some kind of action and change. There was growing support – particularly from right-wing circles – for the Nazis' cry for a tough line on foreign policy and an end to the reparation payments (see document 10).[65] For many the rise of the vigorous Nazis seemed unstoppable. To them, their promise to rebuild a strong and healthy Germany provided the only hope in the middle of a deepening crisis which seemed set to destroy everything. Only the Nazis seemed capable of checking the perceived threat of disturbances and socialist revolution. Officials noted at the end of 1931:

> Generally the people express the opinion that the NSDAP will soon be the strongest of all political parties, and that its rising movement cannot be stopped by anything. The SPD seems to be on the way to perishing ... The majority of the peaceful population is very embittered about the bloody terror of the KPD. There is surprise that the government does not introduce decisive measures.[66]

In 1932 the crisis worsened further and business reached more or less a 'standstill' in the district of Schwarzenberg. In February four out of five large factories were either struggling or closed. Social tensions deteriorated due to rising unemployment and poverty. A report stated: 'There was and still is great anger among those who receive social benefits because of the cuts in aid. In some places in the district the local police, sometimes backed up by the riot squad, was kept ready on pay days to keep public order.'[67] Political opponents clashed more frequently too, particularly in strongholds of the KPD and SPD where the Nazis faced stiff resistance. For instance, two Nazis were seriously wounded by activists of the *Reichsbanner* and KPD in the town of Lößnitz, a Marxist bastion.[68] However, the swing towards the NSDAP continued. Early in 1932 more and more people believed that 'only this party seems to be able to change the current extremely bad economic and political situation.'[69] A few weeks later a report revealed: 'The NSDAP is winning a growing number of supporters through the determined and purposeful appearance of its speakers in its frequent meetings.'[70] This confirms findings from other regions in Germany that Nazi propaganda – which included the readiness for violence and sacrifices, the military-like character of the SA, and the new quantity of meetings – gave the Nazis an 'image of determination' and organisational competence which made people believe that the Nazi party was able to realise what other right-wing parties only talked about.[71]

The majority of the population voted for Hitler as President of the Reich (51.3 percent) in the district of Schwarzenberg in April. Their disappointment over Hindenburg's election was short-lived because the dissolution of the Reichstag revived their political expectations. During the campaign for the July 1932 Reichstag elections the local Nazis focused on a variety of topics in their meetings, such as women, religion and the economy in the forthcoming Third Reich, and did not follow Goebbels' targeting of the SPD.[72] The weak local Social Democrats did not seem to make this necessary. The Nazi party gained 49.1 percent of the vote and only lost 2.3 percent in the November Reichstag elections.

It was striking that the Nazis received less than one-third of the seats in the district's local elections in mid-November.[73] This remarkable decline in the polls stemmed from the Nazis' negative attitude towards local affairs and their comparatively bad organisation in them. In the late 1920s an activist from the Erzgebirge had complained to the Munich headquarters about their poor material on local affairs compared with that of the Marxist parties, and the *Gau* published a very thin 'Correspondence for Local Council Members' only from late 1931 onwards.[74] Equally important, the NSDAP's tactic in the local councils – 'Not positive cooperation, but strict opposition!'[75] – was too negative. The Nazis' tendency to blame the other parties and the system for all problems, their avoidance of discussing detailed solutions, and their sweeping promises of improvements once they were in power, did not reap the same electoral success in local as in general elections. Paradoxically, people voted for them in order to set up a completely new system, but preferred the traditional parties to look after the street in front of their houses. Radical change at the heart of the state machinery in Berlin seemed more remote and hence easier to support than changes in community affairs. Long-standing networks, traditions and interests in local communities seemed more resistant to breaking down during the crisis than their national equivalent.

The economic depression continued in 1933, and the whole region suffered additionally due to the lack of snow in their ski resorts during the winter holidays. Hitler's appointment as

Chancellor enhanced the polarisation in society. Whereas the majority greeted the news and officials observed a unity among the citizens with nationalistic sympathies, the left moved closer together in its opposition to the new government. Before the Reichstag elections in early March, SPD and KPD activists formed the 'Socialist Fighting Union', while nationalist organisations staged parades with 'unprecedented participation' in all villages and towns.[76] The majority of the voters (51.9 percent) gave the Nazis the mandate to create the Third Reich and celebrated the election result. Officials recorded that many people displayed flags from their windows and that 'despite the enormous misery many eyes were watering with joy.'[77]

(iv) Challenging Nazism: Class, Religion and Popular Politics in the Crisis

It is crucial to look at Nazism as a movement which promoted a national revival for most Germans and not for a specific class (see also documents 9 and 10). The Nazis presented themselves as the only party that aimed to overcome the class divisions in German society, which their political opponents had traditionally fostered or at least accepted. One Saxon Nazi expressed this in the Landtag:

> The left has managed to do one thing: it has torn the German workers as a class out of the German *Volksgemeinschaft* [national community] and separated them as a class-conscious proletariat from the same German *Volksgemeinschaft*; the bourgeois parties have split the remaining nationalist Germans into the Peasant Party, the Democratic Party, the Party for Reevaluation, and the Business Party. They have always put forward new slogans in new elections, and have always spoken about the needs of farmers, of the needs of the middle classes, but never about the needs of the whole German *Volk*.[78]

National Socialism, according to the Nazis, was the only ideology which provided a solution to this and aspired to replace class struggle with harmony and unity, because it meant:

> Love for the blood-related *Volksgenossen* [ethnic comrades] ... If this love is transferred from the individual to the whole *Volk* and into all hearts, it embraces everyone who shares the same blood and soul and lives in the same country: in the fatherland![79]

It is obvious that the Nazis' claim to be forming a new unity was subject to their own arbitrary and scientifically bogus racial criteria which excluded Jews – but also other groups in German society – from belonging to the racially 'fit' nation. These steps would eventually lead to a dictatorship based upon racial principles: an attempt to restructure a 'class' society along racial lines (see document 19 and chapter 4 [vi]).[80]

Besides the propaganda of having found a unifying ideology for Germany – the vision of a *Volksgemeinschaft*, which in fact they had hijacked from other groups (see chapter 3 [v]) – the Nazis also had to appeal more specifically to the various social groups in society. Their skill was to adopt some of the most popular themes of the left (anti-capitalism and social justice) and the right (nationalism and authoritarianism), and to use them in a more radical and uncompromising manner than all other parties.

Before the election in June 1930 the local Social Democrats threw down the gauntlet to the Nazis with confidence and a touch of mockery: 'If National Socialism wants to become powerful in Saxony, the land of the proletariat, it needs to win the soul of the proletariat.'[81] The Nazis' dramatic electoral success in the state delivered to the national SPD 'the first real shock at Nazism's advance'.[82] Some Social Democrats also began to get concerned about the source of the Nazi gains. In an illuminating article the SPD leader Paul Löbe tried to explain why 'petty bourgeois people, civil servants, employees, and unfortunately also workers' had voted for the NSDAP. According to him, opposition to socialism and Marxism, or to the Republic, were not sufficient reasons as other parties had similar aims. Löbe concluded:

> There remain only social reasons ... lively speeches against big capitalism ... accusations against companies and trusts, price fixing and exploitation, criticism against high pensions, salaries, other incomes – these abuses, which we also attack, found a storming applause in their rallies and for their speakers who debated in our meetings.[83]

Henceforth, the Saxon SPD admitted what was previously thought to be impossible: there were workers who supported Nazism. According to the Social Democrats, however, these were 'workers, whose views were not trained enough', i.e., 'misguided class comrades'.[84] Workers had formed a consistent and substantial part of the Saxon Nazi membership (around 37 percent) since the refoundation of the NSDAP in 1925; however, the Nazis had not been very successful in attracting workers to vote for them until 1930. Thereafter this changed dramatically and by 1932 more workers voted for the NSDAP than for the SPD or KPD (for this see chapter 5 [ii–iii]).

Considering that the working classes were by far the largest group in Saxon society, it is not surprising that the local Nazis wooed workers more than any other class (see document 12). In spring 1929 the Social Democrats in southwestern Saxony noticed that the Nazis made great efforts to attract workers and portrayed themselves as true socialists and enemies of capitalism.[85] Before the 1930 state election the Nazis appealed to 'all honestly fighting working-class members' to vote for them.[86] A year later the Nazi party proudly reported that the former Marxist bastion of the Erzgebirge had developed into a National Socialist stronghold.[87] The Nazis literally tried to attract workers with the notion of German 'national socialism' as opposed to Marxist internationalism. In a meeting in northwestern Saxony a factory worker appealed to his class brothers:

> The reason why we workers stand with Adolf Hitler today is because we have realised how Marxism, which apparently looked after the German worker to fight for a better life for him, has betrayed him and has led to today's misery ... And because of this realisation we national socialist workers have joined the great movement of Adolf Hitler, who does not fight for one class or profession, but for the whole *Volk* and therefore for each individual *Volksgenosse*. Those German workers who still stand apart should, instead of indulging in international class consciousness, join the front of national socialism.[88]

The Nazis promised workers a safe and prosperous future: protection from the painful effects of the process of modernisation in the form of a new social unity (*Volksgemeinschaft*) which would enhance the prosperity of all and guarantee employment to everyone.[89] Only an authoritarian state system would be able to deliver this by wiping out the harmful internal divisions. The need to abolish free trade unions was part of this process. The Saxon Nazis pledged to local workers:

> Your right to live will be secured in the nationalist socialist state. The unbounded exploitation through profit-seeking employers ... will be stopped. The trade unions, who have by now lost the trust of their members due to the policies of Marxists or the Centre Party, will be built up to true representatives of the employees.[90]

Only an able dictator could guarantee the welfare of the masses. A Nazi speaker argued in the late 1920s:

> The dictator should not be a tyrant, but he must be the best of all Germans with a deep emotional link to the *Volk* ... The realisation that things cannot go on like this has led to the call for a dictator from the heart of the true *Deutschtum* [Germandom], which is a truly healthy phenomenon. The struggle for this dictatorship must be led with all available means, otherwise the extinction of the German *Volk* will be inevitable.[91]

In a state with more people out of work than anywhere else in Germany, it was crucial that the Nazi party included the unemployed in its propaganda too. The KPD – as in the rest of Germany – was the most active party campaigning for the unemployed in Saxony. In the district of Schwarzenberg it organised at least seven well attended meetings for this group during the slump. The Nazis only organised two meetings specifically for the unemployed in the district, but built up the image of caring for those who were hit worst of all by the slump. The deputy Nazi *Gauleiter* in Saxony, Karl Fritsch, declared: 'We National Socialists regard the unemployed as true *Volksgenossen* who ... have a right to work, a right to a wage, and a right to property.'[92] The Saxon Nazis 'unreservedly supported' Communist motions in town councils for winter aid for the unemployed, and organised similar schemes for their own unemployed followers. They even set up party cells and issued a circular for the unemployed.[93] The increasing competition between Nazis and Communists to woo those who were out of work eventually led to severe clashes between both sets of activists in front of employment offices.[94] The Communists were the clear winners in this battle and – as in the rest of Germany – were supported overproportionally by the unemployed in elections (however, see also document 16). Whilst the Saxon Nazis managed to attract many unemployed to serve as Stormtroopers, they were not very successful in convincing them to vote for them in elections (see chapter 5 [iii]). Even the Saxon Social Democrats, who only started to adopt a more active approach towards the unemployed in autumn 1932,[95] received more electoral support from this group. However, unemployed members of the largest consumer cooperative in Leipzig – which was an essential part of the SPD milieu in the city – received free bread and vouchers for goods during the slump.[96] It is likely that this was common throughout

Saxony. To the unemployed, the traditional Marxist parties offered more than Nazism: the former put a lot of emphasis on practical help in the form of social benefits; socialism promised a more radical shake-up of society in favour of the dispossessed than national socialism; and finally, the Nazis' support for compulsory work schemes[97] – which was vehemently opposed by KPD and SPD – could not have been very popular among unemployed.

One of the most serious challenges to the success of Nazism in attracting workers' support was the great effort the Communists made in describing a 'heaven-like' situation in the Soviet Union, compared with the crisis-ridden capitalist world. The Communists organised around two dozen talks on this topic in the district of Schwarzenberg alone in the early 1930s. The Nazis had to respond to this. They agreed with the KPD about overthrowing the existing system (see document 11). But more than anything else, the Nazis' success depended on their ability to convince the masses that their vision of a future state, i.e., a National Socialist state, was the only positive alternative to the misery. They benefited from the fact that the interpretation of the situation in the Soviet Union was a traditional battlefield between left and right. Throughout the Weimar years the bourgeoisie had painted the picture of a barbaric, unchristian, and anarchic state which threatened the German *Volk*. The *Dresdner Nachrichten* warned its readers before the elections in September 1930:

> This fight is about ... Germany's future, about all our futures, about whether the coming winter will spread a shroud of unutterable misery and slow languish over our fatherland from which will arise the red blood-soaked face of Russian Bolshevism ... This fight is not about the destiny of parties, it is about the destiny of our *Volk*.[98]

The Nazis put forward the same line of argument (of course no-one ever mentioned that most Social Democrats were strongly opposed to a soviet-style Germany), and turned it into a powerful campaign to advocate their alternative to the existing system. They organised a massive campaign throughout Saxony about 'The true face of the Soviet Union' from mid-1931 onwards and described horrific conditions in the country. The main speaker in these meetings was Klötzner, who came from a well-known Communist family in Chemnitz.[99] Apparently, Klötzner had become disillusioned with Communism during a visit to the Soviet Union where he had worked for the secret police. Suspected of being counter-revolutionary, he had managed to flee the country in a dramatic manner. All this was bound to arouse much publicity, particularly as Klötzner appeared in the uniform of the Russian secret police, presented his official papers to the audience, and gave first hand accounts from the Soviet Union. The Nazi party organised fourteen of these meetings in the district of Schwarzenberg and attracted crowds of up to 700 people. The campaign not only hyped up anxieties and strengthened the desire for a strong state, but also demolished the Communists' vision of a future German state.

To become a 'catch-all party' the Saxon Nazis also needed to attract the middle classes. Their basic strategy was to attack organised labour and big capitalism and to show how both of them damaged the middle classes. The Nazis accused local consumer cooperatives – Saxony possessed an extremely elaborate consumer-cooperative movement – and department stores for ruining middle-class business, and uncovered endless cases of how apparently Marxist corruption misused taxpayers' money. Between the two state elections in May 1929 and June 1930 the local Nazis focused heavily on accusing the bourgeois government – and in particular the DVP – of keeping the 'administration filled with Marxists', and 'wasting millions in the Ministry of Labour and Welfare under Elsner [ASP]'.[100] Before the June elections they proclaimed: 'There is no great difference between the Marxists and the DVP ... The DVP betrayed the bourgeoisie' (ibid.). It was crucial that the Nazis' objective of raising the living standards of the whole nation did not challenge property and wealth – unlike the Marxists' concept of nationalisation – but sought to create private wealth for anyone who belonged to the *Volksgemeinschaft*.[101] The Nazis took the initiative on the streets and in public rallies and made the traditional bourgeois parties appear passive. Middle-class people were attracted by the Nazis' dynamic appearance, their nationalist sentiments, their resolute stance against Marxism, and their determined response to the crisis whilst the other bourgeois parties seemed to have failed their constituencies.

A DNVP meeting in southwestern Saxony in 1929 highlights how the Nazis exploited the half-hearted attitude of one of their more radical bourgeois competitors and seized the initiative with an even bolder and more uncompromising approach. Although the DNVP speaker expressed his dislike for the political system, he argued that circumstances made it necessary to participate in parliamentary life. The local newspaper reported how the Nazi Göpfert attacked this stance in the debate:

> Göpfert referred to the proud tradition of the former German nationalist movement, but he regarded their essential approval of the current situation as a weakness which would never stem the spread of Marxism. If the will wants to master the danger, it must be brutal, hard as steel, free of any compromise and ready to fight to the extreme. Only the creation of conditions of power politics [*Machtpolitik*] would make the rebuilding of Germany possible.[102]

The way in which the Nazis and the other politicians responded to the catastrophic economic crisis was crucial in explaining how the NSDAP became the largest party in the region. As mentioned previously, the Nazis almost completely neglected local issues. They only organised four meetings which centred around local affairs (outside local election campaigns) in the district of Schwarzenberg between 1926 and July 1932 (see also tables 2.1 and 2.2). This is surprising as the local population faced very specific and extremely grave economic problems. Workers in the widespread cottage industries led an appalling existence. As a Communist described: 'The food of the poorest of the poor is normally nothing but potatoes and herring, potatoes with linseed oil, potatoes and cabbage, potatoes with onions. It is not unusual that a family of eight only has half a pound of meat for dinner, and that is on Sundays only.' [103] (Also see document 15.) Whole families – including children from the age of six – worked up to fourteen hours a day for an extremely low wage. Some industries perished during the slump: by mid-1930 the toy and embroidery industry had totally collapsed and the beadwork industry was nearly at a standstill.[104] One-and-a-half years later the 'once prosperous enamel industry in the area of Schwarzenberg ... a significant source of income for many workers' was 'completely wiped out'.[105]

There was thus a wide choice of gloomy problems in the district of Schwarzenberg. But the Nazis did not organise a single meeting on these issues. In parliament in Dresden they made it clear that 'they can only find a solution to these problems in their own state' – i.e., they would only be able to implement their unorthodox measures of large-scale government-initiated investments and a mixture of state socialism, autarkic economic development and *Lebensraum* (living space) in the Third Reich (see chapter 4 [v]) – but that they were willing 'to give provisional support' to measures which were designed to ease the catastrophic situation in the Erzgebirge.[106] This was a clever and opportunist tactic because they were not caught in the insoluble problem of how to overcome the crisis in the Republic. The government and the bourgeois parties frequently discussed the enormous misery in the Erzgebirge and the border regions. They were not in a financial position, however, to cure the problems of what were largely old-fashioned and declining industries and admitted that – if at all – only intervention from the Reich could change things.[107] Behind closed doors they agreed that foreign competition and machine production had sealed the extinction of some local industries – like the chip basket industry.[108]

The SPD tried to win support with an honest political debate. A Social Democrat played down the negative impact of Czech competition and argued in parliament: 'The fact that there is considerable unemployment in Saxony is not only caused by our large number of small business, but also by the exceptionally unproductive work of these firms.' He went on to explain:

> Nowadays the piano industry only uses about 20 percent of its production capacity, not because the wages are too high, but because there simply is no demand. Demand has decreased due to the spread of mechanical music, radio, gramophone, etc. ... neither the German and the Saxon economic crisis, nor the world economic crisis, is caused by economically harmful Marxist union and wage policies, but it is caused by ... the nature of the capitalist system. And on top of this comes direct capitalist mismanagement.[109]

Already before the First World War Saxon industrialists had explained the 'severe crisis' of the local embroidery and lace industry – the export from the Vogtland to the U.S.A. had slumped by half in 1913 compared with the previous year – with economic dislocations caused by the process of modernisation: i.e., changes in fashion, political insecurity and international competition which produced cheap and/or better quality products.[110] Those who faced extreme misery or anxiety were aware of these critical explanations of the economic problems, but were not prepared to accept their consequences. In fact, this would have amounted to acceding to their professional extinction because it meant that some industries would inevitably perish while others would continue to suffer because there would be no investment available to modernise them. The Nazis were aware that people's main concern was not to demand generous welfare measures to ease their decline, but to get themselves out of the hole they found themselves in and to regain a belief in the future. A former Saxon SA leader reflected on his experience with those who lived in villages where most employment opportunities were depressed or had ceased:

> A party speaker who used rational arguments was hardly able to sway an audience who faced misery ... To tell these people that the welfare rates had to be raised was not what they really desired. After all they wanted a future for themselves and their families. Their own experiences told them that this could not be secured with those who had been in charge of politics.[111]

More and more people became attracted to the cure that the Nazis offered: a nationalist revival. It seemed to make sense that only new and bold measures – a break with the past, but one in which familiar nationalist values were taken along – could overcome the severe crisis and re-establish the welfare of the people. A Nazi speaker told his audience in southwestern Saxony before the Reichstag elections in July 1932:

> Soldiers of German freedom! ... Adolf Hitler has built the front of German destiny, because we want life and freedom. To secure life and freedom we need to acquire the control over the state, to send those to hell who ruled as they liked. We are going to get rid of those rulers on 31 July. We want to build a state of pride and work, and to do this we must give the German man a sword in his hand so that he is able to defend himself [*Wehrhaft*] and with that become upright [*Ehrhaft*] again. On 31 July we are going to build the fundament: pride, religion, fatherland, family, protection. We will forge an Empire of social justice, of national freedom.[112]

In contrast to this determined message, the local SPD seemed torn between defending the Republican system and dreaming of a future socialist state. Whilst the SPD had extremely mixed success in holding on to its traditional working-class constituency in various parts of Saxony (see chapter 3), its ambition to attract large middle-class support failed due to its orthodox Marxist doctrine. Indeed, the old middle class – farmers, shopkeepers, merchants and artisans – must have felt extremely concerned about the SPD's policies. Saxon Social Democrats showed no sympathy whatsoever for the 'continuous disintegration of middle-class existence', which they regarded as an inevitable and positive economic development that would eventually lead to a socialist revolution.[113] They were also in favour of department stores and rationalised commerce so that goods would be cheaper for the working classes.

Hence the SPD specifically rejected proposals to protect shopkeepers from the competition of department stores and cooperatives.[114] These consumer-orientated views were also supported by members of the new middle classes – salaried employees and civil servants. This may help to explain why a significant number of them became part of the socialist milieu (e.g., nearly one-third of the members of the large Plagwitz consumer cooperative in Leipzig were not workers, and around one-sixth of the membership of the SPD in Leipzig came from the middle classes)[115] and voted for the SPD (see chapter 5). Most members of this class, however, were certainly not keen on the idea of a socialist revolution and the attack on property and thus supported non-Marxist parties.

The SPD proved completely immobile and clung to its traditional and idealistic principles even during the most severe crisis. Goebbels – who followed the dictum 'the greater the lie the better' – would have enjoyed reading the report about the discussion between Social Democrats in Chemnitz regarding their campaign strategy for the September 1930 elections:

> When a comrade suggested that the party should answer the lies of the enemy with its own lies, a loud laughter went through the hall. And the answer of comrade Kuhnt that the party of August Bebel will not fight with lies, but with honest, open truth was followed with loud applause.[116]

Although many Social Democrats were aware that the Nazis' emotional approach struck a cord with many people, this was simply not a political style they found acceptable. Their report about the speech of a leading Saxon Nazi was full of contempt and bewilderment:

> Studentkowski talked very long and very loud. He ... emphasised his words with completely exaggerated theatrical gestures, nonsense and body twists ... And despite this, or more precisely because of this, the attending swastika supporters celebrated the speaker with an applause of shouting and stamping at the end which came close to obsession and fanaticism. One had the feeling that the audience would have applauded in the same way if he had spoken in Russian or Arabic.[117]

The Communists were the only ones – apart from the Nazis – who reacted to the crisis with a certainty and a vision. Again and again they stated what they regarded as the only remedy for the misery of the people:

> It will not help them if the Saxon government will give them … one or several million in subsidies. This will not help at all, they will not shake off their misery but the misery will still continue. It seems clear that if one wants to get rid of it one has to tackle the root of it, one has to get rid of the capitalist system.[118]

A growing number of Saxons favoured the removal of the existing system and turned their back on Weimar. The majority of them, however, did not want a socialist state in place of the Republic, but were prepared to give the Nazis' Third Reich a chance because it promised a combination of nationalist values and individual prosperity. The Saxon Communists were not in a position to stage a realistic revolutionary challenge. They consisted of a small and extremely devoted cadre which made a lot of noise and action but – like a smoke screen – had no depth or real core to it because it lacked a stable and widespread network of members and branches. The KPD's drift to the radical left in the late 1920s and the continuous internal purges and changes in direction helped to explain this. It is true that more and more Saxons voted for the KPD in elections when the crisis unfolded, but most of these sympathisers were not prepared to march for a revolution on the streets (see document 16). The KPD was slowly closing the electoral gap on the SPD – the former received 19.6 percent of the vote in November 1932 in Saxony, while the SPD gained 27.6 percent – but continued to play a clear second fiddle within the workers' movement until the end of the Republic (see document 17).

The Nazis' championship of a strong, nationalist state was decisive for their popularity. They were helped by the fact that Germans who lived in border regions, like many Saxons, tended to be more nationalistic than elsewhere in the Reich.[119] To a growing number of people the belief in the fatherland and in Germany's future assumed quasi-religious proportions and turned into an emotional panacea during the crisis (see document 18). No-one was better at celebrating and exploiting this than the Nazis. The way in which one Nazi ended his speech in southwestern Saxony was typical:

> I believe in my German fatherland, in my German *Heimat*, in the German present, in all the good and the noble, in Germany's future, youth and resurrection! Germany must become free and if we need to die for it, then we will![120]

So widespread was this nationalist appeal and so devastating seemed the crisis, that only a remobilisation of all the available energies – similar to a decisive battle in a war – seemed to promise a way out. The militarisation of ideas and language – but also the feeling of betrayal due to the consequences of the First World War – was a widespread phenomenon in which the traditional Marxist parties also played a significant part. Before the July 1932 elections some Social Democrats talked of a 'decisive battle',[121] and a Communist proclamation could have come from the Nazis themselves:

> Our red freedom banner flaps proudly in the wind despite hatred and slander; it is not stained with the approval of the Versailles pact of disgrace, it is not stained with the policy of toleration and emergency. Our flag shines red and bold for the coming fights. The future is ours – one fight – one front – one victory![122]

The Nazis in the district of Schwarzenberg tried to attract people to their meetings with slogans against the November system and the misery it caused for Germany, and by emphasising the qualities of their own party and of their leader Hitler (see table 2.1). These were broad themes which potentially appealed to nearly every group in society. It is striking how little they focused on specific

Table 2.1 NSDAP Meeting Topics in the AH Schwarzenberg between November 1925 and July 1932[1] (percentage in brackets)

	November 1925–May 1928		June 1929–September 1930		November 1930–July 1932	
November system/ Germany's misery	29	(44.6)	73	(41.2)	93	(19.8)
NSDAP/Hitler	9	(13.8)	33	(18.6)	119	(25.4)
Anti-Marxist	9	(13.8)	21	(11.9)	46	(9.8)
Specific group/topic[2]	11	(16.9)	23	(13.0)	89	(19.0)
Specific party	0	(0.0)	0	(0.0	15[3]	(3.2)
Others	7	(10.9)	27	(15.3)	107	(22.8)
Total	65	(100.0)	177	(100.0)	469	(100.0)

[1] Topic of 711 meetings is known; [2] See table 2.2; [3] SPD: 10, KPD: 5.
Source: STA D, AH Schwarzenberg, Nr. 1940–1945.

issues or classes. The more the movement grew and the Third Reich became a serious possibility, however, the more the Nazis were under pressure to explain their position a little clearer on aspects like religion, the economy, or workers and women.

The skill of the Nazis was to remain vague about problems where there were no immediate solutions, and to fight very determinedly on issues where they felt they could argue a point. One of the most distinctive features of their meeting topics in the district of Schwarzenberg was that by far the largest number dealt with the relationship between the NSDAP and religion (see table 2.2). There was a good reason for this. The area was a stronghold of the

Table 2.2 NSDAP Meetings which Appealed to a Specific Group or Dealt with a Specific Issue in the AH Schwarzenberg between November 1925 and July 1932

	Nov. 1925–May 1928	June 1929 Sept. 1930	Nov. 1930–July 1932
Religion	0	4	29
Workers	3	1	10
Farmers	2	0	10
Youth	0	3	7
Local affairs	1	6	2
Middle Classes	1	1	6
Freemasonry	0	3	5
Women	0	0	7
Anti-Semitism	2	1	2
Military/W.W.I.	0	0	5
Harzburg Front	0	0	3
Cooperatives/warehouses	1	1	0
Invalids/pensioners	0	0	2
Housing	1	0	0
Culture	0	1	0
Insurance	0	1	0
Machines	0	0	1

Source: STA D, AH Schwarzenberg, Nr. 1940–1945.

Christian Social People's Service (CSVD: Christlich sozialer Volksdienst), a Protestant movement of nationalist workers, white-collar workers and former DNVP politicians. This new splinter party, which was founded at the end of 1929, aimed for the spiritual and Christian regeneration of Germany's political life, and wavered between support for the Republic or for the Monarchy.[123] When the CSVD gained a remarkable 11.2 percent of the vote in the June 1930 election in the district of Schwarzenberg, this was a serious challenge for the local Nazis. The party appealed to dissatisfied and religious people – including women – across all classes, and seemed to absorb and unite former voters of the other bourgeois parties (DNVP, SLV, DVP and WP). Although the CSVD had only gained 57,000 votes in the elections in Saxony (2.2 percent of the votes), it had received two crucial seats in parliament. The Nazis' response was to organise three meetings about their stance towards religion during the September election campaign in the district of Schwarzenberg. Then, after the CSVD still gained 10.6 percent at the polls, local Nazis organised twenty-nine meetings about this topic over the next two years. Additionally, they presented themselves as good Christians and supported the 'Christian lists' during the elections of parents' councils (see chapter 4 [iii]). The CSVD was simply overwhelmed by the Nazi onslaught. It was not able to organise more than five meetings in the whole district between September 1930 and July 1932 and its vote dropped then to below 5 percent. Like all other Saxon splinter parties, the local Nazis had crushed and absorbed the CSVD by 1932 (see chapter 4 [v]).

The NSDAP targeted female voters with issues concerning religion and tradition. The Nazis made it clear that they believed that women should concentrate on what they saw as their natural role – i.e., as mothers to raise children – and pledged to enhance the status of women because of their 'deep respect for the enormous significance of the work of the German housewife.'[124] They promised, however, to protect all women, whether single, married, housewife or working in the labour force. Considering that there were marginally more female voters than male voters, the Nazis had every reason to focus on women. And, as in most parts of Germany, they did so with growing success: whilst the female vote for the Saxon NSDAP was slightly behind their male counterparts in 1930, women had reversed this situation by 1932.[125] The Saxon Nazis also received votes from working-class women, in particular from non-unionised workers in the textile industry and home workers. According to Jill Stephenson, the harsh effects of the slump, but also extremely lively Nazi women groups in Leipzig and Chemnitz, mobilised these women to support Nazism.[126]

(v) Economic Crisis and Propaganda: An Explanation for Nazi Success?

The district of Schwarzenberg offered a typical example of the crisis in the Erzgebirge/Vogtland, a region which became one of the Nazis' greatest electoral bastions in Weimar Germany. There seemed to be a clear relationship between the unfolding slump – which led to mounting misery and anxiety among the population – and the simultaneous rise of Nazism. Paradoxically, however, this assumption could not be confirmed at the micro level: there was no link between the economic situation of individual villages and towns – good or bad – and the strength or weakness of the Nazi party. Some small towns which faced a particularly severe recession in their main industries, like beadwork in Eibenstock, were Nazi strongholds. Others, like Johanngeorgenstadt with its depressed glove industry, were places where the Nazis' election results were far below their average in the district.[127] Neither did the Nazis' electoral performance seem to depend on the predominance of a particular industrial sector. In July 1932 the Nazi party obtained the majority at the polls in places where the metal industry, textile industry or paper industry dominated. Looking at the whole of Saxony, however, there was a positive correlation between the NSDAP's voting success and a high percentage of local people working in the textile industry, cottage industries, and agriculture.[128] There was no link between the grade of industrialisation in the various regions in the state and the strength of the local Nazis. Furthermore, it did not seem to matter for the Nazis' showing in elections, if villages or towns were dominated by large factories (more than fifty employees) or small businesses.

If one looks at the number of people in need (*Hilfsbedürftige*) who received some kind of welfare benefit, it becomes apparent that the Nazis' ability to exploit the economic crisis varied considerably in the various Saxon districts.[129] In southwestern Saxony, the Nazis did well in the July 1932 elections where the support for *Hilfsbedürftige* was high. Most importantly, the Vogtland, whose once flourishing embroidery and lace industry was experiencing such a painful decline, became the greatest Saxon Nazi bastion. In the KHs Dresden and Leipzig, the Nazis' performance was extremely bad in nearly all areas where more people depended on the welfare service than the Saxon average. Overall, the NSDAP only received an above average voting percentage in three (Freiberg, Chemnitz and Plauen) of the ten electoral districts with the highest number of people receiving state support in Saxony. It is striking that in seven of these places (the towns of Pirna, Chemnitz, Freital, Wurzen, and the districts of Leipzig, Meißen, and Pirna) the combined vote for the Marxist parties was extremely solid, if not high. The next chapter argues that these were places of a strong socialist milieu in which the Marxist parties managed to defend their position against Nazism even during the brunt of the crisis.

The Nazi party, however, was strong in nearly all areas with the highest rates of registered unemployed in Saxony.[130] Only in Freital, the greatest SPD bastion in the Reich, did the Nazis have election results below their state average. Nevertheless, statistically there was no link between unemployment levels and the electoral strength of Nazism, because the Nazis also flourished in most areas with the lowest unemployment rates (compare with chapter 5 [iii]). The findings suggest that the Nazis did best in a polarised environment and under extreme conditions. Finally, there was a small link between the amount of debt the Saxon communities accumulated in the slump and the strength of the local NSDAP: overall, the Nazis seemed to score better election results in communities with very low debts than very high debts.[131] It is striking that nearly all places with the lowest debts in Saxony were Nazi strongholds.

The district of Schwarzenberg was economically not one of the most afflicted regions. The number of people who received welfare support was below Saxony's average, the number of unemployed was only slightly above the state average, and the new debts of its communities were not the highest in Saxony. Nevertheless, the district became an area where the Nazis scored comparatively high election results from 1928 onwards. It seems that only a combination of factors can help to explain this. The worsening recession certainly provided the necessary breeding ground. Economic distress – if combined with political grievances – was traditionally the most potent force for radicalisation and mass protest. In 1905/6 the Saxon SPD had exploited economic hardships to organise demonstrations against the backward political system. The distress had temporarily united various classes – workers, employees, shopkeepers and artisans – in protest against the government.[132] It seems that from the late 1920s onwards the Nazis were able to do something similar, but far more successfully, that is, to channel economic misery and anxiety into a political mass mobilisation which toppled the existing system. Some people turned to Nazism in the hope that a Third Reich would end their economic misery. Others supported Nazism due to fear of economic hardship and social disturbances and expected that the Nazis' bold approach would bring tranquil times. Economic factors alone, however, were not sufficient to fully explain the success or failure of Nazism among individuals, or in certain villages, towns and regions. Other aspects, which will be discussed in the following chapters – such as the depth of the socialist milieu, the attitude of bourgeois groups and the influence of nationalist sentiments – need to be considered in order to gain a fuller picture.

This chapter has suggested a clear link between the Nazis' propaganda and their electoral performance in Saxony. To be sure, though, the influence of propaganda is difficult to quantify because it is impossible to measure its actual impact on human behaviour. Additionally, public meetings – which were predominantly scrutinised in this chapter – constituted only one aspect of propaganda. A public meeting was normally preceded by leaflets, posters and announcements in newspapers, and was subsequently followed by reports in the press and talks at the workplace or during leisure time. Of course all this could also have taken place without a meeting. Indeed, some historians argue that informal recruiting processes were more important for the Nazis than formal propaganda in meetings.[133]

It seems certain that relentless Nazi propaganda helped to give the movement the image of activity, decisiveness, devotion, and the ability to do something. The Saxon Nazis pursued an extraordinary amount of agitation. According to the SPD, this seemed to attract young voters in particular,[134] while some groups blindly embraced Nazism in sheer desperation. A provincial newspaper observed in 1929:

> There is an incredible lack of clarity and ignorance among large parts of the population, particularly farmers, about the true nature of the National Socialist movement ... But it is a fact that National Socialism managed to particularly infiltrate a few agricultural circles. It seems obvious that the often extremely active and noisy movement is regarded as an instrument people hope to be able to cling on to in times of economic crisis.[135]

In Saxony, the Nazis were strongest where they were most active, and in particular where, from late 1930 onwards, their propaganda completely outpaced their opponents, that is, in southwestern Saxony.[136] Eight out of nine electoral districts where the NSDAP received the absolute majority in July 1932 were in this area. Relentless Nazi activity also enabled them to mobilise a substantial number of former nonvoters, one of the key reasons for their dramatic electoral gains in 1930, but particularly in 1932 (see chapter 5 [iii]). Nazi propaganda was far less dominant in the Marxist bastions of northwestern and central Saxony. These were areas where the Nazis found it comparatively difficult to attract mass support. For instance, in the district of Leipzig – a solid Marxist stronghold and the Nazis' worst district in the July 1932 elections (SPD: 34.3 percent, KPD: 24.6 percent, NSDAP: 30.0 percent) – the Nazis were beaten by the Marxists in terms of the number of public meetings (see table 2.3 and document 13). The lack of a Nazi party network and propaganda in rural northwestern, but particularly eastern Saxony, helped to explain the low votes for the Nazis in these areas until 1930. In this environment the Nazis were only able to do reasonably well in towns, where even a small group could pursue effective propaganda. This explained why they were able to win roughly 17 percent of the vote in Mittweida, Bautzen and Zittau in June 1930. All three towns possessed active Nazi party branches. In many villages and small towns, however, the vote for the NSDAP preceded the appearance of Stormtroopers on a propaganda trip or party speakers in local

Table 2.3 The Number of Public Meetings of Various Parties between 1 January and 5 March 1933 (percentage in brackets)

	AH Leipzig	AH Schwarzenberg
NSDAP	90 (34.0)	84 (66.8)
SPD	81 (30.6)	15 (11.9)
KPD	59 (22.3)	19 (15.1)
Bourgeoisie	7 (2.6)	4 (3.1)
Others	28 (10.5)	4 (3.1)
Total	165 (100.0)	126 (100.0)

Source: STA L, AH Leipzig, Nr. 2673; STA D, AH Schwarzenberg, Nr. 1944, Januar 1933; ibid., Nr. 1945, Februar-März 1933.

meetings. It is most likely that knowledge of the Nazis had spread there through newspapers and by word of mouth (see chapter 4 [iv]). After surprising electoral gains in previously neglected areas in June 1930, a Nazi leader in Leipzig appealed for the integration of these sympathisers into the party:

> The votes hurried on ahead by a long distance. In some places hundreds of votes were cast for the NSDAP, even without a local party branch ... Surprising are the gains in the many small villages, and an army of speakers is essential to organise the success here and to anchor the idea of National Socialism.[137]

The development of the Nazi propaganda machine in Saxony was not only a success story, but also one which faced great problems, particularly before the Nazis built up a centralised party structure. The propaganda headquarters in Munich was frequently unable to cope with the amount of work, which slowed down the progress in the *Gaue*. In 1927 Himmler apologised to a Saxon activist for a late answer and pointed out that his office was too small.[138] The party's policies and its strategy to respond to attacks from opponents were often unclear: followers were frequently embarrassed when local citizens asked them to explain contradictory leaflets in different neighbourhoods.[139] Propaganda activities were frequently hampered by financial and organisational limits. Some branches – like the one in Leipzig – had problems in paying the rent for meeting venues,[140] others prepared public rallies badly and wasted the time of speakers. In 1929 a Reich speaker complained bitterly that he had to wait for several days in a Saxon district before he could address a meeting.[141] There were also constant procedural problems: some branches did not follow the official instructions on how to apply for prominent speakers and, instead of contacting the *Gau* headquarters, got directly in touch with Munich or the speakers themselves.[142]

Not all the problems were resolved by the early 1930s. In fact, the Saxon *Gau* only started to build up an efficient propaganda apparatus – with propaganda leaders and propaganda circulars for each district and party branch – at the end of 1930.[143] In mid-1930 Himmler informed a Saxon party branch that Munich had run out of leaflets for local elections.[144] A few months later the *Gau* leadership lamented that one party branch had decorated a venue black, white and red for a nationalist celebration while only displaying two small swastika flags and signing the programme with 'celebration committee' (*Festausschuß*). Plauen warned that they did not want to see similar 'military club-like manners' any more.[145] Nazi sympathisers in a small village in the northwest felt abandoned and recalled from this period that 'no-one in the party looked after them.'[146] They had to take the initiative to buy party leaflets and brochures in Leipzig themselves. The distribution of this material in their village before the September election paid off and they suddenly became the second largest party.

Saxon farmers provide one of the best examples of how the Nazis exploited the radicalisation (due to economic grievances) of a middle-class group, crushed their traditional party, and absorbed its constituency. First signs of a serious crisis in Saxon agriculture were felt in 1927.[147] One year later, as in other parts of Germany, angry Saxon farmers demonstrated against high taxes and for cheaper credit and higher tariffs on agricultural imports, and made clear their readiness to use anti-democratic means to put through their demands.[148] The Saxon Rural League (*Sächsischer Landbund*), which had been closely associated with the DNVP, responded to the radicalisation among the farmers and the founding of a new agrarian party in neighbouring Thuringia by building up the image of an unpolitical professional interest party, and formed the Saxon Landvolk (SLV). From 1928 onwards the SLV participated with own lists in elections and effectively terminated its alliance with the DNVP in 1930. By the early 1930s this attempt had all but collapsed at the cost of the NSDAP.[149] During the elections to the Agricultural Chamber (*Landwirtschaftskammer*) in Saxony in May 1931, the SLV suffered a heavy defeat at the hands of the Nazis. The Nazis won twenty-two of the forty seats, although this was the first time that the NSDAP had participated in elections to Agricultural Chambers in a whole state in Germany. The only reason why the Nazis did not gain an absolute majority in the Saxon Agricultural Chamber was because another eleven members of the chamber were elected by small professional bodies[150] which had not yet been infiltrated by the Nazis.

The Saxon Nazis had already wooed farmers in the 1920s and by early 1931 possessed a sophisticated agricultural organisation. In mid-March Plauen gave orders to concentrate propaganda on rural regions,[151] and mobilised a large group of speakers with expertise in agricultural questions (eight Saxon *Gau* speakers and twelve *Gau* speakers from outside Saxony, and additional speakers from the rural *Gau* Ostmark) for the actual campaign from late April onwards.[152] *Der Freiheitskampf* introduced a special supplement for the election, and Plauen instructed followers to deliver one leaflet and a ballot paper to each farm in their district, to tell farmers when and at what time voting took place, and to place an activist in front of each polling station for late canvassing.[153] No other political party was able to match such widespread rural propaganda or could hope for similar electoral success. The SPD did not even participate with their own lists, and the KPD only managed to put up lists in Bautzen and the Erzgebirge, though unsuccessfully. In reality there was only a choice between the SLV – which had previously controlled the Agricultural Chamber – and the NSDAP.

In the months before the elections the Nazis avoided direct confrontation with the SLV in order not to alienate potential voters. Their campaign was a mix between a concrete manifesto for improvements, and nationalist and racist appeals. They put forward the idea that the current Agricultural Chamber had not pursued a coherent policy and that it had betrayed its constituencies regarding the tax on milk. They promised to get rid of the large bureaucratic machinery, to be economical and in close contact with the constituencies, to close the small and expensive agricultural schools, and to enhance the farmers' interests in the commodity exchange and cattle markets.[154] Here was one of the rarer instances where the Nazis addressed local issues head on and put forward specific solutions. Additionally, the Nazis pledged and argued: 'Agriculture will become the corner stone of the Third Reich ... The cooperation of farmers will decide if German soil will be occupied by a healthy German race or slaves of international Jewish capitalism.'[155] Germany, according to them, could only recover through its 'blood and soil'.[156] To be exact, the SLV held similar views. A former director of the SLV had argued that 'living space and power' were 'essential for the thriving of a *Volk*.'[157] Compared with the SLV, however, the Nazi party appeared more determined, radical, uncompromising, dynamic, fresh and promising.

What about the crucial claim of recent studies that Nazi propaganda only worked with people who already possessed similar values? The extreme nationalist sentiments of most Saxon farmers was certainly an essential precondition for the Nazi victory in the elections to the Agricultural Chamber. For instance, the association of farmers in the district of Marienberg had proclaimed in 1923: 'The German Reich and *Volk*, our *Heimat* and fatherland are on the brink of ruin and disintegration; the aim of our sworn enemy, the French, is the destruction of Germany and is close to becoming reality.' [158] In the district of Schwarzenberg there was also a correlation between the strength of local nationalist/conservative milieus in political elections at the beginning of the Republic, and Nazi success ten years later. Villages or towns where the DVP or DNVP had done comparatively well and the Marxists comparatively badly in the general election in June 1920 – a time when the most resilient forces on the right had re-emerged after the 'shock' of the revolution – tended to be good electoral ground for the Nazis in 1930. Equally, nearly all places where votes for the Nazis were lagging behind in 1930, had been a stronghold of the SPD and/or KPD ten years earlier and had kept this position. This refuted the SPD's frequent claim that Communist bastions were the breeding ground for Nazism.[159] This picture remained to some extent during the July 1932 Reichstag election. By then, however, the Nazis had also conquered new strongholds where the vote for both Marxist parties had either collapsed or had continued to be solid. Similarly, strong local support for Hindenburg, Wilhelm Marx or Ernst Thälmann in the second ballot to the elections for the Reich President in April 1925 indicated the existence of a specific milieu that hardly changed until the end of the Republic: former strongholds of Marx and Thälmann remained SPD or KPD bastions respectively, while large parts of the nationalist milieu that had backed Hindenburg in 1925 became Hitler supporters seven years later. (See also chapter 5 [iii]. For the relationship between a right-wing press and the rise of Nazism, see chapter 4 [iv].)

The example of the village of Bockau in the district of Schwarzenberg underlines the powerful influence of deep-rooted traditions. The Protestant Nationalist Workers' Association (ENAV) – who aimed at winning workers away from the SPD with the nationalist appeal 'the fatherland above parties' [160] – made some headway in the village from 1910 onwards. The SPD found it difficult to mobilise workers in this nationalist environment. In 1912 its candidate for local councillor was handsomely beaten by the bourgeois contender, even though around 90 percent of the electorate were workers.[161] Before the Great War only the National Liberals under Stresemann made some attempts to woo nationalist workers – including the ENAV – while the Saxon conservatives were suspicious about any contact with workers *per se*.[162] Although the SPD continued to face problems in Bockau during the Weimar Republic and was only able to attract a few citizens to their local sports club,[163] none of the traditional nationalist and conservative parties tapped into this pool of nationalist workers. In the late 1920s the Nazis found a fertile ground and a political vacuum in Bockau and turned it into one of their earliest strongholds. A few years later they were just short of the absolute majority.[164]

Far from only focusing their propaganda at communities with a right-wing and nationalist electoral tradition in Saxony,[165] the Nazis made great efforts to hold meetings in every political environment, including Marxist strongholds. In fact, it was crucial for the success of Nazism in Saxony to make serious inroads into the working-class milieu. The next chapter will look at the reasons why many villages or towns that had been solid Marxist strongholds at the beginning of the Republic, or even in the late 1920s, turned into Nazi bastions by 1932, while others continued to be difficult ground for them.

Violence was certainly a crucial part of Nazi, but also of Communist, propaganda. What was the link between violence and the disintegration of democracy and/or the rise of Nazism? After 1929 the amount of violence between political opponents (particularly between Nazis and Communists), and clashes between demonstrators and the police (mainly with Communists) clearly increased. The growing use of knives and firearms made the nature of these fights more and more brutal: twelve demonstrators and two policemen lost their lives in confrontations in northwestern Saxony in 1930,[166] and five people died in clashes between political opponents in the state in the second quarter of 1931 alone (also see document 14).[167]

Why did violence flair up so dramatically? On a general level, the enormous crisis aggravated tensions in society and fostered an atmosphere in which violent means became more attractive. There was also the extremely aggressive behaviour of followers of radical parties. The Stormtroopers were combat units who aimed at defeating their opponents in street battles and possessed emergency aid for followers who were imprisoned and injured.[168] The SPD complained that the violent activities of the Nazis in and around Chemnitz had created 'Balkan-like conditions', and reported that even in Leipzig their brutality towards Republicans and Socialists had created an atmosphere of fear.[169] The Communist hard-core reacted to this challenge by taking the counter-offensive with their slogan, 'Beat the fascists wherever you meet them'. The police commented about violent incidents in central Saxony:

> The followers of the NSDAP often appeared in a provoking manner which contributed heavily to these kind of disturbances and clashes. However, it cannot be denied ... that the KPD was prepared and determined to use violence right from the start in order to prevent the infiltration of fascists into working-class districts.[170]

At times, the Communists appeared to be even more desperate to carry the fight to the opponent because they were far less successful in exploiting the crisis than the Nazis. But they were fighting a losing battle against an opponent who was rapidly outnumbering them and whose Stormtroopers were only banned for a short period by the police. Any realistic chance of winning a physical confrontation with Nazism was destroyed by the lack of a united front on the left, and the fact that the overwhelming majority of the Social Democrats stuck to legal means and tried to avoid any confrontation on the streets.

Also crucial for the development of violence was the irresponsible behaviour of influential parts of the Saxon bourgeoisie: from the beginning of the Republic it painted unrealistic nightmare scenarios of a socialist revolution and claimed later that the *Reichsexekution* against the SPD-KPD coalition government in 1923 had prevented this by a small margin (see also document 3). This greatly contributed towards the polarisation of society and prepared the way for the use and toleration of violence. Eventually, the bourgeoisie and the government seemed to lose control of events and were no longer capable of guaranteeing security and order – which was, after all, the most important criteria on which they rested their legitimacy. An account from a village in eastern Saxony in early 1931 stated:

> Due to the recently uncontrollable spread of left-wing radical elements and their appearance in large numbers, the local organisation of the *Landbund*, *Stahlhelm* and NSDAP united to form a self-defence force ... In the event of looting, as it had occurred in 1923, they would be able to protect the citizens until the arrival of stronger police forces.[171]

The anxieties of the population intensified and there was a longing for tranquillity. A growing number of citizens tolerated Nazi violence as a means of clearing the streets once and for all of the Marxist threat. The threat of a civil war sparked off by the left, however, was nothing but a myth. The local Communists were not strong enough, and the SPD stood firmly on Republican ground. Most of the brutal incidents were the result of the activities of a comparatively small number of radicals who managed to capture public attention. The police assessed the situation in northwestern Saxony in 1931:

> The great majority of the population has nothing to do with these unpleasant disturbances, in particular the unemployed and those who receive benefits were, on the whole, totally uninvolved. Nearly all disruptions of the public law and order stemmed from the party disputes of the two radical-wing parties and are mostly limited to their supporters and a few recent members.[172]

(vi) The Reality of the Third Reich

The Third Reich did not turn out to be what many citizens in the district of Schwarzenberg had unrealistically hoped it would: an era of prosperity and tranquillity. What follows are only a few observations about the development in the district, as other aspects of Saxony during the Nazi dictatorship will be discussed in the following chapters. Economically, there was no upturn from 1933 onwards and large parts of the local population did not benefit from a boom in the armaments industries. Unemployment only fell in the few years before the war, and even those in work moaned consistently about bad working conditions and the low wages compared to the high prices. At the beginning of the war the grumbling centred around the insufficient food supply.[173]

The disappointment that no economic revival had set in and the repressive nature of the regime were the main causes for the bad mood in the district,[174] and why more and more people distanced themselves from politics. Disillusioned farmers withdrew gradually from public life, and some cancelled the 'Weekly Paper for Saxon Farmers' because it did not tell the truth.[175] There was a growing reluctance to participate in the enormous number of rallies and meetings organised by the Nazis.[176] A few even released their grievances in public: workers in Eibenstock expressed their annoyance when a meeting was held about 'the work struggle of workers in the cottage industry' but the Nazi speaker hardly referred to their specific problems.[177] However, only a few citizens went into active resistance and distributed leaflets against the regime. Former Marxists were under constant observation, which made any move against the regime extremely risky.[178] A growing fear and suspicion about informers affected more and more people. Officials recorded in April 1934:

> The mood among the population is not always as bright as it is reported in newspapers and other reports. It can be described as very reserved and withdrawn. This stems from the fact that many people ... fall victim of unfounded suspicion. It is said that no person can express his opinion openly any more.[179]

Whereas the daily economic struggle lessened the expectations many had invested in the Third Reich, the Nazis managed again and again to spark enthusiasm by exploiting nationalist sentiments and capturing ever wider circles of the population with it. However, these were limited moments during which the existing shortcomings were only temporarily disguised. Many citizens took part in celebrations when the result of the plebiscite in the Saar region (to rejoin the Reich) was announced in early 1935. Officials reported a 'sea of flags' and 'torchlight processions' and explained:

> These rallies, which were accompanied with thanksgiving services in some places – have left a deep sense of community [*Gemeinschaftsgedanke*] among the population. It should be specifically mentioned that a large part of former Marxists, who had remained aloof during other nationalist celebrations, also participated at these celebrations. The working population is still complaining that the wages are too low compared to the price of food.[180]

Similarly, Hitler's bold approach in foreign affairs met nearly unanimous approval and rallied and unified large parts of the population. When the Nazis unveiled their new plans for the army in mid-1935 there was a 'storm of enthusiasm' which only a few resisted: 'All *Volksgenossen* are enormously grateful to the *Führer* that he has given our Fatherland its honour back. Only a few voices have raised concern because they see in these new measures a danger of war.'[181] When German troops marched into the demilitarised Rhineland a year later, or when Bohemia and Moravia came under 'Reich protection' in March 1939, there was similar euphoria.[182]

Earlier we argued how deep-rooted nationalist sentiments among workers in the village of Bockau helped to prepare the ground for Nazism. The example of the town of Lößnitz, which suffered even more under the slump than Bockau, will show the continuous problems the Nazis could face if they did not find such favourable conditions: the Nazis had become the largest party in Lößnitz in 1932, but the local SPD had defended its position very well – more than twice as many citizens per head were organised in its sports club than in Bockau – and the combined Marxist parties had kept their absolute majority.[183] Marxist traditions provided a serious obstacle for creating enthusiasm for the Third Reich. Many local citizens voted with a 'no' in the plebiscite in August 1934 which led to the imprisonment of former Marxist party officials.[184] Several corruption scandals – one linked with the local winter aid collection – robbed the population of the little confidence that was left towards the new rulers.[185] Henceforth, officials in the district noted Lößnitz for a 'lukewarm' atmosphere at meetings and rallies, the fact that the Hitler greeting was not often used, the purge of eleven Stormtroopers who had neglected their duties, and the disputes among party members over special dues and the selling of badges.[186]

Notes

1. H. James, 'Economic Reasons for the Collapse of the Weimar Republic', in I. Kershaw, ed., *Weimar: Why did German Democracy Fail?* London, 1990, 30f.
2. E.g. see Pridham, *Bavaria*; Böhnke, *Ruhrgebiet.*
3. D. Orlow, *The History of the Nazi Party, Vol. 1: 1919–1933*, Pittsburgh, 1969, 5.
4. G. Paul, *Aufstand der Bilder. Die NS-Propaganda vor 1933*, Bonn, 1990, 255. Also see D. Ohr, 'War die NSDAP-Propaganda nur bei "Nationalistischen" Wählern erfolgreich? Eine Aggregatanalyse zur Wirkung der nationalsozialistischen Versammlungspropaganda', *Kölner Zeitschrift für Soziologie und Sozialpsychologie*, 46 (4) (1994), 646–67; I. Kershaw, 'Ideology, Propaganda and the Rise of the Nazi Party', in P.D. Stachura, ed., *The Nazi Machtergreifung*, London, 1983, 162; R. Bessel, 'The Rise of the NSDAP and the Myth of Nazi Propaganda', *Wiener Library Bulletin*, 33 (1980), 20–29.
5. These unpublished reports were – as in other districts – compiled by the local police and administration and kept the government in Dresden up to date with developments in the region. Although the reports in the district of Schwarzenberg indicate a slight bias towards right-wing and nationalist ideas and parties and need to be used with care, overall they seem to present a fairly accurate picture of contemporary society. For instance, during the Third Reich they also reflected views within the population which were highly critical of the government and some of the developments under Nazism. See also Lapp, *Revolution*, chapter 8.

6. Around 70 percent of the population in the district of Schwarzenberg were employed in industry and less than 10 percent in agriculture. Its 132,000 citizens lived in fifty-one small towns and villages and produced various goods including machines, metal, enamel, men's wear, embroidery, paper, brushes, chemicals, paint and wood carving.
7. STA D, Wirtschaftsministerium, Nr. 1970, Plauen, 13.9.1919.
8. B. Poste, *Schulreform in Sachsen, 1918–1923. Eine vergessene Tradition deutscher Schulgeschichte*, Frankfurt/Main, 1993, 92.
9. Bracher, *Dictatorship*, 161.
10. E. Kolb, *The Weimar Republic*, London, 1988, 165.
11. STA L, AH Döbeln, Nr. 2409, Jahresbericht der KH Leipzig 1926.
12. STA D, KH Zwickau, Nr. F1496/1, März 1926.
13. STA D, AH Schwarzenberg, Nr. 1940, Juni 1926.
14. *Erzgebirgischer Volksfreund*, Nr. 217, 16.9.1933; *Zehn Jahre NSDAP Schwarzenberg im Erzgebirge (1924–34)*, 10.
15. BA, NS 18, Nr. 5022, 8.9.1926.
16. Ibid., 8.10.1926.
17. STA D, MdI, Nr. 11126/2, April–Mai 1928.
18. STA D, AH Schwarzenberg, Nr. 1941, Mai 1928.
19. STA D, MdI, Nr. 11126/2, April 1928.
20. STA D, AH Schwarzenberg, Nr. 1941, März–September 1928.
21. *NSDAP Schwarzenberg*, 16.
22. After the Jewish chief of the Berlin criminal police, Dr Bernhard Weiß, who became Goebbels' major scapegoat in Berlin under the nickname 'Isidor'. See H. Heiber, *Goebbels*, New York, 1972, 62f.
23. *NSfS*, Nr. 4, 23.1.1927; ibid., Nr. 7, 13.2.1927; ibid., Nr. 14, 3.4.1927.
24. BDC, Pillmayer, 'NSDAP Raschau', 2.
25. STA D, AH Schwarzenberg, Nr. 1941, Februar 1928.
26. BDC, Pillmayer, 'NSDAP Raschau', 2.
27. *NSfS*, Nr. 19, 13.5.1928.
28. STA L, AH Döbeln, Nr. 2409, Jahresbericht der KH Leipzig 1929, 4.
29. A price comparison of basic foodstuffs in Saxony and Czechoslovakia at the end of 1929: a pound of bread: 0.19 *Reichsmark* (Saxony)/0.16 *Reichsmark* (Czechoslovakia); one litre milk: 0.38–0.40/0.35; one egg: 0.16–0.20/0.12; a pound of beef: 1.20–1.60/0.90–1.10; a pound of pork: 1.40–1.60/1.30. STA D, AH Schwarzenberg, Nr. 1942, Dezember 1929.
30. For the above see the monthly reports from October 1929 onwards.
31. *Sächsische Industrie* (*SI*), Nr. 5, 31.1.1931, 93.
32. Ibid., Nr. 8, 21.2.1931, 142; ibid., Nr. 33, 1930, 755.
33. From April 1932 the people who lived in the border region were allowed to buy a limited amount of food tax-free on two weekdays only. This was then restricted to one weekday only from May onwards. See STA D, AH Schwarzenberg, Nr. 1945, Mai 1932.

34. *SB*, Nr. 9, 3.3.1929; ibid. Nr. 15, 14.4.1929; BA, NS 18, Nr. 5022.
35. For this see BA, NS 18, Nr. 5022.
36. BA, Sammlung Schumacher (SlSch), Nr. 208, Plauen, 29.4.1929.
37. The court of justice had annulled the 1926 state elections after a complaint from the SPD that it should have headed the ballot papers as the largest party and not the ASP. See Schmeitzner, 'Freistaat', 99.
38. *SB*, Nr. 19, 12.5.1929.
39. BA, NS 18, Nr. 5022.
40. *Dresdner Volkszeitung* (*DVZ*), Nr. 111, 15.5.1929.
41. STA D, MdI, Nr. 11126/3, April 1929.
42. *SB*, Nr. 19, 12.5.1929.
43. BA, SlSch, Nr. 208, 26.4.1929.
44. BA, NS 18, Nr. 5004, 13.12.1928.
45. D. Harsch, *German Social Democracy and the Rise of Nazism*, London, 1993, 67.
46. STA D, AH Schwarzenberg, Nr. 1943, Februar 1930.
47. STA L, AH Döbeln, Nr. 2409, Jahresbericht der KH Leipzig 1930, 1, 5.
48. STA D, AH Schwarzenberg, März, Mai, August, Oktober 1930.
49. Ibid., Juli 1930.
50. STA D, MdI, Nr. 11126/4, Juni 1930.
51. For the complete list of names see Szejnmann, 'Nazis in Saxony', 298.
52. STA D, MdI, Nr. 11126/4, September 1930.
53. Ibid., Dezember 1930.
54. *FK*, Nr. 35, 10.9.1930.
55. STA D, AH Schwarzenberg, Nr. 1943, November 1930.
56. Ibid., Dezember 1930.
57. STA D, MdI, Nr. 11126/6, Juni 1931.
58. For the following see STA D, AH Schwarzenberg, Nr. 1944, Februar, Juli, August, Oktober, November, Dezember 1931, Januar 1932.
59. Ibid., November 1931.
60. Ibid., Juli 1931.
61. BA, SlSch, 7.1.1931. Nazi activists who wanted to speak at NSDAP meetings required an official certificate. For instance, *Gau* speakers carried a certificate from the *Gauleiter* permitting them to use the title and to speak inside their *Gau*. See Orlow, *Nazi Party*, 160.
62. *Erzgebirgischer Volksfreund*, Nr. 217, 16.9.1933. See also chaper 4 (iv).
63. W. Fabian, 'Arbeiterführer und Arbeiterbildungswesen im Freistaat Sachsen. Ein Beitrag zur Führungsproblematik in der Arbeiterbewegung der Weimarer Republik', *Herkunft und Mandat*, Frankfurt, (1976), 123f.
64. *NSfS*, Nr. 22, 3.6.1928.
65. STA D, AH Schwarzenberg, Nr. 1944, Oktober 1931.

66. Ibid., November 1931.
67. Ibid., Nr. 1945, Mai 1932.
68. Ibid., August 1932.
69. Ibid., Nr. 1944, Januar 1932.
70. Ibid., Nr. 1945, Februar 1932.
71. Ohr, 'NSDAP-Propaganda', 649f.
72. STA D, AH Schwarzenberg, Nr. 1945, Juni 1932. Compare with Paul, *NS-Propaganda*, 100.
73. *FK*, Nr. 22, 26.1.1933.
74. BA, NS 25, Nr. 329, 23.8.1929; BA, NS 22, Nr. 1067.
75. *NSfS*, Nr. 24, 5.8.1928.
76. STA D, AH Schwarzenberg, Nr. 1950, Februar-März 1933.
77. Ibid., März 1933.
78. *VdSL*, 5. Wp, 27. Sitzung, 3.2.1931, 1044.
79. *Oelsnitzer Volksbote*, Nr. 177, 30.7.1932.
80. See Burleigh, *Racial State*.
81. *DVZ*, Nr. 125, 31.5.1930.
82. Harsch, *Social Democracy*, 76.
83. *DVZ*, Nr. 149, 30.6.1930.
84. Ibid., Nr. 249, 24.10.1930; *LVZ*, Nr. 10, 13.1.1932.
85. *Sächsisches Volksblatt* (*SVB*), Nr. 80, 6.4.1929.
86. *SB*, Nr. 94, 15.6.1930.
87. *FK*, Nr. 106, 8.5.1931.
88. *Dahlener Nachrichten*, Nr. 40, 17.2.1932.
89. Also see Joachim Bons, 'Der Kampf um die Seele des deutschen Arbeiters. Zur Arbeiterpolitik der NSDAP 1920–1933', *Internationale Wissenschaftliche Korrespondenz*, 25 (1) (1989), 22.
90. *Oelsnitzer Volksbote*, Nr. 177, 30.7.1932.
91. *Vogtländischer Anzeiger und Tageblatt*, Nr. 86, 13.4.1929.
92. *Oelsnitzer Volksbote*, Nr. 108, 11.5.1929.
93. *FK*, Nr. 104, 2.12.1930; ibid., Nr. 259, 6.11.1931.
94. STA D, MdI, Nr. 11126/4, September 1930.
95. Harsch, *Social Democracy*, 214.
96. Adam, 'Arbeitermilieu', 197.
97. *VdSL*, 5. Wp, 74. Sitzung, 12.5.1932, 3212.
98. *Dresdner Nachrichten*, Nr. 432, 14.9.1930. See also chapter 4.
99. For this see BA, SlSch, Nr. 208, 22.5.1931.
100. *SB*, Nr. 76, 23.5.1930.
101. See also Bons, 'Kampf', 20.
102. *Glauchauer Tageblatt und Anzeiger*, Nr. 100, 30.4.1929.
103. *VdSL*, 3. Wp, 31. Sitzung, 12.5.1927, 1059ff.
104. STA D, AH Schwarzenberg, Nr. 1943, März, Mai 1930.
105. *VdSL*, 5. Wp, 104. Sitzung, 14.2.1933, 4537.
106. Ibid., 22. Sitzung, 15.1.1931, 872.
107. Ibid., 16. Sitzung, 27.11.1930, 578.
108. Ibid., 4. Wp, 102. Sitzung, 24.1.1929, 3805.

109. Ibid., 5. Wp, 22. Sitzung, 15.1.1931, 857–59.
110. *SI*, Nr. 18, 20 Juni 1914.
111. Bennecke, 'SA Sachsen', 76f.
112. *Oelsnitzer Volksbote*, Nr. 160, 11.7.1932. For the role of nationalist values see chapter 4.
113. *VdSL*, 4 Wp, 113. Sitzung, 21.3.1929, 4286ff.
114. Ibid., 5 Wp, 101. Sitzung, 2.2.1933, 4416ff.
115. Adam, 'Arbeitermilieu', 202, 294.
116. *Chemnitzer Volksstimme* (*ChVSt*), Nr. 223, 24.9.1930.
117. *LVZ*, 22.7.29.
118. *VdSL*, 5. Wp, 48. Sitzung, 25.6.1931, 1894.
119. H.A. Winkler, *Der Weg in die Katastrophe. Arbeiter und Arbeiterbewegung in der Weimarer Republik 1930 bis 1933*, Bonn, 1990, 698. Also see chapter 4.
120. *Oelsnitzer Volksbote*, Nr. 160, 11.7.1932.
121. Ibid., Nr. 176, 29.7.1932.
122. Ibid., Nr. 177, 30.7.1932.
123. L.E. Jones, 'The Dying Middle: Weimar Germany and the Fragmentation of Bourgeois Politics, *Central European History*, 5 (1972), 42; J.W. Falter, T. Lindenberger and S. Schumann, *Wahlen und Abstimmungen in der Weimarer Republik*, Munich, 1986, 54f.
124. *Oelsnitzer Volksbote*, Nr. 176, 29.7.1932.
125. See the separate voting statistics available from selected villages and towns during the 1930 Reichstag elections and the elections for the Reich President in April 1932 in Saxony: *StDR*, vols. 382 and 427. Compare with J.W. Falter, *Hitlers Wähler*, Munich, 1991, 136–46.
126. See J. Stephenson, 'National Socialism and Women before 1933', in Stachura, *Machtergreifung*, 37f.
127. The NSDAP gained 54.8 percent of the vote in Eibenstock and 37.4 percent in Johanngeorgenstadt in July 1932.
128. For the following see Szejnmann, 'Nazis in Saxony', 322f; see also chapter 5 (iii).
129. *Hilfsbedürftige* were mainly war invalides, pensioners and the unemployed. See A. Betterlein, 'Die Statistik der Fürsorge in den Rechnungsjahren 1927 bis 1931', *ZSäStLA*, (1932/33), 189. The following is calculated from ibid.; and A. Betterlein, 'Die Wohlfahrtserwerbslosen in Sachsen', *ZSäStLA*, (1931), 220f. See Szejnmann, 'Nazis in Saxony', 324ff.
130. It is only possible to determine roughly if Nazis did well or badly in the employment districts because they normally did not coincide with electoral districts.
131. Calculated from G. Hoffmann, 'Die Schulden von Land, Gemeinden und Gemeindeverbänden in Sachsen', *ZSäStLA*, (1932/33), 103–105. See Szejnmann, 'Nazis in Saxony', 327–29. The debt included debt to the Reich, the state, the communities, banks and private individuals. This seems to contradict Falter, who found a positive link between

debts in agriculture and business and the electoral success of the NSDAP. See Falter, *Wähler*, 314ff.

132. C. Nonn, 'Arbeiter, Bürger und "Agrarier": Stadt-Land-Gegensatz und Klassenkonflikt im Wilhelminischen Deutschland am Beispiel des Königreichs Sachsen', in Grebing, *Demokratie*, 106f.
133. Ohr, 'NSDAP-Propaganda', 660, 663.
134. E.g. see *DVZ*, Nr. 111, 15.5.1929; *ChVSt*, Nr. 286, 10.12.1929.
135. *Der Oschatzer Gemeinnützige*, 23.5.29.
136. Recently Ohr also established a positive link between the NSDAP's campaign intensity and its electoral success in Hesse-Darmstadt. See D. Ohr, 'Political Meetings of the National Socialists and the Increase of the NSDAP Vote. Analysing Conditions of Propaganda Effects with Aggregate Data', *Historical Social Research*, 22 (1) (1997), 29–58.
137. STA D, Zeitungsausschnittsammlung (ZAS), Nr. 464, (name of newspaper was not legible), Nr. 156, 3.7.1930.
138. BA, NS 18, Nr. 5022, 2.2.1927.
139. Ibid., 23.4.1927.
140. Ibid., 27.2.1928.
141. BA, SlSch, Nr. 208, 11.6.1929.
142. BA, NS 18, Nr. 5022, 23.8.1928; ibid., Nr. 5006, 13.3.1928.
143. BA, SlSch, Nr. 208, 23.12.1930; ibid., 22.1.1931.
144. BA, NS 18, Nr. 5009, 15.7.1930.
145. BA, SlSch, Nr. 208, 23.10.1930.
146. NSDAP Hauptarchiv, Sachsen, 'Geschichte der Ortsgruppe Belgershain', (1934) .
147. K. Lobmeier, 'Die sozialökonomische Lage und das politische Verhalten der "alten" Mittelschichten in der Kreishauptmannschaft Chemnitz 1927 bis 1935', Ph.D. diss., University of Leipzig, 1989, 23 ff.
148. Ibid., 84 ff. For the following also see Lapp, *Revolution*, 166ff; Jones, 'Saxony, 1924–1930'.
149. The SLV's election results: 1928 Reichstag election: 3.2 percent; 1929 state election: 5.2 percent; 1930 state election: 4.6 percent; 1930 Reichstag election: 4.0 percent; July 1932 Reichstag election: 0.2 percent. Also see chapter 5 (iii).
150. *Sächsische Landwirtschaftliche Zeitung*, Nr. 12, 22.3.1931, 159.
151. BA Koblenz, SlSch, Nr. 208, 15.3.1931.
152. Ibid., 20.4.1931.
153. Ibid., 7.5.1931.
154. Ibid., 25.4.1931.
155. *FK*, Nr. 109, 12.5.1931.
156. Ibid., Nr. 99, 29.4.1931.
157. Ibid., Nr. 39, 16.2.1931.
158. STA D, AH Glauchau, Nr. 24, 10.
159. *ChVSt*, Nr. 139, 18.6.1929.
160. *Sächsisches Evangelisches Arbeiterblatt*, Nr. 6, 1911.
161. *Obererzgebirgische Zeitung*, Nr. 43, 22.2.1912.

162. *Sächsisches Evangelisches Arbeiterblatt*, Nr. 6, 1911; *Sächsische Industrie*, Nr. 17, 5 Juni 1914.
163. Only 2.3 percent of Bockau's citizens were members of the SPD sports club. See *Geschäftsbericht über die Jahre 1928/29 des Arbeiter-Turn- und Sportbundes e.V.*, Leipzig, 1930, 216.
164. The NSDAP gained 49.6 percent, SPD 8.8 percent, and KPD 24.8 percent of the vote in Bockau in July 1932.
165. Ohr, 'NSDAP-Propaganda', 661.
166. STA L, AH Döbeln, Nr. 2409, Jahresbericht der KH Leipzig 1930, 2.
167. STA D, MdI, Nr. 11126/6, Juni 1931.
168. STA D, MdI, Nr. 19087, NSDAP 1930–32.
169. *LVZ*, 14.4.1932; ibid., 5.7.1932.
170. STA D, KH Dresden, Nr. 263, Juni 1930.
171. STA D, MdI, Nr. 19087, NSDAP 1930–32, 12.3.31. Also quoted in Lapp, *Revolution*, 170.
172. STA L, AH Döbeln, Nr. 2409, Jahresbericht der KH Leipzig 1931, 1. Also see document 16.
173. STA D, AH Schwarzenberg, Nr. 1954, Oktober-Dezember 1939.
174. *Sopade*, Oktober 1935, 1218; STA D, AH Schwarzenberg, Nr. 1953, Januar 1936; ibid. März 1936; ibid., Nr. 1954, Januar 1939; ibid. Mai 1939; ibid. Juli 1939; ibid., Nr. 1954, Oktober 1939.
175. STA D, AH Schwarzenberg, Nr. 1955, Mai 1937; ibid., September 1937.
176. Ibid., Juli 1935, August 1935.
177. Ibid., Februar 1935.
178. Ibid., Nr. 1951, Januar 1934; ibid., März 1934; ibid., Nr. 1953, August 1936; ibid. Nr. 1955, Juni 1937. Also see *Sopade*, Juli 1937, 963.
179. STA D, AH Schwarzenberg, Nr. 1951, April 1934. Also see *Sopade*, April 1936, 421.
180. STA D, AH Schwarzenberg, Nr. 1952, Januar 1935.
181. Ibid., Nr. 1951, März 1935.
182. Ibid., Nr. 1953, März 1936; ibid., Nr. 1954, März 1939.
183. 5.4 percent of all citizens in Lößnitz and 2.3 percent in Bockau were organised in the ATSB (see *Geschäftsbericht über die Jahre 1928/29 des Arbeiter-Turn- und Sportbundes e.V.*, Leipzig, 1930, 216f). The NSDAP gained 39.4 percent, SPD 34.2 percent and KPD 17.3 percent of the vote in Lößnitz in July 1932.
184. *Sopade*, August/September 1934, 393.
185. STA D, AH Schwarzenberg, Nr. 1951, November 1934. Also see *Sopade*, Januar 1935, 98f; ibid., September 1936, 1158.
186. STA D, AH Schwarzenberg, Nr. 1953, Juni-Juli 1936.

Chapter 3

'Forward into the Working-Class Districts!' The Brownshirts in 'Red' Saxony

> The Revolution was the salvation for the working class who had torment in their blood, and were harassed and deprived of their rights.
>
> (R. Lipinski, *Der Kampf um die politische Macht in Sachsen*, Leipzig, 1926, 11)

> We do not want humans to starve anymore;
> We do not want there ever to be a war again;
> We want a free body and a free spirit
> And we want to make vows again:
> Struggle for Freedom!
> Struggle Class against Class!
> Join us brothers, forward to the sun and to Freedom!
>
> (Solemn promises given by the 12,000 participants of the SPD's revolutionary celebration in Leipzig on 9 November 1929)

(i) Political and Cultural Oppression: The Development of a Socialist Milieu

For a long time historians have disagreed about the role of the labour movement in modern German society. Günther Roth and others argued that the Social Democratic milieu during Imperial Germany – despite building up a 'negative' subculture – actually imitated bourgeois culture and hence stabilised the existing society.[1] Other historians have argued that this interpretation understates workers' experiences of political and social repression, and denies working-class culture any independence and originality.[2] The creation of a network of organisations around the SPD could be a response to a reactionary bourgeoisie who excluded workers from their clubs – e.g., workers in Leipzig started to set up their own gymnastics organisations after bourgeois clubs had refused to issue new membership cards to workers for fear of socialist infiltration in the early 1890s[3] – or because Marxists wanted to be separate and to establish an alternative to the existing social norms and arrangements.[4] Both was true for Saxony where there was a greater polarisation between the workers' movement and the bourgeois forces than elsewhere, and where labour had to endure harsh oppression (see also document 1). This background is essential to understand why the electoral support for the left remained comparatively stable in Saxony from the end of the nineteenth century until the Nazi seizure of power,[5] and why in some areas there were extremely strong bonds between local citizens and Marxist parties which the Nazis found nearly impossible to crack. Indeed, in the mid-1920s the Nazis reported 'that the deep seated, or rather injected hatred, amongst the masses against Adolf Hitler and his National Socialism assumes an unparalleled form of fierceness' in Saxony.[6]

Until November 1918 the Saxon government used two powerful tools to clamp down on the labour movement: restrictions of the electoral franchise and restrictions on the workers of freedom of organisation and assembly. Working-class activists faced constant harassment and had to endure enormous personal sacrifices. In the 1880s the Social Democrat August Kaden was blacklisted by employers and could not find work in and around Dresden. He was expelled from several pubs and his flat and shop were frequently searched. The Saxon state attempted several times to bring Kaden to court, his family lost their flat twice due to his political activities, and former friends of the family turned their back on them.[7] The notorious Saxon Association and Assembly Law from 1850 restricted the workers' movement from building up an organisational network for half a century until it was reformed in 1898, and finally replaced by the Reich Association Law in 1908. Only then did the mutual association of men and women become legal, and only then did the widespread ban of Social Democratic organisations end.

The overall atmosphere of repression, however, continued. Until the outbreak of the First World War, teachers who worked for Social Democratic associations lost their jobs; the Social Democrats were barred from using public buildings such as schools and gymnasiums; they faced great difficulties in hiring rooms in pubs or houses, and the authorities frequently prohibited working-class gymnastic clubs from giving lessons to children and juveniles.[8] Contrary to bourgeois clubs, workers' associations were only rarely allowed to carry out festival parades, and the police and administration regularly banned a number of songs and plays from festival programmes – sometimes only hours before the performance.[9]

The growth of mass politics brought an increasing awareness of and ability to respond to reactionary policies and economic grievances, which meant that tensions and polarisation in Saxon society clearly increased in the decades before the First World War. Whereas the elite continued to ally against the growing labour movement, the latter moved closer together and became more politicised in the face of the growing social contradictions. The Social Democrats managed to channel the growing economic grievances into political mass demonstrations against the reactionary electoral system in 1905/6 for the first time. It is crucial that the experiences of oppression lived on in the memories of working-class activists and remained an important part of their identity during the Weimar Republic. When in 1921 the SPD discussed possible coalition partners for a national government, the left-wing Seydewitz-group in Zwickau opposed a cooperation with the DVP on the grounds of its conservative nature, as seen in the National Liberals' toleration of the electoral laws from 1896 and 1909.[10]

Indeed, during the Weimar Republic the polarisation between labour and the bourgeoisie continued in Saxony and manifested itself in two completely different visions of how society should be organised and what kind of values it should promote. The Social Democrats' programme of progressive legislation was vehemently opposed by the majority of the bourgeoisie, whose determination to reverse the reforms rallied them behind the slogan 'Against a Soviet Saxony'. This struggle was about power, and the bourgeoisie was desperate to create a framework which would protect their interests. The growing economic crisis, which led to public unrest, and the questions of who was responsible for it and how to react to it, turned this conflict into a bitter confrontation.

A large proportion of Saxon industrialists, farmers, professional middle-class organisations and bourgeois opposition parties were prepared to exploit critical crises in post-war Germany – most importantly the Ruhr occupation and hyperinflation in 1923 – to sacrifice the democratic framework and to get rid of the legally elected left-wing government.[11] After the war they exploited every example of disturbances, strikes, and looting to build up the image of a 'bolshevist situation' in Saxony. For instance, they accused the government of allowing the charismatic revolutionary Max Hölz to 'terrorise' the Vogtland – Hölz had carried out a number of spectacular terrorist activities in the region between 1919 and 1921 and was a popular hero amongst radical workers[12] – and demanded the use of the *Reichswehr* to crush social protest and unrest. In the course of 1923 – when the left-wing Zeigner became Prime Minister, the economy reached a critical situation and a string of social disturbances swept the region – the bourgeoisie literally bombarded the government with attacks. It complained about a 'state of terror' and that the government was 'unable to preserve or at least restore law and order',[13] it claimed that Proletarian Hundreds 'intimidated' the population, and most importantly, it started to lobby the Reich for the forceful dismissal of the government in Dresden. In sharp contrast, the Social Democrat Walter Fabian described the situation in 1923 in the following way:

> There were, to be sure, conflicts; the widespread despair had to find some sort of outlet, but these conflicts did not approach an organized revolt or a revolution. The police proved itself to be strong enough to protect the propertied classes. In Saxony, where unemployment was far higher and the widespread need much greater, it was actually quieter than in many other parts of Germany.[14]

Indeed, overall it seems that the bourgeoisie's evaluations were often exaggerated, were not honest about the actual reasons for the disturbances, and did not account for the serious attempts by the government to curb the crisis. Although there were many hunger riots, food thefts, demonstrations for wage rises (see document 3a) and 'degradation ceremonies' with employers (the employer or director of an industrial plant would be forced under the pressure of demonstrators to march in a demonstration, often forced to carry a red flag or a sign on which was inscribed such a slogan as "I am a slavedriver" or "I am a scoundrel"[15]), there was comparatively little violence. The democratic *Leipziger Tageblatt* described the bourgeoisie's campaign as an 'unjustified generalisation of local incidents which were no worse in Saxony than in other densely populated regions in the Reich.'[16] The bourgeoisie never acknowledged that Saxony's government was hardly to blame for the growing economic crisis – which was the obvious cause for the disorder – and never distinguished whether the disturbances were economically or politically motivated. Indeed, most of these incidents were not initiated by the workers' movement but were caused by those who had been unsettled by the war, i.e., unemployed soldiers, war invalids, and others who suffered economic or social impoverishment.[17] For instance, in early 1923 the police reported that groups of thirty to fifty unemployed men from Werdau forced farmers in the surrounding villages to give them potatoes free of charge, and threatened town bakeries with smashing their shop windows if they did not get free bread.[18]

The Social Democrats put their finger on a sensitive issue – which did not go down well in Berlin – by arguing that 'the real guilt for the hunger riots ... lay not with the workers or the government but, rather, with the financial and foreign policies of the Reich.'[19] There could have been no doubt, however, about the democratic credentials of the Saxon labour governments: indeed they saw themselves as the defenders of the Republic against the activities of the anti-Republican right. They tried hard to curb social disturbances, and unanimously condemned activities of the radical right and left, including those of Max Hölz. When the massive crisis unfolded in 1923, however, the government seemed overwhelmed by the explosion of incidents. The historian Benjamin Lapp concluded: 'The lack of police protection was usually caused by inadequate supply and excessive demand rather than malicious intent, as was often implied in bourgeois testimonies to the Reich.'[20]

Whereas the bourgeoisie felt increasingly alienated by developments in post-war Saxony, the labour movement was equally unhappy about certain developments. Most importantly, it was appalled at how brutally the army – supported by the bourgeoisie – handled the situation. For instance, in August 1919, in what became known as the 'Chemnitz blood bath', 9,000 troops ruthlessly put down a peaceful protest against food shortages, maltreated the population and left fifty dead.[21] The Kapp Putsch in 1920 left hundreds dead in Leipzig and Dresden. Finally, in the largest military operation since the end of the First World War,

60,000 *Reichswehr* troops moved into Saxony and toppled the left-wing government in October 1923. Every sign of resistance was brutally suppressed, resulting in many casualties. In the town of Freiberg thirty-one people died and many were seriously wounded (see document 3b). The organised working class was left with a bitter hatred of the bourgeoisie, who had helped to provoke the incident and welcomed the army with open arms.

The *Reichsexekution* was a turning-point in Saxony's history: after a unique five-year spell in power the organised working class was back in opposition, and the violent 'showdown' in October made the prospect of a genuine collaboration between labour and the bourgeoisie extremely unlikely. The situation was further exacerbated because at the end of the year Zeigner was arrested and charges were brought forward against the former Minister of the Interior Hermann Liebmann.[22] The attempt by the twenty-three SPD 'rebels' to overcome the deadlock by entering a great coalition had an extremely slim chance of long-term success. Finally, the Communists came increasingly under the control of the Stalinist wing of the party, which caused a widening political division of the workers' movement and made any further alliances between SPD and KPD unrealistic.

Whereas the new coalition government moved to the right and slowly replaced Social Democratic reforms with conservative legislation, the supporters of the Marxist parties were back to square one and felt pursued and constrained in their activities again. New Reich legislation encouraged local authorities to deny working-class sports organisations access to public sports grounds or gymnasiums.[23] Indeed, the Social Democrats in Zwickau complained that the bourgeoisie used its majority in the town council to prohibit the traditional annual party festival in the forest clearing close to the town. Instead, they had to celebrate on a sports ground.[24]

There were some examples of cooperation between labour and bourgeoisie: the SPD theatre organisation in Chemnitz and Dresden worked together with the bourgeoisie; and even in the city council of Freital, a major SPD stronghold, the Social Democrats frequently fixed secret deals with the bourgeoisie.[25] But the overall picture was one of division. The bourgeois state theatres imposed their programme on the rest of the society and hardly ever took the wishes of the workers' movement into consideration (see chapter 4 [iii]); the majority of the Social Democrats in Freital regarded the Communists as class comrades and the Democrats as class enemies; and anyone who wanted to register as a member in the central workers' library in Leipzig, needed to present the SPD or ADGB (Socialist Federation of Trade Unions) membership card.[26] The Saxon Workers' Gymnastic and Sports Union (ATSB) refused any cooperation with the bourgeois German Youth Hostel Association and accepted not only high financial costs for the building and maintenance of their own homes, but also that their members lacked the choice of the latter's network. According to the local ATSB, it was impossible to experience a sense of proletarian solidarity when 'one was forced to sleep under the same roof as the bourgeoisie.'[27]

With the growth of the SPD during Imperial Germany a whole network of ancillary organisations had developed in the fields of leisure, culture, sport and commerce. During the Weimar Republic Saxony was probably the most significant centre of workers' culture in Germany. Seventy-five percent of all members of the Association for People's Health were organised in the region and had its headquarters in Dresden, and the Workers' Samaritan Union was based in Chemnitz. The local Socialist Working-Class Youth (SAJ), the Freethinker and the ATSB – the biggest of all socialist leisure organisations – boasted the largest membership in Germany.[28] Finally, Saxony had the most dense network of consumer cooperatives in Germany. These socialist organisations provided the working class with an alternative to the strong bourgeois organisations. An SPD sympathiser was not only approached as a political citizen, but the aim was to reach him or her as a complete human being. The SPD attempted to remove education, leisure time, family, even romantic life, in fact, the whole private sphere, from the influence of the bourgeois class enemy and its spiritual-ideological agencies, particularly the church.[29] The effect of the development of separate organisations for different groups and classes in society was twofold. On the one hand these organisations provided security and an identity for their particular members, but on the other hand they tended to isolate their members in their specific surroundings and prevented communication with other groups in society. In Saxony, but also in Thuringia, the organised working class cut itself off from the rest of society to a greater extent than in any other region in Germany.[30]

Peter Lösche and Franz Walter have described the development of a 'unified community' (*Solidargemeinschaft*) among the socialist working class. They defined it as a consciousness, a feeling of solidarity and practical, mutual support resulting from similar living conditions or political experiences, which created mutual requirements and interests.[31] Both historians distinguish between this 'unified community' and a socialist milieu. Whereas the former was a more loose-knit community of people with a similar identity and set of interests, but where divisions and competition still existed, the milieu was a much stronger and tighter centralisation of working-class culture. A socialist milieu was able to develop in working-class districts where active members and voters for Marxist parties lived close together and where this even led to the development of a specific socialist family culture.[32] If this milieu was threatened, those who were embedded in it had a lot to lose: their friends, a traditional solidarity, duties and responsibilities, and a cultural identity.[33]

The concept has been criticised on the grounds that it lacks a precise definition and fails to account for the divisions between SPD and KPD (particularly after 1923).[34] To some extent this criticism seems justified. Most models, however, have some problems of definition – e.g. modernisation theories – and are still useful in analysing historical developments. Basically, the concept of milieu attempts to encapsulate the predominant contemporary views of society and reveals the bourgeoisie's perception of a united left on the one hand, and workers' shared identification due to their class and class consciousness on the other hand. Indeed, the strong traditions of the labour movement and the polarisation between left and right limited the Nazis – who of course presented themselves as Germany's most radical anti-Marxist force – in their ability to attract working-class members and voters in Saxony: compared to the rest of the Republic, workers were extremely under-represented amongst the local NSDAP electorate until 1930.[35] This only changed in 1932, when the Saxon Nazis managed to attract a substantial working-class electorate for the first time – around 27 percent of all their voters. Although this matched the national average, Saxon workers remained more under-represented amongst the NSDAP electorate than in the rest of the Republic (owing to the large number of workers in the state). Working-class membership in the Saxon NSDAP followed a different pattern and was fairly stable at around 38 percent between 1925 and 1932. In numeric terms, however, the Nazis recruited substantially fewer party members in bastions of the Marxist parties than their own strongholds (see chapter 5 [ii]).

The Nazis were able to make major inroads into working-class areas, where at most a socialist *Solidargemeinschaft* had developed. This was particularly the case in large parts of southwestern Saxony (see table 3.1). In areas where the Nazis encountered a solid socialist milieu (especially in central and northwestern Saxony) they faced enormous resistance from the labour movement.[36] Here, instead of falling apart, the organised working class pulled together (however, not in a united front) and took on the Nazi challenge.

Several factors – including the impact of the unfolding slump, the growth of the Nazi movement, and different opinions on how to react to the crisis – posed a serious challenge for the socialist milieu in Saxony from the late 1920s onwards. The Social Democrats' exemplary social welfare system in Freital ended when the financial resources dried up in 1929, and the SPD in Chemnitz had to cut the free theatre tickets for the unemployed in autumn 1930.[37] More generally, the economic depression took an increasing toll among workers' clubs who lost some of their members – particularly the youth – and had to limit their activities.[38] The crisis also enhanced ideological differences. The German Workers' Choir Association expelled whole choirs from its organisation in Dresden after they had demanded a more revolutionary political attitude.[39] When from 1929 onwards the radicalised KPD attempted to take control of labour organisations, it led to the expulsion of Communist activists and split – and in some respects paralysed – the workers' movement. Instead of forming a united front on the left, the SPD and KPD engaged in bitter attacks against each other during the rise of Nazism. During a large SAJ meeting, with 1,500 visitors, about 'the Fascist danger and working-class youth' in Leipzig in late 1930, around 200 Communists started disruptions and brawls.[40] To make matters worse, the combination of austerity measures and right-wing government policies led to a dismantlement of the welfare state and a policy of restrictions on the labour movement from mid-1930 onwards.[41] Simultaneously the Nazis emerged as a serious competitor for mass support among workers.

There were deep-rooted reasons why labour seemed so vulnerable and divided when the slump unfolded. Although the local workers' movement had expanded overall during the 1920s, the growth had begun on somewhat shaky foundations. First of all, party activists with firm political and ideological convictions had always been in a minority. The Saxon KPD only possessed a hardcore of activists and suffered from an extremely fluctuating membership. Franz Walter estimated that at the heart of the workers' movement in the Social Democratic bastion of Freital, there were around 20 percent committed party members who pulled along all the others and held the movement together. Even in Freital only 10 percent of all workers were SPD members and the great majority were rather unpolitical and not interested in theoretical debates.[42] Indeed, the majority of borrowed books from Saxon working-class libraries were fiction and not standard works of socialist ideology.[43] Despite the great progress of the workers' cultural movement, the bourgeoisie still had a powerful hold over this sphere in public (see chapter 4 [ii-iv]). Besides the differences between the SPD and KPD, there were also schisms within the Social Democratic movement: the decision of the twenty-three party 'rebels' to work in a Great Coalition from 1924 onwards had the support of the ADGB and the *Reichsbanner*. More generally, the ADGB increasingly distanced itself from the Social Democratic emphasis on class consciousness.[44]

The unity of the workers' movement was further hampered by the desire for independence, self-interest and also envy. There was an ongoing struggle for more influence within the Saxon ATSB between workers' gymnasts and water polo players on the one hand, and workers' footballers on the other.[45] In Dresden, concerts of workers' choirs were normally badly attended because of the extreme fragmentation of their local movement: smaller choirs stubbornly resisted joining the larger ones.[46] The process of modernisation also stimulated a retreat into private spheres and an individualisation of freetime. In Freital some workers' families made trips into the countryside rather than joining the socialist mass organisations, and the newly built one-family and two-family houses opened up the possibilities of retreating into a private niche.[47]

(ii) The Social Democrats and the Rise of the Nazis: Fight or Perish

Saxony was one of the greatest strongholds of the SPD in Weimar Germany. The Social Democrats possessed by far the biggest party organisation in the state (and left the Communists a long way behind),[48] were by far the largest group in the Saxon parliament, and were the most resolute defenders of the Republican system. Indeed, the Saxon Social Democrats were the first among their national party colleagues who concentrated on the growing Nazi threat from early 1930 onwards.[49] There were four SPD districts in the state which covered the equivalent KHs: the SPD districts of Leipzig, Dresden/Bautzen, Chemnitz/Erzgebirge and Zwickau/Plauen. Each of these SPD districts was independent in the management of its internal affairs and possessed varying party networks. Each district also faced distinct challenges and responded differently to the slump and to the Nazis' aggressive activities. What then was the role of the SPD in the rise of the Nazi party in Saxony?

Looking at the SPD's local and regional election results in Saxony at the end of the Weimar Republic, one notices two phenomena: the electoral turnout in Nazi bastions grew nearly twice as fast than in SPD strongholds between 1928 and 1932. Furthermore, in many regions where the SPD gained high election results the Nazis remained comparatively weak, whilst in other regions the opposite was the case. Large parts of the SPD districts of Dresden/Bautzen, and especially of Leipzig, were extremely successful in defending their position against the challenge from the Nazis, and proved to be the SPD's greatest bastion in the last Weimar elections. However, a comparative collapse of the SPD vote occurred in many areas of the SPD districts of Chemnitz, and particularly Zwickau, but also in the eastern parts of the district of Dresden/Bautzen (former KH Bautzen). The party nearly disintegrated in many of these areas – especially in the Vogtland and the Erzgebirge – and lost up to 20.5 percent of its vote between the May 1928 and July 1932 Reichstag elections (see table 3.1 and also Walter, 'Stammland').

The radical parties, in particular the Nazis, were able to absorb former SPD supporters, and were successful in mobilising former nonvoters (see chapter 5 [iii]). Southwestern Saxony became one of the greatest strongholds of Nazism in Weimar Germany. In late 1931 the police in the Erzgebirge reported that the SPD was 'perishing' and that it 'continuously loses members who join the NSDAP, KPD and the newly founded SAP.'[50]

The dramatic decline of the SPD's vote in southwestern and eastern Saxony from the late 1920s onwards was the second stage of a process which had started in the immediate postwar years. Basically, government participation had lost the SPD its major asset of Imperial Germany: its function as the party of protest. The 1919 state election had still attracted a protest vote against war, defeat, misery and disorder and reflected hopes of a new beginning. As soon as the harsh realities of life became apparent, many

Table 3.1 Percentage of the Votes for NSDAP, SPD and KPD in the Top Ten Nazi Districts and all KHs (Former KHs Bautzen and Dresden Listed Separately) in Saxony in the July 1932 Reichstag Elections

	NSDAP	SPD	KPD		Electoral turnout 1932[1]		Left's loss 1919–1920/ 1920–1928/ 1928–1932	SPD's loss 1919–1920/ 1920–1928/ 1928–1932
AH Auerbach	57.9	10.6	19.1	(+4.8)	86.3	(+18.7)	11.8/10.1/15.0	14.7/21.5/19.8
AH Oelsnitz	57.5	12.2	18.4	(+0.5)	88.6	(+19.7)	11.4/6.0/6.6	18.9/16.4/7.1
AH Plauen	56.2	14.9	13.9	(+6.3)	89.8	(+9.4)	7.8/10.1/14.2	9.8/15.7/20.5
AH Marienberg	54.4	20.3	17.7	(+2.7)	87.6	(+17.0)	7.6/5.7/9.7	12.4/15.9/12.1
AH Freiberg	53.7	29.0	9.1	(+3.5)	88.1	(+11.5)	8.4/1.8/7.4	9.8/6.0/10.9
Werdau	53.3	20.0	16.1	(+1.7)	90.8	(+9.8)	7.4/10.5/10.7	25.9/6.4/12.4
AH Annaberg	52.5	22.3	15.9	(+7.6)	89.7	(+12.0)	8.9/10.0/3.3	10.9/16.3/10.9
Plauen	50.7	15.8	21.5	(+4.4)	87.4	(+7.8)	5.7/8.8/4.0	9.4/22.2/8.4
AH Dippoldiswalde	50.1	25.0	11.7	(+3.6)	87.6	(+8.9)	6.9/1.9/5.1	7.9/5.2/8.7
Freiberg	49.7	28.2	7.8	(+2.4)	90.3	(+8.5)	13.0/+1.4/3.4	13.1/3.9/5.8
KH Dresden	39.4	32.9	13.7	(+2.5)	86.4	(+6.7)	5.7/0.8/4.1	6.7/11.0/6.6
KH Bautzen	39.0	24.9	16.2	(+8.8)	83.7	(+7.0)	6.6/+–0/4.0	7.9/6.1/12.8
KH Leipzig	36.1	33.1	18.7	(+2.6)	89.8	(+6.3)	6.0/0.5/1.3	8.4/14.2/3.9
KH Chemnitz	45.0	24.8	20.9	(+3.1)	89.7	(+12.0)	6.7/8.5/5.4	18.6/14.4/8.5
KH Zwickau	49.5	19.4	18.1	(+3.8)	88.6	(+11.7)	6.9/8.8/10.6	13.4/16.6/14.4
Vogtland	55.5	13.2	18.7	(+4.6)	86.8	(+13.9)	8.8/9.3/10.0	12.5/20.2/14.1
SAXONY	41.2	28.4	17.4	(+3.4)	88.3	(+8.7)	6.2/3.3/4.8	10.6/12.9/8.2
REICH	37.3	21.6	14.3	(+3.7)	84.1	(+8.5)	3.8/1.3/4.5	5.9/9.8/8.2

[1] Percentage gains since May 1928 in parentheses.
Source: calculated from *StDR*, (1928–32).

Saxons became disillusioned with the Social Democrats – who had taken over responsibility for the new framework of society – and turned towards opposition parties. Between the 1919 and 1920 Reichstag elections the SPD lost votes to the bourgeois parties and the KPD, and this process continued throughout the 1920s. When the crisis unfolded at the end of the 1920s, the SPD's vote plummeted to unprecedented lows in southwestern Saxony – to as little as 10.6 percent of the overall poll in the district of Auerbach in July 1932. Nine out of the SPD's ten worst electoral districts in Saxony were in this region, and it was also here where SPD and KPD together lost up to 36.9 percent of the vote between 1919 and 1932. The Saxon Nazis analysed the dramatic electoral drift to the right in the southwest:

> The belief in the Reich, more specifically in the government, was eroded in the years after the November revolution amongst the people of the Erzgebirge. They had heard the promises which were made at that time and ... many even followed the Marxists, because their agitators made most pledges. Year after year the *Erzgebirgler* waited in vain for the promises of the various parties to be fulfilled. But they saw with their own eyes that things increasingly got worse.[51]

The SPD itself seemed to disintegrate in the southwest. This was a result of fierce internal disputes over how to respond to the economic crisis and to frantic Nazi activity. When Max Seydewitz, the prominent local leader of the left wing, became one of the founding fathers of the SAP in October 1931, the SPD district of Zwickau lost about one-fifth of all members to its new rival. The strong party district of Leipzig, on the other hand, only lost about fifty party members to the SAP.[52] Furthermore, the Social Democrats in Zwickau and Chemnitz were confronted with economic misery and Nazi attacks from early 1929 onwards, while their colleagues in Leipzig did not mention growing Nazi activities before September of that year.[53] In mid-1929, an SPD official blamed the terrible economic situation in the Erzgebirge/Vogtland for the loss of working-class support for his party. According to him, the depression 'took the income from thousands of formerly secure existences. These people ran into the arms of the first prophet that came along. This explains, why ... Hitler found conditions so favourable.'[54] Indeed, people who needed the Social Democrats most, those who lived in miserable conditions in the valleys of southwestern Saxony, found it more difficult to find help from the SPD's welfare association than residents in other parts of the state. The party's Workers' Welfare Associations in the district of Zwickau were far more loosely spread than those in the Leipzig district.[55] The Communists reported at the end of 1930 that the workers' support for the NSDAP was particularly strong in regions, 'where there is a numerous, impoverished working class.'[56]

Party disunity, the timing and scale of Nazi activities, and the extent of the crisis in southwestern Saxony, however, cannot solely explain the SPD collapse in the Erzgebirge/Vogtland. It was also crucial that in this area the network of socialist party and leisure organisations did not prove strong and elaborate enough to withstand the Nazis' offensive, in contrast to many parts of central and northwestern Saxony. There were fewer SPD party members per head of the population in the SPD district of Zwickau than in the rest of Saxony (see table 3.2). Whereas the membership figures in the SPD districts of Dresden, Chemnitz and Leipzig rose considerably between 1926 and 1929 and stayed fairly stable until the end of 1931, membership grew slowly in Zwickau and collapsed dramatically thereafter: by 1931 the district had lost more than one-third of its members.

Table 3.2 Percentage of Party Membership to Population in the SPD Districts of Saxony

Year	Leipzig	Dresden	Chemnitz	Zwickau
1926	2.9	2.4	2.2	1.8
1929	3.2	3.0	2.6	2.0
1931	3.4	2.9	2.6	1.4

Source: Jahrbuch der Deutschen Sozialdemokratie, 1926, 1929, 1931; *StJbSa*, 1924/26.

There was a clear link between the SPD's membership ratio to the population and its ability to withstand the Nazi onslaught. The party sub-districts with the worst SPD membership figures per head of the population in the KHs Leipzig and Dresden – Freiberg and Döbeln – were the ones where the Nazis were most successful. The membership of the SPD and its affiliated organisations in the Erzgebirge/Vogtland, once one of the heartlands of the German labour movement, had not grown in the twentieth century as it had done in central and northwestern Saxony. One of the reasons for this was that the Erzgebirge/Vogtland, with its many valleys and its peripheral position on Saxony's border with Czechoslovakia, was isolated from the rest of the state, and also developed specific regional features and interests. For instance, at the turn of the century the local Social Democrats experienced difficulties in establishing a party press because of rivalries between various towns in the district of Zwickau.[57] It was in this area that the Social Democrats lost a massive proportion of their electoral support and the Saxon Nazis were able to establish their greatest strongholds from mid-1925 onwards. By the June 1930 state elections the Nazis were already the strongest party in the districts of Oelsnitz (31.3 percent of the vote), Plauen (30.0 percent) and Schwarzenberg (20.3 percent), and the towns of Werdau (36.0 percent) and Plauen (35.6 percent). They were not far behind in the towns of Glauchau, Crimmitschau, Freiberg, Zwickau and Chemnitz, places which were the cradle of the German working class.

It is true that there were more SPD branches compared to the number of villages and towns in southwestern Saxony than in most other parts of the state, but this network was essentially a 'remnant' of the flourishing late nineteenth century era after which the local Social Democrats failed to tie more people to the party or other affiliated organisations. At the end of 1930 there was only one SPD member for every hundred citizens in the district of Annaberg and 1.2 in the district of Marienberg. There were even some blank spots on the map where the SPD lacked any representation whatsoever. The Social Democrats of the district of Marienberg reported that there were only sixteen party branches in the thirty-five villages in their district. When the slump unfolded, the party network was far too loose and there were not enough SPD activists to respond to increasing Nazi frenzy: party officials expressed the desire to 'counter the attack of the Nazis through loyalty'.[58] With this tactic they also hoped to be able to 'attract the thousands of uprooted middle-class citizens'.

Areas which had no Social Democratic party branches secured an SPD vote far below even the average obtained in the Erzgebirge/Vogtland. The Chemnitz SPD reported after the 1928 Reichstag elections, in which it had polled 33.3 percent of the total vote, that it had only received an average of around 20 percent of the vote in the eighty-nine villages where it had no party branches.[59] In the same report the Social Democrats praised the small town of Glösa, situated at the northern periphery of Chemnitz, as having the best membership ratio, with 15.3 members for every one hundred inhabitants. This was due to a large housing scheme in which many party officials lived; a place where a deep-rooted socialist milieu had developed and which remained a solid socialist stronghold even in the depths of the crisis. The SPD still scored 50 percent of the votes in July 1932 (a loss of 6.8 percent since 1929), while the Nazis only managed to win 23.3 percent. The left combined, polled 69.6 percent of the vote (a loss of 3.8 percent since 1929).[60]

The SPD encountered major obstacles in its organisation and operation in southwestern Saxony. In the district of Chemnitz the SPD headquarters complained at the end of 1928 that 146 out of 203 party branches had not reported the results of the traditional annual campaign week to attract new members.[61] It is likely that they either did not participate in the campaign or that there was simply no success to report. In the district of Annaberg, sixteen SPD party branches organised as few as thirty-five public meetings throughout the whole of 1929. The remaining twelve branches of the district did not hold even a single public meeting.[62] SPD officials described their own performance as 'unsatisfactory' and concluded in a resigned manner: 'Although there was a willingness to work, there were too many difficulties.'[63] Whereas the Social Democrats in Leipzig were able to match the Nazis' increasing propaganda activities and put up a determined fight against them, their colleagues in the Erzgebirge/Vogtland could not respond adequately to the continuous Nazi onslaught. The comparatively sluggish Marxist parties in the Erzgebirge/Vogtland enabled the local Nazis to dominate public campaigning and to mobilise former nonvoters (see chapter 2 and table 2.3).

In most parts of Germany the SPD encountered severe limits to its expansion in rural areas which were far removed from urban working-class strongholds. In Saxony, the existence of the 'industrial village' together with a long-standing socialist tradition also made the SPD strong in many rural areas. This was particularly so around its urban strongholds in Meißen, Riesa, Leipzig and Dresden. In other rural regions, however, the local SPD only possessed a very loose organisational network. These were places where party officials found it most difficult to attract female supporters and the youth. A quarter of all SPD branches in the district Chemnitz-Erzgebirge had not a single female party member, and the party had a very low youth membership.[64] It was precisely here that the Nazis were most active and successful. In 1929 Social Democrats from an area nearby warned that the National Socialists 'need to be closely watched. Unfortunately, if workers face poverty and distress, [they] run into the arms of ... the Hitler guard.'[65]

In places where long-standing socialist traditions combined with strong party and organisational activities, Nazi electoral success was limited even in the Erzgebirge/Vogtland. In the small town of Auerbach, located south of Chemnitz, the workers' movement began to develop during the time of Bismarck's anti-Socialist laws. For some years seven local Social Democrats trekked fifteen kilometres to the SPD meeting in Chemnitz once a week. Usually they came back late in the night with leaflets and Socialist newspapers in their rucksacks. In 1899 they founded their own party branch and other working-class organisations developed very quickly. During the Weimar Republic these organisations were joined by the Workers' Samaritan Union, Freethinkers, the Socialist Youth Organisation, a building cooperative, a house-renting club, and a socialist theatre group.[66] This small town, with roughly 4,100 citizens, was one of the region's many textile towns, and nearly all of its workers were employed in sock making. This was the perfect place for a socialist stronghold: it was predominantly working class (less than 5 percent of the population was employed in agriculture) and possessed a long socialist tradition, celebrating the First of May from 1893 onwards and experiencing its first strike in 1907. Furthermore, in contrast to most other places, Social Democrats and Communists often cooperated to secure a socialist majority in the town council or to fight the growing threat of the Nazis. The latter encountered difficulties in that kind of environment, even in the Erzgebirge. The SPD managed to retain more than 30 percent of the vote and the combined left kept its majority until March 1933. Still, the Nazis managed to make major inroads even in this 'model working-class community' by scoring more than 36 percent of the vote and becoming the biggest party in July 1932.

Although the Saxon Nazis were active in urban and rural areas from 1925 onwards, they naturally found it much easier to recruit mass support in the 'organisational vacuum' of the countryside. Seven of the Nazis' top ten electoral strongholds in Saxony in 1932 were rural districts (see table 3.1), and the local Nazis were able to attract more workers as party members in villages and small towns than in large towns and cities (see chapter 5 [ii]). Due to the enormous resistance the Nazis encountered from the labour movement in many urban areas, they were often simply forced out into the countryside in the 1920s. In 1926 the Nazis in Freiberg admitted that their SA was not able to protect two local party meetings, 'which would have been a sweeping success if they had not been disturbed by the Marxists.'[67] Instead, the SA was beaten up twice on these occasions by Marxist followers. Henceforth, 'the activities of the Freiberg SA were limited mainly to meetings in villages' (Ibid.).

The towns of Freital, Meißen, Dresden, Leipzig and Döbeln – and their surroundings – and also the towns of Riesa and Pirna, were all areas with a high level of Social Democratic activity, where the Nazis found it difficult to obtain a level of electoral support which accorded with their national average.[68] The SPD in the city of Leipzig was probably pursuing the most sophisticated and effective socialist educational work in Weimar Germany. The Workers' Education Institute trained party officials and organised events throughout the whole country, and a Local Educational Committee organised an enormous amount of educational events. The local Social Democrats attracted high calibre national and international speakers throughout the year and supported their educational efforts with a network of about forty-five libraries, bookshops and the use of mass media, which included the showing of 130 films in 1930.[69] The Nazis admitted encountering most difficulties in this environment: 'In and around Leipzig ... the clashes were at their most severe and took the heaviest toll of human life.'[70] Mass participation in the First of May celebrations, one of the cultural and political climaxes in the Social Democrat calendar, underlined the deep-rooted socialist conscience and tradition of workers in Leipzig. The SPD, and both Marxist parties combined, managed to mobilise far more supporters at these events in Leipzig than could their party colleagues in Plauen.[71] Plauen was the headquarters of the Saxon Nazis and a town where the NSDAP was already by far the biggest party in 1930.

Other SPD strongholds promoted a range of activities similar to those in Leipzig. They organised many educational courses and lectures, and in addition a very high percentage of local pupils participated in *Jugendweihen* (literally, 'Youth Consecration'), which expressed open rejection of the bourgeois state and of the traditional role of religion and the church. One of the most active party organisations in Saxony was the SPD in Freital. In 1929 alone, local Social Democrats organised thirteen educational courses, ninety-two single lectures, and 45 percent of all pupils participated in *Jugendweihen*.[72] The town remained one of the most solid SPD bastions and a relative wilderness for the Nazis until the end of Weimar. In the July 1932 Reichstag elections the SPD scored 43.8 percent of the vote, the NSDAP only 21.6 percent. In Bautzen – a slightly larger town – where the Social Democrats only organised four educational courses, and thirty-three lectures, and where only 14 percent of the pupils participated in *Jugendweihen* in 1929, the NSDAP received 42 percent of the vote in July 1932, compared with 24.4 percent for the SPD.

SPD strongholds were normally areas with the highest rate of people leaving the church, and contrasted sharply with regions with a solid Protestant and nationalist following. Between August 1919 and December 1926, 21.3 percent of all Protestants left the church in Freital, 17.3 percent in Leipzig, and 15.7 percent in the district of Leipzig.[73] In these places the combination of socialist traditions and dense party and organisational networks had created socialist milieus which the Nazis found nearly impossible to infiltrate. Finally, the participation in workers' sports clubs was also an important indicator about the strength of the local labour movement. In rural northwestern Saxony – an area of great SPD activities and a difficult terrain for the Nazis – there was an ATSB club in every third village in which nearly six out of every hundred citizens were organised. In the Vogtland, only every fifth village had an ATSB club and only two out of every hundred citizens were members.[74]

The traditional strength of the Saxon SPD made it extremely immune against Nazism until 1930 (see also document 17). This changed by 1932, when the local SPD lost significantly more voters to the NSDAP than its national average. (Compare table 5.3 with Falter, *Wähler*, 111.) The Nazis found extremely favourable conditions for attracting mass support amongst workers in southwestern Saxony (see table 5.5). Particularly in the Vogtland and the Erzgebirge, the Nazis were able to overrun and absorb a substantial proportion of the SPD's supporters.[75] The local Social Democratic party and organisational network was not sufficiently widespread, determined and united to ward off and respond successfully to the enormous challenges posed by the Nazis and the slump. A large number of small-scale and cottage industries in the area did not help to foster the growth of working-class milieus. In contrast to this, the Social Democrats in Meißen, Freital, Riesa, Döbeln and Leipzig proved that a deep-rooted and sophisticated organisational network enabled them to mobilise their support in defence of the Republican system even in the face of an unprecedented crisis.

(iii) Nazis at the Workplace: Socialists with a Nationalist Purpose

A crucial area requiring examination in any investigation of working-class support for the Nazi party is its strength in the actual workplace, on the factory councils. Claiming to be a working-man's party, it seemed a logical step to get a foothold in this important area. It was only in spring 1931, however, that the National Socialist Factory Cell organisation (NSBO) officially participated in the factory council elections for the first time. It did very poorly in these elections and only began to develop in earnest from late 1931 onwards. Overall, the NSBO remained an insignificant force and was not able to challenge the powerful position of the ADGB, until the latter was forcibly dissolved by the Nazis in May 1933. The reason for the delayed and half-hearted development of the NSBO was that it presented something of a contradiction for the Nazi strategists in Munich. Hitler wanted workers to vote for the NSDAP, become members of the party and join the SA, but was far less enthusiastic about the creation of autonomous Nazi trade unions for a number of reasons: he foresaw few dividends arising from taking on the ADGB; he sought power through elections to the Reichstag (unlike the Communists who were planning a revolutionary general strike); he felt that getting directly involved in industrial relations was bound to alienate one side or another; and lastly, he believed there was a contradiction between forming employee unions and advocating a *Volksgemeinschaft*.

As Saxony was the most industrialised region in Germany, one would expect the local Nazis to be particularly active in attempting to establish a foothold amongst workers in their workplace. However, the NSBO leadership's newspaper, *Der Betrieb* (The Factory), stated that Saxony only ranked sixteenth amongst all Nazi *Gaue* in terms of NSBO membership in May 1931, although it was tenth in June and third in July and August of the same year.[76] Several factors explain the late and slow development of the NSBO in Saxony. First of all, as in the Ruhr area, there were no influential personalities like Engels or Muchow, who did so much in fostering the development of the NSBO in Berlin.[77] Secondly, the urban centres in Saxony possessed a dense trade union network and were a stronghold of the ADGB.[78] Success for the NSBO seemed very unlikely. Finally, the Nazi stronghold in Saxony, the Erzgebirge/Vogtland, was dominated by small- and medium-scale industries where union organisations were not widespread at all. To put it crudely, there was no need for NSBO cells in these areas. When local Nazi officials met for a district meeting in the Erzgebirge in late 1931 there was no NSBO representation. Instead, a group for 'trade, business and industry' discussed the latest policies.[79]

This could explain why the propaganda of the Saxon Nazis was generally aimed at winning over the working class as such, until the end of the 1920s, rather than at trying to gain a foothold in the actual workplace. Still, there were some Nazi efforts to establish themselves in the factories during this period. Saxon Nazis targeted factory workers with leaflets as early as 1923 (see document 7), and the police reported Nazi factory cells in 'industrial and agricultural workplaces' for the first time in July 1929.[80] The whole development seemed to have gained a decisive impetus from the NSDAP's stunning success in the September 1930 Reichstag elections. The next day the Saxon Nazis issued the slogan: 'National Socialism against Marxism. *Bürgertum* is crushed! ... We are going into the factories, we are going to the unemployed.'[81] Soon afterwards official orders to create NSBO cells were issued.[82]

On a general level, the aim of the Nazis was to win over workers from the Marxist parties (see document 12). More specifically, they clearly aimed to attract disillusioned workers with nationalist sentiments. The Nazis in Dresden explained to their party members the task of the NSBO: 'Our fight is against Marxism which destroys every aspect of the *Volk* ... We must expose the guilt of the Marxist parties, their leaders and supporters, for this endless misery and poverty of the German *Volk*.'[83] There was a clear tension between a revolutionary and a reactionary line in Nazi trade union policies: they tried hard to square the circle of equally promoting socialist values, and the interest of the whole nation. One Nazi leaflet emphasised that a Nazi was 'a socialist', but that he did not want 'to ruin his employer' (see document 7). It was clear, however, that the ultimate priority of Nazi ideology was the nation: social peace and a strong nation would create prosperity for all individuals and classes in German society (see documents 9, 10, and 12).

By the end of 1931 the police noted lively Nazi propaganda for the NSBO.[84] However, these seem to have been rather isolated efforts in certain major Saxon towns. There was only one small article in *Der Freiheitskampf* devoted to the elections to the factory councils in spring 1931, which attempted to rally party members behind the NSBO.[85] Handwritten leaflets for a public NSBO meeting in Leipzig in August 1931 do not give the impression of very sophisticated NSBO propaganda capabilities at that time.[86] This stood in sharp contrast to the Nazis' massive propaganda campaign for the elections to the Agricultural Chambers in Saxony in May of the same year (chapter 2 [v]), and was a pitiful effort by comparison with what Wilfried Böhnke described in the Ruhr as an 'incredible propaganda effort' for the 1931 factory council elections.[87] The fact that the Saxon Nazis hardly published any results of these elections suggests that overall they did very badly.

Although the NSBO showed increased activity by the end of 1931, its impact remained very limited and – as Saxon officials noted – the ADGB continued 'to be decisive for the economic life and union movement.'[88] As hardly any elections to factory councils took place in 1932 because of government fears of political disturbances, it is very difficult to assess the further development of the NSBO in Saxony before the Nazis seized power. Some growth and success, especially in the southwestern part of the state, must be assumed. Gunther Mai argued that Saxony was one of the five most important regional NSBO strongholds in early 1933.[89] The economic structure of the region determined the specific spread of Nazi cells. For instance, in mid-1932 one quarter of Saxon NSBO members worked in the textile industry,[90] and in Dresden – the administrative capital of Saxony – local Nazis were particularly active within the 'civil service'.

Nazi activists openly admitted their difficulties in setting up a dense NSBO network in Saxony. The NSBO district leader of Leipzig and the surrounding area complained at the end of 1931 how slow and 'difficult' the creation of the NSBO had been in this traditional Marxist stronghold. In every 1,000 companies in the area there were only six NSBO cells.[91] The situation was similar in other regions. NSBO activists found it 'incredibly difficult in the … "red bastion" of Crimmitschau. Only about five to six workers came from workplaces with several hundred employees to our factory council meetings … at the end of 1931 the membership had risen to 120, and by the middle of 1932 it had only exceeded 300.'[92] Counting only the seventy-three large-scale factories with 10,122 workers, the NSBO had only thirty members for every 1,000 workers in this traditional textile town. However, as the

NSDAP received 41.7 percent of the vote in the July 1932 Reichstag elections, beating the SPD's 32.6 percent to become the largest party in this very industrialised town, it seems likely that a substantial number of workers who were organised in the Social Democratic ADGB must have voted for the Nazis. This was not necessarily a contradiction: workers could well believe that the ADGB looked after their interests at their workplace best, but that they would also benefit in the Third Reich under the Nazis.

In early 1932 the Saxon Nazis reported that 'nearly 1,000 NSBO cells were created in the province in 1931.'[93] Even taking this probably exaggerated figure as true, it would mean that there were only thirty-four Nazi cells in every 1,000 middle-sized and large-scale company in Saxony. In large areas the NSBO did not even exist before 1932 or even 1933. In Markneukirchen, the first town to bring the Nazis an overall majority in elections in the 1920s, the NSBO was only founded in February 1933 by a mere four party members.[94] As the town was dominated by small- and medium-scale industry which normally lacked union organisation, it did not seem necessary to establish NSBO cells.

(iv) Nazis in Working-Class Neighbourhoods: Fists and Open Arms

The Nazis frequently also faced stiff resistance in their attempts to recruit followers in working-class neighbourhoods. When on rare occasions they organised meetings in the 'red West' of Leipzig before 1930, this tended to turn into wild brawls between the SA and Marxist supporters and the Nazis had to leave again, highly frustrated (see also document 14).[95] Even in Plauen, their headquarters, the Nazis faced tough resistance in solidly working-class areas. In their autumn campaign of 1931 Nazis in Plauen specifically targeted factory and non-factory workers and ordered: 'Forward also into the working-class districts!'[96] Directing the campaign at working-class homes rather than the workplace seemed to promise greater success for the local Nazis. It was also effective in reaching both male and women in a working-class family. The task was expected to involve a hard physical battle which could only be attempted after a 'mobilisation of all ... party members ... to wake up the many *Volksgenossen* who are still so far away from us.'[97] *Der Freiheitskampf* reported how residents in a working-class district in Plauen reacted when Nazis marched through their neighbourhood: 'There was amazement amongst the extremely "red residents" of the Lange- and Herderstraße ..., as we came so unexpectedly they could not demonstrate their skill in building street barricades and limited themselves to throwing beer bottles ... [and] the usual shouting of "Red Front" and "Down! Down! Down!"' (Ibid.) Similar was the account by Nazis in Dresden of their activities in 'red Pieschen', a working-class district, only three months before Hitler became Chancellor:

> The fight in our district is incredibly hard. Marxism defends it as its rightful domain. SA members who walk home alone are attacked; party members, as soon as they are known as such, are watched every step they make; their family members are hounded, even children suffer due to the terror from the red comrades; business people are boycotted ... the pack does not even shrink back from attacks in apartments.[98]

This reinforces our earlier contention that overall the Nazis did worst and faced stiff resistance in large working-class districts which traditionally supported the Marxist parties, places where a socialist milieu existed. The Nazis' relentless and flexible efforts to gain a foothold even in the most solid Marxist strongholds, however, helped to dilute and break down the initially strong resistance in some places. To be sure, even solid working-class areas were never completely controlled by the Marxist parties. In 1928 the Social Democrats in Chemnitz complained: 'It is an unpleasant phenomenon, but we do not have outright success in proletarian districts which ought to be ours.'[99] They illustrated this with reference to the housing estate of Chemnitz-Gablenz where around 17 percent of its residents had voted for bourgeois parties. Workers, however, could often not show their sympathies for the Nazis openly due to the pressure exerted on them by their environment. They chose instead to vote quietly for the NSDAP in secret parliamentary ballots. Nazis from Belgershain, near Leipzig, noted:

> The discipline of the workers who were organised in ... Marxist [i.e. SPD] organisations was so good that the NSDAP did not manage to attract these workers to its meetings. It is beyond doubt, however, that a good part of them had voted for the NSDAP who already achieved an absolute majority in the elections of July 1932.[100]

In other areas in northwestern Saxony the police reported that one could see various party flags – red with three arrows (SPD), red with hammer and sickle (KPD), and red with swastika (NSDAP) –

'hanging peacefully next to each other' from workers' windows during the July 1932 Reichstag elections.[101]

The Nazis were extremely flexible in adopting propaganda methods in working-class districts according to the local strength of the Marxist parties. In places where they faced overwhelming resistance they often avoided outright confrontation. As parades or public meetings in the west of Leipzig only fuelled tough resistance from Marxist activists, they preferred to be active 'beneath the surface' in several local party branches and a women's group.[102] In working-class areas where organised resistance against Nazi infiltration was not so tenacious, the Nazis were much more prepared to use violence to conquer new terrain. In Chemnitz, where in addition large sections of the police sympathised with their cause, the Nazis wore down Marxist followers in a brutal battle for control of the streets by the end of 1931.[103] The exceptionally fierce confrontations between Nazis and KPD and SPD activists became evident in the enormous wave of violence which spread through Saxony in the last years of the Republic. According to Nazi records, 48 out of 129 violent attacks against National Socialists in the Reich took place alone in Saxony between 8 March and 25 April 1931.[104]

We have seen that the Saxon Nazis had limited success in establishing widespread support for the NSBO and had apparent problems in infiltrating large working-class districts. Nevertheless the local Nazis were still able to mobilise a significant following among workers, which was a crucial precondition for becoming a mass party in Saxony. They rejoiced after the state election in 1930: 'Particularly gratifying is the enormous success of the National Socialists in purely working-class areas.'[105] This referred to their stunning gains in the Erzgebirge/Vogtland, which was predominantly working class. The Communists diagnosed, 'that a great part of the National Socialist vote is recruited from the proletariat ... Especially in the Vogtland a number of our voters definitely switched over to the fascists.'[106] Two years later in the July 1932 elections, forty of the forty-nine administrative districts in Saxony polled above the Nazis' average national result of 37.3 percent. During the November Reichstag elections the electoral district of Chemnitz-Zwickau became the NSDAP's second best district with 43.4 percent of the votes. Saxony, however, was the state with the sharpest divisions and polarisations in Germany. Whereas many parts of working-class Saxony had become a Nazi stronghold, substantial areas in the state continued to hold up the banner as 'red' Saxony, in fact as the 'reddest' regions in Germany (excluding the city of Berlin): in Weimar's last elections in March 1933, the electoral districts of Leipzig and Dresden became the SPD's top two strongholds, and the Communists scored some of their best results in the electoral districts of Chemnitz-Zwickau and Leipzig.

The Nazis did particularly well in attracting workers' support in the 'industrial villages' of the Erzgebirge/Vogtland, which were dominated by small-scale, medium-scale and cottage industries. Eight out of the nine Saxon districts in which the NSDAP scored an absolute majority in July 1932 were of this type, and all were located in this area (see table 3.1). Seven of them were extremely industrialised, rural districts and the remaining two were the towns of Werdau and Plauen.[107] Furthermore, seven of these districts were dominated by the textile industry which faced a deep-rooted crisis. The Saxon Nazis florished in this kind of environment. The small villages of Pillmansgrün and Kottengrün in the district of Auerbach provide good examples of the dramatic collapse of the SPD's support in a solidly working-class environment over the fourteen years of the Republic and of how workers rapidly turned to the Nazis at the end of the 1920s. Most of the 831 inhabitants were producing embroidery or weaving at home (only 14 percent of the population worked in agriculture). In the election to the National Assembly in 1919 the SPD gained nearly three-quarters of the vote in both villages combined. This fell to less than half of the votes by 1920. By mid-1930 the SPD's vote had completely collapsed when a mere five citizens supported the party (3.8 percent) in the state elections. The Nazis were already close to an absolute majority. Complete triumph came for the Nazis in July 1932 when they received 79.5 percent of the vote. The combined vote of the left was reduced to 15.8 percent (5 percent for SPD). The Nazis were also very successful in many urban areas, particularly in southwestern Saxony. The NSDAP scored a higher percentage of votes in the very industrialised towns of Werdau, Plauen, Glauchau, Aue and Chemnitz than it achieved at Reich level in July 1932. These were towns where the SPD – as in the rural areas of the Erzgebirge/Vogtland – had lost enormous voting support during the Weimar era, but particularly after 1928.

The Nazis mounted a massive propaganda campaign to attract workers' support (for the following see also chapter 2). Throughout the Weimar Republic the Saxon Nazis directed more meetings and other propaganda at workers than at any other group. Equally important, Nazi propaganda mainly concentrated on broad themes which appealed to all groups in Saxon society, including the working classes: they either criticised the existing misery, or promised a better future in a National Socialist state. The SPD's response to the crisis – a mixture of an honest political debate and Marxist ideology – drove many workers virtually into the hands of the Nazis. For instance, the Social Democrats sympathised with the extremely miserable situation of Saxon cottage workers, but at the same time welcomed rationalisation ('thank God!') which would destroy this profession as a natural step on the road towards the large-scale concentration of industries.[108] It was fateful that the SPD stubbornly clung to the Marxist doctrine that the forces of history determined events and – one day in the future – would lead to a socialist state. This theory did not accommodate those cottage workers who suffered or felt threatened by the process of modernisation, had nationalist sentiments, and were not embedded in an SPD milieu. Many of them began to support the Nazis, who described them as 'hard working and diligent people' who deserved financial support to maintain their traditional trade,[109] or they joined the Communists who were very clear about their intentions of setting up a socialist society as soon as possible.

(v) Workers and the *Volksgemeinschaft*: Social Peace in a Strong Germany

The Nazis in Saxony – as in the rest of Germany – received significant support from all classes in German society at the end of the Weimar era. Why did people, who were divided by so many other things, unite to support Nazism? And in particular, why did a large number of workers, rather than supporting the traditional working-class parties, join the Nazi bandwagon? The Nazis' unique success was based on their ability to mobilise the most powerful sentiment that united many Germans – nationalism – and to exploit the concept of the *Volksgemeinschaft*, which offered a vision how to overcome the ills in society (divisions and hatred) and to secure prosperity for all. (See also chaper 2 [iv] and 4.) The asset of the Nazis was the weakness of their greatest opponent: organised labour. Neither SPD nor KPD could reconcile themselves with the concept of nationalism and the vision of a *Volksgemeinschaft.*

The Saxon SPD developed from a background that was fundamentally opposed to any nationalist sentiments. It resisted a Prussian-dominated Germany and opposed the war against France in 1870/71. Whereas the emphasis on Saxon particularism had been an important appeal of the local SPD, more and more Saxons were swept away by nationalist sentiments after the victory against the French and the foundation of the German Empire. Large parts of the population – including members of the SPD – became involved in veterans' associations.[110] By 1913 the Saxon Veterans' Associations had a staggering 220,446 members and 1,751 branches, and had outpaced the SPD's 178,000 members.[111] Furthermore, the Protestant Nationalist Workers' Associations, who had a comparatively small number of 8,123 members and 109 branches in Saxony in 1912, tried to attract workers with nationalist and religious sentiments away from the SPD with help schemes, festivals, and the building of allotments.[112]

Indeed, the SPD's official anti-nationalist stance, its championing of internationalism and emphasis on class divisions, which contradicted the sentiments of a growing number of party followers, led to ruptures within the party. The idea of uniting all Germans in a *Volksgemeinschaft* attracted a growing number of right-wing SPD and trade union supporters in the decade before the First World War. They shared the belief that a powerful foreign policy (*Weltpolitik*) was a remedy to overcome 'economic strangulation' by opening up foreign markets and acquiring colonies, and they hoped that the concept could reintegrate the party back into the nation.[113] The approval of war credits on 4 August 1914, and the alliance between all parties at the beginning of the war (*Burgfrieden*) was thus seen by them as a natural union in defence of the German nation. Unlike the majority of the organised working class, they spontaneously committed themselves positively to the war effort: the police in Leipzig noted a 'nationalistic attitude' among some Social Democrats, and the *Chemnitzer Volksstimme* under Ernst Heilmann suddenly postulated radical nationalist ideas.[114] During the war, the concept of *Volksgemeinschaft* was used by all political parties to emphasise their commitment to unite in the fight for the survival of the nation and to drop the class war in favour of solidarity and partnership.[115] Although the leftwing of the SPD quickly distanced itself from this attitude due to the official annexation policies, large parts of organised labour stuck to this new alliance for much longer. For instance, the German Metal Workers' Union promoted the policy of 'defence of the fatherland' until the end of 1917.[116]

The crisis-ridden beginning of the Weimar Republic led to a brief continuation of the consensus behind the concept of *Volksgemeinschaft* and explains the cooperation between MSPD and *Reichswehr*, and between trade unions and employers at the national level in Germany. This consensus only manifested itself in Saxony in the immediate postwar years because of the extreme polarisation between left and right. Earlier than in the rest of the Republic, each party continued to search for support among specific classes in their own social milieus, not realising that traditional loyalties had started to disintegrate due to continuous crises and the impact of modernisation.[117] By the mid-1920s the local Nazis had become the only political force – with the exception of the ASP – who clung to the 'war spirit' and continued to embrace the whole nation. Again and again the Nazis repeated their aim of establishing a nationalist community that would get rid of the internal divisions in society. Internal unity was seen as the precondition for creating a strong nation that could overcome the humiliations and setbacks suffered after the First World War (see documents 9, 10 and 12). It was crucial for the eventual success of Nazism that the wider nationalist milieu – bourgeois clubs, associations and newspapers – also continued to cultivate the idea of the *Volksgemeinschaft* (see chapter 4).

In the meantime, right-wing Social Democrats – followers of the Saxon ASP – also attempted to establish a government of nationalist integration by recreating the war experience and integrating 'proletarian nationalism' into a great coalition.[118] However, the ASP found it impossible to square the circle between Marxism and the concept of the nation: it found itself caught between faithful SPD supporters and those who distrusted former Marxists and were looking for a more radical solution. It is no surprise that the most extreme nationalists within the ASP joined the Nazi movement when their party disintegrated in the early 1930s, while those who were not able to break with Marxism eventually rejoined the SPD.

The idea of a strong nation and a prosperous, unified *Volk* attracted people from all sectors of Saxon society – including many workers. The Nazis were particularly successful in attracting those workers – and they were the majority of the working class – who were either not affiliated to parties or organisations, or were not firmly embedded in a socialist milieu. For many of these workers the Nazis' promotion of strong nationalism and 'class unity' of left and right was far more appealing than the Marxists' principles of 'internationalism' and 'class struggle'. In the late 1920s the Marxist parties experienced the impact of working-class nationalism during the NSDAP's anti-Young Plan campaign. Local Communists felt let down by their party during the campaign and reported a loss of support to the Nazis.[119] Meanwhile, the SPD openly attacked nationalist sentiments. In the second half of the 1920s in the Landtag a Social Democrat stressed the need to protect the youth from the 'spirit of nationalist contamination', and the ATSB accused its bourgeois competitor of a long history of inciting the youth with nationalist and militaristic propaganda.[120]

It was not possible to reconcile the Marxist world view with the concept of the *Volksgemeinschaft*. In 1930, a representative of the left-wing Saxon ATSB publicly rejected the idea of the *Volksgemeinschaft* and upheld the idea of socialism:

> I am opposed to the propaganda of the so-called *Volksgemeinschaft*. We as the Workers' Gymnast and Sport Association are in fact specifically aiming to win over the proletariat with our education of class-conscious thinking and to offset class antagonism with socialism.[121]

Indeed, the ATSB regarded each gymnasium it had built as 'a stepping stone towards socialism' (ibid., 398). The SPD shared this view and argued: 'As long as the exploiter and the exploited faced each other in sharp class antagonism', the idea of the *Volksgemeinschaft* was 'a phrase without content'.[122] In contrast to this, the Saxon Nazis emphasised the comradeship which 'overcame all class differences' in their party.[123] Nazis from Bautzen aimed at 'the restoration of a strong and united *Volk*.' They claimed to be 'moving forward, towards a nation in which everyone enjoys honour, freedom and justice.'[124] This vision appealed to a growing number of Saxons from all groups and classes, people to whom the traditional Marxist parties had nothing to offer.

(vi) The Workers' Milieu during the Dictatorship: Coercion, Social Integration and Workplaces

It is impossible to do justice to the complex relationship between workers and Nazism during the twelve years of the dictatorship in the framework of this book. It makes sense, however, to continue focusing on the major themes of this study and to ask relevant questions: what happened to the working-class milieu under Nazism? What was the workers' attitude to the regime? And what happened to the concept of *Volksgemeinschaft*?

The Nazis' treatment of the workers' movement was uniquely repressive and brutal, but it did not come out of the blue. The Kingdom of Saxony had been an extremely coercive environment for the labour movement. Even during the Social Democratic honeymoon between the end of 1918 and October 1923, workers suffered at the hands of the *Reichswehr* (see document 3b), who eventually toppled their government illegally. From 1924 onwards, the rights of the workers' movement deteriorated step by step. This tendency accelerated during Schieck's government from 1930 onwards, and again after Hitler's appointment as Chancellor in January 1933. The day after the Reichstag election in March, however, a comprehensive and brutal all-out attack on organised labour followed. In the space of a few months the Nazis destroyed a significant part of the society that had been painstakingly growing for about eighty years.

In a series of bans the Nazis swiftly knocked out the whole infrastructure of the workers' movement. The Communists had already been driven underground before the March elections. All Social Democratic paramilitary organisations were banned on 13 March, the SAJ on 18 March, the ATSB on 28 April, and on 5 May, two days after the ban of trade unions, workers' sports and cultural organisations were officially dissolved and declared illegal.[125] The SPD was officially banned in Saxony on 23 June 1933, three weeks before the national ban on 14 July.[126] By the end of March most of the property that had belonged to organised labour had been seized by the SA and the police and was transferred to the newly created German Labour Front (DAF). Whatever slipped through the net at the time was confiscated, piece by piece, by the state in the following years.

The destruction of the working-class infrastructure was accompanied by a large-scale assault on the rank and file of Marxist followers, Jews and others. Many were taken into custody and often ended up in concentration camps, where they faced horrific ill-treatment and torture. Particularly notorious was the Hohenstein concentration camp, where the guards were even tried for the brutal atrocities they had committed on inmates (also see document 23).[127] By mid-April nearly 9,000 people had been taken into 'preventative detention'.[128]

Terror and intimidation continued to be an integral part of the Nazi Dictatorship. When in late summer 1934, in eastern Saxony, an anti-Nazi slogan was found in the men's washroom of a company the police were called in and took fingerprints and handwriting specimens of suspect Marxists.[129] Particularly in the countryside, where everyone knew each other, former Marxists were constantly observed, and there was mounting pressure on workers and their children to join NSDAP organisations.[130] Those who had been punished because of their political beliefs were socially isolated as they could not easily join a club and were not issued with passports.[131]

It is well known that the size of the organised resistance and its activities was a secondary phenomenon in German society during the Third Reich.[132] What about workers' resistance in 'red' Saxony to the Nazi seizure of power and the dictatorship? In February 1933 the prominent guest speaker, Albert Grzesinski, ended an SPD rally in Leipzig with the slogan: 'We want to be free as our fathers were. Rather dead, than a slave!'[133] But like the rest of the *Reich*, the great majority of the rank and file of the Saxon SPD and trade union stuck to legality, remained passive, and shelved their beliefs when their integrity was put to the test from March 1933 onwards. A report of a Nazi informer in April 1933 summarised the indecisive and often self-delusory attitude: 'Social Democrats and members of the working-class sport organisations keep saying that they will behave quietly during the next half a year in order to see how they can win over those with resentments once again.'[134] As time went by the feeling of hopelessness only increased. At the end of 1935 most former Social Democrats believed that the regime would last for a while. A *Sopade* writer elaborated: 'Many former Social Democrats are full of resignation, and regard illegal work as pointless and the sacrifices as worthless. They refuse to participate in illegal activities and deter others from any participation.'[135] There were also numerous reports about former Marxist officials who accommodated themselves to the new regime;[136] some even joined the Gestapo.[137]

Of course the labour movement had already been weakened by increasing division, disintegration, and a lack of strategy in the years before 1933. Nevertheless, some were prepared to fight. Approximately 2,000 members of the *Kampfstaffeln* (Fighting Units) in Leipzig – an SPD paramilitary organisation which had been set up to combat the Nazis by violent means – were prepared to occupy streets and public buildings. After the March 1933 elections, however, they waited in vain for three days for a signal to strike because their party leadership had decided against the use of violence.[138] It is also noteworthy that the Social Democrats continued to defy Nazism in parliament: six of the twenty-two SPD members of the Landtag who were able to attend the session on 23 May 1933 (eleven members were imprisoned and five had fled to Czechoslovakia), voted as the only parliamentary party against the emergency decree.[139] Only a few workers' activists, however, continued to engage in resistance during the dictatorship. Hans-Dieter Schmid estimates that in the SPD bastion of Leipzig, only about one percent of the former party members participated in organised opposition.[140] Nearly all of these, however, fell victim to Nazi purges and often faced extremely brutal treatment by SA, police, and Gestapo. Some – like the Social Democrat Otto – were beaten to death.[141] The harsh persecution explained why a number of SPD officials fled into exile: at least six SPD members of the Landtag were murdered or tortured to death, and more than twenty spent time in prison or concentration camp.[142]

The Saxon Communists were the most active group in the resistance movement. In Leipzig alone at least 1,600 Communists from various groups were caught and their organisational structure was largely destroyed in a series of arrests between summer 1934 and March 1935.[143] Many Communists faced brutal torture and blackmailing by the Gestapo. This explained the many confessions which allowed the Gestapo again and again to round up whole Communist networks in one sweep.[144] For several years the officials also found it difficult to stem the smuggling of printed material by opposition groups from Czechoslovakia into Saxony. Tighter control of this border region, however, led to increasing arrests.[145] Illegal activities continued – like the distribution of leaflets with the slogan 'down with the warmonger Adolf Hitler' in Eibenstock (Erzgebirge) in 1937[146] – but these were isolated cases (like that of the Social Democrat who was arrested twelve times by mid-1937).[147] (Also see document 20).

Generally speaking, the few who became involved in the workers' resistance movement had been a part of the socialist milieu before 1933. For them the belief in socialist ideals, or other more personal reasons – such as the arrest of a close relative – seemed to have been the primary motivation.[148] The overall effectiveness of workers' resistance was extremely limited due to the organisation's small size, inadequate strategies (the Communists in

Leipzig even continued to keep membership books)[149] and the remaining divisions in its ranks. Even years into the dictatorship the traditional differences among Marxist circles – between supporters of SPD and KPD – but even within these two camps, seemed as pronounced as ever.[150]

The violent persecution and bans completely destroyed the visible network of the labour movement, that is, its public organisations and assets. What happened to the more invisible side of the workers' milieu, to friendships, socialist traditions and values, and forms of solidarity – the aspects that were far more difficult to control and eliminate in a dictatorship that aspired to be totalitarian? There are many examples that the spirit of the socialist milieu still lived on to some degree in Saxony. In 1934 all the workers of a Chemnitz company left the room when a Nazi speaker insulted the Marxist movement and some of its former leaders,[151] and when a year later the well-known Leipzig Social Democrat Hermann Liebmann died shortly after his release from a concentration camp where he had been ill-treated, 1,200 people – mainly older citizens – attended his funeral.[152] It was also striking that by mid-1935 the HJ had recruited a much lower percentage of youth in working-class neighbourhoods than in predominantly bourgeois parts of Leipzig.[153]

To some extent a socialist milieu still lingered on, but faced increasing obstacles. The relatively small group of activists who had formed the hard-core of the socialist milieu before 1933, decreased further and, when the Nazis destroyed their network, inevitably lost touch with other workers. Further research will be needed to establish whether the case of the town of Freital – where the Social Democratic elite came from a few families who retreated into the domestic sphere where they continued to discuss politics and kept their socialist values during the dictatorship[154] – was typical or the exception. A wider milieu was bound to disintegrate or shift in other directions under the new conditions. It is ironic that the church suddenly became a place of refuge, even for former Marxist leaders. A *Sopade* report from Saxony in 1935 complained:

> It is 'not even possible to get some information from formerly reliable people on what they are doing and seeing. They want to be cautious and not to lose work again .... The hopelessness is the reason why many workers turn to the church and all kinds of other sects.'[155]

The totalitarian dictatorship forced workers into an environment that was determined by Nazi ideology and in which particular efforts were made to attract their sympathies. The Nazis' offer of cheap holidays and a whole variety of entertainment with its *Kraft durch Freude* (Strength through Joy; KdF) enjoyed great popularity among many workers, even though only a few could afford all the subsidised trips.[156] A Social Democrat reported in mid-1936 that 'one can hardly avoid the KdF if one wants to do sport or wants to travel', and that many former members of the SPD's Friends of Nature (*Naturfreunde*) used the opportunity to travel with the KdF.[157] Meanwhile, the People's Welfare Organisation (*NS-Volkswohlfahrt*; NSV) took over the public welfare system at a local level, and mushroomed into a massive organisation of 480,000 members and 100,000 helpers by May of 1936.[158]

Even within the family it became more and more difficult to uphold a socialist environment due to the Nazis' increasing hold over the youth. Schools became tools for the Nazis to indoctrinate the new generation with their racist objectives and national socialist principles. The *Sopade* reported from western Saxony:

> Parents are very concerned about the influence of the school and HJ on their children. Parental influence over children has decreased considerably. Frequently children are seduced into giving information about parental activities which are regarded as being in opposition to the state. In many families this led to a tense relationship between parents and children.[159]

Workers were most directly exposed to Nazi rule at the work place. The Nazis' main vehicle to reach workers in companies was the DAF which had replaced the traditional trade unions and also offered a whole range of social activities. The DAF's tasks in companies included the rewarding of successful workers, the organisation of festivities, theatre visits, trips and comradeship evenings.[160] Company units (*Werkscharen*) aimed to foster the *Volksgemeinschaft* by organising mutual visits to other companies and relaxing evenings. In many companies, sport was compulsory and often served to create harmony and distraction from hardships and grievances. Some companies forced their workers to attend training courses which also devoted time to Nazi ideology.[161] The destruction of the trade unions network led to individual wage bargaining between workers and employers (one large metal company had up to forty different hourly wages[162]) and a loss of working-class values. Both were in the interest of employers, as one observer argued: 'For, firstly, they save themselves the costs which would arise from general wage agreements. And, secondly, the workers are atomised through this system, class solidarity is destroyed, each man becomes the enemy of the other and envies him and that is what the employers want.'[163] In mid-1934 a faithful Social Democrat in eastern Saxony complained that the 'old trade union virtues of solidarity have been lost in a shocking way.'[164] Two years later a typical Sopade report painted a devastating picture of the state of the Saxon labour movement:

> Workers knuckle under the brown creatures to gain a little advantage, or to gain or to keep a job, they are even prepared to hand over class brothers to the Gestapo ... The interest in class faith has largely disappeared, it has been replaced by pedantic self-interest and concern for the family. It is obvious that one cannot expect proletarian sacrifices for a revolutionary struggle or any support for just a little illegal work.[165]

Typical was the situation in one quarry in 1938 where the relationship between workers was overshadowed by a fierce competition for the few available resources. After explosions there were 'real races between workers' to get to the biggest stones which would secure a higher wage, and workers needed to arrive early in the morning because there was a risk that their colleagues would add their stones to their own stock.[166] Terror and the threat of informers led to widespread mistrust at the workplace and enhanced the trend towards individualism. When in 1937 a company organised a day-trip for its workers into the Erzgebirge, hardly anyone joined the guided tours that had been arranged for them at their destination. Instead, the workers split up into small groups and individuals who went their own way, unthreatened by informers.[167] Considering the comparatively tiny size of the Gestapo in Saxony – in early 1937 a total of 495 Gestapo officials observed a population of more than 5 million[168] – it seems certain that, like in many other regions in Germany, denunciations kept the machinery of terror going.[169] In the face of the selfish and conformist behaviour of many workers under Nazism, even some Marxists started to have their doubts about the validity of their own worldview. Two years into the dictatorship the *Sopade* reported that some local Social Democrats asked themselves if socialism was 'not merely a noble illusion?'[170] The Nazis too continued their efforts to undermine socialism as a possible alternative to their own system. For instance, they circulated an alleged letter from the Soviet Union in which a worker complained about the local situation and expressed how he longed for freedom in Germany.[171] Indeed, secret reports argued frequently that it was largely the effect of anti-Bolshevik propaganda which made 'large parts of the population' fear that the Nazi dictatorship would be replaced by a much worse Communist dictatorship.[172]

Changes in the economic structure of Saxony, especially after 1936 and during the war years, also contributed to the dissolution of the working-class milieu. There were high levels of migration within Saxony, but also migration from Saxony to other regions in Germany. In 1936/37, 43,000 skilled workers left Saxony alone.[173] There were also frequent tensions between the long-established workforce and new workers who had come from elsewhere. Germans from Bohemia (*Sudetendeutsche*) and Saxon workers did not seem to get on. Local workers feared for their own workplace, and the *Sudetendeutsche* were often extreme Hitler followers who frequently informed on their Saxon colleagues to the Gestapo.[174] Additionally, the retraining of workers for new jobs in armaments industries – e.g., from a radio salesman to a job in the metal industry[175] – and the growth of large-scale companies with new workforces having different background and experiences, disrupted the homogeneous milieus that had existed among the previous permanent staff.[176] During the war the social environment at the workplace changed further as more and more Saxon workers were conscripted, a growing number of women and older men flocked into the armaments industries, and there was a dramatic influx of foreign workers. Of the 154,119 workers who were employed in armaments industries in and around Leipzig in 1943, 43,905 were foreign workers.[177]

Every worker was affected by these developments in a different way and it was hardly possible – even less than before – to speak about a homogeneous working class. Older and skilled workers were the first to benefit from rearmament and higher wages, whereas younger workers experienced labour camps and conscription.[178] Whereas armaments industries boomed in some areas, most parts of the textile industry continued to face depression and its labour force suffered from extremely low wages.[179] Younger workers who had only little or no experience of the time before the dictatorship, seemed less critical about the regime, and responded more enthusiastically to the Nazis' militaristic and nationalist policies.[180]

It is difficult to establish to what extent Saxon workers supported the Nazi regime or were even 'converted' to Nazi ideology. Democratic elections did not exist and plebiscites were carried out amidst great terror. However, we know that more workers had voted for the NSDAP in free elections than for the SPD or KPD at the end of Weimar. On the whole, workers did not seem particularly interested in Nazi ideology during the Third Reich. Company roll calls in which workers were rallied and forced to listen to Nazi slogans were unpopular: e.g., in Chemnitz the slogan for Friday 7 December 1934 was: 'We want to earn the revival of our nation honestly through our diligence, our perseverance, and our unshakeable will'.[181] Only around seventy-five workers out of a total of two thousand in a precision-tools company turned up to informative talks about the NSDAP and its ideology.[182]

Contemporary sources do not suggest that the majority of workers were particularly receptive to the Nazis' racial beliefs and policies.[183] During the first years of the dictatorship the treatment of Jews often met with an unsympathetic response, and later during the war there were several reports of illegal, friendly contact between German and foreign workers.[184] Over the years, however, the enormous amount of Nazi racial propaganda and indoctrination seemed to have a growing impact on people's attitudes (for anti-Semitic attitudes see document 22). It is worth mentioning here that nearly 1.3 million Saxons possessed a radio by 1941.[185] The near silence surrounding non-Jewish victims of racial policies – e.g. the treatment of Sinti and Roma or the handicapped – suggests a widespread indifference to, if not approval, of their fate. The protest by a Communist in Carlsfeld (Erzgebirge) when a girl with 'hereditary disease' (*Erbkrankheit*) was taken away for compulsory sterilisation, was a rare exception.[186]

Workers' attitudes towards the regime depended on time, circumstances and the issues involved. Their dissatisfaction was mainly economic and concerned unemployment, low wages, the pressures of fast work, high prices and food shortages. There were cases of work refusals and strikes after 1933, but most of them were quickly dispelled by coercion. In September 1936 a unit of 150 workers in a Saxon armaments factory – including forty Stormtroopers and twenty SS men – went on strike against the low wages and fast work. All workers were fired on the same day and the SA and SS men who had participated were arrested and sent to a concentration camp.[187] As in other parts of Germany,[188] there was widespread working-class dissatisfaction – largely economic – with the Nazi regime, at least until 1935. A typical *Sopade* report from Saxony during that year stated: 'There is a lot of grumbling in the companies about the low wages and the rising prices, about the militaristic treatment, about the fast pace at work.'[189] In areas where large parts of the population did not benefit from a boom in the armaments industries, many citizens complained about their economic plight throughout the six 'peace years' of the dictatorship, and continued to voice criticism during the war because of shortages and restrictive regulations.[190] The police even described the ongoing economic depression as a 'fertile ground' for Communism in the Erzgebirge.[191]

In early 1939, *Gauleiter* Mutschmann complained to the Ministerial Committeee for the Defence of the Reich about the effects of the new War Economy Decree, which aimed at reversing the trend towards rising wages and increasing bonuses. Mutschmann warned: 'This measure has produced unrest in the economy' and 'has a negative influence on people's enthusiasm and productivity.'[192]

After 1935, however, more and more workers who had a job seemed in some respects content and got on with their lives because their situation was not too bad when compared with that of the unemployed and the young. For most, economic security was of primary importance, and it seemed a natural deal that under Nazism this was traded in against the loss of political freedom (see document 21). Indeed, unemployment fell year by year during the dictatorship: from 718,586 unemployed in 1933, to 388,119 in 1935, to 134,302 in 1938.[193] Even in the former SPD bastion of Gornsdorf near Chemnitz, where the Nazis had not made great inroads into workers' behaviour by late 1934 (for example no-one greeted with 'Heil Hitler') an observer admitted that the maintenance of full employment was the workers' top priority and that this hindered political activity against Nazism.[194] A *Sopade* writer observed in Saxony:

> Workers ... do not perceive the political dissatisfaction and repression as bad because they were persuaded that the democratic freedom for which the working class had fought for decades had not been able to give them economic prosperity.[195]

A similar report dated one-and-a-half years later noted:

> [People] just want to live and are not interested in what is happening around them ... It is not only the terror that explains the lack of interest of the broad masses, but also the fact that Fascism has given millions of unemployed some kind of employment.[196]

The popular marriage loans (e.g., 27 in every hundred newly wed couples took out a loan between 1938 and 1940 in Saxony)[197] were another important financial incentive that served to bind the population to the regime. The fact that the majority of workers were eager to work in the well-paid and expanding armaments industry was another indication of how little influence remained of the socialist vision of international class unity. Nazi propaganda depicting a Bolshevik threat from the East contributed to the acceptance of Germany's rearmament. Many former SPD followers were fully integrated in the nationalist front by supporting the introduction of military service because they felt there was a need to catch up with the other powers, and because it would 'do the youth no harm to get polished a little'.[198] But the Nazis also employed more sophisticated methods to motivate their labour force by appealing to their sense of pride in their skills. Indeed, many workers in a vehicle factory were proud to hear that the Nazis reported how well their vehicles had performed in the Poland campaign and that they had received many letters of gratitude from German soldiers.[199]

An admiration for Hitler and some of the Nazi policies were also crucial reasons why many workers seemed to have gone along with the dictatorship. A growing number of people felt a new sense of pride, purpose and a fresh beginning. After the execution of Röhm and other SA leaders in summer 1934, former SPD followers praised Hitler's tough line.[200] Foreign policy successes and the image of a strong and respected Germany were enthusiastically supported by most Saxons – including workers – and tended to push critics onto the defensive. According to a report from Dresden, a Hitler speech during the war in late 1940 'made a great impression particularly on workers' and was treasured as 'best Christmas present'.[201] However, strong anti-Nazi feelings in the state also continued to exist, particularly in former Marxist strongholds. Leipzig in particular remained a difficult territory for Nazism: the local police reported that in several streets which were inhabited by 'Communists', 50–70 percent of the electorate handed in blank ballot papers during the plebiscite in March 1936 (also see document 20).[202] In mid-1940 a physician reported:

> Here in Saxony there are many who lament the fact that it appears we will defeat England, and not she us. For if the latter was the case, National Socialism – which they despise so much – would disappear and that is more important to them than anything else.[203]

The Nazis made great efforts to appear to be creating a *Volksgemeinschaft* in which everyone had equal rights. Many took this ambition seriously: when the conditions of workers did not improve in the first few years of the dictatorship, local workers – and also Nazis – asked when the regime would fulfil its socialist promises.[204] The DAF under Robert Ley made efforts to overcome – at least symbolically – the separation between workers and employers. When Ley attended an anniversary celebration of a rolling mill in southwestern Saxony in 1937, he criticised the arrangement that both groups were to eat their celebratory dinner in different halls. Henceforth the local DAF leader felt encouraged – despite the presence of the old-fashioned director who refused to participate in a 'common swill' – to announce that everyone would eat together in the same hall.[205] Companies organised comradeship evenings with music and dance, and some directors stressed their idea of a company community in their addresses to their workforce.[206] But whereas workers were called 'working comrades', they saw nothing of the free cigarettes that were given out, during a celebration, to the company management and distinguished guests.[207] The 'Heil Hitler' greeting was also used for a symbolic dilution of titles and ranks. In the mail service, where traditionally great importance had been attached to address the upper echelons of the administration with the correct title, this was replaced by the commonly used 'Heil Hitler'.[208] Hierarchies continued to exist, however, even if in other forms: members of the uniformed police were only allowed to respond with the 'Heil Hitler' greeting after their superior had said it.[209]

The concept of a *Volksgemeinschaft* was a useful tool for Nazis and employers as an aid to discipline workers and to push them to hard work and greater quality. Any disapproval – from not giving support to the regime in plebiscites to complaints from the workforce – was described as 'harming the *Volksgemeinschaft*'.[210] The way in which the Nazis skilfully portrayed themselves as guardian of the people earned them widespread acclaim: when the Saxon Nazis publicised the arrest and prosecution of four mining directors because of their neglect of safety regulations in late 1937, the act was favourably received amongst workers. When no verdict was heard for a while, the Nazis reacted by making it known that they would press for a quick trial. This earned them a reputation for speeding up justice in favour of miners and it was said: 'Previously the judges were untouchable, now the *Volk* can also criticise the judges.'[211]

The day-to-day experience of Saxons inevitably disclosed many contradictions of an alleged *Volksgemeinschaft* and people became tired of the continuous Nazi efforts to mobilise the masses. In 1935 many citizens still enthusiastically gave in donations because the Nazis put particular pressure on more well-off people to give according to their means.[212] Several years later many had become critical about the collections and suspected that most of the money went into rearmament, even party members complained about the frequent additional contributions.[213] Only a few dared to voice public criticism, like one woman who had queued in vain for a bit of bacon for several days, and complained loudly that nothing had changed under Nazism: 'We poor are always the stupid ones, whereas the rich have got everything they want.'[214]

During the Second World War the contradictions increased further and at times the Nazis were at the receiving end of their own propaganda. During a meeting of the Zwickau shoemaker guild one participant complained about the poor quality of the material that was available and that this was 'a betrayal of the *Volk*.'[215] The working-class milieu was further eroded by bombing raids, destruction, shortages of food and consumer goods, and dramatic demographic changes. Nevertheless, important aspects of the Saxon socialist milieu survived the twelve years of illegality in the dictatorship. In the immediate post-war years there was a revival of this milieu, although with some crucial changes: despite there being familiar names on the SPD's electoral lists in Freital in 1946, two-thirds of local party members were new recruits.[216] However, the resurgence of the Social Democratic milieu did not last long: it quickly disintegrated irreversibly from 1949 onwards due to the SED dictatorship, under which it was no longer possible for political groups to retreat into the private sphere. One figure speaks volumes: while the Gestapo in Leipzig had 114 employees in 1937, the East German State Security Police (Stasi) had 2,401 employees in the 1980s.[217]

This chapter is a greatly amended and extended version of my piece 'The Rise of the Nazi Party in the Working-Class Milieu of Saxony', in Fischer, *Working Classes*, 189–216.

Notes

1. G. Roth, *The Social Democrats in Imperial Germany. A Study in Working-class Isolation and National Integration*, Totowa, 1963.
2. R.J. Evans, 'Introduction: The Sociological Interpretation of German Labour History', in R.J. Evans, ed., *The German Working Class, 1888–1933: The Politics of Everyday Life*, London, 1982, 15–53.
3. Adam, 'Arbeitermilieu', 124
4. F. Walter, 'Freital: Das "Rote Wien Sachsens" ', in F. Walter, T. Dürr and K. Schmidke, eds., *Die SPD in Sachsen und Thüringen zwischen Hochburg und Diaspora*, Bonn, 1993, 56; Heidenreich, *Arbeiterkulturbewegung*, 50. The continuing dissatisfaction of working-class women in Leipzig about the bad quality and high prices for foodstuff in local shops led to the foundation of consumer-cooperatives. See Adam, 'Arbeitermilieu', 167.
5. The percentage of the votes for the left in all Reichstag elections between 1890 and 1933 in Saxony ranged between 42 percent in 1890 to 60.1 percent in 1919 and 42.7 percent in 1933.
6. *NSfS*, Nr. 15, 13.6.1926.
7. S. Lässig, '"Mit jeder Faser seines Lebens gehörte er zur Arbeiterbewegung'. August Kaden (1850–1913)', in Grebing, *Demokratie*, 87ff.
8. Heidenreich, Arbeiterkulturbewegung, 100ff.
9. J. Seidel, 'Leipziger Maifeiern, Gewerkschafts- und Arbeitervereinsfeste im letzten Jahrzehnt des 19. Jahrhunderts', in K. Keller, ed., *Feste und Feiern. Zum Wandel städtischer Festkultur in Leipzig*, Leipzig, 1994, 191, 195.
10. B. Häupel and M. Seidel, 'Der Konflikt der Weimarer Sozialdemokratie aus der sächsischen und thüringischen Perspektive', in Bramke, *Mitteldeutschland*, 418f.
11. Similarly Lapp, *Revolution*, 77.
12. See Max Hölz, *Vom 'Weißen Kreuz' zur roten Fahne. Jugend-, Kampf- und Zuchthauserlebnisse*, [original 1929] repr. Halle, 1984.
13. Lapp, *Revolution*, 77, 88ff.
14. W. Fabian, *Klassenkampf um Sachsen. Ein Stück Geschichte 1918–1930*, Löbau, 1930, 171; quoted from Lapp, *Revolution*, 88.
15. Lapp, *Revolution*, 89.
16. SPD Sachsen, *Vier Jahre Sächsische Politik*, 1926, 49.
17. Rudolph, *Sächsische Sozialdemokratie*, 228.
18. STA D, AH Glauchau, Nr. 24, Halbwochenbericht, 9.3.1923.
19. Lapp, *Revolution*, 84.
20. Ibid., 88.
21. Rudolph, *Sächsische Sozialdemokratie*, 234–36.
22. Lapp, *Revolution*, 112.

23. Heidenreich, *Arbeiterkulturbewegung*, 343.
24. *SVB*, Nr. 156, 8.7.1929. Also see chapter 4 (ii–iii).
25. Heidenreich, *Arbeiterkulturbewegung*, 294f, 344; Walter, 'Freital', 87.
26. Walter, 'Freital', 87f; Heidenreich, *Arbeiterkulturbewegung*, 221.
27. Heidenreich, *Arbeiterkulturbewegung*, 397.
28. P. Lösche and F. Walter, 'Zur Organisationskultur der sozialdemokratischen Arbeiterbewegung in der Weimarer Republik', *Geschichte und Gesellschaft*, 15 (4) (1989), 525.
29. D. Klenke, 'Hermann Liebmann (1882–1935). Vom Architekten der "proletarischen Mehrheit" in Sachsen zum "Tolerierungs"-Politiker der Ära Brüning', in P. Lösche et al., eds., *Vor dem Vergessen bewahren. Lebenswege Weimarer Sozialdemokraten*, Berlin, 1988, 205.
30. F. Walter, 'Thüringen – Einst Hochburg der Sozialistischen Arbeiterbewegung?', *Internationale Wissenschaftliche Korrespondenz zur Geschichte der Arbeiterbewegung*, 28 (1) (1992), 21–39. Adam, however, makes a valid point in arguing that within the socialist milieu various classes also got to know each other. For instance, he observes a *rapprochement* between workers and civil servants in building associations and allotment clubs. Adam, 'Arbeitermilieu', 234.
31. Lösche, 'Organisationskultur', 521.
32. Ibid., 535; F. Walter, 'Sachsen – Ein Stammland der Sozialdemokratie', *Politische Vierteljahresschrift*, 32 (2) (1991), 213.
33. Walter, 'Freital', 21.
34. C. Hausmann and K. Rudolph, 'Trotz allem: Sachsen, die rote Hochburg', *Politische Vierteljahresschrift*, 34 (1) (1993), 92–7.
35. Estimated percentage of workers amongst the total NSDAP electorate in Saxony (estimates for the Reich in brackets): 1928: 15 (32), 1930: 18 (27). Compare table 5.5 with Falter, *Wähler*, 225 .
36. For this argument also see Walter, 'Stammland'.
37. Walter, 'Freital', 92ff; Heidenreich, *Arbeiterkulturbewegung*, 298.
38. *DVZ*, Nr. 39, 15.2.1930.
39. K. Bauer, 'Umrisse der Arbeitermusikbewegung in Dresden von 1878 bis 1933', *Sächsische Heimatblätter*, 30 (5) (1984), 215.
40. STA D, MdI, Nr. 11126/4, Oktober 1930.
41. Heidenreich, *Arbeiterkulturbewegung*, 212, 411–13; Walter, 'Freital', 92ff.
42. Walter, 'Freital', 55–9.
43. H. Gebauer, 'Arbeiterbibliotheken in Leipzig', in R. Florstedt, ed., *Leihbibliotheken, Arbeiterbibliotheken, Bücherhallen. Bibliothekarische Bemühungen um die Volksbildung vom Anfang des 19.* Jahrhunderts bis 1933, Leipzig, 1989, 38f.
44. Schmeitzner, 'Freistaat', 92.
45. Heidenreich, *Arbeiterkulturbewegung*, 370ff.
46. Bauer, 'Arbeitermusikbewegung', 214.

47. Walter, 'Freital', 67, 84f.
48. In the early 1930s the Saxon KPD only had between 20,000 and 27,000 members (Heidenreich, *Arbeiterkulturbewegung*, 247) compared to the SPD's 140,000. See document 17.
49. Harsch, *Social Democracy*, 71.
50. STA D, AH Schwarzenberg, Nr. 1943, Dezember 1931.
51. *FK*, Nr. 250, 6.11.1931.
52. *SVB*, Nr. 44, 22.2.1932; *LVZ*, Nr. 38, 15.2.1932.
53. *SVB*, Nr. 28, 2.2.1929; *LVZ*, Nr. 214, 13.9.1929.
54. *SVB*, Nr. 165, 18.7.1929.
55. Ibid., Nr. 30, 5.2.1932; *LVZ*, 28.5.1932.
56. C.J. Fischer, 'Gab es am Ende der Weimarer Republik einen marxistischen Wählerblock?', *Geschichte und Gesellschaft*, 21 (1) (1995), 65.
57. F. Heidenreich, ' "... Das Wichtigste Agitationsmittel für die Partei." Zur Geschichte der Sozialdemokratischen Presse in Sachsen vor 1933', *Internationale Wissenschaftliche Korrespondenz zur Geschichte der deutschen Arbeiterbewegung*, 27 (2) (1991), 148f.
58. *Jahresbericht der sozialdemokratischen Bezirksorganisation Chemnitz/Erzgebirge. 1929*, 27.
59. *Jahresbericht 1928 Sozialdemokratische Bezirksorganisation Chemnitz/Erzgebirge*, 8.
60. *ChVSt*, 13.5.1929; ibid., 1.8.1932.
61. *Jahresbericht 1928 Sozialdemokratische Bezirksorganisation Chemnitz/Erzgebirge*, 9.
62. *Jahresbericht der sozialdemokratischen Bezirksorganisation Chemnitz/Erzgebirge. 1929*, 9.
63. Ibid., 27.
64. *Jahresbericht 1928 Sozialdemokratische Bezirksorganisation Chemnitz/Erzgebirge*, 8ff.
65. *Jahresbericht des Bezirksvorstandes der SPD Bezirk Leipzig 1929*, UB Rochlitz-Burgstädt-Mittweida.
66. H. Dittmann, 'Zur Geschichte der Arbeiterbewegung in Auerbach', *Der Heimatfreund für den Kreis Stollberg/Erzgebirge*, (März–Juli) (1963), 57–9, 74f, 93f, 115–17, 133–35.
67. *NSDAP Freiberg*, 14.
68. The NSDAP stayed below its national average in the following Saxon AHs and self-governing towns in the July 1932 Reichstag elections (NSDAP/SPD percentage in parentheses): Freital (21.6/43.8), AH Leipzig (30.0/34.3), Riesa (31.1/41.9), Leipzig (32.3/34.1), Meißen (32.6/46.1), AH Zittau (32.9/26.0), Pirna (33.5/24.2), AH Dresden (36.3/34.8), Döbeln (37.2/34.1). The combined left gained an overall majority in all these electoral districts, except the AH Zittau.
69. *Jahresbericht des Bezirksvorstandes des SPD Bezirk Leipzig 1930.*
70. Seven Nazis lost their life in political clashes in the area before Hitler came to power. See *Der Gau Sachsen*, 125.

71. The SPD mobilised 2.5 percent of the population (the combined left 3.7 percent) during the First of May celebration in Leipzig in 1931. Equivalent figures for Plauen: SPD, 1.5 percent, combined left: 3.2 percent. See STA D, MdI, Nr. 11126/4, Mai 1930, April 1931. See also chapter 4 (ii).
72. For this discussion see *SPD Bezirksverband Dresden. Geschäftsbericht vom 1. Januar bis zum 31. Dezember 1929.*
73. Calculated from F. Burkhardt, 'Die Kirchenaustritts- und Kircheneintrittsbewegung im Zeitraum 1919 bis 1930 mit einem Rückblick auf die Entwicklung der kirchlichen Statistik', *ZSäStLA*, (1931), 194.
74. Calculated from *Geschäftsbericht 1928/29 Arbeiter-Turn-und Sportbund*; and *StDR*, 1933, 10/59–10/76.
75. Table 5.3 does not account for variations within Saxony and the electoral district of Chemnitz.
76. See V. Kratzenberg, *Arbeiter auf dem Weg zu Hitler? Die Nationalsozialistische Betriebszellen-Organisation. Ihre Entstehung, Ihre Programmatik, Ihr Scheitern 1927–1934*, Frankfurt/Main, 1989, 209.
77. Böhnke, *Ruhrgebiet*, 171f.
78. Forty-three percent of the industrial work force in Saxony (27 percent in the *Reich*, excluding Saxony and the Saarland) were members of the ADGB. See Heidenreich, 'Agitationsmittel', 141.
79. *FK*, Nr. 250, 6.11.1931.
80. STA D, MdI, Nr. 11126/3, Juli 1929.
81. *FK*, Nr. 39, 15.9.1930.
82. Ibid., Nr. 54, 2.10.1930.
83. Ibid.
84. STA D, MdI, 11126/4, November 1931.
85. *FK*, Nr. 58, 10.3.31.
86. BA Koblenz, NS 26, Nr. 2113.
87. Böhnke, *Ruhrgebiet*, 174.
88. STA L, AH Döbeln, Nr. 2409, Jahresbericht der KH Leipzig 1931, 9.
89. Together with Berlin, Westphalia-North, Silesia and Cologne-Aachen. See G. Mai, 'Die Nationalsozialistische Betriebszellenorganisation. Zum Verhältnis von Arbeiterschaft und Nationalsozialismus', *Vierteljahreshefte für Zeitgeschichte*, 31 (4) (1983), 596.
90. Kratzenberg, *Arbeiter*, 228.
91. *FK*, Nr. 264, 12.11.31.
92. *Fünfzehn Jahre Ortsgruppe Crimmitschau*, 1937, 29.
93. *FK*, Nr. 1, 2.1.1932.
94. *NSDAP Markneukirchen*, 65.
95. *FK*, Nr. 79, 1.11.1930.
96. Ibid., Nr. 227, 29.9.1931.
97. Ibid., Nr. 228, 30.9.1931.

98. Ibid., Nr. 242, 14.10.1932.
99. *ChVSt*, Nr. 29, 4.2.1929.
100. NSDAP Hauptarchiv, 'Ortsgruppe Belgershain'.
101. STA L, AH Döbeln, Nr. 2409, Jahresbericht der KH Leipzig 1932, 6f.
102. *LVZ*, Nr. 194, 22.8.1931; ibid., Nr. 6, 8.1.1932.
103. E.g. see *ChVSt*, Nr. 197, 25.8.1931.
104. *VB*, Nr. 130/31, 10/11.5.1931.
105. Ibid., Nr. 151, 27.6.1930.
106. *Der Bolshewik*, 1, Nr. 7, August 1930.
107. Similarly, more workers joined the Saxon NSDAP in rural communities than in towns or cities. See chapter 5 (ii).
108. *ChVSt*, Nr. 57, 8.3.1930.
109. *FK*, Nr. 12, 14./15.1.1933. Workers in the cottage industries were extremely susceptible to vote for the NSDAP. See chapter 5 (iii).
110. E.g. the majority of the SPD branch in Chemnitz were members of the local veterans' association. The social benefits and support that came with the membership, however, were also an important explanation for this. See T. Rohkrämer, *Der Militarismus der "kleinen Leute". Die Kriegervereine im Deutschen Kaiserreich 1871–1914*, Munich, 1990, 37ff.
111. Rudolph, *Sächsische Sozialdemokratie*, 87.
112. *Evangelischer Volksfreund*, Nr. 18, 15.9.1912.
113. G. Mai, ' "Verteidigungskrieg" und "Volksgemeinschaft". Staatliche Selbstbehauptung, nationale Solidarität und soziale Befreiung in Deutschland in der Zeit des Ersten Weltkrieges (1900–1925)', in W. Michalka, ed., *Der Erste Weltkrieg. Wirkung, Wahrnehmung, Analyse*, Munich, 1995, 585ff.
114. Rudolph, *Sächsische Sozialdemokratie*, 94ff.
115. Mai, 'Verteidigungskrieg', 590f.
116. Heidenreich, *Arbeiterkulturbewegung*, 91.
117. Also see Mai, 'Verteidigungskrieg', 594f.
118. SPD, *Vier Jahre Sächsische Politik*, 114. Also see Lapp, *Revolution*, chapter 5.
119. C.J. Fischer, *The German Communists and the Rise of Nazism*, London, 1991, 112.
120. Heidenreich, *Arbeiterkulturbewegung*, 215, 356.
121. Ibid., 400.
122. SPD, *Vier Jahre Sächsische Politik*, 236.
123. Lang, 'Annaberg', 228f.
124. *15 Jahre Kampf der NSDAP, OG Bautzen* (1922–37), 49.
125. Heidenreich, *Arbeiterkulturbewegung*, 417.
126. STA L, PP-St, Nr. 19.
127. BDC, Mutschmann, OPG, Wettengel an Oberstes Parteigericht, 4.12.1936.
128. Heidenreich, *Arbeiterkulturbewegung*, 416.
129. *Sopade*, August/September 1934, 438.

130. STA D, AH Schwarzenberg, Nr. 1951, Mai 1934; *Sopade*, April 1936, 504; ibid., Juni 1935, 699.
131. *Sopade*, August 1938, 855.
132. H.-D. Schmid, 'Der organisierte Widerstand der Sozialdemokraten in Leipzig 1933–1935', in Schmid, *Hannover und Leipzig*, 26.
133. STA L, PP-St, Nr. 19, 24.2.1933.
134. Ibid., April 1933.
135. *Sopade*, November 1935, 1273.
136. E.g. see ibid. Juni, 1936, 747; ibid. Juli 1936, 853.
137. Schmid, *Gestapo Leipzig*, 29.
138. See PDS Archiv Leipzig, Nr. 15/329, 'Die Kampfstaffeln'.
139. Schmeitzner, 'Freistaat', 108f.
140. Schmid, 'Widerstand', 26.
141. *Sopade*, März 1935, 369.
142. Schmeitzner, 'Sozialdemokratische Landtagsabgeordnete in zwei Diktaturen (1933–1952/89)', in Schmeitzner, *Geschichte*, 125.
143. S. Höppner, 'Leipziger Jugendliche im antifaschistischen Widerstand 1933/34 – die "Zelle Zentrum"', in Schmid, *Hannover und Leipzig*, 119.
144. Schmid, *Gestapo Leipzig*, 29ff. See also, W. Bramke, 'Der unbekannte Widerstand in Westsachen 1933–1945', *Jahrbuch für Regionalgeschichte*, 13 (1986), 220–53.
145. STA D, AH Schwarzenberg, Nr. 1951, März 1934.
146. Ibid., Nr. 1955, April 1937.
147. *Sopade*, Juli 1937, 920.
148. Höppner, 'Jugendliche', 133ff.
149. Ibid., 124f.
150. *Sopade*, September 1938, 984f.
151. Ibid., August/September 1934, 438.
152. STA L, PP-St, Nr. 19, Juli 1935.
153. *Sopade*, Juni 1935, 687.
154. Walter, 'Freital', 111ff.
155. *Sopade*, März 1935, 283.
156. E. g. see STA D, AH Schwarzenberg, Nr. 1951, Juni 1934.
157. *Sopade*, Juli 1936, 884.
158. Ibid., September/Oktober 1934, 528; ibid., Mai 1936, 631.
159. Ibid., September/Oktober 1934, 579.
160. Ibid., Dezember 1937, 1689.
161. Ibid., Oktober 1938, 1078f.
162. Ibid., März 1938, 288.
163. J. Noakes and G. Pridham, *Nazism 1919–1945. Volume 2: State, Economy and Society 1933–1939*, Exeter, 1984, 373.
164. *Sopade*, Juni/Juli 1934, 208.
165. Ibid., Juli 1936, 836.
166. Ibid., Oktober 1938, 1102f.
167. Ibid., September 1937, 1276.

168. Schmid, *Gestapo Leipzig*, 20.
169. K.-M. Mallmann and G. Paul, 'Omniscient, Omnipotent, Omnipresent? Gestapo, society and resistance', in Crew, *Nazism*, 166–96.
170. *Sopade*, Juni 1935, 666.
171. Ibid., Mai 1936, 540.
172. Ibid., August 1936, 972.
173. Hess, 'Rüstungswirtschaft', 83.
174. *Sopade*, Oktober 1938, 1090.
175. Ibid., Juni 1939, 754.
176. Heß, 'Rüstungswirtschaft', 87.
177. Kürschner, 'Leipzig', 206.
178. *Sopade*, Juni 1935, 659.
179. E.g. see ibid., Juni 1936, 693ff.
180. Ibid., November 1935, 1255.
181. Ibid., März 1935, 290f.
182. Ibid. Juni 1936, 728.
183. For the receptiveness of the nationalist milieu to Nazi racism see chapter 4 (vi).
184. Boberach, *Meldungen*, 2.9.1943, 5703.
185. *Sachsen im Spiegel der Statistik*, 14.
186. AH Schwarzenberg, Nr. 1955, Juni 1937.
187. *Sopade*, September 1936, 1173.
188. E.g. see S. Hinze, ' "Die ungewöhnlich geduldigen Deutschen". Arbeiterleben 1934–1936 im Spiegel ausgewählter Gestapodokumente (Regierungsbezirk Potsdam)', in D. Eichholtz, ed., *Brandenburg in der NS-Zeit. Studien und Dokumente*, Berlin, 1993, 32–62.
189. *Sopade*, September 1935, 1061.
190. E. g. see STA D, AH Schwarzenberg, Nr. 1953, Januar 1936; ibid., Nr. 1954, Oktober 1939.
191. E. g. see ibid., Nr. 1953, August 1936.
192. J. Noakes, *Nazism 1919–1945. Volume 4: The German Home Front in World War II*, Exeter, 1998, 109.
193. *Sachsen im Spiegel der Statistik*, 10.
194. *Sopade*, August/September 1934, 437f.
195. Ibid., Juli 1936, 835.
196. Ibid., Januar 1938, 26f.
197. *Sachsen im Spiegel der Statistik*, 3.
198. *Sopade*, Mai 1935, 528.
199. Ibid., Februar 1940, 128. Also see A. Lüdtke, 'The "Honor of Labor": Industrial Workers and the Power of Symbols under National Socialism', in Crew, *Nazism*, 67–109.
200. *Sopade*, Juni/Juli 1934, 210.
201. Boberach, *Meldungen*, 12.12.1940, 1859.
202. STA L, PP-V, Nr. 4943.

203. G. Aly, 'The Posen Diaries of the Anatomist Hermann Voss', in G. Aly, P. Chroust and C. Pross, eds., *Cleansing the Fatherland. Nazi Medicine and Racial Hygiene*, London, 1994, 114.
204. *Sopade*, November 1935, 1267.
205. Ibid., September 1937, 1277ff.
206. Ibid., April/Mai 1938, 466.
207. U. Heß, 'Jubiläen Leipziger Firmen im 20. Jahrhundert – Zwischen Gründungsmythos und Traditionsbewußtsein', in Keller, *Feste*, 266, 275.
208. *Sopade*, Dezember 1935, 1483.
209. *SVBl*, Nr. 19, 8.3.1935.
210. *Sopade*, Juli 1935, 853.
211. Ibid., Dezember 1937, 1703.
212. Ibid., Februar 1935, 180.
213. Ibid., Januar 1938, 80, 99; STA D, AH Schwarzenberg, Nr. 1955, Juli 1937. Nevertheless, the total amount donated to the winter aid increased every single year in Saxony between 1933 and 1941. See *Sachsen im Spiegel der Statistik*, 4.
214. *Sopade*, September 1935, 1052
215. Boberach, *Meldungen*, 14.2.1940, 763f.
216. Walter, 'Sachsen und Thüringen: Von Mutterländern der Arbeiterbewegung zu Sorgenkindern der SPD. Einführung und Überblick', in Walter, *Sachsen und Thüringen*, 30f.
217. Schmid, *Gestapo Leipzig*, 20f.

Chapter 4

'Vote for Whom You Want, but Do Not Vote for the Left!' The Nationalist Milieu and the Nazis

> We want Germans to feel German again, think like Germans and act German.
>
> (a Protestant church paper in Saxony in 1929: *Sächsisch evangelisch-soziale Blätter*, Nr. 20, 1929)

> Fight Marxism! ... Two broad fighting fronts are facing each other, on the one hand international Marxism, on the other hand a sense of duty by the national citizen towards the *Volk* and the Fatherland.
>
> (*Vogtländischer Anzeiger und Tageblatt*, Plauen, Nr. 86, Nr. 95, 24.4.1929)

During the Weimar Republic the national right was united by its rejection of the democratic system and its support for an authoritarian state in which outstanding leaders would rise above the masses. Central to its political belief was the fight against the Marxist working-class movement and the peace of Versailles, which was regarded as a national disgrace.[1] The greatest obstacle for the anti-democratic right was that it was organisationally divided and hampered by internal conflicts. When the NSDAP made astonishing gains in the September 1930 Reichstag elections, it became clear that Hitler's movement had legitimate prospects of leading Germany out of the Weimar 'swamp' into a new future.[2] This chapter looks at the powerful nationalist milieu in Saxon society. The nationalist milieu stood often in sharp confrontation with the socialist milieu, was firmly embedded in bourgeois-elitist circles, and provided an essential breeding ground for Nazism. Our knowledge of the nationalist milieu at the local and regional level is still very limited because most of the studies which deal with these aspects cover the national level and focus predominantly on intellectual history.[3] Furthermore, investigations about the 'radicalisation of the centre' have largely focused on political parties and political pressure groups up until the late 1920s without dealing with the wider nationalist network.[4]

(i) Bourgeois Clubs and Organisations: Fountains of Nationalism

The development of modern clubs was linked with the emergence of bourgeois industrial society at the beginning of the nineteenth century. The vast number of clubs and their influence not only at a local, but also a national level, ensured them a powerful position in German society. Clubs developed along class divisions in society, were an instrument of social control, and were often used to put forward the particular interests of their members, including political ones.[5] Voluntarily created clubs were dominated by the upper and middle classes in Germany. The development of working-class clubs in the last quarter of the nineteenth century created an 'alternative' organisational network to the existing bourgeois one. Nevertheless, bourgeois clubs continued to dominate society, particularly in rural areas and in small and medium-sized towns.

Most bourgeois clubs in Saxony – if professional or leisure-orientated – had an extremely nationalistic and conservative nature before the First World War. In 1913 a swimming club in Chemnitz celebrated the 100th anniversary of the defeat of Napoleon's army at the battle of Leipzig and proclaimed: 'We want to be German, we want to cultivate German mentality ... We need motivation which reminds us to really give the best for our *Volk*, be it work, property or blood.'[6] It was typical too that in August 1914 the Agricultural Organisation for the Oberlausitz and the Saxon industrialists joined the war effort with flags flying in defence of the nation, and – although members of both organisations suffered economic and social hardships – repeatedly expressed their deep loyalty to *Kaiser*, King and Fatherland during the war years (also see document 2).[7]

Some bourgeois clubs continued to postulate extreme nationalist convictions after 1918. The disappointing outcome of the war, the terms of the Versailles Peace Treaty, and the unstable postwar years seemed to make these beliefs more essential than ever. However, this was more the exception than the rule. Leisure clubs in particular tended to avoid expressing nationalist sentiment or covering political matters in their club publications after the war. Most leisure clubs – but also many professional organisations – had a policy of focusing on club affairs only and of leaving politics out of their organisation. A large section of members in bourgeois leisure clubs were workers,[8] and an unpolitical stance seemed to be the best strategy to keep political disputes outside of club life at a time of great political tensions. This is why one club emphasised: 'Sport is free. It serves no political and religious tendencies.'[9]

The activities and membership numbers of most bourgeois clubs – like those of workers' clubs – reached a peak in the 1920s. Thereafter, most clubs plunged into a dramatic crisis due to the devastating effects of the slump and – like the political parties – radicalised. Professional organisations politicised, adopted an increasingly anti-government and anti-democratic stance, and moved to the right. Whereas many leisure clubs tried to resist politicisation, more and more joined those who voiced radical nationalist beliefs. By the early 1930s there was an almost unanimous front of bourgeois clubs in Saxony who put forward extreme nationalist, anti-democratic and aggressive sentiments, expressing their desire for change and their readiness to support a radical nationalist solution headed by a strong leader (see also document 18). Anti-Marxist sentiments played an additional and crucial role among professional clubs. Because they were far more divided along class lines than leisure clubs, they did not have to pay much attention to the feelings of working-class members. Moreover, due to the very nature of their function, professional organisations were much more closely tied to the political process.[10]

A random survey of twenty-eight magazines (*Mitteilungen*) of bourgeois professional and leisure clubs in Saxony in the final years of the Republic found that all could be classified as nationalist/authoritarian or extreme nationalist/authoritarian. Starting with magazines of professional organisations, the Higher Civil

Servants in Saxony announced in mid-1931: 'We all want to believe that an historic hour is awaiting us at which a *Führertum* [leadership principle] ends the tedious, corrupting material competition of the *Stände* [estates]'.[11] In Dresden, one of the largest garrison towns in Germany, with strong economic and social ties between the army and the local population, a magazine for *Reichswehr* members called on its readers in late 1932 to 'get rid of the pacifist madness' and 'if necessary to fight for German freedom with blood.' The article elaborated:

> History is made by men, not by majority decisions, parties, ideologies and demagogues. Only the strong will of the conscientious, God-sent leader ... who rests on the divine power of the *Volkstum*, is able to lead a *Volk* from deep misery to ascent, and from slavery to strength.[12]

Most bourgeois leisure organisations postulated a more aggressive nationalism during the slump too. When the Saxon members of the German Gymnastics Association organised a gymnastics meeting in June 1929, the participants used the occasion to demonstrate against Germany's war guilt.[13] The organ of Saxon Rifle Clubs advised all members in early 1932: 'Hold out, because the last period of conflict for Germany's freedom has come ... This final fight can only be successful, when the German *Volk* is united on the soil of the German fatherland.'[14] A swimming club proclaimed:

> We must regard sport as a substitute for general military service ... We practice sport to be able to give the fatherland a strong and vital man who will be prepared to give his life for the *Heimat* one day.[15]

Some bourgeois clubs had expressed nationalist beliefs and a dislike of the Republican system throughout the Weimar years. For instance, farmers' organisations blamed the revolution for the bad situation in agriculture after the war.[16] The development of a broadly radical nationalist front in the early 1930s, however, was linked to the massive crisis which the bourgeois clubs faced. To be sure, each club had its own specific history, faced different problems and responded differently to them. Generally speaking, clubs became radicalised by the worsening economic situation of their members, and leisure clubs in particular faced serious financial problems that often threatened their whole existence. The Saxon Nazis – who had good reasons to include an extensive sport section in *Der Freiheitskampf* – benefited from the crisis of bourgeois leisure clubs.

Leisure clubs had already gone through a difficult time when the First World War disrupted club life and many male members did not return from the front. Then came the unstable postwar years during which club life was revived with great effort and personal sacrifice, only to subsequently suffer heavily during the time of hyperinflation in 1923.[17] From 1924 onwards most clubs seemed very active and expanded again. Long-term investments in new and expensive sports grounds and club houses were not unusual. A few years later these same clubs faced enormous financial problems when suddenly the economic crisis caused unemployment and drove members away – e.g., the membership of the Sport Association Leipzig-Lindenau declined from 3,166 to 2,775 in 1931 alone[18] – and led to a serious decline in the income and activities of clubs. (See chapter 3 [i] for the impact of the slump on working-class leisure organisations.)

During the 1920s many bourgeois sport clubs – like Marxist clubs – had used an emotional appeal to enhance the loyalty of their members and to attract more people to join. Whereas the SPD had appealed to the members' duty to the Republic,[19] the bourgeoisie had emphasised the moral link between the activity in the club and 'a love and duty for the fatherland'.[20] In the course of the slump this appeal assumed an increasingly aggressive tone and the traditional emphasis on an unpolitical stance became more and more farcial.[21] Since its first issue in 1924 the magazine of the Police Sport Club 21 Leipzig had only reported about sport results and club affairs. When in the early 1930s fewer and fewer members paid the membership fees and a growing number of members left the club for good, it responded by printing an aggressive political and emotional vision under the title 'sport as a service for the fatherland', which linked sport with the fight for a better future for Germany:

> The first and equally most noble aim lies in the following lifelong pursuit: The welfare of our own *Volksgenossen* and – as its precondition – the freedom and powerful development of the fatherland. The immense scale of our task is revealed when we see that our German fatherland is currently not free and by the kind of obstacles which are blocking its development ... We feel like soldiers in a war which has continued by other means, of equal quality to our German brothers who have given everything they had for the fatherland during the world war. We too should devote all of our strength to a renewal of our fatherland.[22]

The longing to realise 'the great idea of the *Volksgemeinschaft*' that would unite all classes was expressed by a growing number of clubs (see also document 18).[23] Meanwhile, some leisure clubs were infiltrated by Nazism. The 'neutral' Gymnastic Club Leipzig-Schleußig carried Nazi swastikas at a march through the town in late 1932.[24]

Although all clubs treasured the youth and had the unanimous opinion that the future belonged to it, it is striking how difficult many bourgeois clubs found it to maintain a good relationship with young people and to keep them within their ranks. Frequently there was a lack of understanding for the young and their needs and desires in a modernising society. The old-fashioned leaders of one swimming club – whose own principle was 'discipline is necessary, the tougher the better' and who had a long history of losing young club members – were completely aloof from the new generation and even ridiculed them in their club magazine:

> Now look at the youngsters who are growing up! They give in to every desire and craving, puff away at English cigarettes, buy the first tasty titbit, dance, and throw away every activity that requires some effort. Do not carry through anything under any circumstances! Weak body and soft will! And they want to fight for freedom and retain it? Poor Germany![25]

In 1924 the Gymnastic and Sport Association 1848 Leipzig-Lindenau mentioned for the first time that children were 'running away from them' and explained this with their failure to attract them with new fashionable sports gear.[26] During the slump a wave of young people turned their back on their traditional clubs, and were never to return again.[27] The reasons were not always financial. In 1932 the Gymnasts in Leipzig-Lindenau admitted that 'the stormy youth feels inhibited by the contemplation of the older'.[28] In a desperate move to keep the remaining youth, the club invited unemployed youngsters for get-togethers in the afternoons. But the clubs' 'resolutions' as to what should and should not be done during these meetings sounded so paternalistic and restrictive – the youth were asked to tell each other their experiences and to read from books; smoking, card-games and political discussions were prohibited – that no-one turned up. Working-class organisations faced similar problems: in the late 1920s Social Democrats in eastern Saxony reported difficulties in organising the eighteen to twenty-five-year olds due to 'psychological obstacles', and working-class allotment clubs organised strictly 'systematic play' for their youth which limited the freedom of childish behaviour.[29] The growing problems most clubs faced in attracting and keeping young people stood in sharp contrast to the youthful and dynamic appearance of the Nazis, who – at least in the public image – increasingly seemed to have won the battle over the youth. (This also reflected the young membership of the Saxon NSDAP. See chapter 5 [i–ii].)

Professional bourgeois organisations and their members also radicalised, albeit generally earlier than the leisure clubs and normally with more openly political overtones. They felt squeezed by the effects of the hyperinflation, a sluggish economy with high unemployment rates, new taxes, increased rationalisation and the competition from organised labour and big business. During the latter half of the 1920s a growing number of bourgeois organisations became disillusioned with the bourgeois parties they were traditionally allied with – including the government. In western Saxony members of the old middle class – artisans, shopkeepers and house owners – demonstrated against high taxation and government favouritism to big business and labour in summer 1926.[30] They also started to look for help elsewhere. For instance, Saxon professionals founded a working group for craft, trade and business in 1928 because they were dissatisfied with their traditional representatives.[31] During election time the main aim of these organisations was to prevent a Marxist victory. Before early 1930 they only rarely expressed a preference for any bourgeois party in this task.[32] Before the 1929 state elections the leadership of the Saxon crafts stated:

> If you are clear where you belong, that you have to stand on the right if you do not want to help digging your own grave, you easily recognise that the differences between the bourgeois parties are not very great ... the essential question is: vote and vote at all costs bourgeois! ... You know the meaning of a 'social economy'. Should the crafts become proletarian? Do you as a free and independent man want to become a mere number in this social economy?[33]

As the Great Slump worsened, organisations radicalised and slowly moved towards the NSDAP. Before the September 1930 Reichstag elections the powerful Saxon Home and Land Owner Association – which had 501 local branches and more than 100,700 members[34] – warned: 'The home owners will be driven to despair by the bourgeois parties and many will turn to the radical parties if nothing is done to improve the situation of home owners.'[35] According to the association, many home owners, particularly young people, had already joined the NSDAP. It is not surprising that the same Home Owner Association, but also organisations such as the State Committee for Saxon Handicraft and the Saxon Farmer's Union, called for a coalition of the bourgeois parties with the NSDAP in the Landtag after the June elections.[36] By late 1931 the Association of Saxon Craft blamed the bad situation on the 'total failure of politics' and concluded: 'We can only recover with a government that is detached from any compromises with Marxism.'[37] The Higher Civil Servants in Saxony discussed alternatives to the parliamentary system after the September 1930 Reichstag elections, and made the first sympathetic remarks about the Nazi party at the end of the year.[38] By mid-1931 they were praising the NSDAP's educational programme as 'an emotional idealism which aims to create a politically strong Germany with German citizens', and after the July 1932 Reichstag elections they grieved that the NSDAP had not gained an absolute majority.[39]

The single most powerful professional interest group in Saxony, the Association of Saxon Industrialists which had representatives in all major bourgeois parties, had a history of undermining parliamentary democracy and helped to prepare the ground for the Nazi dictatorship.[40] The negative attitude of many local industrialists towards the Republic and their pronounced hatred of the working-class movement were caused by their deep-rooted bourgeois-elitist and nationalist views, their long-standing refusal to accept organised labour as an equal partner in the running of society, and Saxony's particularly uneasy economic and political development after the Great War. The mainly small- and medium-scale Saxon industrialists also felt frustrated by a number of disadvantages and a lack of influence in the Reich compared with that of the big capitalists in the west.

Between 1919 and 1923 the VSI used all of its influence to get rid of the legally elected left-wing governments in Dresden, and afterwards it did everything to ensure that the bourgeoisie stayed in power by rallying middle-class groups against a 'Soviet Saxony' during election campaigns. It was no coincidence that the VSI gained a new chairman in the late 1920s – Wilhelm Wittke – who turned out to be one of the fiercest critics of the Republic. Soon after his appointment in late 1928, Wittke described the parliamentary system as 'deplorable and unbearable',[41] and later that year suggested the deactivation of parliament with an emergency law.[42] Henceforth, the VSI became a trailblazer amongst industrial organisations in Germany, determined to exploit the crisis and replace the democratic and costly welfare state with a dictatorship.

When the growth of the NSDAP became apparent in late 1929, the VSI examined in detail Mussolini's economic policies and expressed 'a certain admiration for this organically built economic theory'.[43] The interest that the VSI showed in 'fascism' was checked by the NSDAP's role in overthrowing the Bünger and Schieck governments which eventually led to new elections in June 1930. More than anything else the Saxon industrialists feared instability and uncertainty, and blamed the Saxon Nazis for the fall of two 'excellent governments'.[44] Although the VSI allowed several economic experts of the NSDAP to speak in front of the organisation over the years, it did not openly support the Nazis. The Nazis' political opportunism and some of their radical features – but also their unorthodox economic approach (see chapter 4 [v]) – seemed to have prevented this.

Crucially, however, the VSI too adopted increasingly radical, emotional and nationalist language in the face of the desperate economic situation, and a growing number of representatives openly cried for a change in the system. In mid-1931 the VSI's branch in Annaberg demanded a strengthening of Germany's military power and an end to any discussion of pacifist ideas, and praised Mussolini as the best statesman of the time.[45] Aggressive expansionism – what the Nazis promised – seemed a remedy to revitalise the depressed export of textiles and machinery. The representative of the district of Zwickau stated in early 1932: 'We cannot win this struggle to the death if we do not regain breathing space [*Luft und Raum*] for our development at home and beyond the borders ... The system has to be changed.'[46] Only a few weeks later, Wittke gave a blank cheque for a dictator – including Hitler – and stated: 'The precondition for every recovery remains that the economy is finally allowed again to follow its own laws, and any leader who restores this possibility for our economy, no matter where he comes from, is welcome.'[47] Unlike the leaders of the Ruhr heavy industry,[48] the VSI did not voice implicit support for the NSDAP before Hitler's appointment as Chancellor, but it severely undermined the democratic framework and broadened support for a dictatorial solution to the crisis.

Heinrich A. Winkler described how the Nazis gradually came to control many artisan and small trade middle-class interest organisations by infiltrating them at a local level and mobilising the members against their leaders until the whole organisation was run on NSDAP lines.[49] Similar developments could be observed in Saxony. In early 1932 a trade council in northwestern Saxony reacted to internal pressure by some members in favour of a move towards the NSDAP and warned: 'Our organisation should only have economic objectives and has to remain completely free from party political influence.'[50] But its repeated appeals fell on deaf ears and the NSDAP – as in other parts of Saxony – won a majority of seats when it broke the tradition of single lists and competed in the elections to the trade councils in autumn 1932.[51]

Professional organisations and leisure clubs of the bourgeoisie faced a variety of severe problems and had no constructive answers to offer in the final years of Weimar. In early 1932 the Electrotechnical Club in Chemnitz openly admitted its inability to help its unemployed members and to stem the flow of those who left the club because of financial difficulties.[52] Traditional clubs and their club life were depressed and disintegrating. Some members left club life altogether, some deserted to join the dynamic Nazi movement, and some clubs were infiltrated by Nazism. Many club managers and/or members radicalised in the face of economic pressures and opened themselves to an extreme nationalistic solution. Certain deep-rooted beliefs and values seemed to offer a natural panacea in this difficult time: extreme nationalism, the stress on the subversion of the individual to *Volk* and fatherland, the emphasis on tradition, obedience and discipline (even the ATSB had copied the bourgeoisie's militaristic club discipline),[53] the warning against the dangers of modernisation in the form of large cities and youths who grew up without discipline but with alcohol and cigarettes, and the perceived threat of socialism.

A growing number of those who were part of the traditional bourgeois club life regarded the Nazis' vision of the Third Reich as a logical conclusion to the ideals that had been preached for many decades. This explained the smooth nazification of many bourgeois clubs, and how, with much enthusiasm, some of them gave up their independence and welcomed their obsoletion. By the end of 1933 most bourgeois clubs had been incorporated into the totalitarian dictatorship, some of them – like the Christian Parents Associations in Saxony – toadied to the Nazis and printed whole lists of resolutions they had already suggested in previous years and which had finally been realised in the Third Reich.[54]

Most bourgeois clubs were allowed to carry on, but they slowly withered away. The main aim of professional organisations – to promote the interests of their members – had become a contradiction in itself in a centralised totalitarian regime. Those clubs and club members who had hoped that they could revive their organisation in an authoritarian nationalist state, had a sober awakening. The organ of the Saxon industrialists – *Sächsische Industrie* – became an instrument to promote Nazi economic policies, and its frequent emphasis on the importance of export for Germany[55] was meaningless in an economy that was geared towards self-sufficiency and the preparation for war. Sports clubs, too, lost their function in a dictatorship that undertook to physically train a population for the coming war. The clubs lost their members – particularly the youth – to company sport clubs and Nazi organisations, and their financial difficulties worsened further under Nazism. A secret report summarised some of the developments after four years' dictatorship:

> All the *gleichgeschalteten* [coordinated] sports clubs are doing badly. They all complain about a large loss of members and no money. The Reich's Sports Association demands an extremely high fee from the various clubs. The lack of members stems from the fact that most youth who are fit and want to do sport are with the SA, labour service or in the *Reichswehr* ... A large bourgeois sports club in Heidenau with 1,500 members before 1933 had to sell its meeting place due to its high debts and the fact that its membership had shrunk to several hundred.[56]

(ii) Celebrations and Symbols: Battlefields between Left and Right

Festivals and celebrations occupy a central role in the rhythm of life of any given society.[57] Among other things, they serve as symbols which highlight traditions and beliefs, and frequently establish a link between past, present and future. At no time were the divisions in Saxon society more evident than during public celebrations, when the completely different attitudes and values of various groups became apparent. Early in the twentieth century, a Leipzig company saw itself forced to abandon its yearly summer celebration because it so frequently ended in political arguments.[58]

Festivals with direct political associations led to a particular polarisation and heightened politicisation within society. This was especially true during public holidays which expressed identification with the democratic system and the Republic. The most important ones were the annual celebrations to commemorate the start of the revolution and the day when Germany was declared a Republic, 9 November 1918, and the passing of the constitution on 11 August 1919. On the republican side of the political spectrum the Social Democrats and liberals celebrated these occasions with mass parades and festivals, while the national right expressed their open hatred. In 1928 a police report captured the long-standing tensions in Saxon society on 9 November: 'Everywhere the SPD staged well attended Revolution celebrations ... This caused the NSDAP, Stahlhelm and Alldeutscher Verband to organise several commemoration rallies.'[59] A year earlier, the Nazis in Zwickau had used the occasion for a propaganda campaign against the Republic. This had included a parade through the town, the handing out of leaflets, the laying down of wreaths for comrades and soldiers who had died, and speeches in which they made clear that workers had not been freed but made slaves by the revolution.[60]

The significance which left and right attached to public festivals and their symbolic meaning made these celebrations one of the major battlefields during the Weimar Republic. When the Socialist government in Saxony declared 1 May (the traditional celebration of the European working class) and 9 November official state holidays with mandatory observance in April 1922, the bourgeoisie was furious and organised a petition (*Volksbegehren*) to force new elections through a referendum.[61] Whilst the Social Democrats regarded 9 November as a 'day of the liberation of all oppressed and progressive democratic circles', the bourgeoisie argued that it 'encouraged social antagonism and highlighted class tensions'. In fact, most members of the bourgeoisie associated the day with 'cowardice, treachery, and national disgrace.' Whilst the workers' movement regarded 1 May as the symbol of international workers' solidarity, the bourgeoisie condemned its internationalism and its emphasis on class conflict. The labour movement and the bourgeoisie rallied behind two completely different world views which led to a dramatic political polarisation: the bourgeoisie agitated against the dictatorship of the Socialists and Socialist class-rule in Saxony, whilst the left mobilised against the counter-revolutionary forces. Indeed, the petition – the first of its kind in the Weimar Republic – which needed 276,000 signatures to force a referendum, received more than 800,000 signatures. The Landtag voted to dissolve itself and initiated new elections, rather than submit the issue of new elections to a referendum.

The extent to which festivals reflected the mood and atmosphere in Saxon society became evident by an apparent link between the number of celebrations – up-and-down-and-up-again roughly for the periods 1918/19–1925, 1926–29, and 1930–33 – with political and economic developments during the Weimar years. The number of participants for the left could go into the thousands, as events were centrally organised by SPD and KPD and their affiliated organisations. The nationalist milieu was far more fragmented, but used these occasions to create a united front and frequently also managed to attract large crowds. Most importantly, there were around 120,000 participants from the whole of Germany at the parade of the *Reichskriegertag* (Reich War Day) in Leipzig in 1925.[62]

During the first five years, which experienced social, political and economic instability, the left and right put enormous efforts into staging celebrations that served to underpin their position. The left normally celebrated its achievements and demonstrated its vision for an even better future. The right used festivities to express disappointment and dissatisfaction with the current situation and a longing to restore past glories. The Saxon workers' movement treated the nationalist milieu with suspicion and did not tolerate anything that seemed to threaten their rule or which was in sharp contrast to their beliefs. In 1923 this caused enormous tensions between both groups when Proletarian Hundreds – which were set up to counter anti-democratic activities of the far-right – disrupted conservative and nationalist celebrations. The police reported about two incidents in the Erzgebirge:

> Two Hundreds visited two towns, allegedly to counter National Socialist intrigues. The former Sergeant Schüler had organised a memorial consecration in Marienberg ... and in Röhrsdorf the Association of Young Farmers celebrated its 25th anniversary ... To negotiate, both localities turned to the state commissioner in charge ... In the first town it was possible to avoid disturbances although both sides carried out parades ... This was not the case in Röhrsdorf ... More than 100 persons from Chemnitz disrupted the parade. Knife fights took place. One of the injured had to be taken to hospital.[63]

In Plauen the police complained that Proletarian Hundreds were pursuing tasks which only the police had the authority to carry out. Members of the organisation had carried out identity checks and searches among nationalist citizens who had visited a meeting in Hof at which Hitler was present.[64]

At a time when the Nazis only possessed an extremely small following and no central party organisation, celebrations of the nationalist milieu were an important opportunity to meet other like-minded people and to establish links with the wider nationalist network. Such occasions unified these 'outsiders' from the existing political system and enhanced their radical right-wing beliefs and their opposition to the Republic. Besides participating in nationalist celebrations in Saxony, the local Nazis came to the *Deutscher Tag* (German Day) in Coburg in October 1922, and many went to the above-mentioned *Deutscher Tag* in Hof in September 1923. It is worth noting how many local Nazis participated at the German Gymnastic Festival in Munich in 1923 and came across the Nazi movement on this occasion (see document 4).

After the left-wing government was overthrown at the end of 1923, it was their followers who felt pushed onto the defensive in their activities. Most significantly, in late 1929 the bourgeois majority in the parliament in Dresden abolished the holiday on 9 November, the day which commemorated the anniversary of the 1918 revolution.[65] The abolition of this celebration – which many citizens regarded as the symbol of democracy and unity of the Republic, and which had traditionally been one of the most important events in the working-class calendar – caused enormous resentment on the left.

Generally speaking, public celebrations were at their lowest during the second half of the 1920s. The comparatively tranquil situation did not seem to make political manifestations in public an urgent necessity.[66] Additionally, the increasing strains between Social Democrats and Communists had fragmented the left, and both parties needed time to recover from the setback of the *Reichsexekution* and to sort out internal disputes. Then, in the final years of Weimar, there was a significant revival and radicalisation of public activities. The SPD mobilised in defence of the Republic and against the Nazi threat. The KPD prepared for a socialist revolution, and the nationalist milieu became agitated and more outright than ever about its dislike of the system they lived in. Meanwhile the Nazis had become by far the busiest campaigner on the political right and were increasingly identified with representing the nationalist milieu.

The most important celebration of the nationalist right during the Weimar era was 18 January, the day the German Empire was founded in 1871 ('Day of the Fatherland'). The Nazis frequently participated in these celebrations with other supporters of the national right. For instance, the Saxon war hero and Nazi leader Hellmuth von Mücke was invited by the national right in Freiberg to commemorate the event in early 1927, and spoke about his war adventures in front of 500 guests.[67] *Deutsche Tage*, which took place at weekends throughout the year, were occasions where various groups of the nationalist right came together and celebrated their beliefs. In Saxony *Deutsche Tage* featured particularly frequently between 1923 and 1925 in both small and medium-sized towns. In the southwest the Nazis played an important part in these celebrations. The *Deutscher Tag* in Crimmitschau was visited by 450 people in February 1925. Among others, the subsequent Nazi leader Killinger gave a speech. The participants honoured the dead soldiers at the war memorial, there was a service and the consecration of flags, and 1,100 people marched in the parade.[68]

Another powerful unifying experience for the national right was the cultivation of war memorials in commemoration of soldiers killed in the war. Here too, the Nazis were sometimes successful in assuming a leading role. They reported the consecration of a war memorial in Ruppertsgrün, near Zwickau, at the end of 1927:

> A large number of local inhabitants participated at the consecration of the memorial for the heroes killed in the world war ... It was a special day for us National Socialists. We had helped to create the warrior memorial with pick and shovel. All local bourgeois organisations, the United Military Association of Werdau-Leubnitz with flag bearers and the local branch of the NSDAP with twenty Stormtroopers and several civilian party members took part. The consecration began with a service in our church. After the service the participants, led by our Stormtroopers with banners, marched to the memorial square, where General Schönfels ... gave the consecration speech. The local priest then consecrated the memorial. It was a solemn moment when the memorial was unveiled while the National Socialists saluted, the military association stood to attention, and the drum rolled. Afterwards ... our leader Gräßer spoke with powerful words about those killed in the war.[69]

In these moments the deep divisions of Saxon society became most apparent. Whilst the nationalists celebrated and the Nazis used the occasion to strengthen their influence in this milieu – Ruppertsgrün became one of the earliest Nazi strongholds in Saxony[70] – the organised working class regarded war commemorations as a cynical performance by those who were guilty of the death and injury of millions of innocent people. The SPD had expressed its disgust about a similar consecration of a war memorial by a large nationalist crowd in Plauen in the early 1920s:

> Ugly! Ugly like the whole system which had caused this murder of the nations and now even plays hell with the corpse of the murdered! ... So ugly that it would be desirable at the first possible opportunity, to put a detonator up the backside of this disgraceful monument.[71]

Another issue of constant dispute between the nationalist milieu and Republican supporters concerned the use of colours and flags. Even colours of sports gear led to disputes and one swimming club, whose 'anti-republican' stripe on the swimming trunks had 'caused offence' in 1922, was forced to introduce more 'neutral' (blue-yellow) colours.[72] The nationalist milieu often expressed their dislike of the Republic by showing the 'black-white-and-red' flag of Wilhelmine Germany, or carrying their own consecrated flags – e.g., the Nazis' swastika flag – to which they swore allegiance. But even the Social Democrats were not completely united behind the symbols of the Republic. In 1926 the ATSB in Saxony unsuccessfully attempted to stop the display of the Republican black-red-gold flag next to the red flag on the national headquarters of its organisation in Leipzig. It argued that only the red flag had a uniting meaning for the proletariat and that the colours of the Republic symbolised the compromise with the bourgeoisie.[73]

There was a heated discussion in the Saxon parliament about the hoisting of the French national flag in the town of Meißen in April 1931. A Social Democratic sports club had invited a French boxing team to an international competition. As a welcome, the town council had granted permission to hoist the French 'Tricolour' and the German national flag opposite the station, and to put up a placard between both flag posts with the slogan: 'Welcome, French Brothers!'[74] This was done on the morning of the guests' arrival. By lunch, however, after one member of the Meißen town council had demanded the removal of the French flag, the Saxon Ministry of the Interior intervened and ordered its removal. The ministry justified its decision by pointing out that it was 'undoubtedly backed by the majority of the population' and that it 'served to prevent disruptions of the public peace'. All the bourgeois parties and the NSDAP fully supported the government's action. The DVP called it a 'monstrosity ... that the flag had been hoisted in the German fatherland', and the Nazis were outraged that 'the colours of the French blood enemy [had] waved above a town in Saxony.'[75]

Reunion celebrations of war veterans also played an important part in the annual agenda of the nationalist milieu. The Saxon Military Association was possibly the largest organisation in the state, claiming 1,624 local branches with 206,325 members in the mid-1920s.[76] The Saxon police frequently reported well-attended regimental celebrations in all major towns during that time. Elliot rightly argued that if one considers that members were 'honour-bound to turn out on national and church festivals, funerals of comrades, local *Kreisverband* events etc., here was to be found a significant source of irritation to the supporters of the Republic.'[77] The Saxon Nazis also participated on these occasions (they were, however, not always welcomed by all veterans) and used similar aspects – for instance the Stormtroopers used the same numbers for their units as former local army regiments[78] – and rituals for their own propaganda. They proclaimed that it was necessary to re-create war socialism (*Frontsozialismus*) – which in their opinion was National Socialism – in order to overcome the problems German society was facing.[79]

A brigade meeting of Stormtroopers in the town of Markneukirchen in 1931 was a festival in which all citizens were encouraged to participate, and 'the streets were decorated with garlands and flags … there was a concert and German dance in the evening'.[80] The swastika flag was the symbol of the rejection of the Republic and the desire for a new National Socialist State. Markneukirchen's economic and cultural background as a centre for the production of musical instruments provided the link with local tradition, the field service by a local priest provided the religious blessing, and the march by 3,000 Stormtroopers through the town gave the image of discipline, order, military strength and the memory of glorious days. The Nazis reflected: 'Again and again it was said, that it was like in the good old peaceful days, when the military marched with ringing steps through the streets during exercises … (war veterans from 1870/71 received seats of honour).'

Public political celebrations had always been about the display of strength and the vision of what a society should look like. During the Third Reich the Nazis followed this tradition, but took it to extremes and raised it to new quantitative dimensions. The monopolisation of public festivals not only served to mobilise and indoctrinate the population, but also to wipe out all oppositional views and traditions. In contrast, public workers' culture disappeared and had no chance of being experienced by a new generation.[81] Public life in Nazi Germany seemed to revolve around public celebrations. Even appointments and promotions of civil servants, employees and workers had to be made on one of the major festive days.[82] The amount of celebrations and new regulations was such that it often led to confusion among the Saxon population. For instance, people were unclear about the difference between *Totengedenktag* (the last Sunday before Advent commemorating the dead) and *Heldengedenktag* (commemoration of the sixteen Nazis who died during the attempted Hitler putsch in Munich on 9 November 1923).[83]

Whether official festivities or the numerous other celebrations – celebrations on the day when the Empire was founded, after the Saar referendum in January 1935, or when conscription was reintroduced in March 1935 – the local Nazis exploited these occasions to indoctrinate the population and to cover up various shortcomings. To do this, they were not inhibited about picking up the thread of various traditions. In Schneeberg-Neustädtel, where an ongoing economic depression led to resentments against the regime, the Nazis attempted to defuse the situation by organising an historical mountain march of miners.[84] In early 1938 when the Nazis put great efforts into organising a carnival, a Social Democrat interpreted this as a cover-up for the terror and an attempt to give the impression that much was legal again.[85] Solstice celebrations at which a Greater Germany was idolised and which were held directly at the border,[86] were preparations for the annexation of the *Sudetenland*. Public celebrations were also the perfect occasion to promote the idea of the *Volksgemeinschaft* and the harvest festival became a celebration in which people from all social classes were encouraged to participate.[87] In the end, everything was subordinated to Nazi goals, including the dismantling and melting of Bismarck's monuments to support the war effort.[88]

The Nazis were not always successful in mobilising the population according to their wishes. There were reports that many places did not show sufficient flag-waving on 1 May, and the decree for hoisting the flag to commemorate the death of the Swiss NSDAP leader was scarcely adhered to in Saxony in 1936.[89] At the same time, the Nazis were even forced to curb some citizens who outpaced their own cult of nationalism. War memorials, local heritage museums and home town museums sprang up throughout the state, and the Nazis introduced legislation to stem this 'uncontrollable increase', because many of these activities were based on commercial interests.[90]

The May the First celebration was a prominent example of how the Nazis used this most important workers' festival for their particular purposes. The cynicism of this became obvious when the Saxon Nazis hastily abolished the day as a public holiday in late March 1933,[91] something they had already fiercely demanded in the Dresden parliament in 1929.[92] Overjoyed by this news the local industrialists boasted that they themselves had repeatedly tried to get rid of this 'revolutionary celebration' in the previous years.[93] The embarrassment came in April when Goebbels declared 1 May 'public holiday of national work'. Saxon employers and Nazis put on a brave face and several weeks later they all celebrated the occasion with Goebbels' motto that the day would establish the *Volksgemeinschaft* and get rid of the class struggle. Whereas 25,200 Social Democrats and Communists had participated at separate May the First Celebrations in Leipzig in 1931, three years later 280,000 people were forced to parade under Nazism.[94]

After the collapse of Nazi Germany, the SED revived some of the workers' celebrations which had been banned since 1933. But of course the SED's style was as opportunistic as their predecessor's. The short revival of the March celebrations (for the victims of the Kapp putsch) in 1947 were used to highlight the anti-fascist and democratic bloc policy of the SED, and from 1949 onwards the November celebrations related to the Russian October Revolution.[95]

(iii) Nationalist Culture: Education, Religion and Theatre

Education stood at the cutting edge of politics because whoever controlled it was able to convey his values and beliefs to a new generation. The way schools were run and what kind of curriculum was used became one of the great conflicts between the traditional and progressive forces in modernising societies. Whereas the left and most liberals in Saxony demanded the strict separation of school and church and an emphasis on equal opportunities, tolerance and democratic values, the conservative forces vehemently clung to the confessional character and hierarchical structure of the school system and an emphasis on obedience, fear of God, and the idolising of the fatherland (see also document 1).[96] The close link between church and priests with schools – particularly in the countryside – had ensured that the church had an enormous influence in the educational sector until the beginning of the twentieth century.

In the years before the First World War the Saxon Conservatives prevented the attempt by Liberals and Social Democrats to reform elementary schools.[97] In fact, the state openly used schools as a political weapon. Social Democrats were not able to become teachers, and teachers who were critical of the political system faced disciplinary proceedings.[98] The Weimar Republic promised favourable conditions to introduce fundamental reforms. Whereas at the Reich level the planned reforms in the school sector ended in a compromise (as with most other things), the Social Democrats introduced a more thorough set of reforms in Saxony: most importantly, school fees were abolished and the profession of teachers and priests was separated. The separation of primary schools along confessional lines was also abolished. Pupils who chose to attend religious lessons rather than the newly introduced lessons in moral studies (*Moralunterricht*) had to present a signed letter from their parents. Furthermore, corporal punishment was banned in schools.[99]

There was an immediate and sharp reaction to these developments. The traditional forces felt that their power and beliefs were being undermined, and they formed a broad conservative and nationalist front – which later included the Nazis – to fight the reforms, to agitate against the socialist government, and to embark on an aggressive ideological offensive. The DNVP argued that there was a need for 'a truly Christian religious lesson and a history lesson which was dominated by the spirit of the fatherland.'[100] In the early 1920s the DVP even focused its election campaigns on the school reforms and warned: 'The school is being de-christianised – songs and prayers have been removed – degraded to a socialist party school; the youth is dissolute.'[101] Similarly, the Saxon Teachers Association asked the electorate: 'Do you want there to be strict discipline and order once again, or do you want an unruly youth to grow up? … The healthy youth of our *Volk* is at stake.'[102]

The attacks against the school reforms were frequently mixed with an assault on the Republican system. The Saxon Teachers Association described the passing of the Weimar Constitution on 11 August 1919 as 'a day of mourning for the German schools and their teachers'.[103] Twelve years later the Saxon Nazis published a proclamation to all Saxon pupils and asked them not to attend the constitutional celebrations on that day.[104] In 1923 the Association of Higher Schoolteachers – who argued that the task of history lessons was 'to awake a deep, loving understanding for *Volkstum* and the state' – indicated very openly that the Republican system was not the only political system which they recommended to pupils.[105] During the Third Reich the Association emphasised its own contribution in the Nazi 'revolution' and claimed that it had 'stimulated it, prepared it and had helped to carry it out by its upright, *vaterländisch* educational work.'[106]

When the bourgeoisie regained political control in Saxony at the end of 1923 the precarious situation in parliament did not allow them to completely undo the Social Democratic reforms. In any case, the bourgeois parties could not agree on a new comprehensive school reform themselves. Hence they moved in small steps to undo many aspects of what the SPD had introduced and to change the overall spirit of education. To mention a few examples: as early as January 1924 the government lifted the ban on religious influencing outside religious lessons at schools;[107] after 1928 '*Deutschtum*' was made the overriding idea of the whole school education;[108] and in 1930 all classes from the fifth year upwards had to celebrate the withdrawal of foreign troops from the Rhineland.[109] The government's austerity measures from mid-1930 led to a further drastic dismantling of the SPD's reforms.

During elections to the parents' councils – which had a similar role for the school system as local councils had on a political level – the socialist milieu had never been able to rally the support they received in parliamentary elections during the Weimar years. Burkhard Poste explains this as being the result of widespread conservative propaganda and tradition.[110] Dietmar Klenke found that the majority of workers were indifferent towards the question of religious education in Saxony and concluded that Social Democratic ideology was not deeply rooted in most parts of the state.[111] Many workers must have had conservative beliefs regarding family matters and education. Moreover, the results of the elections to the parents' councils indicate a continuous drift among Saxons towards right-wing values during the Republic. The only time when more secular representatives were elected than Christian representatives was in 1921, the first year when elections of this kind were carried out. Already a year later the Christian representatives received an overall tiny majority. This majority increased steadily and grew to 61.6 percent of all votes in 1931.[112]

The nationalists usually put forward the choice between Christianity or barbarity in Saxon schools during the election campaigns for the parents' councils. During the May 1931 elections the NSDAP played a radical part in the religious-nationalist front. An article in *Der Freiheitskampf* warned about the evil effects of the spread of unchristian Bolshevism from the Soviet Union – the 'sinister moloch and patroniser of ungodliness' where 'women were turned into whores' – which aimed at wiping out German culture and traditions.[113] The Nazis – like other nationalists – blamed the political system for tolerating the fact that 'values that had been built up and treasured throughout centuries were kicked in the mouth' (Ibid.). They emphasised their attitude as good, Christian, German citizens who treasured family values and made an emotional appeal:

> Parents! If the well-being of your children means a lot to you, if you do not want their open souls to be infiltrated daily and purposely by the ideas of class struggle, if you reject that they are at the mercy of cultural bolshevism, if you are worried that religion, faith, ideals, sense of family and national conviction will be torn out of their hearts, then you should go to the elections of the parents councils and as German parents vote for the Christian list![114]

Two years later – a few days before the March 1933 Reichstag elections – the State Association of Christian Parents in Saxony appealed to the electorate in similar words and gave them the choice between the 'strong front which is built on Christian, *vaterländisch* foundations of the united national Germany and ... the land of Bolshevism, contempt for God, [and] demolition of culture.'[115] By then, the choice for 'Germandom' basically stood for Nazism.

The deliberate exploitation of schools for political indoctrination came to completion during the Nazi dictatorship (see also chapter 3 [vi]). Two weeks after the elections the Saxon DNVP proposed to the Nazi government the removal of all former Communist and Social Democrats from active functions in the educational sector.[116] One of the earliest and fiercest opponents of the progressive educational reforms in the early 1920s, the Dresden school councillor Dr. Wilhelm Hartnacke (DNVP), officially introduced the 'national, *völkisch* and Christian' education in Nazi Saxony.[117] Whereas the SPD government had tried to foster democratic values and an awareness and toleration of other customs and beliefs – it was telling that in 1931 the SPD had supported school trips to France whereas the DNVP, DVP and NSDAP had opposed this on the grounds that France was

Germany's old enemy and that Saxon pupils should only visit Germanic countries[118] – the Nazis indoctrinated the pupils with their beliefs in racism, militarism and leadership. There was the introduction of the Hitler-greetings in schools, lessons in genetics and racial anthropology, and school holidays on Hitler's birthday to enable the pupils to participate at local army parades.[119]

Some teachers were initially rather lax about the implementation of Nazi ideology in their lessons, but young teachers in particular were often enthusiastic about Nazism. There was less and less room for individual teachers to continue with their traditional teaching methods.[120] The Nazis made sure that they were the overall winner in the battle for the youth. A Saxon Social Democrat noted in a resigned manner in early 1936:

> Nowadays most of the youth goes from the Boys' League to the Hitler Youth, from there to the work scheme and then to the *Wehrmacht*. These young people are lost for us in the foreseeable future. This is also true for working-class youth.[121]

The longer the dictatorship lasted, the more this was true. For instance, the Nazis reported in 1943 that HJ induction ceremonies had in general made a deep impact in Saxony and that 'a considerable number of young people who were to be confirmed the following Sunday at the instigation of their parents, rejected the Confirmation after having undergone the induction ceremony.'[122] At the same time, the existence of non-conformist youth gangs in Saxony – most importantly, the Leipzig *Meuten* (gangs) and Dresden *Mobs*, which had grown out of the working-class milieu and constituted a specific sub-culture[123] – proved that the Nazis never managed to control all youth.

Religion and the affiliation to the church also caused a major rift between the socialist milieu and the rest of Saxon society. After the war the Saxon SPD curbed the influence of the Protestant church and made it much easier for citizens to leave the church. This sparked off a wave of church leavers and was seen with growing anxiety by those who supported conservative and traditional values, including the Nazis. The nationalist milieu believed that the whole structure of Christian society was threatened by Communism from the east. In 1928 the local DNVP described the KPD's anti-religious activities as a 'systematic poisoning of the young',[124] and a weekly church paper in the Erzgebirge warned in early 1930:

> The Bolshevist government has carried out a fight against the Church for twelve years; it has not dared to wipe it out yet, but is preparing to do so ... Every state rests on the faith of God. This ultimate belief is abandoned, destroyed and wiped out in Russia ... these developments in Russia, once they are completed, will become a model for Europe. Today Russia, tomorrow and thereafter the other states.[125]

Considering that the Nazis were the most resolute anti-Marxists, it is not surprising that the former bishop of Saxony assessed that already in 1931 'nearly all priests in the state were under the spell of National Socialism.'[126] In that year the NSDAP supported a DVP motion in the Saxon parliament which asked the government to do everything in its power to stem the spread of the ungodly movement,[127] and a year later *Der Freiheitskampf* introduced the small section 'church news'.[128]

Sources suggest that during the Third Reich a significant part of the Protestant church supported the emphasis of nationalist values by the Nazis. One church paper rejoyced:

> Our German *Volk* has rediscovered the meaning of manly and strong creatures, for soldier-like discipline and order. It has re-discovered its best character and has brusquely renounced all weaknesses and incompleteness. We Christians have particular reason for joy about this.[129]

To many Saxon priests these aspects were extremely important and their loyalty to a nationalist, anti-Marxist state was so profound that they accepted that the Nazis gradually broke the church's independence, attacked religion when it did not submit to Nazism, and destroyed the church's remaining hold over the young.[130] However, the Nazis' assault on the church and the attempt to integrate it into their totalitarian project, proved how difficult even the Nazis found it to change deep-rooted values and allegiances. A large part of the population in the Erzgebirge refused to denounce their faith in Protestant Christianity.[131] The imprisonment of priests who resisted nazification led to widespread condemnation in Saxony,[132] and those priests who conformed readily to Nazism were sometimes shunned by the local population.[133] At the same time, there were reports that workers in particular used the new environment to leave the church for good.[134]

Theatre was another ideological battlefield. Nationalists and socialists used the theatre stage as a political platform to express their vision of society or criticism of existing features. Here was another important area where the Saxon Nazis were fully integrated in main-stream nationalist thinking. There was a serious disturbance during the first performance of Ernst Toller's play *Hinkemann* – about a war invalid who goes to rack and ruin in the postwar environment – in Dresden in early 1924.[135] Radical nationalists had disrupted the play with whistling, clapping, singing and shouting, and when they cried 'get out Jews', a Jewish banker from Berlin suffered a fatal stroke. Ensuing inquiries established that the incident had been carried out by DNVP supporters – later on the DNVP described the play as a 'piece of dirt' in the Landtag[136] – and *völkisch* splinter organisations (incl. Nazis), and that the money for it had been collected in bourgeois circles.

The incident proved not only how wide-ranging the nationalist network was, but also how strong were the Nazis' links with it already at that time. The SPD criticised the Minister of Culture for having made comparatively moderate statements about the disruption of the play because of his membership in the Nationalist Club for Saxony (apparently the club had received some of its interior fittings from the same fund which had financed the incident).[137] The Nationalist Club was an elitist organisation that aimed at uniting the activities of the various nationalist clubs and parties in Saxony, including DVP, DNVP, the 'Saxon Association of Fatherland Clubs' and the Nazis. In particular, Manfred von Killinger's connections with the club gave the Nazis respectability in powerful right-wing circles in the state,[138] and even Hitler accepted an invitation and spoke to the club in Dresden in April 1930.[139]

The fact that the workers' theatre movement outside Dresden did not show adequate support for the Hinkemann play and did not react to the intimidation of artists by the far-right – but also the dropping of the play because of a death threat, and the acquittal of the offenders – proved to what extent the left had already been pushed onto the defensive in the cultural sphere by 1924.[140] Here too there was a shift towards an increasingly nationalist environment in which the socialist milieu found it difficult to develop. In the summer of that year the Social Democrats in Leipzig did not dare to play Ernst Toller's anti-war drama *Die Wandlung* in public.[141]

The Saxon Nazis were part of this nationalist conspiracy against socialist plays. In Leipzig they were one of sixteen organisations who disrupted Karl Zuckmayer's *Der fröhliche Weinberg* in early 1926.[142] In the same year the mayor of Leipzig and the town council succumbed to right-wing pressure 'for a German theatre with German plays and German artists', dropping a play which did not fit these criteria.[143] The local Nazis used theatre and culture as a platform to propagate their extreme nationalist ideas. They regularly reviewed the programme of Saxon state theatres in a column in *Der Freiheitskampf*, and made it clear that they regarded theatres as institutes 'that have to preach primarily German feelings and thinking, in contrast to the perverse trends of our time.'[144] The Nazis' Fighting Union for German Culture was devoted to the same aims, and there were also local Nazi theatre groups.[145]

The DNVP and DVP were less radical than the Nazis: in principle both rejected a party political theatre and wanted to leave some room for modern plays. They all agreed, however, upon putting German culture and classic German plays at the heart of theatre programmes.[146] Indeed, on most cultural issues the Saxon Nazis stood in one front with the other bourgeois parties and the government. Most importantly, in late 1930 they all condemned Remarque's book *All Quiet on the Western Front*. They also welcomed the fact that Schieck's government was the first to propose that the Reich censor should ban the Universal Pictures film of the book, which had come out earlier in the year.[147] Instead of distancing itself from the terror of the SA who had initiated brawls during showings of the film in Berlin, the Saxon government argued that the film caused anger among a wide sector in society.[148] A Nazi speaker noted with satisfaction in the Landtag: 'I believe there is no-one in this house who calls himself nationalist who has not rejoiced at the initiative of the Saxon government.'[149] In a follow-up move in early 1931 the majority of the Saxon parliament supported a NSDAP motion to remove the book *All Quiet on the Western Front* from all school libraries and to ban it from the curriculum.[150] Additionally, the Saxon DVP was solidly behind its national party which called for 'state protection against the un-German activities which destroy the moral strength of the nation, against non-culture, dirt and rubbish in radio, theatre and film.' The Saxon government's increasing censorship and surveillance in the final years of the Republic was mainly directed against the socialist milieu and helped to foster the disintegration of the workers' leisure organisations. The little influence Social Democrats had in the programme of state theatres in the 1920s disappeared completely.

During the Third Reich the Nazis continued and eventually perfected this trend towards a Germanic theatre programme.

Private theatres too refrained from any experiments and stuck to proven operas and plays. Entertainment was used for indoctrination and to distract people from the harsh daily life. This was particularly necessary during the Second World War when the Saxon Nazis continued to provide cultural activities, even in the countryside.[151] Because the local leisure associations had been dissolved or had been allowed to wither away in favour of the Nazis' centrally-run mass organisations – the KdF, the *Gau* Film Centre, and the People's Educational Organisation – a local cultural life found it more and more difficult to survive after 1933.[152] Even the cultivation of folk art (*Volkskunst*) and folk studies (*Volkskunde*) was organised through the centrally run cultural organisation *Heimatwerk Sachsen* from 1936 onwards. Local culture and traditions were exploited to enhance nationalist sentiments. In the words of the Nazis, the aim of the *Heimatwerk Sachsen* was 'to strengthen the *völkisch* life with the creative power of the home soil, so that it can master all weathers.'[153]

(iv) The Bourgeois Press and Nazism: Malicious Ink

Most experts accept that the mass media, in particular the press, exerted a powerful influence in political opinion making. Richard Hamilton suggested that the reorientation of the bourgeois press towards the NSDAP helped the party's rise from the late 1920s onwards.[154] However, there have been no systematic investigations about the influence of the press in the rise of National Socialism. Very recently the political scientist Jürgen Falter confirmed that there was a general tendency among bourgeois newspapers to move to the right in the final years of the Republic, and that the press in Protestant rural areas and small towns tended to be NSDAP-friendly or at least not opposed to the party.[155] Overall, Falter concluded that the NSDAP's electoral success was helped by the bourgeois press, but that the influence of the press in voters' decision making was less significant than Hamilton believed.

The press in Saxony was clearly dominated by the bourgeoisie, which published 94 percent of all local newspapers at the end of the Weimar era (see table 4.1). The NSDAP's share of the press was, as in the rest of the Reich, extremely small.[156] The 25,000 copies of *Der Freiheitskampf* competed with more than two million copies of the bourgeois and working-class press.[157] The press in Saxony was much more politicised than in the rest of the

Table 4.1 Newspapers in Saxony in 1931: Party Allegiance and Copies Printed (Number of Newspapers in Brackets for which Number of Copies was Lacking)

	Number	Copies	
NSDAP	5	25,000	(4?)[1]
Nationalist/Right	80	588,791	(31?)
Bourgeois/Neutral	168	606,805	(74?)
Liberal	3	28,300	
SPD/KPD	18	274,200[2]	(6?)
Rest	26	414,300	(17?)
Overall	300	1,937,396	(132?)

[1] The overall number of copies printed by the Saxon Nazis did probably not exceed 40,000 copies; [2] Including the KPD's figure of 119,300 copies, which is likely to be greatly overstated.
Source: Calculated from *Handbuch der deutschen Tagespresse* (1932).

Reich. Whereas a quarter of all newspapers in the Republic were affiliated to a party or a political cause, in Saxony the ratio was nearly half.[158] Particularly striking was that the powerful representation of the Centre Party and the liberals in the middle, which accounted for 13 percent of all newspapers in the Reich, did not exist in Saxony. The only two significant liberal newspapers in the state, the *Oberlausitzer Tageszeitung* (12,300 copies) and the *Zittauer Morgen-Zeitung* (13,000 copies), were published in the eastern towns of Zittau and Neugersdorf. This was an area with a strong liberal milieu which the Nazis found comparatively difficult to infiltrate. Indeed, in late 1930 the Nazis argued that the monopoly of the two liberal papers made the spread of their own press in that region particularly necessary.[159] By contrast, in the electoral district of Chemnitz-Zwickau – which covered roughly a third of the state and was the stronghold of the Saxon Nazis – the political orientation of the press was extremely right wing and nationalistic. More than half of the eighty newspapers in the state which openly declared themselves as supporters of a nationalist or right-wing cause, were published here.

In Saxony, and throughout Germany, newspapers of all political shades of opinion were published in large and medium-sized towns, while independent or right-wing/nationalistic newspapers dominated in the countryside and in small and medium-sized towns.[160] The local press of the left or liberals was only present in fourteen of the more than 200 Saxon towns in which newspapers were published. The only place in Saxony where one of their newspapers had a local monopoly was the above-mentioned liberal *Oberlausitzer Tageszeitung* in Neugersdorf. There was not a single Saxon town where the only local newspaper was left wing.

The poor distribution of the working-class press in rural areas meant that its newspapers were lagging behind in the coverage of local affairs; this allowed the strong bourgeois press, which increasingly sympathised with the Nazis, to exert a quasi-monopoly over public opinion. It is impossible to come up with exact figures, but roughly speaking, even if one copy of an SPD or KPD newspaper was read by three workers every day, half of all Saxon workers would still not have read a newspaper of the left.[161] Many workers read bourgeois newspapers and must have been influenced by them in one way or another. Indeed, after the SPD received some poor results in the local elections in the Erzgebirge in 1929, local activists blamed the press: 'We will only be able to make any progress when we have removed the bourgeois newspapers from working-class houses.'[162]

The right-wing press enjoyed a local newspaper monopoly in forty-seven small and medium-sized towns in Saxony. It is noticeable that most of these places, like Adorf in the Vogtland (NSDAP's poll in July 1932: 60.1 percent), Annaberg (58.2 percent), Marienberg (54.8 percent), Markneukirchen (72 percent) and Thum (59.9 percent), were traditional Nazi strongholds.[163] To be fair, a monopoly for a local right-wing paper was not always a guarantee of Nazi success. For example the NSDAP scored election results far below the state average in the towns of Grimma (35.2 percent), Klassenbach (34.7 percent) and Radeberg (35.2 percent). These were exceptions, however, which can be explained in terms of other factors. A local SPD newspaper was distributed in Grimma (*Volkszeitung für das Muldental*), and Klassenbach and Radeberg (located on the outskirts of Chemnitz and Dresden) possessed a strong SPD press.

Large parts of the bourgeois press helped the Nazis to spread their ideas by frequently announcing their meetings and reporting favourably about them. The *Leipziger Neueste Nachrichten* reviewed a Hitler speech in spring 1926: 'His arguments are delivered carefully ... His speech was intellectually well balanced.'[164] And when in spring 1929 a provincial newspaper argued that the Nazis' attitude regarding private ownership was 'highly questionable',[165] another bourgeois paper quickly allowed the Nazis to publish an article to put things right: 'The National Socialists generally accept the principle of private ownership and put it under state protection.'[166] The respectability of the local NSDAP was enhanced when many nationalist papers supported the Hugenberg-Hitler referendum against the Young Plan at the end of 1929. The Social Democrats warned workers in late November that the 'right-wing' *Chemnitzer Tageblatt*, which normally printed a maximum of 7,000 copies, planned to flood the Erzgebirge with a special edition of 100,000 copies.[167] The warning seemed justified as the referendum was subsequently supported by a substantial number of voters in the electoral district (20.5 percent compared to 13.8 percent in the Reich). After the result became known, the SPD in Chemnitz accused the three local 'independent' bourgeois papers of 'outrageous irresponsibility' because of their 'fierce competition for the favour of swastika and Stahlhelm.'[168] It is worth quoting a longer and not untypical report of a Nazi meeting during the Young campaign by a local bourgeois paper in the Erzgebirge:

> The primary teacher Göpfert from Glauchau, an excellent speaker, spoke to the people of the Erzgebirge about the slavery of the German *Volk* at a meeting of the National Socialists in the 'German House' in Buchholz ... The speaker immediately got down to his theme with great anger and rich economic and political knowledge which was convincing. Whatever one thinks of National Socialism, one had to believe what one heard here. The speaker ended by saying that there was only one conclusion: Men and women should act now! You will have to fight like the soldier at the front to protect the fatherland ... The end of Göpfert's speech released a storm of approval. And this was fitting, because in times like this, whatever party you belong to, you need to judge things as a German first and foremost and yesterday your instinct told you that what this man said was right![169]

Bourgeois newspapers reinforced middle-class anxieties about a socialist revolution, helped to increase the divisions in Saxon society between left and right, and fostered support for the Nazis who stood for violent anti-Marxism. After the First World War they vehemently attacked the SPD government and shared responsibility for its illegal dismissal by the Reich in late 1923. In all subsequent election campaigns, the bourgeois press warned the population about the threat of a socialist revolution if the Marxist parties should win, and produced an enormous flow of stories about alleged 'red terror', disturbances, casualties and looting between the end of 1918 and 1923. In similar fashion, bourgeois newspapers led a continuous campaign against the threat that the 'barbaric' and 'unchristian' Soviet Union posed for Germany and its society. (See also chapter 2 and other sections of this chapter.) Most bourgeois newspapers also rallied behind the 'stab-in-the-back legend' (*Dolchstoß-Legende*), which assumed that the German army was not defeated by the enemy from outside in the First World War, but by the treacherous left from within. The right-wing *Stollberger Anzeiger und Tageblatt* wrote in April 1924: 'The SPD is to blame for the collapse and therefore the shameful *Diktat* (Dictat) of Versailles and the misery of the German *Volk*.'[170] It is striking that those papers who were most vehement with these kinds of accusations were also the first papers to sympathise with the local Nazi movement.

After 1923 all bourgeois papers made enormous efforts to prevent another Marxist government. Before 1930 they rarely expressed an explicit preference for any party in this task. (See section [i] of this chapter for similarities with bourgeois clubs.) Typical was the advice of the right-wing *Oelsnitzer Volksbote* before the 1929 state elections: 'Vote for whom you want, but do not vote for the Communists and Social Democrats. We all have to die one day, but it does not have to be through mass murder or starvation as in Soviet-Russia.'[171] When the economic situation deteriorated at the end of the 1920s, an increasing number of right-wing/nationalistic papers, particularly in rural areas, became sympathetic to the NSDAP. The Nazis pronounced the same anti-Marxist slogans and the same vision of a *Volksgemeinschaft* as other parts of the nationalist milieu. Many papers joined the Nazi bandwagon because it represented a fresh political force with no responsibilities for the political system, whereas the traditional parties and organisations had lost their credibility over the years. The nationalist *Obererzgebirgische Zeitung* reported on a Nazi meeting with the slogan 'Against Corruption! – Never again a Soviet Saxony'. This slogan could have come from any bourgeois or conservative party; however, as the paper argued: 'Whereas other parties do not seem to care, the NSDAP is active against the slavery of Germany.'[172] In early 1930 the *Werdauer Zeitung* turned against Hindenburg after he had failed to join the Hugenberg-Hitler referendum. The paper explained: 'Germany needs a fresh and energetic man as president who is in the prime of his life … We cannot afford to have someone as head of the Reich who is only following representative functions!'[173] Henceforth, the *Werdauer Zeitung* stood at the side of the Nazis as their 'undaunted fighting partner'.[174]

There was widespread disappointment that the NSDAP did not join the bourgeois coalition government – the 'anti-Marxist' front – after the 1929 state elections. But this did not hamper the Nazis' increasing prominence among the nationalist milieu. In fact, the Nazis became more and more successful in 'popularising' the nationalist slogans outside the original boundaries of the nationalist milieu. The result was that a growing number of papers threw their support behind the NSDAP. The *Crimmitschauer Anzeiger* put forward the commonly repeated threats of a Marxist government before the 1929 state elections, but did not declare any specific preference among the bourgeois parties.[175] A year later, the paper rejoiced at the Nazis' stunning performance in the June 1930 state elections ('The victory is ours!') and praised Nazi propaganda and the fact that the NSDAP was not linked with the corrupt system.[176] The Nazis, who had complained about a lack of support from the bourgeois press until late 1930,[177] had less and less reason to do so thereafter.

Jürgen Falter rightly points out that even if one establishes a link between the political leaning of the local press and the electoral success of the NSDAP, it is difficult to determine cause and effect. Was the local press National Socialist because most of its readers were, or was it the other way around?[178] So far we have mainly looked at cases where the bourgeois press was instrumental in spreading nationalist ideas and introducing the Nazi party to its readers. The findings suggest, however, that it was more of a two-way process, which reflected the continuous radicalisation of society. Several local newspapers were more or less forced to adopt a more lenient line towards the NSDAP in the face of its increasing popularity among its readers. Before the September 1930 Reichstag election the 'independent' *Zwickauer Tageblatt* refused to accept National Socialist advertisements or announcements for meetings which were supplemented with 'no entry for Jews' or were in any way anti-Semitic. This changed with the Nazis' electoral gains. According to the Nazis: 'Thereafter the *Zwickauer Tageblatt* had to adopt a friendlier line towards us, albeit reluctantly ... only out of instinct for survival, not because of conviction.'[179] Furthermore, the Social Democrats argued that the *Allgemeine Zeitung* in Chemnitz had supported the Hugenberg-

Hitler referendum at the end of 1929 mainly because local industrialists had backed it and due to its declining subscriptions: 'Subscribers left in their thousands because the attitude of the paper was not sufficiently nationalistic.'[180]

The Nazis faced severe problems when they were not supported by the local bourgeois press. One of their meetings in the Erzgebirge in 1926 was poorly attended because the local newspaper carrying the meeting announcement had been delivered too late.[181] The Nazis also blamed the unsympathetic press in Leipzig for their difficulties there and concluded: 'In no large city in Saxony is there more need for the spread of the National Socialist press than in Leipzig.'[182] It is true that the largest Saxon papers, *Leipziger Neueste Nachrichten* (180,000 daily copies) and the *Dresdner Neueste Nachrichten* (110,000 copies), and many other bourgeois papers did not support the NSDAP. Nevertheless, they often sympathised with its nationalist ideology, appeared to be as helpless as the traditional parties in providing a vision of a brighter future, and were often not explicit enough about the Nazis' radicalism and violence, and about what a Nazi state would look like. The fact that most bourgeois newspapers increasingly withheld any criticism against the NSDAP, was crucial in making the Nazis respectable in Saxon society. Those influential bourgeois circles who felt uneasy about Nazi domination faced the dilemma that the movement which they had once helped to prominence, suddenly seemed to have acquired a powerful monopoly over attitudes and visions that had largely come from a loosely united nationalist milieu with which they shared many sentiments. It was like a snowball they had started to roll down the hill but which had turned into an avalanche which they could no longer control. No-one dared to step in its way from fear being overrun by it. The warnings of the *Dresdner Neueste Nachrichten* (*DNN*) on the day of the July 1932 Reichstag election were half-hearted and too late, and expressed the dilemma:

> The greatest danger a state can face is rule by a single dominating party or even a party dictatorship ... Hatred, or the stirring up of hatred, will not provide any political solution. This can only be achieved by the *Volksgemeinschaft* which will remove hatred and the belief in panaceas.[183]

This cautious and comparatively sensitive approach, however, lost the *DNN* reader, while the local Nazi press was thriving on their simple and aggressive language.[184]

The Third Reich brought enormous changes for the press, and Saxony was no exception. Working-class newspapers – but also bourgeois papers with a liberal-democratic tradition – were seized and incorporated into the Nazi press machinery which grew considerably.[185] Roughly speaking, in 1931 there was one copy of a Saxon Nazi newspaper for every 142 Saxon voters, by 1935 there was one copy for every twenty-two adults. Nevertheless, the increase of the Nazi press did not match the overall decline in newspapers and copies printed. The *Sopade*'s most conservative estimate is that between 1932 and 1935 the number of newspapers in Saxony declined by about 15 percent,[186] and the number of copies in print went down by around 17 percent.[187]

The expansion of the Nazi press had its limits, though, and again it became clear that the Nazis found it very difficult to change people's habits, in this case the reading of their traditional bourgeois newspaper. The larger Nazi newspapers often only grew at the expense of their own smaller provincial papers, of which many folded in 1935. Even the flag-ship of the Saxon Nazi press – *Der Freiheitskampf* in Dresden – was fighting for readers in mid-1935 – while the circulation of the DNN was up to 100,000 again.[188] Strong competition from the bourgeois newspapers forced the Saxon Nazis to issue statements such as the *Dresdner Anzeiger* having no right to call itself a National Socialist daily paper.[189] In a move to appease the population, however, the Saxon Nazis decreed that no-one could be forced to subscribe to a Nazi newspaper, and that the subscription to such a paper should not influence getting a job or any other favours.[190] Although the official Nazi press reached as similar a proportion as the bourgeois press in some areas of Germany, in Saxony this was not the case. In October 1935 the 159,850 copies of Saxon Nazi papers still faced 927,715 copies of the bourgeois press.[191] To be exact, although not all of these bourgeois papers used the same aggressive, violent, racist and anti-Semitic language as *Der Freiheitskampf* (which helps to explain their success compared with the Nazi papers), these bourgeois papers had lost much of their traditional character, had become static and had increasingly turned into the mouthpiece of Nazi policies.

(v) The NSDAP and the Bourgeois Parties: A Maggot in an Apple

The NSDAP was the direct beneficiary of the dramatic collapse of the bourgeois parties in Saxony during the final years of the Weimar era (see also chapter 5 [iii]). This was the end of a process which had started in the mid-1920s with the remarkable political fragmentation of the bourgeoisie: this included the decline of the 'traditional' bourgeois parties (DDP, DVP and DNVP) and the simultaneous emergence of bourgeois special-interest parties (VRP, SLV and WP), and the NSDAP.[192] During the 1929 state election the overall share of the vote for the bourgeois parties still accounted for 46.3 percent – only a minor loss compared with the December 1924 Reichstag elections. Henceforth, however, the bourgeois vote started to decline sharply: during the June 1930 state elections the traditional bourgeois parties lost 9 percent – adding to the 17.3 percent they had lost between 1924 and 1929 – whilst the vote for the still-growing number of splinter parties (the declining VRP, SLV and WP were joined by VNR and CSVD) only rose slightly. By July 1932, the traditional bourgeois parties were decimated to a total of 8.9 percent and the splinter parties had more or less vanished.

When the Nazi movement started to grow noticeably in early 1929, the bourgeois parties showed interest and frequent signs of sympathy. The Nazis were seen as belonging to the nationalist anti-Marxist front. After the NSDAP won five seats and a key position in parliament in May 1929, however, it became clear that the Nazis had their own ambitions. They did not hesitate to disturb the fragile political status quo in parliament – which favoured the bourgeoisie – in order to strengthen their own power. An increasingly unstable relationship between NSDAP and bourgeois parties developed. The Nazis tolerated the DVP-led Bünger government (see document 8), but they continuously threatened to bring it down when their demands were not met. Eventually the Nazis initiated Bünger's resignation in February 1930, and did not show any willingness to overcome the state of 'political limbo' in the following months. Indeed, they helped to bring down the newly formed Schieck government in May, when they withdrew their promised toleration after only fifteen days.

Whilst the bourgeois parties disliked the Nazis' opportunistic strategy, they needed their parliamentary support and also shared many values with them. When one looks at how toughly the bourgeois parties dealt with their Marxist counterparts, one cannot fail to notice their overall extremely moderate stance towards the Nazis who, after all, had pursued consistent and vicious attacks on their parties and leaders, and had helped to bring down two of their governments. During the June 1930 state election campaign a national German newspaper commented about a 'simply laughable neutrality' which the DVP displayed towards the Nazis despite being fiercely attacked by them.[193]

The NSDAP became the second largest party in these elections and seemed in an even stronger bargaining position than before. Indeed, six bourgeois parties – WP, DVP, DNVP, SLV, VRP and CSVD – allied with the NSDAP, hoping to appoint Krugg von Nidda (DNVP) as Prime Minister, with Gregor Straßer (NSDAP) as Minister of the Interior at his side.[194] During this period the Saxon Nazis gave moderate and conciliatory speeches in parliament and emphasised their commitment to legal means.[195] Furthermore, the NSDAP's impressive victory in the September *Reichstag* elections seemed to increase their bargaining position. In the end, however, a political truce developed against the NSDAP: two 'liberal' parties (DDP and VNR, who later united to form the German State Party; *Deutsche Staatspartei*) and the SPD tolerated Schieck's 'neutral cabinet of experts' without Nazi participation in order to prevent the formation of the Nidda-Straßer government.[196] At that moment this was the only option left to continue parliamentary government in Saxony and sealed the Nazis' fate as a powerless parliamentary force until March 1933. The Nazis were fuming and revived their parliamentary obstruction. But while they continued their extremely aggressive behaviour against the left, they always kept a level of conciliation towards the bourgeoisie. Whenever the NSDAP tried to topple the Schieck government with referenda or votes of no confidence, it was also keen to emphasise that this was a move against the system and nothing against members of the government personally, who were 'men of honour'.[197]

After the coalition negotiations with the Nazis collapsed in October 1930, the parliamentary DVP began to distance itself from the NSDAP. The problems their colleagues had with Frick in Thuringia became increasingly evident. To be exact, most Saxon DVP members would have preferred to cooperate with the Nazis. A grass-roots revolt forced the resignation of their parliamentary leader because the DVP members of parliament had failed to support the Nazi candidate Erich Kunz for President of the Saxon parliament in late 1930.[198] Additionally, the call of the Saxon DVP for a more aggressive foreign policy under the slogan 'away with Versailles' emphasised its break with Stresemann's conciliatory policy and its drift to the right from late 1930 onwards.[199]

More than any other bourgeois party, the DNVP cooperated with the NSDAP and undermined the democratic system during the Weimar years. This was not surprising: in parliament, a DNVP speaker even described his party as the 'spiritual home' of the NSDAP.[200] The DNVP used all of its influence to bring about the overthrow of the left-wing government in Saxony in October 1923, and when the NSDAP was declared illegal after Hitler's Beerhall putsch, the Saxon DNVP proposed a motion in parliament to reverse the ban.[201] In mid-1929 a member of the DNVP declared that democracy had failed in Saxony and that it was 'simply a contradiction to implement a system, which had developed in foreign countries, under German conditions and with German characteristics', and demanded a constitution that guaranteed a strong executive.[202] From the anti-Young campaign onwards, both parties frequently allied in the Landtag and local councils to attack the democratic system. A leader of the Saxon DNVP hailed the NSDAP's national breakthrough in September 1930 as a political turning point: 'It was a great, impressive victory for the National Socialists ... The outcome of these elections is the clear awakening of our nation and the victorious penetration of the national idea into the masses.'[203]

It did not really matter to the fate of the bourgeois parties if they cooperated with the NSDAP, or kept a certain distance. The outcome was the same: the Nazis swallowed up most of their voters by 1932. The anti-Republican DNVP and SLV had more or less become obsolete in the face of the more united, determined, dynamic and fresh Nazi party who had put itself at the head of the nationalist milieu, and was not burdened by past failures and collaboration with the Weimar system.[204] Those bourgeois parties who supported Schieck's government from late 1930 onwards – DDP, DVP, WP, CSVD, VRP and VNR – had clearly failed to provide solutions in the crisis and had lost the trust of their constituencies. When the slump worsened in the early 1930s it became clear that the special interest parties had been unable to fulfil the expectations of those who had deserted their traditional bourgeois parties. Meanwhile, the middle classes possessed a completely splintered political representation which was even less able to respond to their social and economic interests than before.

Most of the bourgeois parties clung to a system which their radicalised traditional voters had already abandoned. The WP, for instance, had risen to prominence in Saxony from 1926 onwards because it seemed to offer the old middle class a new economic representation, it was militantly anti-Marxist and a strong proponent of a united bourgeois front against the left, and because it also held anti-capitalist and anti-Republican views.[205] Being part of the Saxon government between 1926 and 1930 and tolerating it thereafter, however, alienated its increasingly desperate constituency. For instance, although the WP demanded tougher action from the Saxon government over the misery in the border region in 1931, it acknowledged that some of the government's measures had 'an easing effect'.[206] More importantly, the WP's continuous support of Brüning's Reich government led to a disintegration of the party in Saxony: in summer 1931 the WP's three Saxon district organisations seceded from the party and reconstituted themselves as the Saxon Business Party, and six months later its two leading members joined the DNVP.[207] By July 1932 the Nazis had more or less absorbed the WP's previous electorate.

It was crucial that all bourgeois parties – as well as the SPD and KPD – pursued an overall passive economic strategy during the slump: they stuck to an orthodox economic policy that adhered to balancing the budget and did not allow for large investment programmes (to 'kick-start' the economy).[208] In a typical fashion, the local WP emphasised its contribution in 'fighting every extravagant spending policy with firm determination' and bringing about a balanced state budget in mid-1931.[209] The right-wing bourgeois parties disliked the principle of state intervention in the economy. The government believed that Saxony itself was unable to overcome the economic crisis and focused much of its energy into lobbying the Reich government – to little avail – to help Saxony with its special crisis.[210] Although the organised working class supported an active role of the state in the economy, it also failed to come up with a concept to tackle the specific problems of Saxony's economic structure. The SPD's work programmes were limited to meeting realistic spending requirements, whilst the KPD attempted to hasten the demise of the capitalist system by pursuing a policy of obstruction during the slump.

Whilst the Saxon Nazis supported many government measures to tackle some of the most pressing problems caused by the depression, they also attacked them as a limited and short-sighted response, and argued that only a radical reform of the existing system (e.g., a tax reform) and large-scale programmes financed by budget deficits (e.g., work programmes) would ensure long-term growth and stability.[211] The Nazis combined these Keynesian economics with what William Brustein called 'nationalist-etatist thinking': state socialism, autarkic development and *Lebensraum* (also see documents 9–10).[212] The Nazis were the only ones who offered an innovative economic programme that presented some kind of hope to overcome the slump. The Saxon Nazi leader Erich Kunz elaborated in September 1930:

> We National Socialists have never believed that it was enough to throw a few beggar Pennies to the unemployed every now and then, a few pittance Pennies which overcome the misery only for a moment ... The most important factor in solving their misery does not lie in the further expansion or a rise of the insurance or the social benefit, but the emphasis lies solely on the fact that in the end one has to do something to create new employment and income opportunities with a different tax course than the current one.[213]

Kunz demanded the lowering of the tax burden for some groups and the increase of tax on capital invested in the stock exchange. More generally, the Nazis' most important economic statement, Gregor Straßer's Immediate Economic Programme from May 1932, publicly challenged Brüning's deflationary policies and suggested a massive public works programme and autarkic development.[214]

Whilst the pro-government parties' approach in economic affairs differed sharply from that of the NSDAP – indeed they expressed extreme scepticism that the Nazis would be able to satisfy their constituencies in a Third Reich[215] – many of their other views (particularly nationalist values) were similar to that of the Nazis. When the Saxon CSVD declared its aims in 1930, they could have come from the mouth of a Nazi follower: to fight 'demonic Marxism' and to 'build a *Volksgemeinschaft*' within the nation in order to 'gain national freedom for our *Volk* externally.'[216] Step by step the government and the other bourgeois parties moved away from the Republican system. After the SA was banned in spring 1932, the 'neutral' Schieck government proposed that Berlin should simultaneously ban the *Reichsbanner*,[217] the largest democratic organisation in support of the Republic. The Saxon government also exploited emergency decrees of the Reich in June 1932, banning parades of working-class sports clubs, while bourgeois clubs and Nazi organisations seemed to have no problem in following their activities.[218] Finally, in mid-February 1933, all bourgeois parties and the NSDAP united in turning down an SPD motion to go to the High Court regarding the illegal dissolution of the Prussian Landtag by the Reich Commissar.[219] Three weeks before the Nazi seizure of power the SPD was the only party left in Saxony, that was prepared to stand up for the democratic system.

The traditional electorate of the bourgeois parties must have found it a natural progression to switch to the NSDAP at the end of Weimar: all bourgeois parties had failed them in the past and present, and had no vision for the future; all bourgeois parties had cooperated and compromised with a political and economic system that had let them down; all bourgeois parties were moving towards a dictatorial system and Nazism in one way or another; and all bourgeois parties supported the idea of creating a strong and united Germany and of forming a *Volksgemeinschaft*, but only represented small interest groups which seemed a great contradiction to this aim. Before the 1926 state election the attempt by the Stahlhelm and the Young German Order to organise a 'bourgeois consolidation from below' failed. Their efforts to unite 'the so-called "patriotic parties" ... in a crusade to free Saxony – and, by extension, Germany – from the insidious yoke of Marxism ... foundered on Stresemann's refusal to countenance any electoral alliance that might jeopardise the prospects of the "Great Coalition" in the Reich.' The ensuing electoral truce for the duration of the campaign – a 'bourgeois consolidation from above' – 'proved inadequate and failed to protect the Saxon bourgeoisie against the centrifugal forces that more than a decade of economic hardship had unleashed within its midst.'[220] In the early 1930s the accelerating fragmentation of the bourgeois parties and their internal divisions stood in sharp contrast to the emerging National Socialist front.

Parliament became increasingly polarised in the final years of the Republic and the bourgeois parties were clearly disintegrating. Simultaneously, the function of the administration and decent codes of behaviour in society fell apart. For example, a Nazi doctor in the Erzgebirge refused to treat a pregnant women because he was on duty for the local Stormtroopers; he was not prosecuted for this.[221] The SA leader Bennecke noted in late 1931: 'Some things which are legal in one place are illegal in other places. At times one can get the impression that the Saxon administration is in the process of disintegration.'[222]

Although the bourgeois parties in Saxony drifted more and more towards the right, some continued to be cautious about integrating the Nazis into the political decision-making process. This became clear during the elections for the president of the Landtag, when the Nazi candidate – Erich Kunz – repeatedly failed to get elected. In November 1930 a decisive minority of bourgeois members of parliament followed, for the last time, the tradition that the largest faction in parliament should provide the president: they indirectly supported the Social Democrat Weckel as candidate by handing in blank ballot papers.[223] At the end of 1931 Weckel was voted president again because the bourgeois parties put forward a candidate of the WP, and did not support the Nazi Kunz.[224] A year later the same thing seemed to be happening when the bourgeoisie put forward a member of the DNVP, and the NSDAP put forward Kunz again. This time, however, some Nazis supported the DNVP candidate in the second ballot, which secured his election as president with forty votes.[225] Most bourgeois parties had moved further away from standard practices of the Republican system and closer towards an authoritarian solution.

(vi) A Nationalist or Racist Unity?

In October 1929 Killinger warned the left in a speech in parliament: 'There will perhaps come a time ... when we will ... throw at you the cut off heads of your bigwigs.'[226] A month earlier he had stated in a public meeting: 'We reject parliament. It is the system of irresponsibility ... every democracy is rotten.'[227] *Gauleiter* Mutschmann prophesied in Weimar in June 1931: 'The day of reckoning will come and the synagogues will go up in smoke.'[228] Later that year the Nazi Werner Studentkowski put forward an analogy about those who were of 'pure race' and those who were not, by comparing pure-bred dogs with pigs in parliament. He elaborated that one could house-train dogs, but this was not possible with pigs, who were 'normally stabbed.'[229] In the previous parliamentary session the Social Democrats had described a series of Nazi atrocities, including an incident in the town of Riesa, where eight Nazis had ambushed two activists of the organised working class and had stabbed one of them to death.[230] In mid-1932 the Nazi Arno Schreiber declared at a meeting in Dresden: 'If someone shows us his fist we will break it open and will also break his neck. Our slogan is: forward with Adolf Hitler, forward over graves.'[231] And finally, a few days before the March 1933 Reichstag elections *Der Freiheitskampf* promised on its front page that the 'Marxist murder plague will be ruthlessly exterminated!', and screamed: 'We are fed up with voting!'[232] The NSDAP gained 45 percent of the votes in the elections in Saxony.

How do we explain that, despite these open threats and violence, many Saxons, clubs, organisations, newspapers, parties and parts of the state administration supported, sympathised or at least tolerated Nazism? The staff in the sanatorium in Gottleuba (district of Pirna) adopted the Hitler salute in early 1932 (long before Hitler became chancellor), and even the government openly admitted the sympathetic attitude of the police in Chemnitz and Dresden towards the NSDAP.[233] Nazism shared far more beliefs and values with a broad nationalist milieu than most historians seem to realise, while others seem to play down the consequences of generally shared aggressive nationalist sentiments.[234] Lothar Kreyssig, who as a young man belonged to this nationalist milieu in Saxony, reflected with horror in the 1970s upon his and many others' attitudes during the Weimar Republic:

> It was fatal, how natural it was to act 'nationalistic' and to be against anything that was left ... The socialist government in Dresden were dreadful people for us, a disease that had to be overcome as quickly as possible, which in fact also happened. Yet these were respectable people who in my present view had a fantastic attitude.[235]

The nationalist environment provided the breeding ground for Nazism (also see document 18). There was a widespread idolising of everything that was German, and in some respects an exclusion of anything foreign. One swimming club even argued in 1920: 'Sport is not something foreign.'[236] Eleven years later the Nazi Studentkowski claimed in the Saxon parliament that music had no international character but had developed from the spirit of a particular *Volk*.[237] Opinion leaders and influential people of Saxony's elite frequently formed a united 'nationalist front' with the NSDAP. In early 1932 Prime Minister Schieck earned great applause from this group when he demanded that Germany should have 'equal rights with other nations and finally be freed from the *Tributfesseln* [indemnity chains] ... which our honour and conscience cannot bear any longer.'[238] Curt Fritzsche, a member of parliament who had left the DNVP because of its Nazi-friendly line, described two cases in parliament where the Saxon judiciary and police had acted with open sympathy towards Nazism. He concluded that an inquiry into these cases was pointless because a majority of the civil servants took the view that:

> The National Socialist Party is a fine party, after all it is national. If someone uses the word national he immediately encounters favourable assessments by all other people who are nationalist too, and the police officer and the judge tell themselves: nationalist people cannot be criminals, these things are impossible among nationalist people ... After all the National Socialist Workers Party is a legal party! [239]

No-one would deny that the Saxon Nazis stood out for their extremism. However, the commonly held distinction between the 'radical' Nazis and a 'decently behaved' bourgeoisie[240] plays down the bourgeoisie's own radical language, ideas and methods. For instance, the Stahlhelm was not exactly over-sensitive, and the bourgeoisie encouraged the *Reichswehr* to put down the workers' movement mercilessly during the first years of the Republic. When in late 1931 the Saxon Minister of the Interior described clashes between political opponents as 'unworthy of our *Volk*, a *Volk* whose character used to be one of decency and gallantry',[241] the statement did not account for the widespread hatred that existed in Saxon society between various groups, and in particular between the nationalist and the socialist milieus.

After the Saxon bourgeoisie managed to oust the left from power in Dresden at the end of 1923, it faced two basic problems: to keep the left out of power, and to keep their own support bound to their parties. In order to achieve this, the bourgeoisie fostered anxieties about the possibility of a new Soviet-style government in Saxony. Mounting economic pressures, however, led to a gradual fragmentation of the bourgeois party system. Only an increasingly radical rhetoric seemed to be able to rally the bourgeois electorate. A bourgeois newspaper commented approvingly before the state elections in 1929: 'The best method to get a German burgher to the ballot box is, and will continue to be, fear.' [242] Yet several weaknesses of this strategy became obvious during the elections. Even the threat of a 'Soviet Saxony' did not halt the disintegration of the centre. For the first time bourgeois parties could not agree on a united front against the left, and instead, campaigned with single lists and only concluded a vague pact not to attack each other.[243] The threat to their survival forced them temporarily to try their luck with a more independent stance. Henceforth the animosity between various bourgeois parties increased.[244] But it was too late to convince the electorate that the bourgeois parties had given up long-established conventions. Throughout the 1920s the bourgeois parties had pursued an unimaginative and passive political style that had served the interest of local dignitaries. The *Leipziger Neueste Nachrichten* captured this during the 1929 campaign:

> The [bourgeois] party is without its own political will and only a sum of professional organisations. The electorate is composed of professional groups [*Stände*] which ban any winning over of neighbouring groups. The peace between the bourgeois parties [*Burgfrieden*] ... is nothing else than subordination to the command of the professional organisations and a renouncement of the burgher to any political activity. The bourgeois parties on the right therefore do not regard elections as a struggle in which conquests are made in all directions, but as a purely arithmetical occasion whose task it is to wake up followers and move them to the ballot box. The party offices of the right therefore abstain from any programme and any idea.[245]

In the face of an unfolding crisis a growing number of middle-class people – e.g., farmers and artisans – became active and radicalised because they were not able to find help and vision from their traditional politicians.[246] Eventually they began joining the dynamic Nazi party.

The bourgeoisie's integrative anti-Marxist tactics amplified paranoia about a socialist revolution which simply did not match reality. It is true that the Communists worked for a 'Soviet Saxony', but critical observers noticed again and again their overall weaknesses. The KPD's disastrous move to the ultra-radical left in spring 1929 split the Saxon party and hampered its future development.[247] The Communists consistently failed to mobilise even the poor and unemployed to street demonstrations during the economic crisis – the Saxon police repeatedly described the KPD's influence over the unemployed as 'insignificant' – and even Communist officials complained about the 'unsatisfactory situation' (see document 16). Even the SPD – which stood solidly on democratic grounds and distanced itself from the Soviet Union – was branded as a Bolshevik threat. The Saxon Social Democrats publicly rejected this accusation and declared in May 1929: 'Down with Marxism – Never again a Soviet Saxony! cries the Saxon bourgeoisie in reference to the proletarian "reign of terror" in 1923. Saxon Social Democracy has never thought about turning Saxony into a soviet state along the Russian model.'[248] However, the SPD's own language and its inability to scrap its Marxist rhetoric – for instance five days after the above statement the Social Democrats demanded: 'The aim – a red Saxony! The aim of Social Democratic politics is socialism'[249] – did not help to overcome these old prejudices.

The fact that the bourgeoisie equated the KPD and SPD with Soviet style rule also served to enhance one of the bourgeoisie's most important claims: i.e., that any economic competence rested only with them. In order to maintain this crucial assumption, the bourgeoisie was prepared to undermine Social Democratic economic reforms between 1919 and 1923 *per se*. Any economic success that was linked with the left caused envy and fear among the right and even within the left itself. For instance, the setting up of a large, modern American-style cigar factory that brought employment to at least 400 workers in the town of Döbeln during the slump, was strongly resisted by local industrialists and representatives of bourgeois parties.[250] They attacked the new cigar factory for wiping out the traditional small-scale cigar producers in the area and destroying the link between the worker and his product. In reality the bourgeois elite feared that the SPD mayor of Döbeln would reap the success of the cigar factory which would challenge their monopoly on economic and political competence. This dispute was about power. And indeed, when the bourgeoisie regained the leadership of the local council in early 1933 they suddenly argued vehemently in favour of the mechanical production of cigars and used exactly those arguments which they had attacked previously: the creation of new jobs, the fact that cottage industries were out-dated, and that smokers would get a quality product for little money.

The bourgeoisie's integrative tactic of Marxist-bashing failed: it did not prevent their own disintegration, and after the 1930 state elections the bourgeois government was actually tolerated by the SPD. More importantly, it undermined the Republic because it fostered political polarisation and tensions, and kept the SPD – the largest democratic party – out of government. Anti-Marxist hype drew more and more people towards Nazism as the most explicit enemy of the left. The bourgeoisie, which poured out stereotypes year after year – for instance it claimed before the 1929 state elections: 'Two broad fighting fronts face each other: on the one hand international Marxism and on the other hand the national duty towards *Volk* and fatherland'[251] – could not have prepared a better ground for Nazism (whose choice was: 'Marx or Hitler'; see document 12). The radicalisation also made Nazi violence against the organised working class acceptable. Not only was this increasingly seen as a final battle to clean up Marxism once and for all, but in addition, the Stormtroopers made it possible for most people to achieve this task without getting their hands dirty. These developments had important repercussions for the stability of the Nazi dictatorship. The gratitude of the nationalist milieu for the fact that the Nazis had smashed Marxism – in a typical statement one business man said about Hitler in mid-1934: 'the most important thing is that he has freed us from the Marxists'[252] – became one of the most important factors that made these circles supportive of the Third Reich, despite various aspects they disliked.

The nationalist milieu shared sentiments of nationalism, authoritarianism, anti-Marxism and the idea of a *Volksgemeinschaft*. Most members of this milieu had hoped that the Republican system would be replaced by a dictatorship for a long time. During the Weimar Republic Nazism stood out for offering something positive in a nationalist environment that had a predominantly negative perception of the world: the latter was traumatised by humiliating defeat in the war and never fully identified with the political system; it regarded the ongoing modernisation of society as decadent; it focused on past glorious times and had nothing to offer regarding a better future.[253] Furthermore, the inherent divisions of the nationalist milieu go a long way towards explaining why it was much better at destroying things – most importantly the SPD's progressive achievements – than creating something constructive. In contrast to this, the Nazis offered hope and something positive: the vision of a strong and united Germany that would get rid of all the existing problems under their leadership. The fact that the Nazis were political newcomers and seemed justified in attacking corruption, traditional networks of power and compromises, made this message more powerful. The Nazis' whole appearance: their youthfulness, dynamism, and their enormous activity, stood in sharp contrast to any other political group in society – except the most active Communists or Social Democrats.

Besides extreme nationalism and anti-Marxism, there were of course other aspects that assumed an even more important role during the dictatorship: permanent terror and mobilisation, foreign expansion, violent racism and anti-Semitism (also see documents 9 and 19). To what extent did the nationalist milieu support these features? We have seen that the Nazis had certainly not been shy in proclaiming their beliefs and in stating what they intended to do once they were in power (of course their actual record was even more horrific than their brutal warnings). The general knowledge about Nazism before March 1933 has to be taken seriously, not only in terms of explaining its mass support, but also as explaining why the majority of Saxons refused to support it. However, from the reaction of many nationalists in Saxony during the dictatorship – which was negative about certain features – one can assume that many people had not taken everything the Nazis had said literally, and had not comprehended what a Nazi dictatorship would actually mean, with all its consequences. The generally shared sentiments of the nationalist milieu seemed to have clouded some aspects that were more specific to Nazism. Many Saxon nationalists accepted physical violence against the left as a means of clearing out Marxism for good, but were unprepared for the violence and terror that were integral parts of the Nazi dictatorship. More and more people were caught in Nazi coercion, and by spring 1934 even nationalists did not feel 'safe' any more. The police reported a reserved atmosphere in the Erzgebirge because 'many people with good German and national sentiments fall victim of unfounded suspicion.'[254] However, the unbroken fear of Marxism – and in particular Bolshevism from the Soviet Union – continued to make violence against the left acceptable. Most Saxons were also happy to accept violence when it apparently served the unity and strength of the German nation. There was a widespread positive reaction when the SA leadership around Röhm was killed in mid-1934,[255] and when German soldiers conquered foreign countries and subjugated their people in order to establish a greater Germany.[256] When it became clear that Britain refused to strike a peace deal with Hitler in mid-1940, the Security Service reported from Oschatz, near Leipzig, that 'everywhere people spontaneously demand England's total destruction.'[257]

The nationalist milieu had also shared the idea of a *Volksgemeinschaft*. But this was an extremely vague notion which possessed different interpretations, and nobody seemed clear what this meant in practice. The Nazis' realisation of it was initially disliked by many sectors of the nationalist milieu. For instance, industrialists were not interested in giving up any real power in favour of workers: many felt threatened by the DAF – who in their eyes had moved too far to the left – and secretly criticised the Reich government.[258] Many employers were also reluctant to make material sacrifices for the state or to get involved in Nazi indoctrination.[259]

At the heart of Nazi Saxony – as in other regions in Germany – stood violent racism and anti-Semitism. Nazi race ideology very quickly assumed a crucial importance: e.g., from mid-1935 onwards a whole range of students in social and medical professions needed proof of 'Aryan' descent to be able to enter their chosen profession.[260] From the moment the Nazis seized power Saxon Jews were frequently assaulted in public and lost more and more basic rights.[261] Aggressive and violent anti-Semitism was one of the most noticeable public features in many parts of Saxony after March 1933 (although there were many areas, where hardly any Jews lived, that did not experience anti-Semitic indicents). To what extent was violent racism and anti-Semitism new? Were there any links between the nationalist milieu and this most radical Nazi feature? Sifting through the twenty-eight randomly picked bourgeois leisure and professional journals before 1933 (see section [i]), one does not find anything that directly predicted what was to happen during the Third Reich: the 'cleansing of the fatherland' of those regarded as 'unfit' to belong to the healthy body of the nation (*Volkskörper*): the Jews, Gypsies, handicapped, Slavic people, and other groups.[262]

Some nationalist sports clubs, however, indicated that not everybody could belong to the *Volksgemeinschaft*. Although none of these clubs advocated any punishment for those groups that were excluded from the *Volksgemeinschaft*, let alone the killing of them, one could regard this exclusion as a precondition for accepting – or even a low-key acceptance of – the Nazis' implementation of their racial policies. Nearly all nationalist sports clubs regarded sport as part of the education of the youth: a 'people's education ... which will form a race which is strong, life-loving and hard working.'[263] Some clubs suggested that only the physically fit – those who pursued sport and participated in what was regarded as a 'struggle' – could belong to those who aimed 'to bring about the re-birth of our *Volk* on the basis of a healthy body.'[264] The Swimming Club Chemnitz 1892 celebrated the youths' 'healthy and strong core' and made it clear that its purpose was not for the weak: 'A club that wants to nurse its youth deserves to perish. Who needs to be nursed? The weak, the frail, the ill. But the club is no place for infirmity, no sanatorium.'[265]

This kind of thinking was closely linked with attitudes towards health, race and hygiene that had developed since the mid-nineteenth century. Amongst others, this had been sparked off by the rapid process of urbanisation which had led to poverty, slums and the spread of disease.[266] Considering that Saxony was one of the most industrialised and urbanised regions in Europe, it comes as no surprise that leading local officials took a particular interest in these issues. Dresden, frequently also referred to as the 'city of hygiene', was able to look back on various activities and institutions that had focused on hygiene and health since the second half of the nineteenth century. Most importantly, the enormously successful I. International Hygiene Exhibition in 1911 was visited by more than 5 million people. This led to the creation of the extremely active 'Association of the National Hygiene Museum' two years later and made Dresden an international centre in the field. The success was largely based on a new approach that made science accessible for the general public.[267] During the 1920s and 1930s the Association (meanwhile renamed the 'Society of the German Hygiene Museum') enjoyed an international reputation and organised an enormous amount of broadly acclaimed public lectures, exhibitions (which toured nearly all European countries), excursions, films, radio programmes, records, diagrams and three-dimensional biological models.[268] The II. International Hygiene Exhibition in Dresden 1930/31, which took place in the newly opened, specially designed museum, attracted widespread publicity and was proudly mentioned in contemporary publications. Besides the more mainstream topics, however, it also contained (like its predecessor) a section that was based on the more controversial pseudo-science of 'racial hygiene'. In 1911 the aim of the section was described: 'to enhance the valuable genetic make-up with every means and to fight the inferior ones which threaten to spread at the expense of the valuable ones and could lead to a degeneration of the *Volk* ... and to find ways how to prevent an undesirable racial mix ....'[269]

During the 1920s Saxony also gained a reputation for having some of the most extreme proponents of forced sterilisation. The 'sterilisation apostle' Heinrich Boeters, a medical officer in Zwickau, gave maximum publicity to the illegal eugenic sterilisations that he had initiated, in order to campaign for compulsory sterilisation.[270] In 1924 the nationally minded health experts of the Saxon government formulated the 'most radical sterilisation proposals' of any German state and proposed voluntary sterilisation for psychiatric diseases on the basis of 'racial hygiene' and the premise that 'culture inhibited selective processes in society'. The ideas of 'racial hygiene', which had found a fertile breeding ground in Saxony, also had an impact on the local Nazi movement: Professor Philateles Kuhn (director of the Institute of Hygiene at the Technical University in Dresden and one of the leaders of the Nazi movement in eastern Saxony in 1924) and the Nazi *Gauleiter* Mutschmann supported the idea of cleansing and strengthening the body of the nation by forcefully sterilising those who were regarded as 'unfit' to breed and to prevent other 'inferior' races from mixing with the German race.[271] Additionally, The racist *Ostara* movement spread among Saxon Nazi students.[272] Ideas of racial hygiene, however, also started to make inroads into much wider circles. During a field service for the army in 1924 a priest insisted: 'It is decisive for Germany's ascent that the influx of alien blood is avoided.'[273] Meanwhile a Marxist physician in Zwickau argued enthusiastically that racial hygiene could be used to breed socialist tendencies.[274]

Traits of these beliefs became more and more evident over the years, particularly within the nationalist milieu. In 1930 the *Sudetendeutsche* members of the German Singer's Union emphasised the need to cherish and maintain 'German customs, language and descent' in the face of Czech expansion: 'Every village, every school, every club which will be lost will mean an irreplaceable national loss for the Germans.'[275] In early 1932 a local farmers' paper appealed 'to save the German farmers abroad from extinction',[276] and Saxon artisans organised a state meeting under the slogan: 'Living-space for the artisans serves the self-preservation of the nation.'[277]

Even the Saxon government did its part to enhance racist – in this case anti-Czech – sentiments. To be certain, though, economic considerations played a major role in this. In 1931 it sent a detailed questionnaire to villages and towns on the border for a memorandum about 'the predicament of the border region', in an effort to gain more aid from the Reich government in Berlin. The questionnaire not only sought to establish economic decline and misery, but also the 'danger for ... *Deutschtum* on both sides of the border ... and the infiltration of the national *Tschechentums* in areas of originally purely German population.'[278] The response from several border towns in the Erzgebirge underlined the locals' perceived feelings of threat from the Czech nation and their extreme nationalist and racist attitudes. The town of Jöhstadt reported that '*Tschechisierung* [the process of becoming Czech] proceeds in giant strides ... in several decades the border region with purely German population will be infiltrated strongly, maybe even predominantly, by Czechs. A mix with the German population on the German side will be inevitable.'[279] The town of Oberwiesenthal worried that '*Deutschtum* was seriously endangered abroad, and particularly at the border.'[280] In a similar statement – which reminds of the 'blood and earth' (*Blut und Boden*) ideology of Nazism – a DNVP speaker warned in the Saxon parliament in 1932: 'We must not allow our Saxon border region to bleed to death.'[281] The Saxon Nazis, who cleverly mixed economic grievances with their racial theories – for instance in 1928 they stirred up hatred against 'inferior elements from Poland and Slovakia' who worked in the coal mines of the Zwickau district[282] – benefited from these fears and sentiments. They gained 59.5 percent of the vote in Oberwiesenthal, and 54.1 percent of the vote in Jöhstadt in the July 1932 Reichstag elections.

It is difficult to assess how widespread ideas of racial purity and methods for their implementation were discussed and supported in Saxon society during the Third Reich. We have seen above that a growing part of the population had come into contact with, and were receptive to, these ideas before 1933 (to be sure, this still seemed only a minority of Saxons). Overall, it seems that elitist circles – for instance the Leipzig physician Hermann Voss, who wrote in his diary that all Communists should be 'sterilised', and took part in the Nazi killing programme in the east during the Second World war[283] – were the driving force behind racial policies. The majority of Saxons went along with it, particularly since it rarely had a negative impact on themselves. During the war, more and more people seemed prepared to exploit racial categories for the essential decision over the distribution of resources, which could have repercussions over death or survival. A report by the Security Service about the reaction in Leipzig to the toughness of fighting at the eastern front in August 1941 stated:

> The huge numbers of prisoners are a cause of concern. People consider that these sub-humans infected with Bolshewism can hardly be deployed in our industry and agriculture without endangering our own people. So they will have to be fed without doing any work at the expense of our own population, who are in any case already poorly provided for.[284]

When in 1937 several teachers categorised their village population according to racial criteria in the Erzgebirge, however, this sparked off resentments by the local population.[285]

Considering the strong anti-Semitic traditions in Saxony, it is surprising not to find any trace of it among the mainstream bourgeois magazines we have looked at: Jews did not feature in them, let alone receive the blame for the crisis in German society. Anti-Semitic sentiments, however, had a long tradition in the region (see chapter 1 [iv]), and continued to play a part amongst various groups of the nationalist milieu. For instance, a member of the Saxon DNVP made explicit anti-Semitic statements in the Landtag.[286] Although the Saxon Nazis – as in other parts of Germany – curbed their anti-Semitic propaganda from around 1930 onwards, it far from disappeared and anyone who came into contact with Nazism must have been aware of it. For some, this was certainly an important appeal. Contemporary sources suggest that the majority of Saxons were not particularly receptive to the Nazis' aggressive anti-Semitism during the Third Reich – for instance, the American Consul in Leipzig reported that during the events of the *Reichskristallnacht* (Reich Crystal Night) on 10 November 1938 'all of the local crowds observed were obviously benumbed over what had happened'[287] – but that the high level of propaganda and indoctrination had a growing impact over the years (see document 22). In fact, Saxony was a prime example how the influence of one powerful and violent anti-Semite – *Gauleiter Mutschmann* – led to an earlier radicalisation of anti-Semitic measures (e.g., the erection of anti-Semitic signs in nearly all Saxon villages and towns in summer 1935) than in other areas, such as Berlin.[288] There were also those who – as in the rest of Germany – tried to exploit Nazi anti-Semitism to their own advantage: e.g., in the late 1930s Jewish property was very sought-after because it was sold for a quarter of the real value.[289] By the early 1930s, however, parts of the Saxon nationalist milieu were moving more towards supporting a broad Nazi programme of territorial aggrandisement and a vague racial purification than being fixed on the Jewish question.[290]

Notes

1. K. Reimus, ' "Das Reich muß uns doch bleiben!" Die nationale Rechte', in D. Lehnert and K. Megerle, eds., *Politische Identität und nationale Gedenktage. Zur politischen Kultur in der Weimarer Republik*, Opladen, 1989, 231.

2. K. Sontheimer, *Antidemokratisches Denken in der Weimarer Republik. Die politischen Ideen des deutschen Nationalismus zwischen 1918 und 1933*, Munich, 1962, 357f.
3. See especially R. Woods, *The Conservative Revolution in the Weimar Republic*, London, 1996; S. Breuer, *Anatomie der Konservativen Revolution*, Darmstadt, 1993; Sontheimer, *Antidemokratisches Denken*; A. Mohler, *Die konservative Revolution in Deutschland 1918–1932*, 2nd edn., Darmstadt, 1972.
4. E. g. see Jones, 'Middle'; H. Matthiesen, *Bürgertum und Nationalsozialismus in Thüringen. Das bürgerliche Gotha von 1918 bis 1930*, Jena, 1994; Lapp, *Revolution*.
5. K. Tenfelde, 'Die Entfaltung des Vereinswesens während der Industriellen Revolution in Deutschland (1850–1873)', in O. Dann, ed., *Vereinswesen und bürgerliche Gesellschaft in Deutschland, Historische Zeitschrift*, Beiheft 9, Munich, 1984, 96 ff.
6. *Monatliche Rundschau herausgegeben vom Schwimmklub "Chemnitz von 1892"*, Nr. 10, Oktober 1913.
7. *Mitteilungen des Landwirtschaftlichen Kreisvereins für das Sächsische Markgraftum Oberlausitz*, Nr. 90, August 1915 (20.12.1914); *SI*, Nr. 21, 5. August 1914; ibid., Nr. 2, Dezember 1917.
8. E.g. see Heidenreich, *Arbeiterkulturbewegung*, 346; Adam, 'Arbeitermilieu'.
9. *Mitteilungen Schwimmklub Chemnitz 1892*, Nr. 5, Mai 1924.
10. In his investigation about the Black-Forest region Oded Heilbronner did not distinguish between various forms of bourgeois clubs and argued more generally that 'anti-Socialism' was the most important common feature of bourgeois club rhetoric. See O. Heilbronner, 'Der verlassene Stammtisch. Vom Verfall der bürgerlichen Infrastruktur und dem Aufstieg der NSDAP am Beispiel der Region Schwarzwald', *Geschichte und Gesellschaft*, 19 (2) (1993), 183f.
11. *Mitteilungen der Vereinigung Sächsischer Höherer Staatsbeamter e.V.*, Nr. 7/8, Juli/August 1931, 3. For a complete list of all *Mitteilungen* used see Szejnmann, 'Nazis in Saxony', 226.
12. *Mitteilungen für die Reichswehrangehörigen betreffend dem Besuch von Theatern, Lichtspielen und sonstigen Unterhaltungsstätten im Standort Dresden*, Dezember 1932.
13. *SB*, Nr. 26, 30.6.1929.
14. *Sächsische Schützen-Zeitung*, Nr. 1, 1932, 2.
15. *Mitteilungen Schwimmklub Chemnitz 1892*, Nr. 4, April 1932.
16. *Mitteilungen Landwirtschaftlicher Kreisverein Oberlausitz*, Nr. 95, Juli 1920 (18.3.1920).
17. For this see *Mitteilungen der Turn- und Sportgemeinde 1848 Leipzig-Lindenau e.V.*, Dezember 1923; ibid., Nr. 21, 24.5.1924, *Mitteilungen Schwimmklub Chemnitz 1892*, Nr. 9, September 1923; ibid., Nr. 9, September 1932.
18. *Mitteilungen Sportgemeinde Leipzig-Lindenau*, Nr. 7, 20.2.1932.

19. Schmid, 'Die Märzfeiern für die Opfer des Kapp-Putsches in Leipzig', in Keller, *Feste*, 243.
20. *Mitteilungen Sportgemeinde Leipzig-Lindenau*, Nr. 21, 24.5.1924.
21. Similarly, the Saxon ATSB was keen not to advocate a preference for any party on the left in the 1920s. Only when the divisions between SPD and KPD deepened and the slump unfolded in the late 1920s did it openly support the SPD. See Heidenreich, *Arbeiterkulturbewegung*, 394, 408f.
22. *Mitteilungen. Offizielles Organ des Polizei-Sport-Vereins 21 Leipzig (e.V.)*, Oktober 1931, Heft 10, 5.
23. E.g. see *Mitteilungen Sportgemeinde Leipzig-Lindenau*, Nr. 32, 13.8.1932.
24. *VdSL*, 5. Wp, 88. Sitzung, 18.10.1932, 3917.
25. *Mitteilungen Schwimmklub Chemnitz 1892*, Nr. 6, Juni 1920.
26. *Mitteilungen Sportgemeinde Leipzig-Lindenau*, Nr. 4, 26.1.1924.
27. E. g. see (*Mitteilungen*) *Polizei-Sport-Verein 21 Leipzig*, Januar 1933, Heft 1; *Monatliche Mitteilungen des Allgemeinen Turnvereins Leipzig-Schleußig e.V.*, Nr. 5/6, Mai/Juni 1933, 4.
28. For this see *Mitteilungen Sportgemeinde Leipzig-Lindenau*, Nr. 32, 13.8.1932; ibid., Nr. 48, 3.12.1932; ibid., Nr. 51, 24.12.1932
29. *DVZ*, Nr. 35, 11.2.1929; Adam, 'Arbeitermilieu', 232.
30. Lapp, *Revolution*, 163ff. For the radicalisation of Saxon farmers see chapter 2 (v).
31. Lobmeier, 'Mittelschichten', 90. For the emergence of special interest parties see section (v).
32. Compare the similarities with bourgeois newspapers in section (iv) below.
33. *Sächsische Handwerker und Gewerbezeitung*, 27.4.1929. Quoted from Lobmeier, 'Mittelschichten', 83.
34. *Erzgebirgische Nachrichten und Anzeigenblatt*, Nr. 121, 28.5.1929.
35. Quoted from Lobmeier, 'Mittelschichten', 91.
36. Lapp, Revolution, 202f.
37. *Zeitung für Meißner Hochland*, Nr. 264, 12.11.1931.
38. *Mitteilungen Vereinigung Sächsischer Höherer Staatsbeamter*, Nr. 10, Oktober 1930; ibid., Nr. 11, November 1930.
39. Ibid., Nr. 7/8, Juli/August 1931; ibid., Nr. 9, September 1932.
40. See C.-C.W. Szejnmann, 'Sächsische Unternehmer und die Weimarer Demokratie. Zur Rolle der sächsischen Unternehmer in der Zeit der Weltwirtschaftskrise und des Aufstiegs des Nationalsozialismus', in U. Hess and M. Schäfer, eds., *Unternehmer in Sachsen. Aufstieg – Krise – Untergang – Neubeginn*, Leipzig, 1998, 165–79.
41. *SI*, Nr. 11, 16.3.1929, 249.
42. R. Neebe, *Großindustrie, Staat und NSDAP 1930–1933*, Göttingen, 1981, 64. For Wittke, also see J. Adolph, 'Der VSI-Vorsitzende Wilhelm Wittke', in Hess, *Unternehmer*, 181–92.
43. *SI*, Nr. 9, 1.3.1930, 195.

44. Ibid., Nr. 26, 28.6.1930, 617.
45. Ibid., Nr. 16, 18.4.1931, 270.
46. Ibid., Nr. 11, 12.3.1932, 113.
47. Ibid., Nr. 17, 23.4.1932, 199.
48. D. Abraham, *The Collapse of the Weimar Republic. Political Economy and Crisis*, 2nd. edn., London, 1986.
49. H.A. Winkler, *Mittelstand, Demokratie und Nationalsozialismus. Die politische Entwicklung von Handwerk und Kleinhandel in der Weimarer Republik*, Cologne, 1972, 171ff.
50. *Mitteilungen des Gewerbeverbandes in der AH Borna e.V.*, Nr. 1, Januar 1932, 2.
51. Ibid., Nr. 11, November 1932, 5. In the KH Chemnitz the NSDAP won 68.5 percent of the vote among the 'crafts' trade councils, and 82.1 percent among the 'trade and business' trade councils. See Lobmeier, 'Mittelschichten', 104.
52. *Mitteilungen Chemnitzer Bezirksverein des VdJ Elektrotechnischer Verein Chemnitz*, Nr. 1 Januar 1932.
53. Heidenreich, *Arbeiterkulturbewegung*, '340f.
54. *Mitteilungen des Landesverbandes der christlichen Elternvereine Sachsens, e.V. für die Vorstände der christlichen Elternvereine*, Nr. 4–6, 2, Quartal 1933.
55. E.g. see *SI*, Nr. 22, 3.6.1933.
56. *Sopade*, Juli 1937, 962f.
57. For a summary of recent publications see M. Maurer, 'Feste und Feiern als Historischer Forschungsgegenstand', *Historische Zeitschrift*, 253 (1991), 101–130. Also see G.L. Mosse, *The Nationalization of the Masses. Political Symbolism and Mass Movements in Germany from the Napoleonic Wars Through the Third Reich*, New York, 1975.
58. Heß, 'Jubiläen', 280.
59. STA D, MdI, Nr. 11126/1, November 1928.
60. *NSfS*, Nr. 47, 20.11.1927.
61. For this see Lapp, *Revolution*, 65–71.
62. Bramke, 'Der erste Reichskriegertag in Leipzig 1925', in Keller, *Feste*, 215, 225.
63. STA D, AH Glauchau, Nr. 24, 18.7.1923.
64. STA D, SäStKa, Nr. 128.
65. *VdSL*, 4. Wp, 18. Sitzung, Dienstag, 10.12.1929.
66. There were, however, an increasing number of large protest rallies by artisans, shopkeepers and houseowners. See Lapp, *Revolution*, chap. 7; also see section (v).
67. STA D, KH Dresden, Nr. 262, Januar 1927.
68. STA D, SäStKa, Nr. 131. See also Lapp, *Revolution*, 138ff.
69. *NSfS*, Nr. 50, 11.12.1927.
70. The NSDAP gained 34.2 percent of the vote in Ruppertsgrün in the May 1929 state elections.
71. *Deutsche Zeitung*, Nr. 255, 7.6.1922.

72. *Mitteilungen Schwimmklub Chemnitz* 1892, Nr. 9, September 1932, 74.
73. Heidenreich, *Arbeiterkulturbewegung*, 394.
74. For the following see *VdSL*, 5 Wp, 42. Sitzung, 19.5.1931, 1542, 1554.
75. *FK*, Nr. 105, 7.5.1931.
76. STA D, MdI, Nr.11126/6, Juli 1925.
77. C.J. Elliot, 'The Kriegervereine and the Weimar Republic', *Journal of Contemporary History*, 10 (1)(1975), 114.
78. STA D, MdI, Nr. 19088, SA 1928–1932.
79. *FK*, Nr. 34, 9.9.1930.
80. For this see *NSDAP Markneukirchen*, 29.
81. Also see Schmid, 'Märzfeiern', 230f.
82. *SVBl*, Nr. 40, 21.5.1935.
83. Ibid., Nr. 19, 8.3.1935.
84. STA D, AH Schwarzenberg, Nr. 1952, Juni–Juli 1935.
85. *Sopade*, Februar 1938, 144.
86. Ibid., Juni 1938, 561.
87. STA D, AH Schwarzenberg, Nr. 1951, Oktober 1934.
88. Boberach, *Meldungen*, 15 Oktober 1942, 4336.
89. *Sopade*, April 1934, 415; ibid., Februar 1936, 162f.
90. *SVBl*, Nr. 10, 5.2.1935; ibid., Nr. 39, 17.5.1935.
91. *Neue Leipziger Zeitung*, Nr. 88, 29.3.1933.
92. *VdSL*, 11. Sitzung, 4 Wp, 23.10.1929.
93. *SI*, Nr. 13, 1.4.1933.
94. STA D, MdI, Nr. 11126/4, April 1931; A. Dornheim, 'Emotionalisierung, Uniformierung und Militarisierung – nationalsozialistische Feiern in Leipzig', in Keller, *Feste*, 295.
95. Schmid, 'Märzfeiern', 247f.
96. Poste, *Schulreform*, 584f.
97. Ibid., 42f.
98. Heidenreich, *Arbeiterkulturbewegung*, 116f.
99. Fabian, *Klassenkampf*, 100ff; R. Lipinski, *Der Kampf um die politische Macht in Sachsen*, Leipzig, 1926, 19ff.
100. Poste, *Schulreform*, 181f.
101. Heidenreich, *Arbeiterkulturbewegung*, 194.
102. *Sächsischer Lehrerverein*, 1925, 84. Quoted from Poste, *Schulreform*, 202.
103. *Sächsische Schulzeitung. Zeitung des Sächsischen Lehrervereins und seiner Zweigvereine*, Nr. 28, 1919, 377f. Quoted from Poste, *Schulreform*, 46.
104. *FK*, Nr. 189, 15.8.1931.
105. *Mitteilungen des Sächsischen Philologenvereins*, Nr. 7, 1922, 2; ibid., Nr. 1, 1923, 2. See Poste, *Schulreform*, 185f, 215.

106. *Neue Sächsische Schulzeitung*, Nr. 4, 23.2.1927. Quoted from Poste, *Schulreform*, 228.
107. SPD, *Vier Jahre Sächsische Politik*, 226.
108. D. Gernert, *Schulvorschriften für den Geschichtsunterricht im 19./20. Jahrhundert. Dokumente aus Preußen, Bayern, Sachsen, Thüringen und Hamburg bis 1945*, Cologne, 1994, 214f.
109. Ibid., 222.
110. Poste, *Schulreform*, 208f.
111. D. Klenke, *Die SPD-Linke in der Weimarer Republik: Eine Untersuchung zu den regionalen organisatorischen Grundlagen und zur politischen Praxis und Theoriebildung des linken Flügels der SPD in den Jahren 1922–32*, 2 vols., Münster, 1983, 836–40.
112. *Mitteilungen der christlichen Elternvereine Sachsens, e. V. für die Vorstände der christlichen Elternvereine*, Nr. 2, 2. Quartal 1931, 1.
113. *FK*, Nr. 109, 12.5.1931.
114. Ibid., Nr. 112, 16.5.1931.
115. *Die Christliche Schule*, 1.3.1933. Quoted from Poste, *Schulreform*, 204f.
116. Poste, *Schulreform*, 229.
117. Ibid., 256.
118. *VdSL*, 5. Wp, 29. Sitzung, 10.2.1931; ibid., 30 Sitzung, 12.2.1931.
119. Gernert, *Schulvorschriften*, 224ff; *Sopade*, Juni 1937, 869f.
120. *Sopade*, Februar 1936, 192; ibid., Juni 1937, 869f.
121. Ibid., Februar 1936, 170.
122. Noakes, *Home Front*, 406.
123. D.J.K. Penkert, *Inside Nazi Germany. Conformity, Opposition and Racism in Everyday Life*, London, 1987, 165ff.
124. *VdSL*, 3 Wp, 96. Sitzung, 6.12.1928, 3563.
125. *Mitteilungen für die Kirchengemeinden Nieder- und Oberwürschnitz*, Nr. 2, Februar 1930.
126. G. Prater, *Kämpfer Wider Willen. Erinnerungen des Landesbischofs von Sachsen D. Hugo Hahn aus dem Kirchenkampf 1933–1945*, Metzingen, 1969, 17.
127. *VdSL*, 5 Wp, 42. Sitzung, 19.5.1931, 1543ff.
128. E.g. see *FK*, Nr. 123, 28.5.1932.
129. *Mitteilungen Kirchengemeinde Nieder- und Oberwürschnitz*, Nr. 6, Juni 1934.
130. Ibid., Nr. 5, Mai 1934; *Sopade*, Juni 1935, 681; ibid., August 1937, 1183f.
131. STA D, AH Schwarzenberg, Nr. 1955, Mai 1937.
132. *Sopade*, November 1935, 1293; ibid., April 1937, 499.
133. Boberach, *Meldungen*, 7. Februar 1940, 734.
134. *Sopade*, April 1937, 504.
135. Heidenreich, *Arbeiterkulturbewegung*, 203ff. Ernst Toller was a German Marxist poet and dramatist (1893–1939).
136. Ibid., 205.

137. SPD, *Vier Jahre Sächsische Politik*, 233.
138. BDC, Mutschmann; Killinger.
139. STA D, MdI, Nr. 11126/4.
140. SPD, *Vier Jahre Sächsische Politik*, 233; Heidenreich, *Arbeiterkulturbewegung*, 205, 321.
141. Heidenreich, *Arbeiterkulturbewegung*, 325.
142. Ibid., 326.
143. Ibid., 328.
144. *SB*, Nr. 6, 10.2.1929.
145. *FK*, Nr, 88, 12.11.1930; ibid., Nr. 201, 29.8.1931.
146. T. Liebsch, 'Dresdner Theaterkrise 1929–1933', *Dresdner Hefte*, 12 (39) (1994), 52–63.
147. *VdSL*, 5. Wp, 18. Sitzung, 11.12.1930; ibid., 30. Sitzung, 12.2.1931.
148. Heidenreich, *Arbeiterkulturbewegung*, 217.
149. *VdSL*, 5. Wp, 18. Sitzung, 11.12.1930, 688.
150. Heidenreich, *Arbeiterkulturbewegung*, 218; also 217, 314ff.
151. Boberach, *Meldungen*, 13 Februar 1941, 1995.
152. Ibid., 1996.
153. G. Altmann, 'Von der Löffelschmiede zu den Krauss-Werken im erzgebirgischen Schwarzenberg. Ein Unternehmen in den politischen Umbrüchen und technologischen Wandlungen des 20. Jahrhunderts', in Hess, *Unternehmer*, 201.
154. R.F. Hamilton, *Who voted for Hitler?*, Princeton, 1982.
155. Falter, *Wähler*, 330ff.
156. In the Reich 2.6 per cent of all newspapers sympathised officially with the NSDAP, in Saxony only 1.3 per cent. All figures in this section stem from the end of 1931. See *Handbuch der deutschen Tagespresse*, 1932, here 27, 39.
157. However, it is crucial not to neglect the influence of the wider network of the *völkisch* press in Saxony, e.g., Theodor Fritsch's anti-Semitic publishing house in Leipzig (*Hammer Verlag*). For Thuringia see J.H. Ulbricht, 'Kulturrevolution von rechts. Das völkische Netzwerk 1900–1930', in D. Heiden and G. Mai, eds., *Nationalsozialismus in Thüringen*, Weimar, 1995, 29–48.
158. *Handbuch Tagespresse*, 27, 39.
159. *FK*, Nr, 98, 25.11.1930.
160. Falter, *Wähler*, 333.
161. Calculated from *Handbuch Tagespresse*; *StJbSa*, 1924/1926; also see Heidenreich, *Arbeiterkulturbewegung*, 80.
162. *ChVSt*, Nr. 272, 23.11.1929.
163. For a complete list see Szejnmann, 'Nazis in Saxony', 253f.
164. *Leipziger Neueste Nachrichten*, Nr. 101, 12.4.1926.
165. *Oschatzer Gemeinnützige*, 23.5.1929.
166. *Tageblatt Borna*, 28.5.1929.
167. *ChVSt*, Nr. 249, 24.10.1929.

168. Ibid., Nr. 262, 11.11.1929.
169. *Obererzgebirgische Zeitung*, Nr. 252, 26.10.1929.
170. *Stollberger Anzeiger und Tageblatt*, Nr. 98, 26.4.1924.
171. *Oelsnitzer Volksbote*, Nr. 107, 10.5.1929.
172. *Obererzgebirgische Zeitung*, Nr. 134, 12.6.1930.
173. Quoted from *SVB*, Nr. 64, 17.3.1930.
174. STA D, ZAS, Nr. 429.
175. *Crimmitschauer Anzeiger*, Nr. 84, 13/14.4.1929; ibid., Nr. 100, 30.4.1929.
176. *SVB*, Nr. 144, 24.6.1930; *Crimmitschauer Anzeiger*, Nr. 167, 21.7.1930. Also see Lapp, *Revolution*, 202, 207ff
177. *SB*, Nr. , 5.1.1930; *FK*, Nr. 49, 8.12.1930.
178. Falter, *Wähler*, 327.
179. *FK*, Nr. 49, 27.2.1932.
180. *ChVSt*, Nr. 262, 11.11.1929.
181. *NSfS*, Nr. 13, 30.5.1926.
182. *FK*, Nr. 234, 7.10.1931.
183. *DNN*, Nr. 178, 31.7.1932.
184. According to Ralf Krüger, between the end of 1931 and 1932 the *DNN*'s circulation went down from 110,000 to 98,000 copies, whilst *Der Freiheitskampf* mushroomed from 24,000 to 107,000 copies. See R. Krüger, 'Presse unter Druck. Differenzierte Berichterstattung trotz nationalsozialistischer Presselenkungsmaßnahmen. Die liberalen *Dresdner Neueste Nachrichten* und das NSDAP-Organ *Der Freiheitskampf* im Vergleich', in Pommerin, *Dresden*, 43f. According to the *Sopade*, however, Krüger's figure for the *FK* seem to include that of the *Chemnitzer Tageszeitung* and *Leipziger Tageszeitung*, who were affiliated with the *FK*. See *Sopade*, Juni 1936, 820.
185. For the information below see in particular 'Die Ergebnisse der Nationalsozialistischen Pressepolitik', *Sopade*, Juni 1936, 785–825.
186. The average in the Reich was 27.4 percent. See ibid., 787.
187. The average in the Reich was 23.7 percent. See ibid., 803.
188. Ibid., Juni 1935, 719f.
189. Ibid., 720.
190. *SäVBl*, Nr. 17, 28.2.1936. There were also reports, however, that former readers of left-wing newspapers were forced to subscribe Nazi papers. See *Sopade*, Juli 1938, 785.
191. *Sopade*, Juni 1936, 818.
192. See esp. Jones, 'Saxony, 1924–1930'.
193. *Frankfurter Zeitung*, 28.5.1930. Also see Lapp, *Revolution*, 194.
194. *VdSL*, 5. Wp, 2. Sitzung, 15.7.1930, 25; ibid., 7. Sitzung, 7.10.1930, 197f. In late July the WP had failed to attract the NSDAP into a coalition by offering them the Ministry of the Economy. See Lapp, *Revolution*, 203.
195. *VdSL*, 5. Wp, 4. Sitzung, 22.7.1930, 71.
196. Ibid., 7. Sitzung, 7.10.1930, 200, 203.

197. Ibid., 88. Sitzung, 18.10.1932, 3863.
198. *Meißner Volkszeitung*, Nr. 271, 21.11.1930.
199. *SVB*, Nr. 270, 20.11.1930.
200. *VdSL*, 4 Wp, 113. Sitzung, 21.3.1929, 4292.
201. Stoschek, 'Entwicklung', 271.
202. *VdSL*, 4 Wp, 6. Sitzung, 9.7.1929, 138.
203. *Chemnitzer Tageblatt*, Nr. 355, 23.12.1930.
204. For the DNVP's inability to establish itself as a credible opposition party and its dramatic disintegration see Jones, 'Saxony, 1924–1930'.
205. Lapp, *Revolution*, 163ff.
206. *VdSL*, 5 Wp, 43. Sitzung, 21.5.1931, 1588.
207. L.E. Jones, *German Liberalism and the Dissolution of the Weimar Party System, 1918–1933*, London, 1988, 432, 442.
208. Also see W. Brustein, *The Logic of Evil. The Social Origins of the Nazi Party, 1925–1933*, London, 1996.
209. *VdSL*, 5 Wp, 55. Sitzung, 11.7.1931, 2339.
210. For this section also see M. Rudloff, 'Die Strukturpolitik in den Debatten des sächsischen Landtags zur Zeit der Weltwirtschaftskrise', in Bramke, *Mitteldeutschland*, 241–60.
211. *VdSL*, 5 Wp, 4. Sitzung, 22.7.1930, 100.
212. Brustein, *Evil*, 51ff. Also see chapter 2 (iv) and the conclusion.
213. *VdSL*, 5 Wp, 6. Sitzung, 30.9.1930, 157.
214. Brustein, *Evil*, 145f.
215. This 'scepticism' was the reason why the VRP abstained in the vote of confidence against the government. See *VdSL*, 5 Wp, 55. Sitzung, 11.7.1931, 2339.
216. Ibid., 18. Sitzung, 11.12.1930, 684f.
217. Ibid., 69. Sitzung, 26.4.1932, 2921.
218. Ibid., 88. Sitzung, 18.10.1932, 3916f.
219. Ibid., 105. Sitzung, 16.2.1933, 4588.
220. Jones, 'Saxony, 1924–1930', See also Lapp, *Revolution*, 143–50.
221. *VdSL*, 5 Wp, 70. Sitzung, 27.4.1932, 2970.
222. Ibid., 61. Sitzung, 16.12.1931, 2565.
223. Ibid., 12. Sitzung, 13.11.1930.
224. Ibid., 59. Sitzung, 24.11.1931.
225. Ibid., 89. Sitzung, 19.10.1932.
226. Ibid., 4 Wp, 11. Sitzung, 23.10.1929, 354, 395.
227. *Chemnitzer Tageblatt*, Nr. 254, 14.9.1929.
228. *Zum sechzigsten Geburtstag von Gauleiter Mutschmann. Markante Worte von Martin Mutschmann*, 1939.
229. *VdSL*, 5. Wp, 62. Sitzung, 17.12.1931, 2615.
230. Ibid., 61. Sitzung, 16.12.1931, 2532ff.
231. Ibid., 84. Sitzung, 5.7.1932, 3674.
232. *FK*, Nr. 52, 2.3.1933; ibid., Nr. 53, 3.3.1933.
233. *VdSL*, 5. Wp, 69. Sitzung, 26.4.1932, 2953; ibid., 62. Sitzung, 17.12.1931, 2599.

234. E.g. Elliot questioned whether the widespread activities of military associations in Weimar Germany fostered militaristic attitudes. See Elliot, 'Kriegervereine', 126.
235. S. Willems, 'Widerstand aus Glauben. Lothar Kreyssig und die Euthanasieverbrechen', in Eichholtz, *Brandenburg*, 384.
236. *Mitteilungen Schwimmklub Chemnitz 1892*, Nr. 6, Juni 1920.
237. *VdSL*, 5. Wp, 49. Sitzung, 30.6.1931, 1959.
238. Ibid., 64. Sitzung, 26.1.1932.
239. Ibid., 97. Sitzung, 12.1.1933, 4255ff.
240. E.g. see Matthiesen, *Gotha*, 14.
241. *VdSL*, 5. Wp, 62. Sitzung, 17.12.1931, 2598.
242. *Leipziger Neueste Nachrichten*, Nr. 131, 11.5.1929.
243. STA D, MdI, Nr. 11126/3, März 1929.
244. E.g. during the 1930 state elections the newly formed VNR bitterly attacked the DVP. See Jones, 'Middle', 47.
245. *Leipziger Neueste Nachrichten*, Nr. 131, 11.5.1929.
246. The main theme of Rudi Koshar's, Peter Fritzsche's, and now also Benjamin Lapp's studies, deal with the grass-roots mass mobilisation of the German bourgeoisie in the second half of the 1920s. See R. Koshar, *Social Life, Local Politics, and Nazism. Marburg, 1880–1935*, London, 1986; P. Fritzsche, *Rehearsals for Fascism. Populism and Political Mobilization in Weimar Germany*, Oxford, 1990; Lapp, *Revolution*.
247. STA D, MdI, Nr. 11126/3, März 1929.
248. *LVZ*, Nr. 87, 15.4.1929.
249. Ibid., Nr. 92, 20.4.1929.
250. For the following see C. Kurzweg, 'Unternehmeridentität und regionale Selbstthematisierung: Auseinandersetzungen um die maschinelle Herstellung von Zigarren im sächsischen Döbeln, *Comparativ*, 4 (1995), 127–45.
251. *Vogtländischer Anzeiger und Tageblatt*, 24.4.1929.
252. *Sopade*, Juni/Juli 1934, 199.
253. Also see Rohkrämer, *Kriegervereine*, 182f.
254. STA D, AH Schwarzenberg, Nr. 1951, April 1934.
255. *Sopade*, Juni/Juli 1934, 198.
256. Boberach, *Meldungen*, 1266f.
257. Noakes, *Home Front*, 528.
258. STA D, AH Schwarzenberg, Nr. 1951, Juni 1934.
259. *SVBl*, Nr. 4, 15.1.1935.
260. E.g. see ibid., Nr. 45, 7.6.1935.
261. See *Sopade*, Mai/Juni 1934, 116; ibid., Juli 1935, 807ff; ibid., August 1935, 928ff, 942f; ibid., September 1935, 1027, 1043f; ibid., Januar 1936, 24f, 37ff; ibid., August 1936, 982ff; ibid., Juli 1937, 932, 945f; ibid., November 1937, 1572f; ibid., Februar 185, 199f; ibid., Juli 1938, 746f, 762f; ibid. November 1938, 1183ff, 1196; ibid., Januar 1939, 9ff; ibid., Februar 1939, 225; ibid, Juli

1939, 921ff; ibid., April 1940, 260. See also Boberach, *Meldungen*, 1942, 23. Juli, 4000. Also see Victor Klemperer, *Ich will Zeugnis ablegen bis zum letzten. Tagebücher 1933–1945*, 2 vols., Berlin, 1995; Lässig, 'Judenpolitik'.

262. Aly, *Cleansing the Fatherland.*
263. *Sportgemeinde Leipzig-Lindenau*, Nr. 2, 12.1.1924.
264. *Mitteilungen Schwimmklub Chemnitz 1892*, Nr. 9, September 1920.
265. Ibid., Nr. 11, November 1924.
266. The relative decline in population growth also made some circles fear that their race was dying out or would decline in its purity due to the influx of 'racially inferior' blood. Meanwhile developments in science led to a new emphasis on the role of genetic factors in determining human behaviour. At the end of the nineteenth century the idea of sterilisation ('negative eugenics') was put forward by some radical proponents of the pseudo-scientific 'racial hygiene' as a solution to prevent the mixing of the 'unfit' with the 'healthy' body of the nation.
267. G. Heidel, 'Die Dresdner Internationale Hygiene-Ausstellung 1930/31', *Dresdner Hefte*, 9 (10) (1991), 35f.
268. P. Fäßler, 'Sozialhygiene – Rassenhygiene – Euthanasie: "Volksgesundheitspflege" im Raum Dresden', in Pommerin, *Dresden*, 193–207.
269. C.-P. Heidel, 'Zwischen Naturheilkunde und Rassenhygiene – Dresdner Medizin im Nationalsozialismus', *Dresdner Hefte*, 11 (35) (1993), 39.
270. For this and the following see P. Weindling, *Health, Race and German Politics between National Unification and Nazism 1870–1945*, Cambridge, 1989, 389ff. Boeters also 'formulated a series of proposals, known as *Lex Zwickau*, which would sanction the compulsory sterilisation of (*inter aliis*) idiots, the feebleminded, the blind, deaf and dumb, and illegitimate mothers of low eugenic value.' Meanwhile Ewald Meltzer, director of a Saxon asylum (Katharinenhof), also instigated illegal sterilisations based on racial hygiene. See M. Burleigh, *Death and Deliverance. 'Euthanasia' in Germany 1900–1945*, Cambridge, 1994, 36, 21f.
271. M. Lienert, 'Der Einfluß des Nationalsozialismus auf die Technische Hochschule Dresden während der Weimarer Republik', *Neues Archiv für sächsische Geschichte*, 66 (1995), 287f.
272. *LVZ*, Nr. 222, 22.9.1929. *Ostara* refered to a periodical by Adolf Lanz which contained bloodthirsty race mythology. It is likely that Hitler read it when he lived in Vienna. See Bracher, *Dictatorship*, 86.
273. *Sächsisches Militärvereinsblatt*, Nr. 14, 25.7.1924.
274. J.-C. Kaiser, K. Nowak and M. Schwartz, *Eugenik. Sterilisation, 'Euthanasie'. Politische Biologie in Deutschland 1895–1945. Eine Dokumentation*, Buchverlag Union, 59.

275. *Jahrbuch des Deutschen Sängerbundes 1930*, 82–5.
276. *Landwirtschafltlicher Anzeiger für Sachsen und Thüringen*, Nr. 21, 24.3.1932.
277. *Dresdner Nachrichten*, Nr. 193, 25.4.1932.
278. STA D, AH Annaberg, Nr. 592, 10.6.1931.
279. Ibid., Jöhstadt, 19.2.1931.
280. Ibid., Oberwiesenthal, 23.2.1932.
281. *VdSL*, 5. Wp, 43. Sitzung, 21.5.1931, 1585.
282. *NSfS*, Nr. 27, 8.7.1928.
283. Aly, 'Voss', 105.
284. Noakes, *Home Front*, 534.
285. *Sopade*, Juni 1937, 869f.
286. *VdSL*, 4 Wp, 113. Sitzung, 21.3.1929, 4292ff.
287. Noakes, *State*, 554–56.
288. Lässig, 'Judenpolitik', 163, 175. For some examples of Mutschmann's violent anti-Semitism, see ibid., 151f. Apparently Mutschmann had already suggested during the Poland campaign, to force all Jews to wear an identifying Star of David. This was two years ahead of its time. See D. Orlow, *The History of the Nazi Party, Volume II: 1933–1945*, Pittsburgh, 1973, 281. For one remarkable example how some leading members of the Saxon bourgeoisie openly defied the Nazis' anti-Semitism by attending the funeral of the Jewish banker Heinrich Arnhold in Dresden in 1935, see Lässig, 'Judenpolitik', 167f.
289. *Sopade*, Februar 1938, 199.
290. This contradicts the recent findings by Daniel Goldhagen who argues that a widespread and deep-rooted anti-Semitism permeated German society before and during the Third Reich. See D. Goldhagen, *Hitler's Willing Executioners, Ordinary Germans and the Holocaust*, London, 1996.

Chapter 5

'Germans Unite!' The Nazis and Their Constituency

> They came from all professions and classes and shared the bond of men with the same faith, the same hatreds, and the same love for eternal comradeship. They were linked to each other by a life and death struggle. No-one asked what class and profession the person next in line had, everyone shared his bread with another, everyone risked his life when the comrade was threatened.
>
> (The account of a unit of Stormtroopers in Annaberg/ Erzgebirge. E. Lang, 'Kampf und Sieg der nationalsozialistischen Bewegung im Grenzlandkreis Annaberg/ Obererzgebirge!', in *Vom silbernen Erzgebirge*, 228f)

(i) Leaders and Activists

The question of who were the Nazi leaders and activists, and what were the reasons for their extreme devotion to their cause, stands at the heart of any analysis of Nazism. The spread and success of Nazism at the local and regional level was closely linked with the work of party followers. The dominant Nazi in Saxony was Martin Mutschmann, who was born the son of a master locksmith in 1879 in Hirschberg in Thuringia.[1] Mutschmann was brought up in Plauen where he also attended the business school. He then pursued an apprenticeship in embroidery and became a master in the trade. He was a departmental manager in several textile factories before he founded his own lace factory in Plauen in 1907. During the First World War he was wounded at Verdun and subsequently dismissed from the army with the 'Iron Cross', Second Class, in December 1916.

Mutschmann was a classic example of a middle-class business man who became receptive to extreme ideologies and radicalised by economic problems, the unexpected defeat in war, and the subsequent revolution and triumph of organised labour. These developments sparked off particular tensions in heavily industrialised Vogtland, where the once prosperous lace and embroidery industry faced a disastrous decline, where traditionally a strong polarisation between workers and employers, and socialists and nationalists existed, and where anti-Semitic sentiments were widespread. This background helped to explain why Mutschmann found his way from the DVSTB into the NSDAP in 1922 and soon afterwards emerged as one of the most fanatic and anti-Semitic Nazi leaders. In August 1924 he replaced Tittmann as provincial leader of the *völkisch* alliance and became leader of the Saxon Nazi movement.[2] In March 1925 Hitler officially ordered Mutschmann to rebuild the organisation in the state,[3] and soon afterwards he was appointed *Gauleiter of Saxony*.[4]

Mutschmann blamed Marxism and the Jews for the ills of German society. Marxism was held responsible for Germany's humiliating defeat in the war and its disastrous consequences, and for inciting a class war against the bourgeoisie and property. The Jews were seen as dominating international capitalism and squeezing Germany – and in particular the middle classes – with the *Diktat* of Versailles and international capitalism (see also documents 9, 10 and 19). Mutschmann faced the delicate task of fighting socialism and attempting to win over the large working-class constituency at the same time. This study has repeatedly shown that this was not necessarily a contradiction. Mutschmann's answer was to appeal to the nationalist sentiments of workers and to give them the illusion of a fairer society under National Socialism. He assured a factory owner:

> Do not be bewildered by the slogans 'Down with Capitalism' which we write on our posters. These slogans are necessary. You must know that it would be impossible to reach our objectives simply with the catchword 'German-national or National'. We have to speak the language of the embittered socialist workers, otherwise they will never feel comfortable with us.[5]

To Mutschmann, only tough measures promised a revival of society: the crushing of Marxists and Jews would overthrow the November system and open the way for Germany's revival. It helped that Mutschmann's whole family shared these views and became involved in the Nazi movement.[6] Mutschmann's grave financial problems further enhanced his determined fight for the movement.

A number of characteristics made Mutschmann a 'perfect' Nazi *Gauleiter*: he was very loyal to Hitler,[7] a violent anti-Semite, extremely ruthless and determined – even Goebbels respected Mutschmann as a 'decent, brutal leader'[8] – possessed links with local business circles, felt strong sentiments for his region, and was a skilful opportunist. From 1926 he had used the 'left-wing' *Kampfverlag* of the Straßer brothers and their influence as an ideal vehicle to strengthen his position in working-class Saxony. Only four years later he went along with the ousting of the 'left-wing' circle around Otto Straßer, and then dropped Gregor Straßer during the Hitler-Straßer dispute in late 1932. Mutschmann was instrumental in turning Saxony into one of the strongest Nazi *Gaue* which – despite having by far the largest population of all *Gaue* – was never split. He became one of the most important Nazi *Gauleiter*[9] and dominated his state up to the end of the Second World War, when he was captured by the Soviet army (on 9 May 1945) and eventually died in captivity in 1948.[10]

Mutschmann's modest family background and his lack of interest and knowledge in the cultural sphere[11] made him uncomfortable with the traditional elite and led him to desire the creation of a new order in society in which merit and hard work were rewarded and opposition was brutally purged.[12] His collection of a whole range of titles during the Third Reich mirrors his craving for control.[13] Mutschmann's strong attachment to his region, a deep-seated insecurity and intellectual limitations seemed to explain why he never pursued national ambitions and why he defended Saxony's interests in the Reich. From Hitler's point of view, Mutschmann was extremely suitable as *Gauleiter*, but he did not regard him as a particularly intelligent person or a skilful politician.[14] Mutschmann repeatedly requested Goebbels and Hitler – to no avail – to ban jokes about Saxons and their dialect,[15] and in 1943 he attempted to delay the shifting of the armaments industry into Saxony because it increased the risk of bomb attacks.[16]

Erich Kunz became a prominent Saxon Nazi leader as a protégé of Mutschmann and proved what an impact one devoted activist could make, particularly when the movement was still very small.[17] Kunz was born in 1897 near Zwickau, the son of a foreman. When the First World War broke out he interrupted his business studies and volunteered for the front. He was slightly injured twice and received the 'Iron Cross', Second Class. After the war he continued his studies, became a commercial employee (*Handelsgehilfe*) and married in 1921. He joined the NSDAP in 1922 and occupied positions as SA leader and HJ leader before 1928. From 1929 onwards Kunz led the Nazi party district of Zwickau and became a member of Zwickau town council. A year later he became member of the Saxon parliament with responsibility for his party's local affairs in the state. Kunz was elected to the Reichstag in March 1933 and led the first Ministry of employment and social security in Saxony during the dictatorship. He held top senior positions in Saxony's government and civil service before he died in a car accident in 1939.

Why did Kunz develop into such a devoted Nazi activist after the First World War? Experience in the war and serving at the front had a crucial impact on such a young man (like most other Saxon Nazi leaders) and shaped his vision of German culture and society.[18] The war experience – comradeship and excitement at the front, the transcending of class barriers and the suffering for the fatherland – was shattered by the sudden defeat and the political rise of the SPD, which worked to fulfil the terms of Versailles and pursued a policy of pacifism and internationalism. Kunz and many other early Nazi activists never came to terms with these dramatic changes and blamed Marxist betrayal for the defeat and the ensuing misery. To them, the Nazi movement became a means to re-live the war experience and to reverse its conclusion. Kunz believed that only the creation of a strong fatherland – whose citizens would unite behind the interests and pride of a nation that practised social justice – would enable Germany to escape the exploitation of other international powers (see document 10).

Whereas more than 50 percent of the Saxon population, and nearly 40 percent of the members of the Saxon NSDAP, came from the working classes (see the next two sections below), only between 15 and 20 percent of branch leaders – the bottom of the party leadership pyramid – came from this class (see table 5.1). However, there were eight workers among the most influential thirty Saxon Nazis before 1933.[19] The middle classes clearly dominated these highest ranks within the Gau. With Hellmuth von Mücke and Manfred von Killinger, the Saxon Nazi leadership also recruited from the traditional elites.[20]

Table 5.1 Social Composition of Saxon NSDAP Branch Leaders (by Percentage)

Profession	Before 14.9.1930	Between 15.9.1930 and 30.1.1933	1935
Workers	15.4 (19.7)	13.8	13.7
Employees	39.1	34.5	33.4
Self-employed	20.7	16.8	17.8
Civil servants	17.2 (7.5)	16.3	17.5
Farmers	7.6 (7.5)	18.0	16.0
Rest	–	0.6	1.6
Total	100.0	100.0	100.0

Source: NSDAP Parteistatistik, vol. II. See some of Lobmeier's findings in brackets. Lobmeier was able to track down 146 Nazi branch leaders in Saxony around 1930. See Lobmeier, 'Mittelschichten', Anlage 10.

Several features about the Saxon Nazi elite were striking. All of them were either born in Saxony or had lived there for a long time. Most of them had fought in the First World War at a very young age (often at the age of eighteen). Only Hellmuth von Mücke, Martin Mutschmann and Manfred von Killinger – who occupied the most senior posts – were a little older. In the early 1930s the latter two were older than forty and presided over a leadership circle of young men in their early thirties. Many of the Nazi leaders had joined the movement in the early 1920s and had led local HJ or SA groups. The strength of the HJ in Saxony was a crucial precondition for producing a devoted and dynamic leadership core in the region. Professionally, the Nazi leaders were either civil servants and administrators (most importantly the economist Dr. Fritsch as party manager from 1926 onwards) or skilled artisans and farmers. Nearly all had attended further education. The picture confirms Michael Kater's findings that Nazi functionaries were not – as often assumed – outsiders from society.[21] Indeed, most Saxon Nazi leaders risked a better-than-average professional career with their activities in the anti-Republican Nazi party. They were frequently harassed by police, customers, employers or the organised working class. The engraver Franz Pillmayer in Zwickau and the master bookbinder Helmut Böhme in Freiberg – both

NSDAP district leaders – lost their jobs because of their work for the Nazi movement in the 1920s.[22]

The professions of several Nazi leaders, however, seemed to be volatile and depended upon the fluctuations of the business cycle. Most importantly, Mutschmann faced financial ruin due to a severe recession in his trade. For some, the Nazi party opened up a professional career from about 1930 onwards. Heinrich Bennecke became editor of the *Sächsischer Beobachter* in Dresden; Walter Dönicke gave up his trade as a cabinet-maker and became a professional party manager in Leipzig; Martin Mutschmann's decision to close his embroidery factory in September 1930 must have been linked to the income he received as a newly elected member of the Reichstag; and Fritz Tittmann supplied the Nazi movement with propaganda material from his publishing company in the 1920s and was a member of the Saxon, and later Prussian, Landtag.[23] Financial dependence certainly provided an incentive to fight for the victory of the movement.

Overall, it seems that all Saxon Nazi leaders joined the movement for a similar reason: their determined desire to replace the Weimar Republic with a strong nationalist state that would wipe out the defeat, misery and injustices which were apparently caused by the outcome of the First World War. This explains why one of the Nazis' major themes up until 1930 was to blame international finance and capitalism for the exploitation of Germany. International capitalism was equated with the interests of the western powers in the form of the Versailles Peace Treaty (and, subsequently, the Young and Dawes Plans), an international Jewish conspiracy against Germany, and the threat big business, department stores and rationalisation posed to workers and middle-class groups.[24] This message provided a simple explanation and solution to the damaging side-effects of the process of modernisation and held a powerful appeal for many groups in Saxony due to its backwards economic structure. It was a unique formula which united the fears of shop-owners with those of workers, and thrived on nationalist sentiments.

From 1930/31 onwards the Saxon Nazis shifted most of their attacks onto the other main theme they had emphasised throughout the 1920s: the betrayal of Marxism. Traditionally they had accused the Marxists for having betrayed the German population during the war and the revolution – and more generally – for inciting class struggle which weakened the German nation. In the final years of the Republic, the threats against Marxism reached new dimensions with the uncompromising claim that Germany could not prosper under Marxism, i.e., Marxism had to be wiped out before Germany could be revived again.

(ii) A Social Profile of the Saxon NSDAP Membership before 1933 (by Detlef Mühlberger)[25]

Although we know that the first individual to join the Nazi party in Saxony was a university student resident in Leipzig, who entered the party in late September 1920,[26] relatively little is known about the social types attracted to Nazism in its formative years in the region.[27] The data we have on Nazi membership following the formation of the party in Saxony is limited and patchy. The only evidence that has come to light recently from which it is possible to reconstruct the social types recruited by the local NSDAP in the early 1920s is restricted to a number of lists which recorded the membership enrolled by the party in the city of Leipzig.[28] These lists contain the details of those who joined the branch from the time of its formation in late November 1922 to April 1923. With the exception of a handful of Nazis living in small towns and villages in the vicinity of Leipzig, all of the members were resident in the city.[29] The social profile of the exclusively male membership of the Leipzig branch of the NSDAP (see figure 5.1) was markedly different from that of the male working population of the city. Members drawn from the middle classes dominated the branch. Blue-collar workers, even though they accounted for just over one-third of the Leipzig membership, were noticeably under-represented.[30] A similar pattern emerges when one looks at the data available on the recruits who had joined the NSDAP between 28 September and 9 November 1923 in Saxony as a whole (see figure 5.1).[31] Again there is a far from perfect match between the occupational background of local individuals entering the Nazi party on the eve of Hitler's abortive bid for power, and the occupational and social structure of the male working population of Saxony.[32]

The Saxon NSDAP members were even younger than in the rest of the Republic.[33] In both the Leipzig branch and among the entrants into the NSDAP in Saxony in late 1923, those under twenty-one years of age alone made up around half of the entire membership, whilst those under thirty-one years of age accounted for 89 percent and 83 percent respectively. Although Nazis resident in big cities continued to dominate the membership enrolled in

Figure 5.1 NSDAP Membership by Class; Leipzig Compared with Rest of Saxony

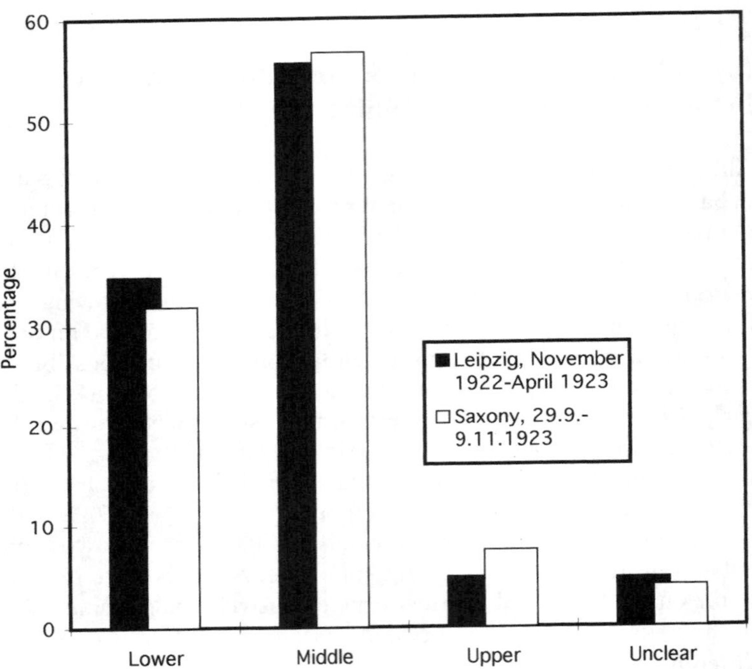

Saxony in late 1923, the available data suggests a spread of the Nazi membership into the smaller towns and rural communities in the region. The membership records of the Saxon NSDAP are noticeable for their lack of female members. Although women formed but a marginal element within the NSDAP in its formative years, accounting for a maximum of 10 percent between 1919 and 1923, it seems that in Saxony even this modest recruitment level proved impossible, making the Saxon NSDAP virtually an exclusively male affair.[34]

The limited evidence that we have on the social background of the Saxon Nazi membership before 1923 broadly shared the social characteristics of the membership attracted by the NSDAP in other parts of Germany on the eve of the putsch.[35] The Saxon NSDAP was a party of youth with a predominantly male membership. The nucleus of the party was undeniably provided by recruits coming from the middle classes, but support from the working class was still considerable. Overall, the party had the characteristics of a *Volkspartei* (People's Party) rather than those of a middle-class party.[36]

The only comprehensive data currently available on the social structure of the membership recruited by the Nazi party in *Gau* Saxony, from the time of its re-formation in February 1925 until Hitler's appointment as chancellor on 30 January 1933, is that contained in the *Partei-Statistik* (Party Statistics) produced by the Nazis in 1935. Overall, historians agree that the *Partei-Statistik* represents an attempt by the Nazi leadership to capture an accurate picture of the social composition of their party.[37] The *Partei-Statistik* data for Saxony suggests that despite the predominantly working-class population and the powerful presence of the SPD and KPD in the region – factors which theoretically should have provided a considerable obstacle to the spread of Nazism – Saxony proved to be the most rewarding recruitment ground for the NSDAP in its so-called *Kampfzeit* (Period of Struggle)[38] phase. According to the *Partei-Statistik*, the Nazis recruited more members in Saxony than in any other *Gau*: the Saxon membership accounted for some 10.3 percent of the entire Nazi membership mobilised between February 1925 and Hitler's elevation to the chancellorship in January 1933.[39] The fact that the Nazi data claims that the middle classes accounted for 55 percent of the Saxon membership enrolled before 30 January 1933 will not, given the dominance of the middle-class thesis of Nazism in the literature from the 1930s to the 1980s, raise any eyebrows.[40] However, a more tendentious aspect of the *Partei-Statistik* data is the suggestion that workers were also attracted to the Saxon NSDAP in some numbers, accounting for 29.2 percent of the membership enrolled by the time of the Reichstag election on 14 September 1930, for 35.8 percent in the period between 15 September 1930 to 30 January 1933, and for 35 percent of the membership mobilised in Saxony in the entire period before Hitler was appointed chancellor.[41]

Until now no data has been available on Saxony for the *Kampfzeit* phase against which one could test the veracity of the *Partei-Statistik* data.[42] The analysis which follows is based on a sample involving 2,999 members recruited in Saxony between 1925 and 1933, part of a larger systematic sample drawn from the Berlin Document Center (BDC).[43] The BDC data confirm the strong support for the Saxon NSDAP originating from the middle

Figure 5.2 Membership of the Saxon NSDAP by Class and Year of Entry, 1925–1933

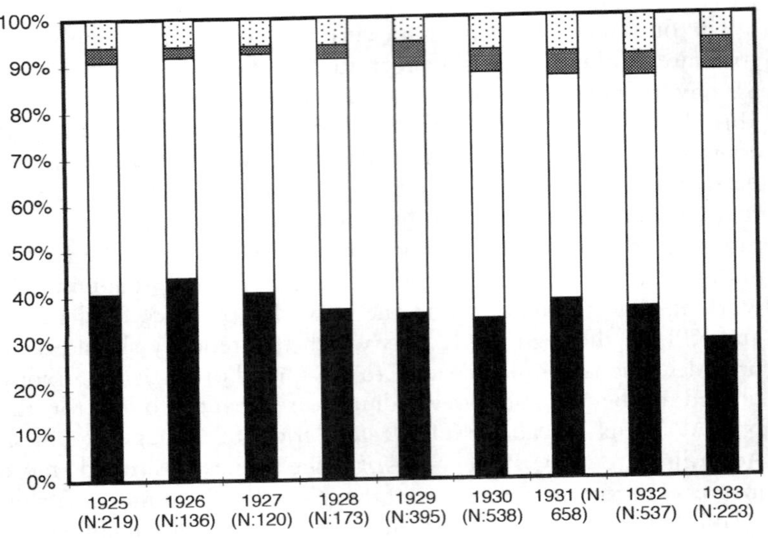

Unclear; Upper; Middle; Lower.

classes in the 1925 to 1933 period (see figures 5.2 and 5.3). The self-employed, nonacademic professionals, lower- and middle-grade white-collar employees and civil servants collectively provided the Saxon NSDAP with the majority of the membership enrolled each year, and the absolute majority in all years except for 1926 and 1931.[44] Supporters drawn from the Saxon elite also began to be more visible in the movement after 1929 (see figure 5.2). The increase in the membership drawn from both the middle and upper classes, which accounted for 58.3 percent and 6.7 percent of the 1933 intake respectively, explains the corresponding decline to 29.5 percent of the proportion of workers entering the NSDAP. The percentage relating to the working-class membership recruited in the period before 14 September 1930 in the BDC data, however, is much higher than that provided by the *Partei-Statistik*.[45] It seems that following its re-formation in 1925, the NSDAP was particularly successful in winning supporters among the Saxon working class in the years 1925 to 1927 (see figure 5.2).

Figure 5.3 Membership of the Saxon NSDAP by Class and Period of Entry, 1925 Onwards

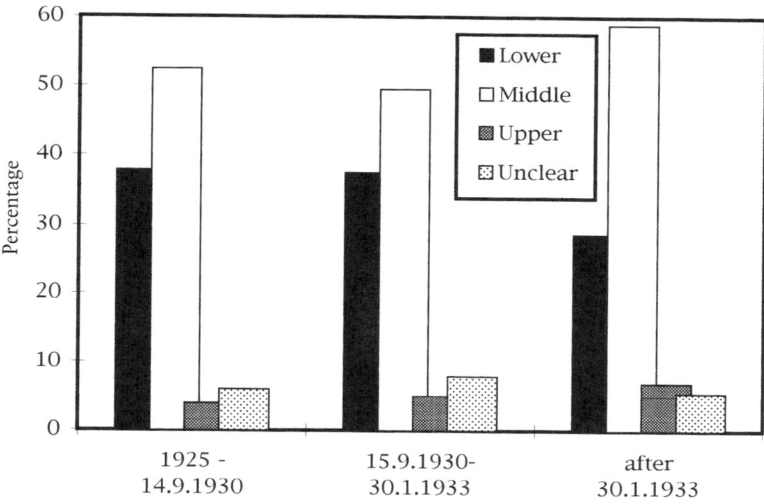

Whereas the Nazis claimed a working-class component of 29.5 percent among its membership in the period 1925 to 14 September 1930, the BDC material provides a figure of 37.8 percent (see figure 5.3).[46] The discrepancy between the percentage values of the workers category in the two sets of data reinforces my argument expressed elsewhere that the Nazis were able to mobilise a considerable working-class membership before their electoral breakthrough in September 1930, but found it more difficult to retain this support over time, giving rise to a significant understatement in the *Partei-Statistik* of the worker element active in the party in the late 1920s.[47] This feature, however, is not apparent in the early 1930s. According to the BDC data, 37.5 percent of the membership of the Saxon NSDAP came from the working class in the period 15 September 1930 to 30 January 1933 (see figure 5.3), which was only marginally higher than the figure in the *Partei-Statistik*.

The membership of the NSDAP in Saxony was much more urban-based than that of the party in Germany as a whole.[48] The few cities in the region with a population of over 100,000 provided

39.4 percent of the total middle-class membership recruited by the party in Saxony.[49] However, the Saxon NSDAP recruited a sizeable proportion, some 39.4 percent, of its working-class membership in the small villages and rural areas. The greater resistance to Nazism offered by the working class in the larger Saxon towns and cities is further suggested by the fact that only three of the top ten electoral strongholds of the NSDAP by the time of the July 1932 Reichstag elections were towns (see table 3.1 and figure 5.4). The social configuration of the Nazi membership between 1925 and 1933 in

Figure 5.4 The Social Structure of the NSDAP Membership in the Top Ten NSDAP Strongholds in July 1932

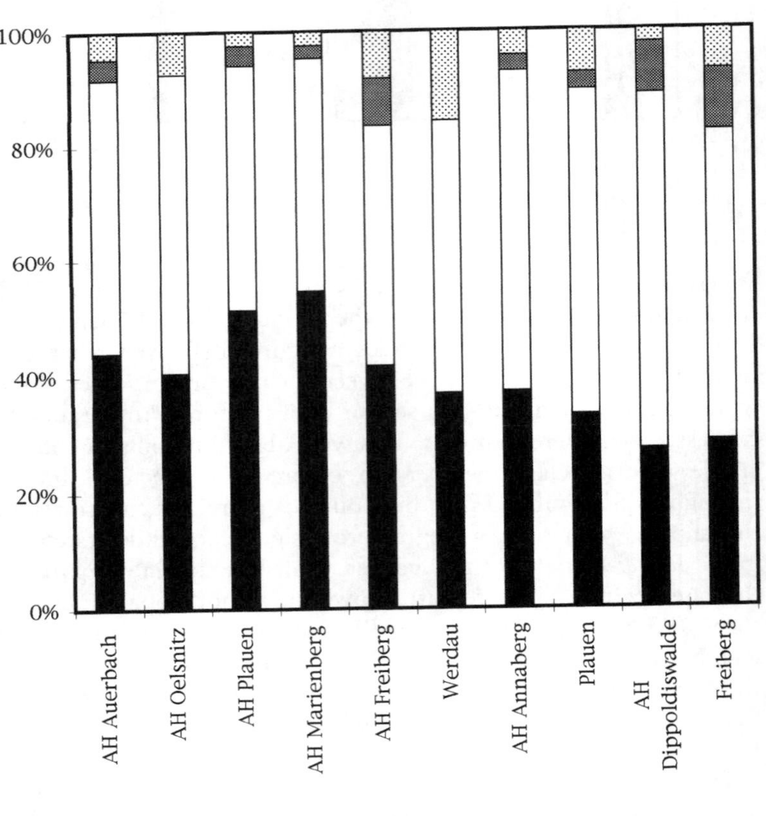

the top ten Nazi electoral strongholds shows significant variations. The percentage of working-class members ranged from a low of 27.3 percent in the district of Dippoldiswalde to a high of 54.5 percent in the district of Marienberg. There was a lower working-class membership in the three towns compared to the seven rural districts. However, in half of these Nazi strongholds the working-class component in the membership exceeded the 37.7 percent average achieved by the NSDAP in Saxony in the period 1925 to 30 January 1933 as a whole. The Saxon Nazis had a much lower party recruitment in areas of SPD and KPD dominance than in their strongholds.[50] In percentage terms, however, they frequently attracted a high working-class membership in Marxist bastions (see figures 5.5 and 5.6). In seven of the top ten SPD, and six of the top ten KPD electoral strongholds, the percentage of workers drawn to the NSDAP exceeded the regional average of the 37.7 percent working-class component. In sheer percentage terms the Saxon Nazi party obtained some of its highest levels of working-class membership support in towns and districts dominated by the left.

Between 1925 and 1933 the Saxon Nazis continued to attract the younger age cohorts of German society, even if the gradual rise in the average age of NSDAP entrants during this period suggests that the party was being subjected to a gentle ageing process.[51] Whereas the 18-30-year-olds provided 62.9 percent of the membership in the period 1925 to 14 September 1930, the percentage declines to 55.4 percent in the period from 15 September 1930 to 30 January 1933. In only one respect did the Saxon NSDAP membership in the post-1925 period show a marked difference from the data we have on its pre-1923 composition. After 1925 the Saxon Nazis began to attract female members in small numbers. Females accounted for between 5.1 and 8.7 per cent of the annual membership recruited into the Saxon NSDAP between 1925 and 1933. This was in line with the data provided for the Saxon NSDAP in the *Partei-Statistik*. It is in gender terms that the NSDAP's membership in Saxony, and this applies to the party as a whole, never managed to reflect the structure of German society.

Following its reemergence in 1925, the NSDAP's social profile saw the further development of the *Volkspartei* characteristic which had been evident in its formative years. The ability of the party to transcend the class divide was strengthened and working-class members became more numerous within the party. However,

Figure 5.5 The Social Structure of the NSDAP Membership in the Top Ten SPD Strongholds in July 1932

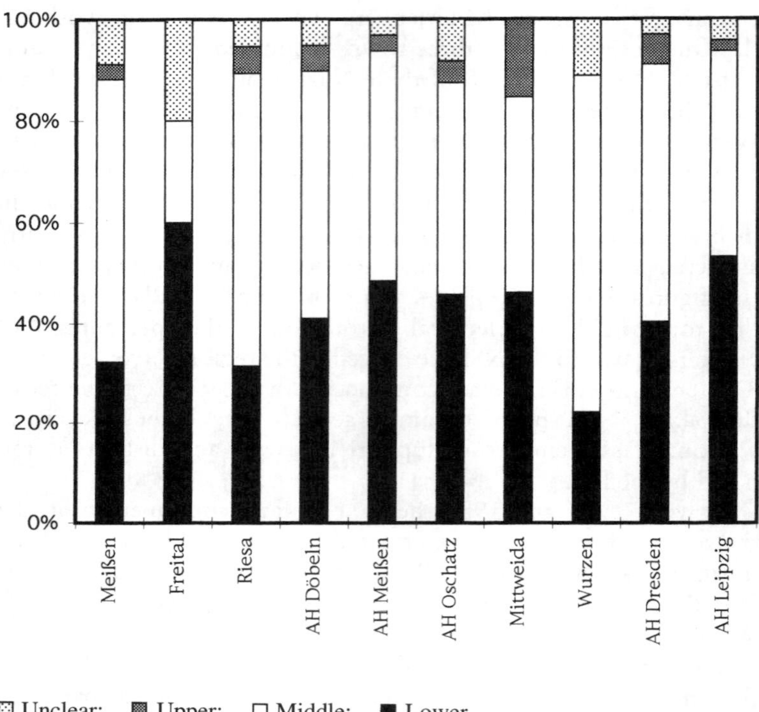

Unclear; Upper; Middle; Lower.

despite its improved performance after 1925 as far as attracting working-class members is concerned, the social configuration of the predominantly male Saxon Nazi party did not correspond with that of the male working population in the region. One cannot ignore the fact that workers continued to be under-represented, and the middle classes over-represented, within the Saxon NSDAP between 1925 and 1933. But the presence of a substantial working-class base within the Saxon Nazi party cannot be overlooked either. Given the social structure of the membership of the NSDAP in Saxony, it is impossible to characterise it as a middle-class movement. In social terms, the Saxon Nazis came from all walks of life, with mechanics and factory workers rubbing

Figure 5.6 The Social Structure of the NSDAP Membership in the Top Ten KPD Strongholds in July 1932

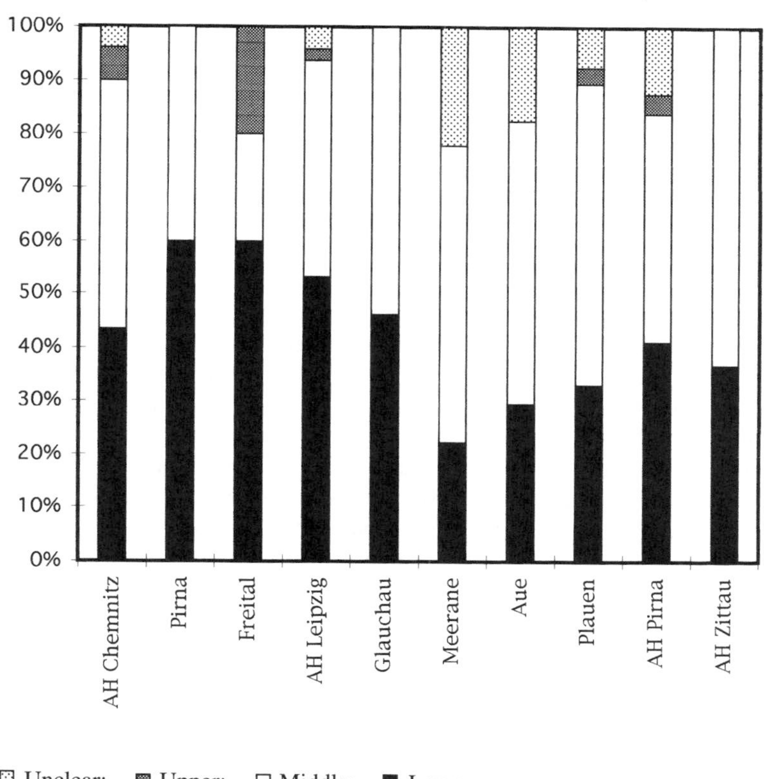

Unclear; Upper; Middle; Lower.

shoulders with clerks and shopkeepers, and with members of the free professions and civil servants of all grades. Overall, the Saxon data confirms the validity of the *Volkspartei* thesis of Nazism.

(iii) A Social Profile of the Saxon NSDAP Voters (by Dirk Hänisch)[52]

Since the early 1980s the empirical analysis of NSDAP voters has moved more and more to the centre of social-historical research concerning the rise of National Socialism. Numerous studies have exploited methods of modern electoral analysis in an attempt to investigate the political and social origins of NSDAP voters during the final phase of the Weimar Republic.[53] The scholarly aim surrounding these studies was to investigate whether the classical interpretation, which saw the NSDAP as a typical middle-class party, would stand up to the findings of modern electoral research. Closely linked to this was the question, whether the electorate of the so-called workers' parties, SPD and KPD, was indeed as immune to Nazism as has been so long presumed. A further question also needed attention: was the radicalisation of the middle and its swing towards Nazism mainly limited to the middle-class parties, or was the mobilisation of nonvoters the main explanation for the electoral rise of the movement?[54] Finally, for a long time specialised literature did not sufficiently clarify if unemployment favoured the electoral fortunes of the Nazis or not.

After the publication of much empirical research in the second half of the 1980s, a consensus has emerged regarding the political origin and social basis of the voters of the German NSDAP.[55] In contrast to the 'classical' middle-class theory (especially Geiger, Speier or Lipset), it is now commonly accepted that the Nazi electorate was much broader and managed to transcend class. Indeed, the NSDAP electorate in the Reich can be described as similar to a people's party in terms of its social background. The middle-class element was noticeably over-represented, but the latest research suggests that a quarter of all Nazi voters were workers. In July 1932, when the NSDAP had reached the peak of its electoral success, more workers voted for National Socialism than for the SPD or KPD.

Below we will discuss a few important results of empirical research about the political origins and the social profile of the NSDAP voters in Saxony.[56] The findings are based on the analysis of the results of the elections to the Reichstag in 1920, 1928, 1930 and 1933, and also the result of the second ballots of the elections for the Reich President (RPW-II) in 1925 and 1932.[57] The social data was taken from the 1925 and 1933 censuses. As some of the official results were in a different aggregate level, there was a need to be flexible with the compilation of the data base. It was also necessary to take account of the numerous territorial reforms in order to establish a comparative longitudinal elevation in the data base.[58] The final results are several data files with the election results and social data of Saxon towns, communities and remaining districts (*Restkreise*: all communities which have less than 2,000 inhabitants in one district), which are longitudinally comparable in respect of the territory.[59]

The electoral rise of the Saxon Nazis was as rapid as in the rest of the Republic. The local NSDAP gained 561,381 votes in the September 1930 Reichstag elections compared to only 74,343 votes in the previous May 1928 Reichstag election. In July 1932 the Nazis achieved their greatest electoral success before their seizure of power. More than 1.3 million Saxons voted for them. In terms of the number of registered voters, which is the only sensible measurement for longitudinal electoral comparison, 2.2 percent voted for Hitler's party in 1928, 15.7 percent in 1930 and 36.1 percent in July 1932 (for the following see table 5.2).[60] These figures were slightly above the national average.

There were clear differences in the NSDAP's election results in the three Saxon Reichstag electoral districts. Most importantly, voters in the electoral district of Chemnitz had much stronger sympathies with Nazism. Whilst this was also the KPD's electoral bastion, the SPD always performed worse here compared to the two other Saxon Reichstag electoral districts, Leipzig and Dresden. A remarkable 61 percent of the electorate in the electoral district of Chemnitz voted for one of the extreme parties which actively fought against the Weimar Republic. In the other two Saxon electoral districts this figure was still below 50 percent.

If one investigates the party-political origins of NSDAP voters, one finds that an early point of crystallisation regarding the National Socialist mobilisation of voters in Saxony – as in the rest of the Republic – was the 1925 RPW-II and the plebiscite about the 'Law against the Slavery of the German *Volk*' in 1929 (also see chapter 2[v]). The votes for Hindenburg in the second ballot and the yes votes for the proposed law correlate more than any other electoral results with the following NSDAP election success. All those anti-Republican forces who were splintered in the various parties and movements rallied behind the German nationalist figurehead Hindenburg. For instance, there was a high correlation coefficient between the Hindenburg electorate in 1925 and those who voted for Hitler seven years later.[61]

These associations, however, do not as yet give any answers to the question of where the Saxon NSDAP voters came from during the final years of the Republic. In a first step, one can establish linear associations through correlations of the percentage losses of various parties with the gains of the NSDAP. In 1930, the correlations were strongest with the losses of the DVP and the nonvoter

Table 5.2 Percentage of NSDAP, SPD, KPD and Nonvoters in the Three Saxon Electoral Districts (in Reichstag Elections)

	Reichstag district			Saxony	Reich
	Dresden	Leipzig	Chemnitz		
NSDAP 1928	1.4	1.6	3.3	2.2	1.9
NSDAP 1930	13.5	12.3	20.3	15.7	14.8
NSDAP 1932, July	33.7	32.1	41.5	36.1	31.1
NSDAP 1933	39.0	36.9	45.6	40.9	39.8
USPD 1920	16.8	34.9	13.7	20.5	13.2
MSPD 1920	21.4	8.9	25.4	19.6	17.0
SPD 1928	30.9	30.6	25.7	28.9	21.5
SPD 1930	29.0	30.7	24.2	27.7	19.5
SPD 1932, July	26.6	29.4	19.8	24.8	18.0
SPD 1933	25.4	27.7	19.4	23.9	15.4
KPD 1920	0.8	2.1	7.6	3.6	1.6
KPD 1928	8.2	13.3	12.4	11.0	7.1
KPD 1930	10.4	15.1	15.7	13.6	9.7
KPD 1932, July	12.2	16.7	17.3	15.2	12.0
KPD 1933	12.0	16.0	17.3	15.0	9.9
Other Parties 1920	40.2	40.6	34.1	37.8	46.7
Other Parties 1928	38.6	37.4	35.0	36.9	43.6
Other Parties 1930	30.9	29.7	25.0	28.3	36.9
Other Parties 1932, July	13.1	10.8	9.7	11.4	22.3
Other Parties 1933	13.4	11.7	9.0	11.2	22.9
Nonvoters 1920	20.8	13.5	19.2	18.5	21.5
Nonvoters 1928	20.9	17.1	23.6	21.0	25.9
Nonvoters 1930	16.2	12.2	14.8	14.7	19.1
Nonvoters 1932, July	14.4	11.0	11.7	12.5	16.6
Nonvoters 1933	10.2	7.7	8.7	9.0	12.0
RPW					
1925–II (Hindenburg)	41.6	38.5	42.1	40.9	37.2
1932–II (Hitler)	31.7	30.7	41.8	35.1	30.5

Percentage basis: registered voters.

camp. In other words: the NSDAP was able to make most gains in Saxony where the nonvoters and the DVP had registered most losses.[62] There are no electoral results from the lower aggregate level for the Reichstag elections in 1932. We therefore correlated the gains of the NSDAP between 1930 and 1933 with the corresponding losses of the other parties.[63] The highest association between the gains of the NSDAP and the losses of most parties in this period was with the SLV (which was more or less smashed by 1932), and again with the loss of nonvoters.[64] The correlation with SPD losses, by contrast, is much weaker. All other bivariate associations are less pronounced or not evident at all.

Bivariate correlations of percentage changes can at best describe linear associations, but they cannot establish quantitative changes or an electoral transfer. Such electoral movements, which are normally calculated on the basis of survey data, can today only be determined by ecological estimates of aggregate data.[65] When it came to chosing a method, we picked Thomsen's 'Logit-Model'. It has several advantages compared to the ecological regression, which cannot be discussed here.[66] The estimated figures which are calculated with this method give details about the grade of affinity and resistance of the parties towards the Nazi mobilisation of voters at different times. They indicate to what extent the voters of one party voted NSDAP in the following elections and what the social composition of Nazi voters was (see table 5.3). Because of the restrictive methodical assumptions, they should certainly not be interpreted exactly according to percentages, but should rather be understood as an indication of the order of magnitude. Because there are no other options than estimates on the basis of aggregate data in historical electoral research, these kinds of calculations – despite all their pitfalls and limitations – are the only way in which to gain at least an approximate picture of the contemporary movement of voters. It is advantageous that the 332 collectives, which were entered into the calculation, were all comparatively small (with the exception of the cities of Dresden, Leipzig and Chemnitz).

According to this estimate, DNVP voters were the most inclined to vote for National Socialism in all three elections. More than two-fifths deserted to the NSDAP in this period. There were also remarkable desertions among the DVP voters and the camp of nonvoters. The volume of the movement from the SPD and KPD to the NSDAP was comparatively small at this time, i.e., both parties were largely (although not completely) resistant. Former SPD voters only comprised around one-tenth of the Saxon Nazi voters in 1930, the figure for the Communists was even smaller. In 1932, the sources of the Nazis' party-political recruitment increased quantitatively (their votes more then doubled compared to 1930) and qualitatively (it broadened). The main reason for this was the

Table 5.3 Movement of Voters to the NSDAP and the Party-Political Background of NSDAP Voters between 1930 and 1933 (in Reichstag Elections)

	Recruitment (rounded percentage)			Composition (rounded percentage)		
	1928/30	1930/32–II	1930/33	1928/30	1930/32–II	1930/33
	NSDAP 1930	Hitler 1932–II	NSDAP 1933	NSDAP 1930	Hitler 1932–II	NSDAP 1933
Saxony						
NSDAP	64	63	73	9	28	28
DNVP	43	48	43	20	5	4
DVP	24	12	19	14	2	3
DDP	15	11	23	4	1	2
WP	8	32	46	4	6	7
SPD	6	19	23	11	15	15
KPD	5	13	10	4	5	3
Others	7	73	81	4	19	18
Nonvoters	23	46	56	31	19	20
Electoral District of Chemnitz						
NSDAP	75	70	81	12	34	36
DNVP	44	36	34	15	3	3
DVP	37	31	37	16	3	3
DDP	20	24	31	3	1	1
WP	10	24	30	4	4	5
SPD	4	22	20	5	13	11
KPD	8	27	18	5	10	6
Others	14	61	78	6	13	16
Nonvoters	29	55	63	34	19	20

Reading example: 6 percent of the Saxon SPD voters from 1928 voted NSDAP in 1930, 19 percent of the Saxon SPD voters from 1930 voted for Hitler in the 1932 RPW-II, and 23 percent of the Saxon SPD voters from 1930 voted for the NSDAP in 1933. Equally, former SPD voters comprised 11 percent of the Saxon NSDAP voters in 1930, and 15 percent of former SPD voters voted for Hitler in the 1932 RPW-II and for the NSDAP in 1933 respectively.

massive influx from the splinter parties, the WP and – compared to 1930 – a significant increase from the nonvoter camp to the NSDAP. Nearly every second nonvoter from 1930 voted for Hitler in the 1932 RPW-II. According to this estimate, one-fifth of former SPD voters from 1930 also voted for Hitler.[67]

There was a decisive transformation of the core of the Saxon Nazi voters between 1930 and 1932. By 1932 the Nazis had managed to absorb voters, though in different proportions, from all parties and all camps. No political camp and no party proved to be totally immune. Former nonvoters and voters of the splinter parties – including those of the SLV – comprised the greatest contingency amongst the NSDAP electorate from 1932 onwards. The middle-class element clearly dominated. Former SPD and KPD voters together made up around a fifth of all Nazi voters. Compared with the size of the overall electorate, they remained under-represented, but still comprised a remarkable part of the Nazi electorate.

We have already noted that the electoral district of Chemnitz was the bastion of the NSDAP in Saxony. The estimates for the electoral movements roughly coincide in this district with developments in the rest of Saxony. Compared with the whole of Saxony, one aspect is particularly noteworthy here: the SPD voters seemed to be slightly more resistant to Nazism than the KPD voters. If our estimates are correct, the reverse was the case in the rest of the state. The desertion of former KPD voters to the NSDAP was not particularly high; however, in the electoral district of Chemnitz it was twice as high as the Saxon average and was even above that of the SPD. The bonds amongst the KPD electorate in Chemnitz seemed weaker than in Dresden and Leipzig. This finding is supported by the fact that in the rest of Saxony the NSDAP tended to do well after 1928, where the SPD had been stronger than the USPD in 1920. This was not the case in the electoral district of Chemnitz: here the NSDAP gained better results in areas where the USPD had dominated the SPD ten years earlier.[68] Left-wing political traditions had completely the reverse effect in the electoral district of Chemnitz than in the rest of Saxony.

The reader of this book is already acquainted with Saxony's economic, social and political character. For the purpose of what follows, it makes sense to reiterate the lack of a strong contrast between town and countryside due to the industrial villages in the region,[69] but also to emphasise Saxony's industrial traditions and the strength of its labour movement. It is therefore a challenging question to investigate how it was possible that the Nazis managed to become comparatively strong in working-class Saxony, particularly in the electoral district of Chemnitz.[70] Empirical electoral research can only give limited answers to this due to a lack of crucial explanatory variables, such as the behaviour of the trade union movement, the network of nonpolitical organisations, or local data about the NSDAP organisation. One can, however, make reasonable assessments about the typical electoral behaviour of all those who were classified as workers, what their proportion in the social composition of the NSDAP was, and how the NSDAP performed in towns and communities with various percentages of unemployment.

It is important to remember that the working classes were not a homogenous social class that shared the same voting behaviour.[71] Equally, the fact that the NSDAP performed better in Saxony than in the Republic as a whole, should not automatically lead to the conclusion that Saxon workers voted over-proportionally in favour of Nazism. To find any answers to this problem, it is probably pertinent to investigate the NSDAP's dependence on workers (see table 5.4). This dependence is put into context with the correlatives of other important social variables from the 1925 census. Additionally, we have carried out percentage counts relating quartiles of varying proportions of workers, and calculated partial correlations under statistical control of the agricultural proportions, to keep constant the effect of this third factor. This seemed necessary, because the NSDAP success was positively linked with the growing size of the agricultural sector from 1932 onwards.

Neither bivariate and trivariate evaluations produce a clear pattern of correlation between the NSDAP mobilisation and working-class proportions in Saxon towns and communities. It seems that it did not matter if a town or a rural community had a low or high proportion of working-class inhabitants: there were no linear associations with Nazi successes. In contrast to this, the proportion of salaried employees and self-employed correlated more markedly; the first surprisingly negative, the latter more positive.

There was a clear positive association between the proportion of cottage workers and the extent of the NSDAP mobilisation. Although this social group did not play a particularly important role according to the 1925 census, it seems to have stood for a specific type of employment which favoured the NSDAP's likelihood of success. This group, which was formerly part of the self-employed, was particularly resident in areas where the textile industry existed. It is therefore not surprising that the NSDAP proportion positively correlated with the proportion of the textile industry: the more local people who were employed in the textile industry, the more successful was the NSDAP.[72]

Table 5.4 NSDAP Mobilisation in Relation to Various Important Social Variables in Saxony (in National Elections)

Quartile					Correlative	
Self-employed	1	2	3	4	Bivariate Correlation	Partial Correlation
1928	2.4	1.7	2.1	2.8	09	18
1930	17.2	16.0	14.5	17.7	05	15
1932 RPW-II	36.1	35.7	33.4	42.6	22	09
1933	39.2	40.9	40.0	49.1	40	29
Breadth of Quartiles	–11.9	11.9–13.6	13.6–14.1	>14.1		
Cottage Workers	1	2	3	4	Bivariate Correlation	Partial Correlation
1928	1.4	1.9	3.2	2.2	12	13
1930	12.8	14.4	18.6	18.4	29	31
1932 RPW-II	35.0	31.3	40.5	41.9	41	43
1933	39.0	38.6	44.7	46.5	40	42
Breadth of Quartiles	–0.6	0.6–1.2	1.2–3.6	>3.6		
Salaried Employees and Civil Servants	1	2	3	4	Bivariate Correlation	Partial Correlation
1928	1.8	1.8	1.8	2.5	09	–07
1930	15.0	15.1	16.1	16.1	01	–25
1932 RPW-II	40.7	35.3	35.6	31.9	–53	–42
1933	46.2	39.7	40.0	38.2	–51	–33
Breadth of Quartiles	–8.3	8.3–17.5	17.5–31.4	>31.4		
Workers	1	2	3	4	Bivariate Correlation	Partial Correlation
1928	2.5	1.9	1.7	2.1	–12	–09
1930	15.7	16.7	15.0	14.3	–08	–05
1932 RPW-II	33.1	39.8	37.1	32.9	12	07
1933	40.3	44.4	41.2	37.2	–04	–11
Breadth of Quartiles	–46.7	46.7–54.3	54.3–58.7	>58.7		

Social variables according to the 1925 census. Percentage figures. Basis for the percentage of the NSDAP: registered voters. Basis for the percentage of the social variables: the employed population. Weighted with the residential population. Basis: 198 diachronic towns and rural communities in Saxony. The average proportion of the self-employed according to the census are 13.2 percent, that for cottage workers 2.9 percent, that for salaried employees and civil servants (together) 19.1 percent, and that for workers 54.0 percent (in employment). The quartiles have the same

number of cases. Control variables of the partial correlatives: agricultural unit according to the 1925 census.
Reading example: the NSDAP gained 15.7 percent in the collective units with the lowest proportion of workers (1. Quartile); 14.3 percent of all registered voters voted for the NSDAP in the collective units with the highest proportion of workers (4. Quartile).

The example of the cottage workers shows that it is not possible to make quantitative assessments on the basis of correlations. The only way of doing this is with ecological estimates. Despite all their limitations and pitfalls, again they offer the only method at this point to gain a rough picture of the social composition of the NSDAP voters. In order to determine the proportion of workers amongst the National Socialists at various times, we have undertaken an estimate with the social variables analogous to the movement of voters (see table 5.5).[73]

It seems certain that in 1932 the NSDAP mobilised more working-class voters in Saxony than the SPD or KPD. This result corresponds with findings for the whole of Germany, which were based on a slightly different method of estimation.[74] Whilst the proportion of workers amongst the Nazi electorate in Saxony was strongly under-represented before 1932, this changed with the elections for the Reich President. Our findings, based on the 154 towns, communities and remaining district in Saxony, show that the proportion of workers amongst the NSDAP electorate was the same as amongst the SPD electorate.

Finally, we want to round off this brief analysis by looking at the role of unemployment (see table 5.6). Unlike for the KPD, recent electoral research has not managed to find a positive association between regions of electoral success for the NSDAP and high unemployment rates. A breakdown of the unemployment rates amongst workers and salaried employees found that the higher the rate of unemployed workers, the weaker was the NSDAP and the stronger was the KPD.[75]

Unlike elsewhere in the Reich, unemployment had no directly positive or negative impact on the NSDAP's grade of mobilisation (see table 5.6).[76] This did not change either, when the proportion of unemployed workers was not considered. It is somewhat surprising that the linear association with the proportion of unemployed salaried employees was negative. Ecological estimates, which can be only mentioned here briefly, gave an average for 1930, and from

Table 5.5 The Estimated Voting Behaviour of Workers and the Proportion of Workers amongst the NSDAP, KPD and SPD Electorate in Saxony and the Electoral District of Chemnitz (in National Elections)

	Estimated voting behaviour of workers for: (rounded percentage)			Affinity Index			Estimated proportion of workers amongst parties' electorate (rounded percentage)		
Saxony	NSDAP	SPD	KPD	NSDAP	SPD	KPD	NSDAP	SPD	KPD
1928	1	31	14	50	107	126	15	31	37
1930	10	30	19	64	108	131	18	31	41
1932 RPW-II	33	?	18	94	?	164	27	?	47
1933	40	23	22	97	98	146	28	28	42
Electoral District of Chemnitz	NSDAP	SPD	KPD	NSDAP	SPD	KPD	NSDAP	SPD	KPD
1928	2	28	15	51	100	111	18	35	38
1930	14	25	22	68	107	134	22	34	44
1932 RPW-II	41	?	20	98	?	147	31	?	47
1933	45	19	24	98	96	138	31	31	44

The proportion of workers according to the 1933 census (sum of unemployed and employed workers). Percentage basis of NSDAP proportions: registered voters. Percentage basis of workers' proportions: residental population in 1933. Affinity index = (working-class electorate/workers in total) x 100. An affinity index below 100 indicates an under-, an index over 100 an over-representation of working-class voters. Weighted with the residental population. Basis: 154 diachronic towns and rural communities in Saxony (80 for the electoral district of Chemnitz). According to this percentage basis, the average workers' proportion in Saxony was nearly 29 percent, whilst in the electoral district of Chemnitz it was 32 percent. No calculations were possible for the SPD in 1932, because it supported the candidature of Hindenburg together with other parties.
Reading example: 10 percent of workers voted for the NSDAP in 1930, 30 percent SPD and 19 percent KPD. The estimated workers' proportion amongst the NSDAP electorate was 18 percent, 31 percent amongst the SPD, and 41 percent amongst the KPD.

1932 onwards a rather under-representative affinity of unemployed workers and salaried employees to vote for the NSDAP.[77] Exactly the opposite was the case for the KPD. The estimated proportion of unemployed workers amongst its electorate was twice as high as its proportion of the electorate. Accordingly, in March 1933 only slightly more than every fifth unemployed

Table 5.6 NSDAP Mobilisation and Unemployment in Saxony (in National Elections)

	Quartile (percentage)				Correlative	
Unemployed	1	2	3	4	Bivariate Correlation	Partial Correlation
1930	14.5	16.5	14.6	18.8	.13	.01
1932 RPW-II	39.4	38.6	30.8	37.5	–.23	.00
1933	44.1	44.1	38.0	40.8	–.29	–.04
Unemployed Workers	1	2	3	4	Bivarate Correlation	Partial Correlation
1930	15.1	14.8	15.2	19.2	.15	.09
1932 RPW-II	38.5	32.1	36.2	38.5	–.02	.15
1933	43.0	39.6	41.1	41.7	–.11	.06
Unemployed Salaried Employees and Domestic Servants	1	2	3	4	Bivariate Correlation	Partial Correlation
1930	16.3	14.9	13.1	16.2	.01	–.19
1932 RPW-II	42.4	36.9	32.9	31.5	–.51	–.37
1933	47.0	42.6	37.8	38.0	–.48	–.26

Unemployment variables according to the 1933 census. Basis for the NSDAP percentage: registered voters. Basis for the unemployed percentage: registered voters in 1933. Weighted with the residential population. Basis: 154 diachronic towns and rural communities in Saxony. The average proportion of the total unemployed was 17.3 percent according to the census, that for unemployed workers 14.4 percent and that for unemployed salaried employees (and domestic employees) 2.9 percent (registered voters in 1933). The quartiles have the same number of cases. Control variables of the partial correlatives: agricultural proportion according to the 1925 census.
Reading example: in 1930 the NSDAP gained 14.5 percent in the collective units with the lowest proportion of unemployment (1. Quartile); 18.8 percent of the electorate voted for the NSDAP in the collective units with the highest proportion of unemployed (4. Quartile).

worker voted for the Nazis, nearly every third for the Communists, and every fourth for the Social Democrats. These estimates imply that the unemployed workers together with the salaried employees belonged to the groups which were most immune to National Socialism. As was the case elsewhere, unemployment did not have a direct, but rather an indirect impact on the rise of Nazism in Saxony.

To sum up, the social composition of the NSDAP electorate in Saxony changed fundamentally between 1930 and 1932. It recruited its voters predominantly from the bourgeois electorate; however, there were inroads into all electoral groups after the elections to the Reich President in 1932. This included a remarkable proportion of former Social Democratic voters. The social composition of the Nazi electorate changed accordingly. Workers were suddenly only slightly under-represented. These estimates suggest therefore that Nazi propaganda was more fruitful amongst employed than unemployed workers. The high proportion of workers and the markedly under-representation of salaried employees does not justify the description of the NSDAP electorate as middle class or petit bourgeois. This was only the case, if at all, until 1930. By 1932 the NSDAP had become an integrative party of protest – as in the rest of the Republic – which reached all social groups, albeit in different proportions.

Notes

1. Unless stated otherwise, the information below is taken from the following sources: BDC; Mai, 'Mutschmann'; E. Stockhorst, *5000 Köpfe. Wer war was im Dritten Reich*, Bruchsal, 1967; K. Hoffkes, *Hitlers Politische Generale*, Tübingen 1986.
2. *NSDAP Zwickau*, 13.
3. See 'Die NSDAP in Sachsen', *Sachsen*, (2) (1938), 2.
4. See Hoffkes, *Generale*, 243. It is possible that Mutschmann was only appointed *Gauleiter* during the NSDAP meeting in Weimar in 1926. See STA D, MdI, Nr. 11126/6, August 1926.
5. Quoted from H.-G. Schumann, *Nationalsozialismus und Gewerkschaftsbewegung. Die Vernichtung der deutschen Gewerkschaften und der Aufbau der "Deutschen Arbeitsfront"*, Hanover, 1958, 45f.
6. Apparently Mutschmann was also heavily influenced by his wife. See M.H. Kater, *The Nazi Party. A Social Profile of Members and Leaders, 1919–1945*, Oxford, repr. 1985, 395.
7. Mutschmann visited Hitler several times in prison in Landsberg (*FK*, Nr. 143, 24.5.1935), and was loyal to the Munich headquarters after the refoundation of the party in 1925. At the end of 1932 Mutschmann spent several days during the Hitler-Straßer dispute with his wife as Hitler's guest in Berchtesgaden and mediated with Gregor Straßer. See *Die Tagebücher von Joseph Goebbels.* Sämtliche Fragmente, ed., E. Fröhlich, Munich, 1987, 29.12.1932–30.12.1932.
8. See *Tagebücher Goebbels*, 23.11.1925.

9. E.g. see P. Hüttenberger, *Die Gauleiter. Studie zum Wandel des Machtgefüges in der NSDAP*, Stuttgart, 1969, 45.
10. Altmann, 'Löffelschmiede', 203. It is not clear how Mutschmann died. See Hoffkes, *Generale*, 244.
11. E.g. *see Hitler's Table Talk 1941–44. His Private Conversations*, ed. H.R. Trevor-Roper, 2nd. edn., London, 1973, 321.
12. This comes across in some of the few documents that exist about Mutschmann. See BDC, Mutschmann.
13. Among others, after 1933 Mutschmann was master of the state huntsmen of Saxony, honorary leader of the SA-Standarte 100, honorary leader of the German labour front, SA-Obergruppenführer and 'Reichsverteidigungskommissar für den Wehrkreis IV' (1.9.1939).
14. [Otto Wagener] H.A. Turner, ed., *Hitler aus nächster Nähe. Aufzeichnungen eines Vertrauten 1929–1932*, Berlin, 1978, 337ff.
15. *Tagebücher Goebbels*, 23.5.1936; 27.6.1936; 21.10.1936; 6.11.1936; 18.11.1936.
16. Hüttenberger, *Gauleiter*, 185f.
17. Unless stated otherwise, the information below is taken from STA D, Druckerei des NS-Gauverlages Sachsen. Zeitungstext- und Bildarchiv. Kunz was the driving force for the spread of Nazism in the district of Schwarzenberg. See chapter 2.
18. E.g. *see VdSL*, 5. Wp, 30. Sitzung, 12.2.1931, 1149.
19. They include all NSDAP members of the Saxon parliament and other prominent local leaders. This seems a large figure compared with the national picture. Compare with Kater, *Nazi Party*, 169ff.
20. This gives the elite an over-representation within the Saxon NSDAP leadership. For similarities with the national level see ibid., 174f.
21. Ibid. 179.
22. STA D, 'NS-Gauverlag', Pillmayer; Kater, *Nazi Party*, 180.
23. See Hoffkes, *Generale*, 349f.
24. E.g. see the speech by Mücke in *VdSL*, 3. Wp, 9. Sitzung, 20.1.1927, 166ff; and the speech by Tittmann in ibid., 113. Sitzung, 21.3.1929, 428ff.
25. Detlef Mühlberger is Senior Lecturer in Modern European History at Oxford Brookes University. He has published widely on the sociology of the Nazi movement, and is author of *Hitler's Followers. Studies in the Sociology of the Nazi Movement*, London, 1991; he has edited *The Social Basis of European Fascist Movements*, London, 1987.
26. This 20-year-old held the membership number 2,106. See 'Adolf Hitler's Mitkämpfer 1919–1921', *NSDAP Hauptarchiv* (*HA*), Hoover Institution Microfilm Collection, reel 2A, Folder 230.
27. The only information available at present relates to the occupational and class breakdown of 174 individuals who joined the NSDAP in

Saxony between 28 September and 9 November 1923. See D. Mühlberger, 'Germany', in Mühlberger, *Social Basis*, 63f.

28. A membership list of the NSDAP branch in Leipzig has survived and it records 214 members on 28 February 1923 (212 effectively, since there are two double-entries). A police report from 8.5.23 provided further information about members who joined in March and April that year. On a previous occasion, the Leipzig police listed forty-five NSDAP members who had met illegally on 7.3.1923. For all three documents see BA DH, Erich Kunz, Z/C 17411.
29. The addresses of the members suggest that Nazi supporters were widely dispersed within Leipzig.
30. The occupational breakdown of the male working population of Leipzig in 1925 (by percentage): workers: 49.89; domestic workers: 0.06; white-collar employees/civil servants: 33.7; self-employed: 16.33; working family members: 0.01. Calculated from *StDR*, 403 (1927), part 10, 87.
31. The data are drawn from a fragment of the central membership register kept by the Munich headquarters (see *HA*, 10/250). Although the NSDAP had been banned in Saxony on 24 March 1923, branches at Chemnitz, Dresden, Leipzig, Mittweida and Plauen were recorded in the NSDAP's central membership register as having enrolled 129 of the 174 Saxon members listed as entering the party between 28 September and 9 November. The remaining members were enrolled directly into the Munich branch. The occupational classification system and class model used here are more refined than the ones which the author employed in the mid-1980s, hence the data presented here shows slight differences from that given in Mühlberger, 'Germany', 63.
32. The occupational breakdown of the male working population in Saxony (by percentage):

year	*1925*	*1933*
workers:	57.82	59.72
domestic workers:	0.05	0.02
white-collar employees/civil servants:	22.16	21.36
independents:	18.14	17.24
working family members:	1.81	1.64

Calculated from *StDR*, vol. 403 (1927), part 10, 4; *StDR*, vol. 454 (1936), part 10, 3.

33. Compare with J.P. Madden, 'The Social Composition of the Nazi Party, 1919–1930', PhD thesis, University of Oklahoma, 1976, 68, 72, 78, 86, 94 and 100; M.H. Kater, 'Zur Soziographie der frühen NSDAP', *Vierteljahrshefte für Zeitgeschichte*, 19 (1971), 154–56.

34. E.g. see Madden, 'Composition', 75, 78, 86, 93 and 107; M.H. Kater, 'Frauen in der NS-Bewegung', *Vierteljahreshefte für Zeitgeschichte*, 31 (1983), 204.
35. Compare with Mühlberger, 'Germany', 62f.
36. The argument that the Nazi party was a *Volkspartei* even in its formative years is advanced by Paul Madden. See especially Madden, 'Composition'. See also D. Mühlberger, 'A "Workers'Party" or a "Party Without Workers"? The Extent and Nature of the Working-Class Membership of the NSDAP, 1919–1933', in Fischer, *Rise*, 57–9. For a contrary view see Kater, 'Soziographie'. For a general review see Peter Manstein, *Die Mitglieder und Wähler der NSDAP 1919–1933. Untersuchungen zu ihrer schichtmäßigen Zusammensetzung*, 3rd. edn., Frankfurt/Main, 1990.
37. Manstein is of the opinion that this source has 'considerable value'; Manstein, *NSDAP*, 143–47. See also Mühlberger, *Followers*, 7f.
38. Nazi term to describe the period before Hitler was appointed Chancellor.
39. The Nazis claimed that some 87,079 members had joined the NSDAP in Saxony by 30 January 1933. See *Partei-Statistik*, vol. 1, 19–21.
40. Calculated from ibid., 148.
41. Calculated from ibid., 28, 30, 86, 146 and 148.
42. There is a general lack of information on the social basis of Nazism in central and eastern Germany. See Szejnmann, 'Missing Pieces'. For some limited data see Kater, *Nazi Party*, 246, 248, 250; and D. Mühlberger, 'The Occupational and Social Structure of the NSDAP in the Border Province Posen-West Prussia in the early 1930s', *European History Quarterly*, 15, 1985, 281–311. Recent regional and local studies on the NSDAP in central Germany have not dealt with the social profile of the NSDAP in any detail: e.g. see Lapp, *Revolution*; Matthiesen, *Thüringen*; Heiden, *Nationalsozialismus*; Eichholtz, *Brandenburg*.
43. The author of this piece and the author of the book are most grateful to Professor Jürgen Falter (and also Professor W. Brustein) for providing the Brustein-Falter sample relating to Saxony. For details about the whole sample and the sampling techniques see Brustein, *Evil*, 210, note 69. One should bear in mind that in any comparison between the BDC material and that of the *Partei-Statistik* one is not comparing like with like, in that the Brustein-Falter sample is representative for the Nazi membership recruited in Saxony as a whole (and includes members who were only temporarily in the party at any stage between 1925 and 1933), whereas the *Partei-Statistik* measures only those members of the NSDAP who were still in the party by the time the census was taken in 1934.

44. For an insight into the occupational classification and class model used in the analysis of the Saxon data see Mühlberger, *Followers*, 19–25. In the BDC data the middle-class members of the NSDAP in Saxony account for the following percentages:

1925: 52.1	1928: 54.3	1931: 48.5
1926: 48.5	1929: 53.2	1932: 50.0
1927: 51.7	1930: 53.3	1933: 58.3

45. In the BDC data workers make up the following percentages of the recruits to the Nazi party in Saxony:

1925: 40.6	1928: 37.0	1931: 38.7
1926: 44.1	1929: 35.9	1932: 36.9
1927: 41.7	1930: 34.7	1933: 29.5

46. The average values derived from the BDC data for the periods 1925 to 14 September 1930 and for 15 September 1930 to 30 January 1933 are not weighted in terms of the proportionality of intake per year. However, given the size of the total sample, and the large number of Nazis recruited each year, the results given here are fairly precise and statistically reliable. Compare with Jürgen Falter, 'The Young Membership of the NSDAP between 1925 and 1933. A Demographic and Social Profile', in Fischer, *Rise*, 80 and notes 6 and 13, 96f.
47. Mühlberger, *Followers*, 82f, 122f.
48. A comparison with the national breakdown of the Nazi party recruits by residence for the period 1925–1932 provided by Brustein, *Evil*, 18, table 1.1, highlights the different pattern to be found in Saxony (by percentage):

community size	Saxony	Germany
<5,000	33.0	44.0
5,000–19,999	20.5	13.0
20,000–99,999	11.1	15.0
>100,000	35.2	28.0

49. Working-class and middle-class membership in Saxony, 1925–1933, by size of residence (BDC data, by percentage):

Community size	Working class	Middle class
<5,000	39.4	29.8
5,000–19,999	23.4	18.9
20,000–99,999	9.5	11.9
>100,000	27.5	39.4

50. The average membership frequencies on the basis of which figures 5.4 to 5.6 are calculated are: for the top ten Nazi electoral strongholds: 66.5; for the top ten SPD electoral strongholds: 31.1; for the top ten KPD electoral strongholds: 40.3.
51. The average age of individuals entering the Nazi Party in Saxony in each of the years 1925 to 1933 was fractionally lower than that of the NSDAP as a whole, but reflects the national trend in virtually identical proportions. See Brustein, *Evil*, 174f., table 5.2b.
52. Dirk Hänisch is one of the first experts to have investigated the NSDAP electorate with modern electoral analysis, and belonged to the staff of the political scientist Prof. Jürgen Falter between 1984 and 1989. He has published widely in the field, and is author of *Sozialstrukturelle Bestimmungsgründe des Wahlverhaltens in der Weimarer Republik. Eine Aggredatdatenanalyse der Ergebnisse der Reichstagswahlen 1924 bis 1933, Duisburg, 1983; Die österreichischen NSDAP-Wähler: eine empirische Analyse ihrer politischen Herkunft und ihres Sozialprofils,* Vienna, 1998; and together with A. Elste, *Auf dem Weg zur Macht. Beiträge zur Geschichte der NSDAP in Kärnten von 1918 bis 1938*, Vienna, 1997. This piece was translated by C.-C.W. Szejnmann.
53. See especially the numerous publications by Jürgen Falter and his staff. The most important results are summarised in Falter, *Wähler.*
54. For these early controversies between Lipset and Bendix, see Falter, *Wähler*.
55. The territorial emphasis on the German Reich is emphasised here because the electoral base of the Austrian National Socialists, in contrast to the German NSDAP, was indeed much more dominated by the middle classes. See Hänisch, *Österreichische NSDAP*.
56. To my knowledge, empirical electoral analyses about the Saxon NSDAP do not exist. The following findings are the first results from the specially constructed data base on Saxony by the author.
57. There is no room here to describe the data base in detail. The electoral results for both Reichstag elections in 1932 and both elections for the Reich President were only systematically compiled on the district level and published in the *StDR*. The electoral results for the 1932 RPW-II for the numerous Saxon towns were therefore painstakingly collected from various Saxon daily newspapers. As for the rest, the author used the data base 'Weimarer Wahl- und Sozialdaten', No. 1510, from the Central Archive for Empirical Social Research in Cologne. See the detailed description by D. Hänisch, 'Inhalt und Struktur der Datenbank "Wahl- und Sozialdaten der Kreise und Gemeinden des Deutschen Reiches von 1920 bis 1933" ', *Historical Social Research*, 14 (1989), 39–67. Additional social data which were added to this data base are from *ZSäStLA*,

(1920), (1921), (1930). The author used the RPW-II in 1932 rather than the Reichstag elections in July 1932 for two reasons: whilst Hitler and the NSDAP received very similar results in both elections, the compilation of the election data was less labour intensive for the RPW-II; because the July election coincided with the summer vacation many guests voted during the election in Saxon holiday resorts.

58. For further methodical requirements of aggregate data and the dangers of the so-called 'ecological fallacy', see Falter, *Wähler*. The construction of fairly stable longitudinal geographical units was done with the data from the *StJbSa* (1921/23), and the data from K. Blaschke, *Historisches Ortsverzeichnis von Sachsen*, Leipzig, 1957.
59. The first file contains 332 Saxon towns and communities with more than 2,000 residents and the *Restkreise* with electoral data of the elections to the Reichstag in 1920, 1928, 1930, 1933 and the 1932 RPW-II. The second file contains additional data from the 1925 census, the data of all rural communities with a population above 10,000 and the synthetically constructed *Restkreise*, which includes all rural communities with a population below 10,000 and towns with less than 2,000 people. The number of cases (*Fallzahl*): 198 collectives. Finally, a further file was created which contains additional information from the 1933 census with a *Fallzahl* of 154 aggregate units. The fourth and last file contains all available electoral and social data on the level of the towns and AHs. Of particular interest are the results of the 1925 RPW-II, which were also only published at the level of the districts (47 districts and towns). All files cover Saxony.
60. The percentage basis is generally the number of registered voters. This method has now gained widespread acceptance in the field, because it is the only way of adequately including the nonvoters and preventing the distortion of percentage results of the parties due to different electoral turnouts. Also see the justified criticism from Hausmann, 'Trotz allem'.
61. Pearson's weighted correlation coefficient was +.70. The AHs and town districts form the basis here. The number of registered voters for the districts and communities with more than 2,000 inhabitants had to be estimated according to the data from 1930 and 1933 (the average was taken).
62. The losses of the DVP (3.7 percent) correlate with the gains of the NSDAP (13.5 percent) by –.64, and with that of the losses of the nonvoters camp (6.3 percent) by –.51. The figures are negative because gains and losses are set in relation and therefore describe a relation outside the first quadrant.
63. Despite the semi-free status of the March 1933 elections, they are extremely important for the analysis of the Nazi electorate, because

they indicate resistance and susceptibility of the parties under repressive Nazi conditions.

64. The gains of the NSDAP between 1930 and 1933 (25.2 percent) correlate with the losses of the SLV (–3.4 percent) by –.73, with that of the nonvoters (–5.4 percent) by –.59, and with that of the SPD (–3.9 percent) by –.36.
65. Survey data were hardly known at the time of this investigation. The dangers of an ecological fallacy were extensively discussed in the literature. Strictly speaking, it can only give information about the context of the voters, but not about their individual motives and their behaviour. E.g. see Falter, *Wähler*, 79.
66. For a critic of the ecological regression model, see S. Rijsberg Thomsen, *Danish Elections 1920–1979. A logit Approach to Ecological Analysis and Inference*, Arhus, 1987. The model Thomsen himself developed has, amongst other things, the advantage that it avoids negative estimates, which inevitably develop with regression methods, so that no artificial smoothing procedures are necessary.
67. Jürgen Falter concluded from a different methodical background that 10 percent of the SPD voters from 1928 voted for the NSDAP in 1930 in the Reich. See Falter, *Wähler*, 111. This increased to 16 percent of SPD voters who switched between 1930 and July 1932 to the NSDAP (Falter did not evaluate the 1932 RPW). The figures for the KPD were 5 percent respectively. These quantitative differences can easily be neglected, and one can conclude that the susceptibility of Saxon KPD and SPD voters to Nazism was hardly more pronounced than the national average.
68. This is shown by a negative correlation between the units of the USPD with those of the NSDAP in the district of Leipzig and Dresden (e.g. 1932 by –.67 and by –.35), whilst there was a positive correlation in Chemnitz (by +.30).
69. This also showed in the electoral behaviour, which was overall very similar in town and countryside.
70. See Walter, 'Stammland'.
71. E.g. see J.W. Falter, 'How likely were Workers to Vote for the NSDAP?', in Fischer, *Rise*, 9–45. This piece is largely based on the findings of an earlier publication: J.W. Falter and D. Hänisch, 'Die Anfälligkeit von Arbeitern gegenüber der NSDAP bei den Reichstagswahlen 1928–1933', *Archiv für Sozialgeschichte*, 26 (1986), 179–216.
72. The correlative coefficients, from which the agricultural share was removed, with the NSDAP were +.37 in 1930, +.43 in 1932 (Hitler) and +.39 in 1933.
73. The various employment rates were translated into percentage figures of the resident population. The figure which was left over (*Restgröße*) consists of all nonactive members of social classes. This

figure acts as reference variable (*Referenzvariable*) in Thomsen's Logit-Model, which was again applied for the estimates.

74. See Falter, 'How Likely'.
75. Falter, *Wähler*, 301f.
76. It is 'silently' implied here that the unemployment level between 1930 and 1933 was equally distributed and structured.
77. The unemployment rates were translated into percentage figures for the resident population. Other percentage bases did not change the fundamental associations that were described.

Conclusion

'Fertile Soil and Unfriendly Desert.' The Nazi Experience in Saxony

The development of the Nazi movement in Saxony – a traditional working-class region and one of Germany's most industrialised areas – proved that Nazism could win mass support in one of the heartlands of the German workers' movement. Saxony played a particular role in the development of Nazism at a time when it was transforming into a mass movement. After the Saxon Landtag election in May 1929, Hitler decided to use the Saxon parliament as an experiment for parliamentary cooperation with the bourgeoisie. This paved the way for Frick's participation in a bourgeois coalition government in Thuringia six months later. The Saxon Landtag election in June 1930 marked the Nazis' first significant electoral triumph in an important state in Germany. The Nazis had used the occasion to stage their first centrally organised campaign under the party's new head of propaganda – Joseph Goebbels – and initiated a new era of mass mobilisation. It was fateful that Chancellor Brüning ignored the clear signs from Saxony that the Nazis had become a formidable electoral force, and dissolved the Reichstag in an electoral gamble which backfired: in the September Reichstag elections his government coalition lost seats and henceforth depended on emergency rule, whilst the Nazis achieved their national breakthrough and crossed a decisive hurdle towards overthrowing the Republic.

The premise of this survey is that if one wants to understand the origins, development, success and limitations of Nazism, one has to combine an analysis of the Nazi movement and the society in which it operated. Although the conclusions presented here have to be seen against the specific context of Saxony and have to be compared with other regions in Germany, of course Saxony itself was also heavily influenced by developments elsewhere. Most importantly, the course of Saxon history was intrinsically linked to the Reich and – more generally – to the process of modernisation which affected societies throughout Europe. In the first half of the twentieth century Saxon society was influenced by specific features which limited the options for its development. Economically, Saxony faced a deep-rooted structural problem: an economy that had failed to modernise following early industrialisation. Politically, Saxony entered the twentieth century with a marked polarisation between a progressive working-class movement and an elite and bourgeoisie who vehemently opposed a democratic political system.

Whereas the majority of the labour movement embraced the new Republican environment after the First World War, many members of the bourgeoisie had enormous problems in adapting to it. Moreover, both had completely different visions of what kind of society they wanted to create within the new political framework. Whereas labour aimed at the welfare of the masses and their integration into the system – a left-Republican project – many members of the bourgeoisie fought this approach vehemently. They pursued policies that clung to traditional values and were marked by a fear of social levelling. Throughout the Weimar Republic, however, neither nationalists nor socialists were able to govern Saxony with a coherent programme that successfully tackled existing economic and social problems over a sustained period of time. Neither side was united enough, nor able to increase a fragile advantage in the Landtag into a long-term domineering position. Eventually the Nazis convinced a large part of the Saxon population that they had found a new cocktail which replaced divisions with unity, and uncertainty with boldness: National Socialism.

The structural problems of Saxony's economy and the political tensions and divisions in society indicate an inability to respond to the process of modernisation. Modernisation led to change, fragmentation, polarisation and anxieties. Whereas those considered to be 'better-off' feared for their status and privileges, the masses themselves often experienced modernity as something negative too: for instance, in the form of unemployment and housing shortages. Both often also shared the same fears: they were anxious about large-scale competition, new consumer tastes and technological inventions which threatened their jobs, businesses or factory ownership.

During the nineteenth century the elite did not adequately respond to the needs of the masses. Indeed, most elite did not think they needed to respond to the 'social question' at all. This led to frequent confrontations between both groups and established the SPD as the voice of the underprivileged. Although there were growing differences between the traditional elite and the bourgeoisie regarding the distribution of power and how to react to the labour movement, both continued to unite behind one priority: to prevent the establishment of a society in which resources and power were distributed democratically. During the Weimar Republic the conflict between labour, bourgeoisie and traditional elites continued with even greater force because the various groups competed for the first time on an equal footing, and – due to Saxony's deteriorating economic situation – chased after fewer resources.

Nowhere in Germany did this lead to a greater radicalisation and polarisation than in Saxony. During the Reichstag election in July 1932, 88.3 percent of those eligible to vote went to the polls in Saxony, compared with 84.1 percent in the Republic. Support for the middle-class parties collapsed to a mere 13 percent of the vote, half of that of the national average. The Nazis had one of their greatest electoral strongholds in the Republic in southwestern Saxony. The Communists also performed very well in the southwest, whilst the German Social Democrats had their greatest electoral bastions in northwestern and central Saxony. The enormous polarisation was accompanied by a striking fragmentation in local society.

Rainer Lepsius has argued that in the late 1920s, various milieus in German society 'slowly disintegrated' due to 'progressive industrialisation, increasing mobility and social differentiation.'[1] This disintegration in turn contributed to the collapse of the traditional party system. The Nazis were the main beneficiary of this development. Many of Lepsius's observations hold true for Saxony. Some parts of the socialist milieu started to disintegrate because they were increasingly unable to perform their primary function: prosperous living and working conditions for the masses in a modernising environment. The Nazis mocked the Social Democrats by reminding them of promises that they had made to workers in the past. In the Saxon Landtag one Nazi read out an SPD leaflet from May Day 1904: 'Workers, one day you will drive your own car, cruise with your own ships as tourists through the seas, climb in the Alps and wander through the tropics in amazement of the beauty of the south.'[2] The Nazis contrasted statements like this with the deteriorating conditions for workers in the Republic. The Nazis blamed this situation on the SPD for not having carried out a proper revolution after the war and for selling out Germany with the Treaty of Versailles. Manfred von Killinger challenged the Social Democrats:

> Well, what did you promise workers with your revolution again? Peace, freedom, bread. Peace? Peace was made with the eternal enslavement of Germany. Freedom? We are slaves. Bread? The worker is much worse off, much worse, than before the war. In fact, he leads a miserable existence.[3]

Another Nazi stated in the Landtag: 'I want to see the worker who declares: I have a right to open my mouth in my factory! – If he says something, he gets kicked out'.[4] Later he asked provokingly: 'What then, is the worker supposed to defend? Should the German worker even bother to defend his misery and desperation?'[5] The apparent distance between the potentially emancipatory Republican project and 'the lived reality of modernity'[6] made many Saxons, including a significant number of local workers, eventually turn to Nazism. The Nazis were seriously challenging the traditional role of the labour movement, and became increasingly regarded as a major voice of protest against anxiety, misery and political failure. Moreover, Nazism seemed to provide a promising alternative to the existing system.

The question as to whether particular Saxons would actually join the Nazi bandwagon depended largely on social and cultural circumstances.[7] The majority of Saxon workers were not tempted by Nazism. Northwestern and central Saxony became the greatest bastion of the German labour movement before the Nazi seizure of power. The deep-rooted socialist traditions in the region explain why local working-class voters were largely immune to Nazism until 1930 – longer than in the rest of the Reich. The local strength of the socialist milieu decided whether the Nazis failed or succeeded in attracting a substantial number of workers as members and voters. The less widespread, deep-rooted and active the Social Democratic party and its organisational network was the less able it was to ward off and respond to the enormous challenges posed by the Nazis and the economic crisis. The SPD (not to mention the KPD) also failed to make significant inroads into the bourgeois constituency and turn itself into a people's party. Although the Social Democrats were committed to the Republic, they clung to an unreal socialist rhetoric, they were reluctant to make compromises with other groups, and they frequently cut themselves off from the rest of Saxon society. With this they contributed to the damaging political polarisation and lack of cooperation between the political players during the Weimar Republic. Moreover, the revolutionary strategy of the Communists split the workers' milieu and weakened its potential to respond to Nazism. While the majority of workers who belonged to the socialist milieu stayed loyal to the Republic, a growing minority demanded nothing less than a socialist revolution.

Whereas the SPD's claim that it could deliver a better world was undermined by the slump and its helpless reaction, the nationalists were poised to benefit from the crisis. Saxon nationalists had a long history of criticising or opposing the Weimar system. However, the many compromises all nationalist parties made with the Republican system during the 1920s, together with their failure to respond to increasing desperation in their traditional constituencies, cost their political representatives dearly. As elsewhere in Germany, the majority of the Saxon middle classes eventually turned their back on the 'stuffy and elitist politics of patronage and personality'.[8] Either they turned to Nazism directly, or they affiliated themselves with it via special interest groups.

During the slump most bourgeois clubs – if professional or leisure-orientated – radicalised. They faced a declining membership, a decline in club activities and growing debts. An increasing number of these organisations expressed the view that an authoritarian, nationalist state was the only solution to the crisis, and began to sympathise with Nazism. Meanwhile, more and more newspapers of the influential bourgeois press were openly supporting the NSDAP. Additionally, many local industrialists and employers finally lost their patience with a Republic which they regarded as an economic liability. This development was fostered by the irresponsible strategy of the bourgeois parties, which defended political majorities against the left by exaggerating the (unrealistic) threat of a 'Soviet Saxony'. The use of an aggressive language to pull together the disintegrating bourgeoisie heightened tensions and polarisation in society, and drew more and more people towards Nazism as the most explicit enemy of the left. Furthermore, the bourgeoisie's Marxist-bashing shattered any chance the traditional parties had in overcoming the divisions between left and right and in tackling the crisis together: the DVP rejected several signals by the SPD to enter a Great Coalition between 1929 and 1930. To be fair, though, the Social Democrats' proposals to join a Great Coalition continued to be wrapped in dogmatic language. They emphasised that their primary interest in such a government would be to look after the interests of the 'proletariat'.[9] All these developments played into the hands of the Nazis: although the Saxon NSDAP managed to attract members and voters from all social classes at the end of Weimar, the middle classes – as on the national level – continued to be over-represented.

The Nazis' fresh image and determined appearance, coupled with their espousal of familiar values – i.e., widespread nationalist, authoritarian, anti-democratic and anti-Marxist beliefs – made them respectable in the eyes of many contemporaries. That respectability led to the increasing perception that the Nazis were the legitimate leaders of the nationalist milieu in Saxony. All other attempts to unite the nationalist circles and to provide a positive vision for the future had failed. More and more members of this milieu, whether they specifically liked the Nazis or not, saw the NSDAP as the only party likely to achieve their main goals: to get rid of the Republican system, to prevent a socialist revolution, and to create a new nationalist, authoritarian state which would revive Germany. Although large parts of the Saxon elite were cautious about the Nazis, they regarded them as part of a wider nationalist milieu with whom they shared fundamental values. Furthermore, when the Nazis seized power, many of them 'immediately threw themselves into the party for fear of losing their jobs.'[10]

Divisions between the nationalist milieu and the socialist milieu constituted one of the most fundamental experiences of Saxon society. However, often they were more perceived than real, and they normally served a political agenda. Most importantly, the nationalists claimed to represent a clear-cut choice between a bourgeois-nationalist government and a bolshevist regime. The SPD, however, firmly backed the Republic. Only the comparatively small KPD stood for a socialisation of society. Furthermore, far from forming a united anti-Marxist block, the bourgeois parties and organisations were bitterly divided. Neither did the socialist milieu only have working-class supporters and the nationalist milieu only middle-class followers. In reality then, there were no clear-cut or static divisions between the socialist milieu and nationalist milieu, or any homogeneity within either one. On the contrary, they were dynamic phenomena that could grow, shrink, disintegrate, shift and even overlap with one another. Indeed, the Nazis' skill was to combine nationalist and socialist values.

So far we have used a long-term perspective to analyse Saxon society and its relationship with Nazism. The persistence of authoritarian mentalities and the legacies of political confrontation proved an obstacle for the acceptance of democratic principles, and made political cooperation between the left and right – a prerequisite for the successful functioning of the Weimar Republic – extremely difficult. Together with long-standing economic problems, this difficulty helps explain why more and more Saxons eventually turned away from the Republican system from the late 1920s onwards, and why a growing number were attracted by the alternative vision of a National Socialist revival in a Third Reich. It would be wrong, however, to construct from this a determinist explanation of misdevelopment along the lines of the German Sonderweg (special path) theory,[11] because this would neglect equally important medium-term and short-term causes and would fail to take seriously the Nazis' own contribution.

Several historians have regarded the enormous crisis German society faced after the First World War to be the primary cause of Nazism.[12] Indeed, the trauma of the 'national humiliation' of November 1918, but also the apparent experience of 'war socialism' and national unification during the war, stood at the heart of the wider *völkisch* movement and its opposition to the Republic. Combined with the shock of the 1917 Bolshevik Revolution in Russia, many of these sentiments and anxieties were shared by a broad stratum of Saxon society. Additionally, the years after the war were marked by economic difficulties, social unrest and political polarisation in Saxony. Labour pushed through left-wing democratic reforms against bitter opposition from the bourgeoisie. The manner in which Social Democratic-Communist rule was illegally and brutally smashed by the Reich in October 1923 – urged on and applauded by large sectors of the Saxon bourgeoisie – left little hope for political compromise or stability in Saxony's future. It became clear that the Saxon bourgeoisie was prepared to undermine the democratic framework to reconquer or defend positions of power. Hence the post-war period revived and deepened traditional battle lines in the new democratic environment.[13] It also allowed extremists such as the Nazis to start linking up with more 'respectable' and moderate segments within nationalist circles. It was only during the enormous crisis which unfolded from the late 1920s onwards, however, that the Nazis managed to become a mass movement.

Although it is widely accepted that the economic depression and the collapse of the Weimar Republic stood in close relation to each other, it is surprising how little attention most local and regional studies of Nazism have paid to the exact linkages between the slump and growing support for the NSDAP. Saxony was hit harder by the economic crisis than any other region in Germany. Nevertheless it is extremely difficult to prove a clear relationship between the severity of the economic crisis and the strength of Nazism at the micro level of villages, towns and cities. It is more fruitful to view the slump as a catalyst that opened up tremendous opportunities for Nazism. The Nazis profited disproportionately from a widespread feeling of anxiety due to the daily experience of misery, insecurity, social disturbances, pressures of change, and fragmentation. In addition, political fragmentation forced the move away from the parliamentary process, and a 'neutral' cabinet of civil servants – Saxony's most right-wing government during the Republic – governed the state from May 1930. The Nazis' radical vision was able to gain popular support because the whole system seemed to collapse.

The Nazis themselves contributed heavily to their rise and success in Saxony. Unfortunately, most historians have played down the Nazis' popular appeal, stressing aspects of manipulation and opportunism, or focusing on the failure and disintegration of their opponents.[14] Geoff Eley has recently rightly emphasised the Nazis' 'ability to bring together and articulate a diverse and hitherto contradictory ensemble of ideological appeals', and called for an examination of 'the connotative principles … that allowed the Nazis to capture the popular imagination so powerfully before and after 1933.'[15] The tendency to look at Nazism with the benefit of hindsight, constantly equating it with barbaric mass murder and extermination, has limited our understanding of the Nazis' appeal, especially before 1933. Nazism has often been described in simple terms: either as something alien to German society (i.e., it was uniquely radical, violent, racist, anti-Semitic, etc.), or – paradoxically, as reflecting the evil nature of German society itself. Variations on the latter view range from the 'moderate' *Sonderweg* theory that Germans were authoritarian and anti-democratic, to the thesis that a bloodthirsty anti-Semitism was entrenched in German society.[16]

Nazism in Saxony was a complex phenomenon. It was a new radical and dynamic phenomenon, but it also possessed features that appeared 'normal' to many contemporaries.[17] The Nazis' most crucial contribution to their own success was that they managed to hijack and monopolise the concept of the *Volksgemeinschaft*. This concept had already attracted those who had attempted 'to reconcile national and social integration or "liberation" respectively' from 1900 onward.[18] The experience of the First World War seemed to confirm that national solidarity was the 'prerequisite to social liberation', for it seemed to guarantee the security and prosperity of individuals and the whole nation. After 1918 this consensus between the political parties disintegrated. The Nazis became the only political force that continued to focus on the nation as a whole and did not follow the other parties' reorientation to particular constituencies. As Saxon society became increasingly fragmented and polarised, the promised *Volksgemeinschaft* appeared able to replace the traditional divisions within German society with harmony and unity.

The concept of the *Volksgemeinschaft* had the potential to capture nearly all individuals, groups and classes in Saxon society because it combined elements of socialism, conservatism, corporatism, authoritarianism and nationalism.[19] In fact, the Nazis offered a 'third way' alongside liberal capitalism and Marxism and promised to establish social justice in a strong nationalist state. To them, and to their supporters, this was not a contradiction in itself, but the only way social justice and solidarity between Germans could be realised. For instance, someone who cared about social welfare could well believe that this would be best looked after in the Third Reich.[20] Of course, nationalist sentiments also appealed to large sectors of the working classes, especially during the national emergencies in August 1914, the Ruhr occupation in 1923, and the slump from 1929 onwards. To more and more Saxon workers the Nazis' promotion of strong nationalism and 'class unity' of left and right was more appealing than the Marxist parties' championing of 'internationalism' and 'class struggle'.

Hardly any expert in the field has maintained that there was a clearly defined Nazi programme. However, it is crucial to see support for Nazism not only as a 'negative' choice – a protest against a system that did not work,[21] or the result of irrational behaviour[22] – but also as an active decision to give the Nazis a chance to put into practice their solution to the problems faced by society. The recent argument that the 'dominant motivation' for

Germans to join the Nazi party was economic,[23] is too extreme. The evidence from Saxony, however, suggests that materialistic motivations played an important role in helping to explain the success of Nazism. During the slump all traditional parties focused on short-term strategies in order to patch up the most severe problems. They were clearly fighting a losing battle because of their financial limitations and their adherence to an orthodox economic approach that focused on balancing the budget. The Saxon Nazis supported many of these measures to ease some of the most immediate burdens, for instance, the particular misery in the region bordering Czechoslovakia. Yet the Nazis also labelled these policies as being a limited and short-sighted response. In their view, only radical reforms and large-scale programmes financed by budget deficits (e.g., work programmes) would pull Germany out of depression and ensure long-term growth and stability.

The Saxon Nazis stood by virtue of their clear identification of the overall causes for Germany's misery and their proposed solutions toward overcoming them. They offered sweeping reforms which would apparently benefit nearly all Germans (though not the Jews and other racially 'unfit' groups). In their view, the western powers had exploited Germany and prevented its revival since the country's defeat in the First World War. Only a united German *Volk* could free itself from this dilemma. Werner Studentkowski declared in late 1930: 'The essential precondition for the removal of the Young-Plan and the Versailles Treaty will always be that the German *Volk* will be liberated first of all from those ... who incite working German against working German. ... German working *Volk* unite ... against the exploitation from outside!'[24] The Nazis portrayed themselves as the only credible force in uniting the nation. All traditional parties had at one point or another accepted Germany's exploitation (in the form of the Versailles Plan, Dawes Plan and Young Plan), had been part of the Berlin government, and had fostered the divisions of German society by inciting the various classes into a 'civil war'. To the Nazis, the Marxists were the major culprits on all these accounts. Hence Studentkowski proclaimed so uncompromisingly during a Nazi rally in Chemnitz: 'Either Germany shall live – then one has to crush the head of Marxism (minute long thunderous applause), or Marxism will win, and then Germany will be lost for ever.'[25]

By getting rid of the burdens of the First World War, the Nazis repeatedly pledged to wipe out international capitalism and to restore an honourable great nation. As Saxony was dominated by small- and medium-scale business, the Saxon middle and working classes felt particularly threatened by unrestricted large-scale capitalism and were desperate for some kind of protection in the rapidly modernising environment. As usual, the traditional bourgeois parties responded to these anxieties when it was too late: in early 1933 they suddenly flooded the Landtag with motions to protect shopkeepers and traders from big business.[26]

Although the Nazis condemned capitalism, unlike the Marxists they did not attack property. In their view, this had contributed to the divisions in society. In fact, they aspired to reconcile property with German society. The deputy *Gauleiter* of Saxony, Fritsch, attacked the left:

> You [i.e. Social Democrats] walked around with red flags and placards carrying the slogan "Fight Capitalism!" and "Down with Capitalism!" With that you equated capitalism with ownership and property. With that you have created a division in our *Volk*, you have created a hatred amongst *Volksgenossen*, against the hated bourgeoisie.[27]

The Saxon Communists were the only other political force that had a similarly clear analysis of the crisis (caused by capitalism), how to overcome it (with a revolution) and what to replace it with (socialism). They were, however, a small bunch of 'smoke-screen' radicals, who mobilised a growing number of Saxons to vote for them, but failed to rally the masses in support of their revolutionary struggle on the streets.

The Nazis' dynamic mass mobilisation also played a crucial role in their electoral success in Saxony. The NSDAP was the first political party within the nationalist milieu to possess propaganda machinery that was broadly-based and active year-round. That machinery carried the Nazi message to all citizens and challenged the left for control of the streets. The skilful mixture of broad themes and specific aspects, combined with a reputation for dynamic youthfulness and unbending determination, helps explain why the Nazis were so successful in mobilising former nonvoters and attracting voters from other parties. In places where Nazi propaganda dominated public life, where nationalist sentiments existed, and where they encountered least opposition from their political opponents, the NSDAP's electoral performance was most successful. The Nazis, however, found it difficult to overcome deep-rooted Saxon traditions that did not conform to their message.

The emphasis on the potential attraction of Nazism in Saxony should not detract from their skilful mastery of opportunism, simplification and deceit with which they exploited the enormous crisis after 1929. Their explanation of the ills of German society: Versailles, high finance capitalism, Marxism and the Jews, was born out of hatred and had nothing to do with sensitive and reasonable analysis. Their actions were ruled by the overriding aim to come to power through the ballot box. In order to mobilise mass support from all groups in society, they promised everything to everyone in sweeping statements which were often contradictory and unrealistic. Detailed proposals for improvements remained the exception.

Although Saxony's democratic system crumbled at the end of Weimar, it did not fall. The Nazis failed to take over the state government as they had done in Anhalt, Oldenburg, Mecklenburg-Schwerin and neighbouring Thuringia. Nevertheless, more and more Saxons supported, or at least approved, the Nazis' 'National Socialist' solution to the crisis. This popular support helps explain why Hitler's followers were guaranteed a comparatively smooth seizure of power and stable rule even in 'red' Saxony. There was an 'enduring hope that the Third Reich was at least a partial realisation of the *Volksgemeinschaft*[28] (which contrasted with the 'failed' capitalist system and the 'horrors' of Bolshevism).

From 1933 onwards, the working-class milieu was smashed and largely disintegrated. In a second wave the traditional nationalist milieu – its clubs, organisations, celebrations, newspapers, etc. – was nazified and often withered away. Both milieus were sucked into the Nazis' integrative and popular nationalism, and their centrally controlled organisations.[29] Simultaneously, the totalitarian terror (which included the justified fear of denunciations that kept the machinery of terror going) led people to retreat into the private sphere and enhanced the process of fragmentation. The Nazis partially succeeded in replacing both milieus with aspects of their *Volksgemeinschaft* which struck a chord with the desires of many Saxons: there was a feeling of pride and confidence in Germany's future, an admiration for Hitler's leadership, and belief in a new unity in the Third Reich. The comparative stability of the dictatorship was linked with the Nazis' ability to provide relative economic security after the Great Depression. Once the high unemployment levels dropped and the seemingly greater job security set in from 1935 onwards, many Saxons seemed content to have swapped a democracy for a dictatorship.

The Nazis found it harder to mobilise the population with aspects which were not as main-stream, yet which stood at the heart of their ideology: racism and anti-Semitism. However, they were able to build on existing foundations. Anti-Semitism had a long history in some nationalist circles and a growing number of Saxons had come into contact with, and were receptive to, racial ideas before 1933. During the Third Reich, the Nazis' relentless racial indoctrination left a mark on the opinions and attitudes of a growing stratum of society (document 22).

Still, the Nazis' totalitarian project faced limitations in Saxony. Some groups in society, particularly the hard-core of the former socialist milieu and many of those who had not benefited from the revival of the economy after 1935, continued to oppose the Nazi regime and its values. The enormous endurance of deep-rooted beliefs, attitudes and milieus became evident when the workers' milieu rapidly revived again after the Second World War. This development was abruptly ended and wiped out by the emergence of an even more thorough totalitarian dictatorship: the GDR.

Did the widespread support for Nazism equal an understanding of what it would mean in power? Were Saxons aware that violence was not a means to end Marxism, but the driving force of Nazism? That the acquisition of more *Lebensraum* would bring war? or that the Nazis' racism would lead to the creation of a racial state in which Jews and all those who were regarded as 'inferior' were segregated, sterilised and eventually exterminated? Most information for what was to come was certainly available from the Nazis themselves. Many Nazi speeches mapped out their intentions in extremely aggressive warnings and metaphors. In particular, Hitler's speeches in Saxony were dominated by his two favourite themes: that Germany needed to fight for more *Lebensraum*, and that the condition of the race was crucial for the survival of the nation.[30]

Around 40 percent of Saxon voters supported Nazism in free parliamentary elections at the end of the Republic. Some of them certainly identified with its extreme ideas. Others did not take very much notice of its more radical features, hoping that Nazism would benefit them personally, whilst some were captured by the Nazis' extreme nationalism and vision of the *Volksgemeinschaft*; or else it was a mixture of some or of all of these aspects. Looking back, a contemporary Saxon reflected apologetically: 'Could the *Volk* have guessed, that the *Führer* and his paladins would deceive it so badly behind the mask of true love for the fatherland?'[31]

The Third Reich turned out to have the most extreme, violent and racist features of what was predictable. During the Republic, Nazism had presented itself as an extreme mixture of radical and comparatively common views. This was rather normal at the time. Contemporary language was noticeably polarised and radical, and there was an apparent gap between language and reality, myths and facts, assumptions and certainties.[32] This situation provided a crucial environment in which Hitler and his followers – who meant everything that they said – were able to flourish. Interwar Germany is a crucial reminder that the survival of a peaceful, democratic system depends on the ability of all groups in society to enter a serious dialogue, to make compromises and to treat each other with respect. We have also seen the irrational, authoritarian and destructive potentials of nationalism. As soon as people are prepared to infringe on other peoples' happiness in order to improve their own situation, they swap humanitarian standards with the barbaric law of nature. This seems to be the greatest danger in modern Europe with its ethnic and cultural diversity.

Notes

1. Lepsius, 'Parteiensystem', 67ff.
2. *VdSL*, 5. Wp, 45. Sitzung, 16.6.1931, 1700.
3. Ibid., 4 Wp, 11. Sitzung, 23.10.1929, 394. The wording was an allusion to Lenin's slogan 'peace, land, and bread' (April Theses, 1917).
4. Ibid., 16. Sitzung, 26.11.1929, 503.
5. Ibid., 5 Wp, 18. Sitzung, 11.12.1930, 700.
6. Graham, *Cultural Studies*, 15.
7. For a similar conclusion for the town of Ettlingen in Baden, see C. Rauh-Kühne, *Katholisches Milieu und Kleinstadtgesellschaft. Ettlingen 1918–1939*, Sigmaringen, 1991.
8. Koshar, *Marburg*, 230.
9. *VdSL*, 4. Wp, 6. Sitzung, 9.7.1929; ibid., 5. Wp, 2. Sitzung, 15.7.1930.
10. From the diary of the Leipzig anatomist Hermann Voss, in Aly, 'Voss', 109.
11. The *Sonderweg* theory sees the primary origins of the success of Nazism and the demise of the Weimar Republic in Germany's specific historical handicaps due to its peculiar development in the nineteenth century. For a guide to the *Sonderweg* debate see R.G. Moeller, 'The Kaiserreich Recast? Continuity and Change in Modern German Historiography', *Journal of Social History*, 17 (1984), 655–83.

12. E.g. see G. Eley, 'What produces fascism: pre-industrial traditions or a crisis of the capitalist state?', in G. Eley, *From Unification to Nazism. Reinterpreting the German Past*, repr. London, 1992, 275.
13. Matthiesen found an even more extreme polarisation between the bourgeoisie and the left in the town of Gotha (Thuringia) during the first five years of the Republic. He argued that this provided the key to why the local bourgeoisie turned away from the Republic. See Matthiesen, *Gotha*, 213ff.
14. E.g. Matthiesen's and Heilbronner's sole emphasis on the 'vacuum' the Nazis were able to fill in the town of Gotha and the Black Forest region seems to neglect the Nazis' own contribution to this development. See Matthiesen, *Gotha*, 218f; Heilbronner, 'Stammtisch', 198.
15. G. Eley, 'Is there a History of the Kaiserreich?', in G. Eley, ed., *Society, Culture, and the State in Germany, 1870–1930*, Michigan, 1996, 30.
16. See Goldhagen, *Willing Executioners*.
17. Matthiesen also emphasised that the Nazis in Gotha were a comparatively 'normal' phenomenon in the local town community. See Matthiesen, *Gotha*, 222.
18. For this see G. Mai, 'National Socialist Factory Cell Organisation and the German Labour Front: National Socialist Labour Policy and Organisations', in Fischer, *Rise*, 124.
19. Ibid.
20. This proves again that a nationalist consciousness could coexist with a socialist consciousness. In the end, it was a matter of making a political decision in which the most overriding consciousness, or a combination of them, were most likely to be achieved.
21. Recently it has been fashionable to describe Nazism as a 'people's party of protest'. See *inter alia* Falter, *Wähler*, 371.
22. E.g. see Mosse, *Nationalization*.
23. Brustein, *Evil*.
24. *VdSL*, 5 Wp, 10. Sitzung, 15.10.1930, 370.
25. *Chemnitzer Tageblatt*, Nr. 212, 2.8.1930.
26. The WP also declared that it had been the wrong economic policy to Americanise the German economy and that they were 'opponents of large, massive machines which replaced humans'. See *VdSL*, 5 Wp, 101. Sitzung, 2.2.1933, 4404f.
27. Ibid., 7. Sitzung, 7.10.1930, 211.
28. Mai, 'Factory Cell', 130.
29. Cornelia Rauh-Kühne also observed that after several years the Nazis had destroyed traditional sociocultural networks of the various milieus in the town of Ettlingen. See Rauh-Kühne, *Ettlingen*, 424.
30. Up until 1930 Hitler gave more public speeches in Saxony than in any other German state, except Bavaria. See also document 9.

31. E. Venus, *Amtshauptmann in Sachsen. Lebenserinnerungen des letzten Dresdener Amtshauptmanns und Landrats*, Reutlingen, 1970, 102.
32. See also T. Childers, 'The Social Language of Politics in Germany: The Sociology of Political Discourse in the Weimar Republik', *American Historical Review*, 95 (2) (1990), 336.

Appendix

Selected Documents

Document 1

The following excerpts are taken from the memoirs of Ernst Venus, who became a higher civil servant in Saxony during the interwar period. We focus on some of his observations from his youth before the First World War. *Source:* E. Venus, *Amtshauptmann in Sachsen. Lebenserinnerungen des letzten Dresdener Amtshauptmanns und Landrats*, Reutlingen, 1970, 16f.

... Parents often had to endure great sacrifices and hardships to finance the enrolment [of their children] into the gymnasium and to the university. They were assisted by grants to help with some of their needs ... However, they were not high enough to enable the children of poorer families to attend, which is why it was said that the 'better-off's' had the privilege of education. Relating to this, I remember from my time how some class-mates ... complained that the son of an engine driver was attending the gymnasium ... A young teacher in the gymnasium, whose mother was an honourable midwife, also went through a hard time. There were rather stark disadvantages regarding promotions, especially in the military and in the government. Basically, sons of primary teachers or of artisans were not promoted to the rank of reserve officer, hardly any one from the middle classes became a *Kreishauptmann* [head of a *Kreishauptmannschaft*]...

Many workers lived in deprived accommodation ... There was frequently a lack of beds for the children, and every now and then two or three children had to sleep in one single bed. A cynical newspaper remarked that the children should sleep in the coal depot and cover themselves with the *Vorwärts* [SPD newspaper]! ...

Document 2

The proclamation of the Swimming Club Chemnitz 1892 at the outbreak of the First World War. *Source: Monatliche Mitteilungen Schwimmklub 'Chemnitz von 1892'*, Nr. 8, August 1914.

There is war! Enemies on all sides! Truly, these are serious times. Nevertheless, are these not the days in which our chest swells with pride, and the heart beats faster? What an enthusiasm! What a calm! What a will to sacrifice! It is not possible to be defeated with such a *Volk*. Every heart sounds and every mouth sings: Germany above all else! I have devoted my heart and my hand to you!

Do we want to stay behind in the face of such widespread enthusiasm? No. During the peace years we have trained ourselves hard to be capable men and to have a healthy and strong youth. We did not do this for ourselves, but for the fatherland. Our members are entering a tough struggle now. Their number is large, only a few will stay back. We are proud that we can place so many who will fight for house and hearth, for *Heimat* and family; they are fathers and sons, husbands and youth ...

Document 3

The following two documents describe the situation in Saxony during 1923 from a completely different viewpoint. The first (a) is an account by Saxon industrialists of how some employers were abused by workers and were forced to sign new wage agreements; the second (b) is a survey from the Saxon SPD on how the army maltreated the population during the *Reichsexekution*.

(a) (*Source: Sächsische Industrie*, Nr. 45, 11.8.1923, 582)

There were severe demonstrations in Schneeberg [Erzgebirge] on 31 July. The woodworkers marched onto the streets, forced their way into the metal and textile factories, rounded up workers and employers and forced the latter to participate in a demonstration and negotiations for a standard wage in the industries of Schneeberg. The textile industrialists were then released due to the interference of the Textile Workers' Association. However, they were brought back again by individual workers to participate in another negotiation, at which about 400 workers suddenly turned up from Oberschlema, armed with clubs and planks. The employers were supposed to sign a wage settlement under the most terrible threats ('you dogs will not get out of here alive if you do not sign!'), first within two minutes and then within ten minutes. They were presented with a piece of paper on which they had to agree a wage for male workers of over 60,000 mark and for female workers of over 40,000 mark. During these 'negotiations' two employers were seriously molested and pushed into a corner with raw violence. The technical director of the municipal wood factory of Neustädtel ... was beaten by demonstrators. A wood industrialist from Schneeberg was beaten on his head and some of his teeth were smacked in. He needed a doctor's examination. ...

(b) (*Source: Vier Jahre Sächsische Politik. Herausgegeben von der SPD Sachsen*, 1926: 27-9).

How the *Reichswehr* established peace and order in the various Saxon villages and towns will be shown in the following survey, which does not claim to be complete:

... 23 October: Invasion in Pirna. Unemployed who wait for the payment of their benefits in front of the town hall are shot at without any reason. One dead, six injured. In other parts of the town there are also a number of injured people as well as those with more serious wounds. Numerous house searches and arrests. The town council, which has a bourgeois majority, protests in a public proclamation against the action of the *Reichswehr*.

Invasion in Freital. Arrested civilians are beaten with a dog whip, others are hit in the face, a coachman is wounded by bullet fire, a worker has his head pushed through a window.

Freiberg. A woman who walks across the upper market with her blind husband is beaten to the ground. A civilian who is carrying an injured woman is beaten by *Reichswehr* soldiers. Numerous people are beaten with a rubber truncheon without reason, including an older worker and a handicapped person, to the extent that they stay on the ground. A small child is run over by a horse without the horseman bothering to look back. The worker Samaritan who looks after the child is beaten and arrested.

Invasion in Plauen. The traffic is closed. The telephone lines cease to function, the border of the town can only be crossed with a passport. Tank vehicles and artillery are positioned. Numerous house searches and arrests, including that of two members of the town council. ...

24 October. A further casualty in Pirna. ...

Freital. The coachman who was wounded by bullet fire has died. The first casualty in the Plauensche Grund since the Revolution.

Two tank trains 'secure' the route between Görlitz and Dresden.

26 October. Freiberg. General strike of the workers because of the ruthless action of the *Reichswehr*. ...

27 October. Bloody Sunday in Freiberg. Fourteen dead and many injured through machine-gun fire. Shortly afterwards there is more gunfire from a *Reichswehr* vehicle without prior warning. Eight dead, including

one Samaritan. The Red Cross flag which had been held up by a Samaritan was shot through.

29 October. Dresden. The *Reichswehr* occupies all ministerial buildings, Landtag and telegraph offices. The ministers are taken out of their offices, the Landtag is banned from meeting. ...

30. October. All political meetings are banned. ...

2 November. ... Freiberg. The number of casualties rose to thirty-one. ...

Overall result: 34 dead, 110 to 130 injured in less than four weeks!

Document 4

Selected branches of the NSDAP in Saxony: background and unifying experience. *Source:* histories of local NSDAP branches; BA DH; newspaper articles.

Place/Founded	*Background*	*Unifying Experience*
Zwickau[1] 11.10.1921	DVSTB, Union of Nationalistic minded Soldiers	Esser and Hitler in Zwickau 1922; Marxist terror and imprisonment 1922-23; DT in Coburg 1922; NSDAP meeting in M; consecration of flag 1923; DTf in M 1923; DT in Hof 1923
Chemnitz[1] 21.02.1922	DVSTB, *Reichshammerbund*, Gymnastic Club Jahn, anti-Semites	DT in Weimar 1920; DT in Detmold; room-brawl 1923; NSDAP meeting in M 1923; DT in Hof 1923; brawl at Goebbels' meeting 1925; Hitler visit
Markneukirchen[1] 16.03.1922	*Orgesch, Brigade Erhardt*	Terror by Hölz; DT in Coburg 1922; NSDAP meeting in M; consecration of flag; DT in Hof 1923; room-brawl in Oelsnitz 1924
Plauen 21.05.1922	DVSTB	NSDAP meeting in Munich 1923; DT in Hof 1923
Freiberg[1] 20.11.1922	Ex-service men, nationalists	Party meeting in M 1923; period of ban; NSDAP meeting in Weimar 1926; Hitler in Freiberg 1930
Leipzig 22.11.1922	*Eiserne Schar*, German Nationalistic Youth Union, *Organisation Consul*, German Socialist Party, *Stahlhelm* (SA)	Police surveillance; Marxist terror; DT in Hof 1923; Hitler speech 1926; NSDAP meeting in Weimar 1926
Colditz 27.12.1922	*Wehrwolf, Bund Sachsen im Reich*, anti-Semites, nationalists	DT in Halle; Hitler speech 1926; Nazi sport meeting 1926
Aue[1]	Anti-Marxists	DTf in Munich 1923; DT in Hof 1923; 1923 hand-shake with Hitler; brawls

Werdau[1] 21.03.1923	'Citizen's leagues', *Stahlhelm*	Marxist terror (searched & beaten up); comradeship; DT in Hof 1923
Schwarzenberg 25.03.1924		Feder speech in Schwarzenberg 1924
Limbach 1925	German Social Party, *Wehrwolf*	DTf in Munich 1923; brawl at DT Hitler speech 1926; NSDAP meeting in Weimar 1926
Annaberg	*Orgesch, Wehrwolf, Brüder von Stein*	DTf in Munich 1923; Marxist terror; hardships; comradeship; links to Hof
Bautzen 02.06.1925	*Wehrwolf, Wiking Bund*, anti-Semites	brawls; Marxist terror; comradeship
Crimmitschau[1] 12.8.1927	*Wehrwolf*	Marxist terror; brawls 1929/30

[1] Founded with the help of Tittmann (Zwickau)
DT: *Deutscher Tag; DTf: Deutsches Turnfest* (German Gymnastic Display);
M: Munich.

Document 5

Proclamation of the Nazis in Leipzig to rejoin the NSDAP after the party was again legalised in early 1925. *Source: Der Streiter*, 17.1.1925.

Proclamation to the National Socialists in Saxony! One year of parliamentary activities of the *völkisch* movement is coming to an end. The result is clearly visible in front of our eyes: disintegration ... of Adolf Hitler's *Volksbewegung*! Should it stay like this? What is our duty? It is to return to the ground of Hitler. The only thing that can still save Germany is the dictatorship of the nationalist will and determination. Our task is to prepare the *Volk* for a dictator when he arrives. Away with the miserable parliamentary system in our ranks! ... National Socialists! The re-legalised NSDAP has arisen again in Saxony too. Become a fighter in this *Volksbewegung* which legally attempts to realise – and it will realise – the old Hitler-programme, issued on 24 February 1920 in Munich. Workers of the brain and fist, those of you who are happy and satisfied today should stay away from us! But whoever is longing for a change and is prepared to accept the struggle for our future at the highest aim, join our ranks as an honest fighter. Down with the international Jewish finance bandits and its serfs! Down with the exploitation of the *Volk* and enslavement of workers! Down with the pimp economy of the parliament! Down with the alien rabble who pushed us into deep misery and created for itself a life of luxurious surplus, while the German *Volk* suffers privations and hungers. We demand: protect those who work in the Republic and create a Greater Germany. Join the NSDAP at its party branch in Leipzig.

Document 6

This document is taken from one of the numerous histories of the local Nazi movement (Annaberg/Erzgebirge) which were written during the Third Reich, and describes the difficulties the first few Nazis had in spreading their ideas and attracting more followers. *Source:* E. Lang, 'Kampf und Sieg der nationalsozialistischen Bewegung im Grenzlandkreiz Annaberg/Obererzgebirge', in *Vom Silbernen Erzgebirge. Kreis Annaberg*, vol. 1, 223f.

It was hard enough to set up a local party branch, but the ensuing struggle against all opposition and enemies to the idea of the *Führer* was infinitely more difficult. The pioneers who had become National Socialists in the party branches had the determined will to convert other *Volksgenossen* with their spirit of struggle, sacrifice and duty for Germany. They wanted to convince men and women that pacifistic weakness, Marxist class-struggle, Jewish dominance, bourgeois half-measures and cowardice would lead to an endless decline of Germany. There was only meant to be one leader in Germany and that was the one who was the best and most capable; only one ideology was meant to be the true faith for Germany. Order, cleanliness, justice, honour and freedom were meant to govern again. The first followers who supported this pure and unselfish idea stood alone. There was canvassing everywhere, wherever people came together. In the factory the canvasser met the working colleague who was an indoctrinated Marxist and who stuck to his crazy ideas. The unemployed who were waiting for their pennies at the employment office laughed and mocked the devotees who talked about leadership and faith, struggle and sacrifice for Germany. A few followers were regarded as crazy dreamers by relatives and acquaintances, were avoided by friends and were banned by so-called 'society' because they had become radical politicians ... Those party members who were unemployed, workers, farmers or artisans saved their few benefits or small wages to pay for the uniform, the party membership, and the party newspaper. When Stormtroopers drove by lorry to party branches which were far away to protect meetings, they had to pay the fares themselves. Leaflets and fliers had to be distributed and sold, placards had to be put up and guarded. Invitations to meetings had to be delivered to all homes ... Initially it was not always easy to find a landlord who would offer a place in which meetings could be held, because they feared for their business. The financial means to carry out these activities was often threatened due to the low cash balance. The membership numbers rose only very slowly ...

Document 7

The following are excerpts from a Saxon Nazi trade union leaflet from 1923. *Source:* STA D, AH Glauchau/Nr. 24, 9.6.1923.

The National Socialist ... regards unions ... as an absolute necessity. He demands, however, that they only deal with economic and not political issues. He supports every reasonable wage dispute and does not act as a strike-breaker when his class comrades fight for their legitimate right to exist. He does not allow himself to be used as a tool for union bigwigs or efforts which aim to ruin his employer ... He is a socialist and is aware that in the struggle against exploitation, he has to fight against the Jews, who are the force behind the exploitation ...

Document 8

Conditions laid down by the Saxon Nazis for tolerating the bourgeois Bünger government from July 1929 onwards. *Source: Sächsischer Beobachter*, Nr. 28, 14.7.1929.

1. That the Saxon government will do its utmost in the *Reichsrat* against all treaties, particularly against the Paris Treaty and all its consequences, through which the German *Volk* has become politically and economically more dependent on international bank- and stock market capitalism.
2. That the Saxon government is prepared to implement austerity measures, i.e., through the simplification of the administration, particularly the withdrawal of the Saxon embassy in Berlin and Munich, and also a lowering of wages and a cut in pensions for those ministers who did not come from the administration.
3. That the Saxon government agrees to work on a sufficient and comprehensive work programme which is suitable to overcome unemployment and to stimulate Saxon industry again, and to take Saxon industries into account when state orders are made.
4. That the Saxon government agrees to feed all rental tax into house building and on top of that, to provide further means which will help to overcome the housing problem.
5. That the Saxon government provides cheap state credits for the agricultural sector.
6. That the Saxon government is prepared to actively support the protection of the middle classes in artisan, commerce and trade, and particularly that it abolishes the tax allowances of consumer cooperatives and introduces a special tax for department stores.

We also demand:

The Ministry of the Interior should not be held by a Democrat ... We National Socialists do not want a ministerial post. You are wrong if you have the opinion that we shirk responsibility. If you wish that we should join the government, we would only consider the Ministry of the Interior. Indeed we would have provided an expert ... (We would have presented party colleague Dr Frick).

Document 9

Hitler gave more speeches in Saxony than in any other German state up until 1930 (except in Bavaria), which indicates the significance of the region for the Nazi movement. Below are some excerpts from some of them. The extremely radical and violent nature of his speeches was striking; however, they clearly became more moderate in the two years before his appointment as Chancellor.

(a) **Annaberg, 17 April 1929** (*Source: Hitler. Reden, Schriften, Anordnungen. Februar 1925 bis Januar 1933*. Vol. III, part 2, ed. K.A. Lankheit, Munich, 1994, 210f.)

... The key to the world market has the shape of the sword. Nations who speculate in the economy, have to be prepared to put all their strength into it ... Germany needs power, three times more power, but no Geneva and no League of Nations ... We only want a peace which will give life to our *Volk*. ...

(b) **Plauen, 1 June 1930** (*Source: Hitler. Reden*, ed. C. Hartmann, vols. III, part 3, Munich, 1995, 216f.)

... When the German *Volk* rises again one day, ... there will be a devastating revenge ... There needs to be a change in attitude, in thinking, and in feeling. A new *Volk* must develop, a new character ... We have our roots in the terms: *Volk*, race, blood. This is why we are a new phenomenon, the only one who will really build bridges. We see the first movement, which is slowly bringing together people from all classes ...

(c) **Chemnitz, 19 June 1930** (*Source: Hitler. Reden*, ed. C. Hartmann, vols. III, part 3, 233.)

... But the factor which really determines the destiny of a *Volk* and its state, is the *Volk* itself, the quality of that *Volk*. This is our immediate difference from Marxism, which is indifferent to the value of people, and declares all humans to be equal. The general thesis of National Socialism is: each *Volk* determines its value through its cultural achievements. Its needs are determined by its efficiency. The second general thesis is, however, that besides the value of the *Volk*, it is also decisive in what space [*Raum*] the *Volk* lives ... National Socialism stands for the world view that each *Volk* has the right to take the earth which it needs and which it is able to cultivate. The time will come when the German *Volk* will cry for those who will give them bread and space ...

(d) **Chemnitz, 23 July 1932** (*Source: Hitler. Reden*, ed. K. Lankheit, vols. V, part 1, Munich, 1996, 261.)

... It is well known to you what they [traditional parties] have done to Germany economically, politically and morally over the last thirteen years. And these parties know it themselves too. It is so terrible, that they do not dare to refer to it. They themselves do not dare to make propaganda out of it and say: we have given this and that to the German people in thirteen years. They could not have given the German people anything else except what they have created: economic misery, the destruction of finance, the ruin of the peasantry, the wiping out of our middle classes, the high debts and mortgages and millions of unemployed. They could not achieve anything different, because how could a *Volk* gain the ability to live, when thirty parties are involved in the decision-making [*Willensbildung*]? When every profession, every class, even every religion has got its own representative? ... The worker has got its own, and not only one, but two or three; the middle classes have also got their special representation, and also the artisans have their own representation; and industry too has to have a special party, and equally the salaried employees and of course also the employers; and then of course the Catholics, and the Protestants can not stay behind either; and then finally the house owners really need their own political representation, and then the tenants, and so forth (amusement).

History will one day judge, if *this* was Germany or if it would not have been more German to get rid of all the parties and to replace this strange happening by establishing *one* political representation for the German nation once more (storming applause). We make no secret that this is our aim. We want this *Volk* to get a unified political leadership [*Willensbildung*] once more. ...

Document 10

Speech by Erich Kunz, a prominent Nazi leader in Saxony, in the Saxon Landtag in October 1930. *Source: VdSL*, 5. Wp, 10. Sitzung, 15.10.30, 377–79.

By accepting the Versailles Peace Treaty you [the SPD] have earned yourself the doubtful merit, not only of sabotaging the socialist wishes of the German worker, but of having sold off the whole German *Volk* and all its working classes, and all its economic assets to international high finance ... We do not see at all that the Young Plan will make things easier, even if it were to be several hundred million marks lower than the Dawes Plan. The figures do not mean anything, what really matters is the principle itself, and the principle remains the same at two-and-a-half billion or two billion ... It is the principle which turned the Revolution against the German *Volk*. It is the principle which was strengthened in the Versailles Peace Treaty. And this principle is called subjugation of the whole German economic area, the gagging of the total German labour force, the exploitation of all German production and labour as a tribute to international high finance. And you have always fostered this principle ...

The precondition for the creation of an economic principle is definitely the freedom of the national workplace ...

We also say that we are happy to apply every means to create the internal political conditions which would then lead to the freedom of the political situation externally; the creation of an internal political front ... is the precondition for the true liberation to and from the outside ...

The right to shape the future will therefore solely fall to National Socialism which ... always has devoted special attention ... to the question of an equal *Volk* ... It is only possible to overcome all this chaos, this confusion in political and economic areas and to break the chains which were laid on us, by organising the total power of the *Volk* ...

Document 11

The official minutes of a speech by the leader of the Saxon Communists, Rudolf Renner, in the Saxon parliament in late 1929. *Source: VdSL*, 18. Sitzung, 4 Wp, 10.12.1929, 561ff.

We do not want to maintain the holiday on the Ninth of November, because we do not believe that one should celebrate this Republic in any special way. (Very true! from the National Socialists) It is not possible to celebrate this Republic. This Republic has to (Member of Parliament von Killinger [NSDAP]: be sent to hell) – has to be destroyed by the masses as quickly as possible. (Very true! from the Communists.) The masses have to break with all the forces which have tried to maintain the Republic. (Very true! from the Communists and from the National Socialists.) They have to respond with the same means and methods which are used to oppress the masses. One cannot respond to machine guns and rubber truncheons with a piece of paper 6 x 8 centimetres in size [ballot paper], one can only answer to machine gun and rubber truncheon with machine gun and rubber truncheon …

Document 12

NSDAP Leaflet for Workers from early 1931 *Source:* BA Koblenz, NS 26, Nr. 2113.

Signals!
for the active German working class
Against a profiteering economy! For the right to work!
Leipzig, January 1931
Marx or Hitler?
Working *Volksgenossen*, this is the question of your destiny, it does not matter if you are 'for' or 'against', or if you are involved in politics at all. In the next few months it may well be decided if Germany will be bolshevist or national socialist. It is up to you to ensure that the **socialism of Adolf Hitler** will surface as the winner from this struggle. For those of you who are still followers of Marx, that Jewish son of a rabbi, it is about time to cut the crazy ideas portrayed to you by this sly Jewish charlatan out of your mind.

The example of the inevitable development and theory of concentration, of the international solidarity of all working people and the necessity of the class struggle, is nothing other than a large-scale Jewish swindle.

The present is the best evidence for the truth of our claims!

If Marx was right with his theory of development and theory of concentration, we could expect the suicide of capitalism in due time, because the whole economy is nowadays monopolised and is full of trusts as never before. No-one could believe that international high finance, that is upholding modern capitalism, will destroy its own system. On the contrary, it has been able to achieve the subservience of leaders of all Marxist organisations and has thereby degraded all Marxist thinking workers to the status of slaves.

Is it for instance anti-capitalist, when the Social Democratic Jew Hilferding _ when he was still finance minister – handed the whole German match industry to the capitalist Ivar Kreuger?

Is it anti-capitalist,when the SPD saves the cabinet and Brüning's catastrophe, which it had been really furious with before the elections to the Reichstag, from every defeat and even agrees to the emergency decrees?!

Is it anti-capitalist, when the KPD only thunders in a theatrical manner against the mean capitalist exploitation through the Young Plan but murders national socialist workers who were actively fighting against Young? No and a thousand times no!

All this is capitalist politics in its most extreme form!

German workers and employees! If you are still waiting for the collapse of the current moneybag system, death through starvation will soon relieve you of the yoke that oppresses you.

Nearly 5 million *Volksgenossen* have been excluded from the process of production. In addition to this number, Germany has the largest army of unemployed in the world. Only gasbags and demagogues can maintain that this is due to the world economic crisis. All hands would have work if we had not been led into the incredible interest rate slavery. There is scope for an infinite number of workplaces in the German domestic market alone. For instance, the building of many hundreds of thousands of houses would overcome the housing shortage.

But this is not possible due to the Young slavery, and millions are condemned to the breadline.

But where is the international solidarity?

Have you ever heard of English, French or Belgian workers being active or demonstrating against the exploitation of the German working population due to the Young Plan?

International solidarity is an empty phrase.

Only the German worker believes it; he sympathises with death and devil in the world, and sacrifices his last penny to support revolting Zulus, but no-one in the world cares about his misery in return. *Volksgenossen* take the necessary steps from this revelation! The 70-year-war of Marxism against capitalism has brought you the opposite of your aims. Leave the false front! Karl Marx was a child of bourgeois dissatisfaction from the middle of the last century – throw him on the scrap heap! It is not too late!

Join the fighting front of the workers' party of Adolf Hitler! This is not about the wellbeing of human kind or of any class, this is about the existence of the German working *Volk*!

Join the fight for national freedom and socialist justice!

Your place is in the National Socialist German Workers' Party and in the National Socialist factory councils.

Document 13

Public Party Meetings and their Number of Participants in the AH Schwarzenberg. *Source:* STA D, AH Schwarzenberg, Nr. 1941–1945.

(**a**) The Number of Public Meetings of Political Parties in the AH Schwarzenberg between 1926–1932

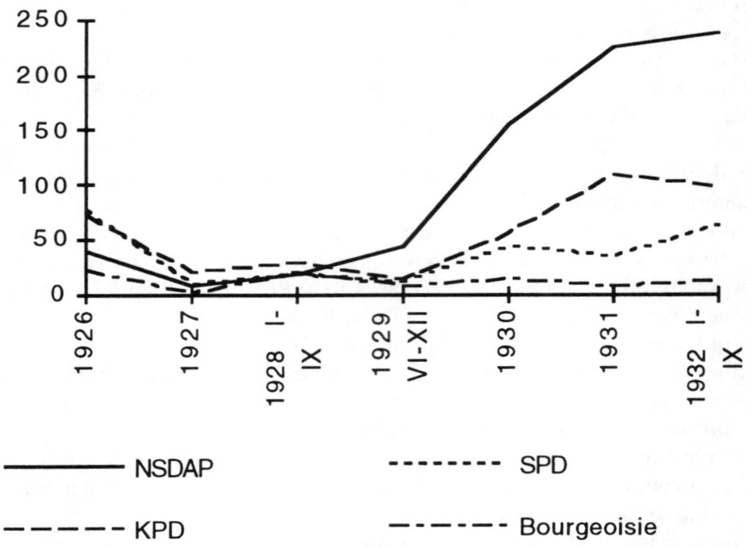

(**b**) The Number of Participants at Public Meetings of Political Parties in the AH Schwarzenberg between 1926–1932

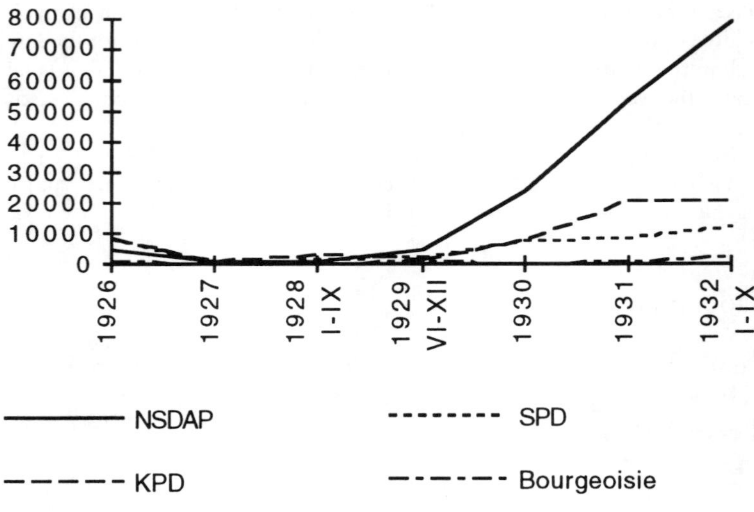

Document 14

Below is a fairly typical police report about one of the numerous party meetings which ended in a brawl. This was an NSDAP meeting in Zschopau in December 1930. The topic was 'The SPD is cheating the *Volk*' and the speaker was Wimmer from Berlin. *Source:* STA D, MdI, Nr. 11126/4, Dezember 1930.

Of the 550 guests there were around 400 supporters of the SPD and KPD ... there were 80 Stormtroopers ... during the discussion it came to a brawl because Wimmer answered the contribution of a Social Democratic speaker with 'you clown', which incited great outrage among the opponents of the NSDAP and increased the already tense atmosphere even further. Whereas the speaker of the SPD asked his followers to leave the venue, the Communists demanded to stay in the hall. At this moment a beer glass flew from the middle of the hall to the stage where the stewards were. A few Stormtroopers grabbed chairs to use them as protection against projectiles. When the brawl started, both sides used chairs, parts of chairs, beer glasses, coffee cups, etc. to beat or to throw. The SA pushed its opponents out of the hall. Overall about twenty persons were injured, three seriously ... When the local police – which was on standby – and the riot squad from Chemnitz entered the hall, the brawl had ended ... the material damage amounted to approximately 2,500 Marks. As many as 139 chairs were destroyed, 250 beer glasses and other glasses, several tables, six windows, and numerous other china disappeared completely.

Document 15

Description by an American journalist who visited an unemployed working-class family in the village of Falkenstein (Vogtland) during the economic depression in the early 1930s. *Source:* H.R. Knickerbocker, *Deutschland So Oder So?*, Berlin, 1932, 39f.

We followed the children through ice-cold corridors which were damp and smelt of wet and dirty washing. We entered with our guide from the local employment office who knew the family.

The head of the family, a builder, sat in the kitchen – the only room of the three that was heated, and he did not turn his eyes away from the pot on the fire. His wife declared with a touch of bitterness, that this had been his only activity for the last two years; he had been unemployed for so long ... The women of the unemployed have to work hardest; day in, day out they have to save, scrape together, darn and wash for sixteen hours in order to get the most out of the benefit ... The pot had food for the man, the women and the five children. The meal was pieces of dough, with which something similar to a dough soup was cooked. This was all they had for Sunday lunch. The sixth child, who was four months old, was laying in the cradle. The mother, a thirty-six old gaunt and wornout woman, was pregnant. The children took off their Sunday clothes; the mother kept them for the next Sunday. They were wearing ragged clothes at home ...

Document 16

Police report about the Communist failure to mobilise the unemployed in Saxony in 1932. *Source:* STA L, PP-St Nr. 82, Polizeipräsidium Leipzig, Abteilung IV, 13.4.1932.

The severe economic crisis made a close observation of the Communist efforts to attract the unemployed ... a necessity. It has become obvious in the last few months that despite the particularly high unemployment figure, Communist influence is not very great. The Communist unemployment bureau was only able to organise larger meetings of the unemployed when they were showing films. No demonstrations by the unemployed took place that were worth mentioning, and illegal attempts were prevented without any problems. The busy attempts to organise and activate the unemployed in so-called unemployment teams, can be regarded as having failed ... Not without reason did the activist Lust from Leipzig complain during the KPD meeting in Leipzig between 25 and 27 March that the KPD had so far failed to carry out an increased mobilisation of the unemployed.

Document 17

Membership of NSDAP and SPD (a), and Number of Party Branches of NSDAP, SPD and KPD in Saxony (b).

(**a**) Membership of NSDAP and SPD in Saxony

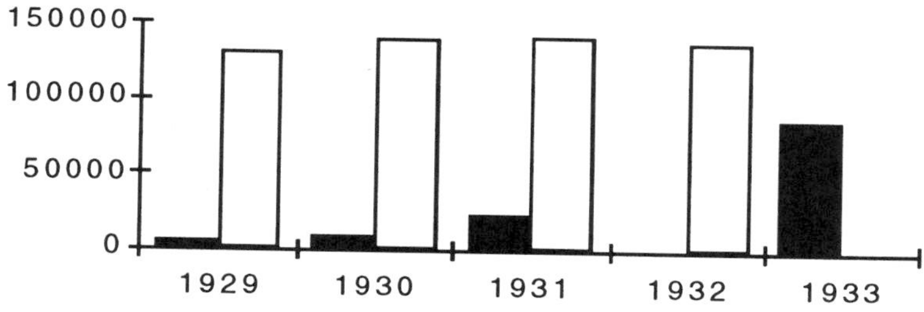

	1929	*1930*	*1931*	*1932*	*1933*
NSDAP[1]	4,609	8,557	22,665	–	87,079
SPD[2]	129,835	139,098	141,603	137,025	–

1: all figures are from January (BA, NS 22, Nr. 1067; except January 1933: *Partei-Statistik*. 1935). The NSDAP figure for January 1933 is likely to be too high. More realistic are around 74,000 members.
2: all figures are from 1 January of each year from *Jahrbuch der Sozialdemokratischen Partei Deutschlands*, (1929–31).

(**b**) Number of Party Branches in Saxony

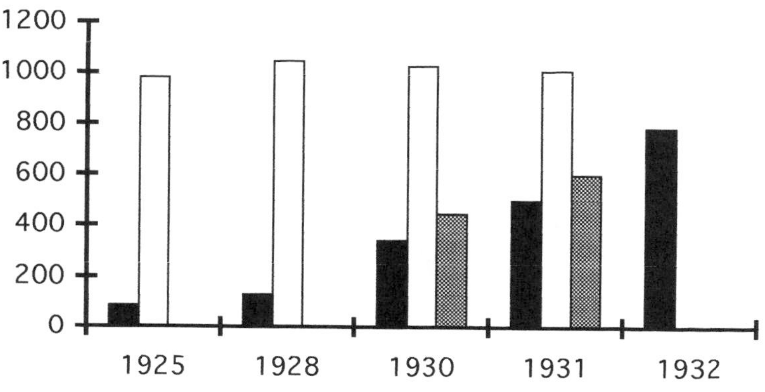

	1925	1928	1930	1931	1932
NSDAP[1]	88	132	341	500	783
SPD[2]	982	1048	1,027	1,011	–
KPD[3]	–	–	446	599	

1: *Partei-Statistik*. 1935 (except 1931: *FK*, Nr. 109, 12.5.1931).
2: all figures are from 31.12. of the previous year. See *Jahrbuch der Sozialdemokratischen Partei Deutschlands*, (1926–31).
3: 1.1.1930: Institut für Geschichte der Arbeiterbewegung Berlin, I 3/8–10/158; 1.1.1931: ibid., I 3/8–10/148.

Document 18

Extract from an article in a bourgeois newspaper in the Erzgebirge before the July 1932 Reichstag elections. *Source: Oelsnitzer Volksbote*, Nr. 171, 23.7.1932.

German Mission

Every *Volk* has a universal mission that it needs to discover in order to fulfil it. The *Volk* cannot rest as long as this mission remains unfulfilled and the road is not free for bigger tasks. The hour of great inner conflict and the wildest dreams is invariably the hour before one wakes up.

Misery throughout the world serves to remind the German *Volk* today of the fulfilment of its destiny. Worldwide suffering begs the German to be alert and to overcome suffering. Changes in the world demands Germany's awakening!

Today's question is not one of political views and systems, but instead is the realisation of the world mission of the Germans. Neither slogans, promises nor wishes of the various parties will save the German *Volk*, only the reflection of its destiny. Nothing superficial will be decisive enough for the destiny of our *Volk* – not name, not form not direction – but only the spiritual attitude, the inner attitude of those who have awoken as German. Not the masses decide, but the spirit.

Today our *Volk* is still its own tyrant. But when the German recognises his mission, a new *Volk* will be created from German earth, a new community [*Gemeinschaft*] which will not know any tyrants and will fear nothing any more ...

To be German means to be heroic, it means: to be free from egoism. It means: to regard life as a task and a sacrifice, not as an end in itself.

To be German means to be a helping brother to everything that lives. It means: to overcome hatred and arbitrariness through a new spirit of love. It means: to recognise, support and foster unity above all divisions. It means to consciously devote one's service to the whole, to rediscover oneself in that whole.

This is the German mission: to return true socialism – the idea of mutual help – to the sick human race who has lost its way in the conflict between materialistic thinking and crazy class-struggle …

It is the German mission to give the struggling world a new spirit and new support, to be the judge of the new human race and to teach it to put idealism first again …

Germanicus

Document 19

Extract from a Nazi's response to a Rabbi's letter that was published two days earlier in the same bourgeois newspaper in the Erzgebirge (one week before the July 1932 Reichstag elections). *Source: Oelsnitzer Volksbote*, Nr. 171, 23.7.1932.

Open letter to Mr Rabbi Dr H. Fuchs, Chemnitz

… We find it really incredible that you claim that not descent and blood, but rather education and environment, country and customs shape the human being. This is too naive, and we cannot accept that you believe this yourself. Lock up a dog of an inferior race or a mixed breed for five years with ten German shepherd dogs and try to teach the beast the noble attitude [*Geisteshaltung*] of a shepherd dog (loyalty, obedience, watchfulness, etc.), and the attempt will fail completely; the cur will always keep its inferior attitude, which is in his blood (unreliability, insidiousness, viciousness, disobedience, etc.), and the same is true for the human race; because the human is like all other creatures a product of nature and is therefore subject to its eternal laws. A Mongolian from the area of Tibet will keep his attitude (dishonesty, insidiousness, cruelty, bloodthirstiness), even if he lives in Germany for fifty years. A Negro also remains a Negro in Germany and a Jew remains a Jew with his inborn physical, mental and spiritual characteristics. A foreigner can adopt the language, customs and rituals of his host nation, but he cannot escape from his skin, no matter how often he would like to do this. Your racial comrade D'Israeli recognised the importance of the racial question for the fate of the nations when he said: 'The racial question is the key to world history' …

Document 20

A sample of what some opponents of the Nazis had scribbled on ballot papers during the plebiscite in Leipzig in August 1934. *Source:* STA L, PP-St, Nr. 23.

'Arse bandit'; 'KPD'; 'Thälmann' [former leader of the German KPD]; 'Hammer and Sickle'; 'Help yourself'; 'Adolf Hitler is one of the greatest seducers of workers and criminals'; 'Red Front'; 'Rather give us some work, so that we have something to scoff. A hungry *Volksgenosse*'; 'God is my leader'; 'Hitler is the executioner of the *Volk*. Long live the candidate for president of all anti-fascists, Ernst Thälmann. "No" on 19.8.!'; 'murderer'; 'Those who converted overnight, those who confess to every state, these are the world's politicians, one could also call them rogues'.

Document 21

A report about the mood among workers in late 1935. *Source: Sopade*, November 1935, 1311f.

Those who are not interested in politics ... do not feel troubled because they do not really care about things, they do not feel oppressed because they were never really passionate about freedom and democracy ... They do not miss democracy and are satisfied when they have a simple workplace. They sympathise with the militarisation of Germany, because it creates workplaces; and anyhow, most of them have become victims of the patriotic slogans of the radio whips. They are mainly interested in their wages; this is the only topic that the worker sometimes participates in with discussions, but only in a manner that he cannot lose his workplace, for which he constantly fears ...

Document 22

The following report captures the numerous accounts about the attitude of Saxons towards the persecution of Jews. This report was written one-and-a-half years into the dictatorship. *Source: Sopade*, September 1935, 1043.

The laws against the Jews are not taken very seriously, because the population has other worries, and predominantly holds the opinion that the fuss over the Jews was produced in order to distract the people from other things and to keep the SA busy. However, one should not maintain that the campaign against the Jews has not had the designed effect on many people. On the contrary, there are plenty of people who are under the spell of the campaign against the Jews and who regard the Jews as the cause of much misery. They have become fanatic opponents of Jews. This opposition against the Jews can often be seen by the fact that *Volksgenossen* who have contact with Jews, are spied on and reported, probably also in the hope of gaining recognition and preferential treatment by the party. However, the mass of the population ignores the campaign against the Jews, they even ostentatiously choose to buy in Jewish department stores and are rather unfriendly towards the controlling SA posts, particularly when they take photographs.

Document 23

The following is an excerpt of one of the many harrowing accounts about the treatment of prisoners in concentration camps; in this case, the concentration camp Sachsenburg (district of Flöha). The majority of the prisoners were former Social Democrats and Communists. There were also around 10 percent who were criminals, and occasionally some Jews. Most prisoners spent eight to sixteen months in the camp, but there were also some who had been there for two-and-a-half years. *Source: Sopade*, Dezember 1936, 1621f.

... It is worse than in a prison. The smallest little thing leads to an order, not to leave the room, smoking bans, writing bans, singing as a punishment, to eat while standing, standing as a punishment, bans on talking, exercises as punishment or a ban on going for a walk on Sundays. A further punishment is to be locked in the bunker with just water and bread between one and forty-two days. The highest punishment is to be in a dark cell with water and bread for forty-two days, and being chained in the cells. There are twenty-five strokes with a stick at the start and at the end of the punishment. There is a special torture stand on which prisoners are strapped. SS-guards deal the blows while the prisoner has to count loudly ... All other inmates have to march in the square during these punishments and watch while standing to attention. Afterwards the prisoner is taken into the bunker. The results are broken kidneys and nervous breakdowns.

The inmates are constantly exposed to the harassment of the guards. While they are working they have to do knee-bends and other torments while running with the cart. Or: while six men have to fill stones into a cart, the other fifteen men have to sing or do knee-bends. Complaints do not exist. Complaints mean mutiny, which would lead to even rougher punishments. …

Most of these prisoners are ill and have broken nerves. Nearly every third inmate in the camp suffers from stomach disease and rheumatism. The nursing quarters are always full with those who have a fever or have been injured in an accident. … The guards only address the inmates with 'swine' or 'criminal', or 'dog' or rabble'.

Bibliography

The availability of contemporary sources for this study was mixed. Generally speaking, the archival situation for the period of Imperial Germany and the Weimar Republic in Saxon archives is good. However, the author was only able to find fragments of Saxon NSDAP documents in several central archives, and most SPD files have not survived either. Adequate sources about the particular role of women and gender issues are few and far between. Research into Saxon society during the Nazi dictatorship is severely limited because most documents from the state administration after 1930 – but particularly from 1935 onwards – were destroyed during the Second World War. Nevertheless, some useful sources have survived. For instance, there are the reports about the political and economic situation in the district of Schwarzenberg until 1940, and the official administrative publications from the Saxon government – the *Sächsisches Verwaltungsblatt* – which contained new legislation introduced by the state. There are also numerous illuminating entries about Saxony in the published *Sopade* reports (*Deutschland-Berichte der Sozialdemokratischen Partei Deutschlands, 1934–1940*, 7th repr., Nördlingen, 1989) and Security Service reports (*Meldungen aus dem Reich. Die geheimen Lageberichte des Sicherheitsdienstes der SS 1938–1945*, eds. Heinz Boberach, 17 vols., Herrsching, 1984). Although both sources – *Sopade and the Lageberichte* – have their drawbacks and need to be used critically, they form a crucial source for the social history of the Third Reich.

Main Archives Consulted

Berlin Document Centre:

Personal files: Bauer, Robert; Böhme, Hellmut; von Killinger, Manfred; Lasch, Kurt; Meyer, Cuno; von Mücke, Hellmuth; Mutschmann, Martin; Pillmayer, Franz (among others 'Geschichte der Ortsgruppe der NSDAP zu Raschau'); Tittmann, Fritz.

Bundesarchiv, Abteilung Potsdam (now Bundesarchiv Berlin, Berlin-Lichterfelde):

Reichsministerium des Innern (15.01).
Reichskommissar für Überwachung der öffentlichen Ordnung (15.07).

Bundesarchiv Koblenz:

Sammlung Schumacher (Nr. 208).
Reichspropagandaleitung (NS 18).
Bestand Reichsorganisationsleiter (NS 22).
Hauptamt für Kommunalpolitik (NS 25).
NSDAP Hauptarchiv (NS 26) (among others 'Geschichte der Ortsgruppe Belgershain').
Kleine Erwerbungen Nr. 569: H. Bennecke 'Die SA in Sachsen vor der "Machtübernahme" '.
Zeitungssammlung (Nr. 103, Nr. 106).

Bundesarchiv, Zwischenarchiv, Dahlwitz-Hoppegarten:

Personal files: Haake, Rudolf; Kunz, Erich (among others BA DH, Z/C 17411, 'Bericht über die nationalsozialistische Bewegung im Freistaat Sachsen').

Institut für Geschichte der Arbeiterbewegung Berlin (former 'Zentrales Parteiarchiv der SED'; now part of Stiftung Archiv der Parteien und Massenorganisationen der DDR im Bundesarchiv, Berlin-Lichterfelde):

Flugblattsammlung.
SPD, KPD (ZPA 9).
SPD, KPD, NSDAP (ZPA 10).

PDS Archiv Leipzig:

Autobiographies of former SPD and KPD activists (‘*Bestand Erinnerungen*’).

Staatsarchiv Dresden:

Ministerium des Innern: among others, weekly or monthly police reports about the political and economic situation in Saxony between 1919 and 1931, and files about the NSDAP. There are many gaps for the period between 1933 and 1945 due to war losses.

Amtshauptmannschaften: among others, reports about the political and economic situation, public meetings, and election reports from the various AHs in the KHs Chemnitz and Zwickau. There are many gaps for the period between 1933 and 1945 due to war losses.

Zeitungsausschnittsammlung (large collection of newspaper clippings from 1919 to 1945): among others, reports about election campaigns, Saxon governments, Saxon towns, political parties and organisations, and the economy.

Sächsische Staatskanzlei: among others, confidential reports about the political and economic situation between 1923 and 1930. There are many gaps for the period between 1933 and 1945 due to war losses.

Newspapers from Saxony.

Druckerei des NS-Gauverlages Sachsen. Zeitungstext- und Bildarchiv.

Staatsarchiv Leipzig:

Reports from police headquarters (PP-V): among others, reports about the activity of political parties in Leipzig.

Reports from police headquarters (PP-St): documents which were stored in the ‘Zentrales Parteiarchiv Berlin’ and returned to Leipzig in 1990.

Judicial inquiries and criminal procedures (PP-S).

Reports from *Amtshauptmannschaften*: among others, reports about the political and economic situation, public meetings, and election reports from the various AHs in the KH Leipzig. There are substantial gaps due to war losses.

Other Archives Consulted

Bibliothek des Stadtgeschichtlichen Museum Leipzig.
Bibliothek für historische und justizgeschichtliche Literatur, Leipzig.
Bibliothek und Archiv der Gewerkschaftsbewegung (Johannes-Sassenbach-Stiftung), Berlin.
Deutsche Bücherei, Leipzig.
Hauptbibliothek Chemnitz.
Ratsschulbibliothek, Zwickau.
Sächsische Landesbibliothek, Dresden.
Stadtarchiv Chemnitz.
Stadtarchiv Dresden.
Stadtarchiv Goslar (Nachlaß Darré).
Stadtarchiv Leipzig.
Stadtarchiv Plauen.
Stadtarchiv Zwickau.
Wiener Library, London.

Contemporary Newspapers and Magazines Cited

Chemnitzer Tageblatt.
Chemnitzer Volksstimme.
Crimmitschauer Anzeiger und Tageblatt.
Deutsche Zeitung.
Dahlener Nachrichten.
Der Bolschewik.
Der Freiheitskampf.
Der Nationale Sozialist für Sachsen.
Der Oschatzer Gemeinnützige.
Der Streiter.
Deutsche Zeitung.
Die Christliche Schule.
Dresdner Nachrichten.
Dresdner Neueste Nachrichten.
Dresdner Volkszeitung.
Erzgebirgische Nachrichten und Anzeigenblatt.
Erzgebirgischer Volksfreund.
Frankfurter Zeitung.
Geschäftsbericht über die Jahre 1928/29 des Arbeiter-Turn-und-Sportbundes e.V., Leipzig, 1930.
Glauchauer Tageblatt und Anzeiger.

Landwirtschaftlicher Anzeiger für Sachsen und Thüringen.
Leipziger Neueste Nachrichten.
Leipziger Volkszeitung.
Meißner Tageblatt.
Meißner Volkszeitung.
Mitteilungen Chemnitzer Bezirksverein des VdJ Elektrotechnischer Verein Chemnitz.
Mitteilungen der christlichen Elternvereine Sachsens, e. V. für die Vorstände der christlichen Elternvereine.
Mitteilungen der Turn- und Sportgemeinde 1848 Leipzig-Lindenau e.V.
Mitteilungen der Vereinigung Sächsischer Höherer Staatsbeamter e.V.
Mitteilungen des Gewerbeverbandes in der AH. Borna e.V.
Mitteilungen des Landesverbandes der christlichen Elternvereine Sachsens, e.V für die Vostände der christlichen Elternvereine.
Mitteilungen des Landwirtschaftlichen Kreisvereins für das Sächsische Markgraftum Oberlausitz, Nr. 90, August 1915
Mitteilungen des Sächsischen Philologenvereins.
Mitteilungen für die Kirchengemeinden Nieder- und Oberwürschnitz.
Mitteilungen für die Reichswehrangehörigen betreffend dem Besuch von Theatern, Lichtspielen und sonstigen Unterhaltungsstätten im Standort Dresden.
Mitteilungen Landwirtschaftlicher Kreisverein Oberlausitz.
Mitteilungen. Offizielles Organ des Polizei-Sport-Vereins 21 Leipzig (e.V.)
Monatliche Mitteilungen des Allgemeinen Turnvereins Leipzig-Schleußig e.V.
Monatliche Mitteilungen Schwimmklub Chemnitz von 1892 e.V.
Monatliche Rundschau herausgegeben vom Schwimmklub "Chemnitz von 1892", Nr. 10, Oktober 1913.
Neue Leipziger Zeitung.
Neue Sächsische Schulzeitung.
Obererzgebirgische Zeitung.
Oelsnitzer Volksbote.
Oschatzer Gemeinnützige.
Sächsische Handwerker und Gewerbezeitung
Sächsische Industrie. Organ des Verbandes Sächsischer Industrieller.
Sächsische Landwirtschaftliche Zeitschrift.
Sächsische Schützen-Zeitung.
Sächsische Schulzeitung. Zeitung des Sächsischen Lehrervereins und seiner Zweigvereine.
Sächsischer Beobachter.

Sächsischer Lehrerverein.
Sächsisches Evangelisches Arbeiterblatt
Sächsisches Militärvereinsblatt.
Sächsisches Verwaltungsblatt.
Sächsisches Volksblatt.
Stollberger Anzeiger und Tageblatt.
Tageblatt Borna.
Völkischer Beobachter.
Vogtländischer Anzeiger und Tageblatt.
Zeitung für Meißner Hochland.
Zittauer Morgen Zeitung.

Contemporary Publications Cited

Adler, H., 'Die Wirtschaftskrise im Spiegel der sächsischen Konkursstatistik', *ZSäStLA*, (1932/33), 305–310.

Betterlein, A., 'Die Statistik der Fürsorge in den Rechnungsjahren 1927 bis 1931', *ZSäStLA*, (1932/33), 189.

Betterlein, A., 'Die Wohlfahrtserwerbslosen in Sachsen', *ZSäStLA*, (1931), 218–22.

Bramstedt, P., *Die Krisis der sächsischen Industriewirtschaft. Veröffentlichung des Verbandes Sächsischer Industrieller,* (67) (1932).

Burkhardt, F., 'Die bevölkerungspolitische Lage in Sachsen Ende 1932', *ZSäStLA*, (1932/33), 300–304.

Burkhardt, F., 'Die Kirchenaustritts- und Kircheneintrittsbewegung im Zeitraum 1919 bis 1930 mit einem Rückblick auf die Entwicklung der kirchlichen Statistik', *ZSäStLA*, (1931), 191–202.

Burkhardt, F., 'Die Sonderstellung Sachsens im Deutschen Reich und die wirtschaftliche Depression der Gegenwart', *ZSäStLA*, (1931), 70–81.

Der Gau Sachsen, 1938.

Deutschland-Berichte der Sozialdemokratischen Partei Deutschlands (Sopade) 1934–1940, 7th repr., Nördlingen, 1989.

'Die NSDAP in Sachsen', *Sachsen*, (2) (1938).

Die Tagebücher von Joseph Goebbels. Sämtliche Fragmente, ed. E. Fröhlich, Munich, 1987.

Fabian, W., *Klassenkampf um Sachsen. Ein Stück Geschichte 1918–1930*, Löbau, 1930.

15 Jahre Kampf der NSDAP, OG Bautzen (1922–37).

Fünfzehn Jahre NSDAP Freiberg, 1939.

Fünfzehn Jahre NSDAP in Chemnitz (1922–1937).

Fünfzehn Jahre NSDAP in Markneukirchen (1922–1937).

Fünfzehn Jahre NSDAP in Zwickau (1922–37).

Fünfzehn Jahre Ortsgruppe Crimmitschau, 1937.

Geiger, T., 'Panik im Mittelstand', *Die Arbeit*, 7 (1930), 643–52.

Geschäftsbericht über die Jahre 1928/29 des Arbeiter- Turn und Sportbundes e.V., Leipzig, 1930.

Geschichte der NSDAP Ortsgruppe Belgershain, Belgershain, 1934.

Handbuch der deutschen Tagespresse, 1932.

Hitler. Reden, Schriften, Anordnungen. Februar 1925 bis Januar 1933, ed. K.A. Lankheit, vols. III, part 2, Munich, 1994.

Hitler. Reden, Schriften, Anordnungen. Februar 1925 bis Januar 1933, ed. C. Hartmann, vols. III, part 3, Munich, 1995.

Hitler. Reden, Schriften, Anordnungen. Februar 1925 bis Januar 1933, ed. K.A. Lankheit, vols. V, part 1, Munich, 1996.

Hitler's Table Talk 1941–44. His *Private Conversations*, ed. H.R. Trevor-Roper, 2nd. edn., London, 1973.

Hölz, Max, *Vom 'Weißen Kreuz' zur roten Fahne. Jugend-, Kampf- und Zuchthauserlebnisse*, [original 1929] repr. Halle, 1984.

Hoffmann, G., 'Die Schulden von Land, Gemeinden und Gemeindeverbänden in Sachsen', *ZSäStLA*, (1932/33), 103–105.

Jahrbuch der Deutschen Sozialdemokratie für das Jahr 1926, 1927, 1928, 1929, 1930, 1931.

Jahrbuch des Deutschen Sängerbundes 1930.

Jahresbericht der sozialdemokratischen Bezirksorganisation Chemnitz/Erzgebirge. SPD Bezirksverband Chemnitz/Erzgebirge 1929, 1930.

Jahresbericht des Bezirksvorstandes des SPD Bezirk Leipzig 1929, 1930.

Jahresbericht 1928 Sozialdemokratische Bezirksorganisation Chemnitz/Erzgebirge.

Kötzschke, R. and H. Kretzschmar, *Sächsische Geschichte,* 2 vols., Dresden, 1935, repr. Frankfurt, 1977.

Knickerbocker, H.R., *Deutschland So Oder So?*, Berlin, 1932.

Lang, E.L., 'Kampf und Sieg der Nationalsozialistischen Bewegung im Grenzlandkreis Annaberg/Obererzgebirge', in *Vom silbernen Erzgebirge. Kreis Annaberg*, vol. I, 218–36.

Lipinski, R., *Die Geschichte der sozialistischen Arbeiterbewegung in Leipzig*, Leipzig, 1931.

Lipinski, R., *Der Kampf um die politische Macht in Sachsen*, Leipzig, 1926.

Meldungen aus dem Reich. Die geheimen Lageberichte des Sicherheitsdienstes der SS 1938–1945, ed. H. Boberach, 17 vols., Herrsching, 1984.

Partei-Statistik, Stand 1. Januar 1935, ed. Der Reichsorganisationsleiter der NSDAP, 3 vols., Munich, no date.

Sachsen im Spiegel der Statistik nach 10 Jahren nationalsozialistischer Führung. Zum 30. Januar 1943 herausgegeben vom Statistischen Landesamt Dresden N6.

Sozialdemokratisches Gemeindeblatt. Mitteilungen für die Gemeindevertreter des Bezirkes Chemnitz-Erzgebirge.

SPD Bezirksverband Dresden. Geschäftsbericht vom 1. Januar bis zum 31. Dezember 1929.

SPD Sachsen, *Vier Jahre Sächsische Politik, 1926.*

Statistisches Jahrbuch des Deutschen Reichs, 1914–1934.

Statistisches Jahrbuch des Freistaates Sachsen, 1919–1934.

Verhandlungen des Sächsischen Landtages.

[Otto Wagener] H.A. Turner, ed., *Hitler aus nächster Nähe. Aufzeichnungen eines Vertrauten 1929–1932*, Berlin, 1978,

Werner, K., *Die deutschen Wirtschaftsgebiete in der Krise. Statistische Studie zur regional vergleichenden Konjunkturbetrachtung*, Jena, 1932.

Zehn Jahre Kampf der NSDAP, Ortsgruppe Bautzen (1922–1937).

Zehn Jahre NSDAP Schwarzenberg im Erzgebirge (1924–34).

Zeitschrift des Sächsischen Statistischen Landesamtes.

Zum sechzigsten Geburtstag von Gauleiter Mutschmann. Markante Worte von Martin Mutschmann, Gauverlag, 1939.

Unpublished Secondary Works Cited (post 1945)

Adam, T., 'Arbeitermilieu und sozialdemokratisch orientierte Arbeiterbewegung in einer Großstadt – Das Beispiel Leipzig', Ph.D. diss., University of Leipzig, 1997.

Habicht, M., 'Verfolgung und Widerstand nichtproletarischer Kräfte im Raum Leipzig-Westsachsen 1933–45', Ph.D. diss., University of Leipzig, 1990.

Lapp, B.N., 'Political Polarization in Weimar Germany: The Saxon Bürgertum and the Left, 1918/1919–1930', Ph.D. diss., University of Berkeley/California, 1991.

Lobmeier, K., 'Die sozialökonomische Lage und das politische Verhalten der "alten" Mittelschichten in der Kreishauptmannschaft Chemnitz 1927 bis 1935', Ph.D. diss., University of Leipzig, 1989.

Madden, J.P., 'The Social Composition of the Nazi Party, 1919–1930', Ph.D diss., University of Oklahoma, 1976.

Mai, T., 'Der faschistische sächsische Gauleiter Martin Mutschmann, die Entwicklung des Gaues Sachsen und der NSDAP', Diplomarbeit, University of Jena, 1984.

Stoschek, H., 'Die Entwicklung der militaristisch-faschistischen Bewegung in Sachsen in den Jahren 1919 bis 1925 unter besonderer Berücksichtigung der NSDAP', Diplomarbeit, Potsdam, 1967.

Szejnmann, C.-C.W., 'The Rise of the Nazis in Saxony between 1921 and 1933', Ph.D. diss., London University, 1994.

Secondary Works (post-1945) Cited and Selected Secondary Literature

Abraham, D., *The Collapse of the Weimar Republic. Political Economy and Crisis*, 2nd. edn., London, 1986.

Adolph, J., 'Der VSI-Vorsitzende Wilhelm Wittke', in U. Hess and M. Schäfer, eds., *Unternehmer in Sachsen. Aufstieg – Krise – Untergang – Neubeginn*, Leipzig, 1998, 181–92.

Altmann, G., 'Von der Löffelschmiede zu den Krauss-Werken im erzgebirgischen Schwarzenberg. Ein Unternehmen in den politischen Umbrüchen und technologischen Wandlungen des 20. Jahrhunderts', in U. Hess and M. Schäfer, eds., *Unternehmer in Sachsen. Aufstieg – Krise – Untergang – Neubeginn*, Leipzig, 1998, 193–204.

Aly, G., 'The Posen Diaries of the Anatomist Hermann Voss', in G. Aly, P. Chroust and C. Pross, eds., *Cleansing the Fatherland. Nazi Medicine and Racial Hygiene*, London, 1994, 99–155.

Allen, W. S., *The Nazi Seizure of Power*, 2nd. edn., London, 1984.

Bach, O., 'Zur Zwangssterilisierungspraxis in der Zeit des Faschismus im Bereich der Gesundheitsämter Leipzig und Grimma', in A. Thom and H. Spaar, eds., *Medizin im Faschismus. Symposium über das Schicksal der Medizin in der Zeit des Faschismus in Deutschland 1933–1945*, Berlin, 1985, 157–61.

Bajohr, F., ed., *Norddeutschland im Nationalsozialismus*, Hamburg, 1993.

Bauer, K., 'Umrisse der Arbeitermusikbewegung in Dresden von 1878 bis 1933', *Sächsische Heimatblätter*, 30 (5) (1984), 213–16.

Bazillion, R.J., 'Liberalism, Modernization, and the Social Question in the Kingdom of Saxony, 1830–90', in K.H. Jarausch and L.E. Jones, eds., *In Search of a Liberal Germany: Studies in the History of German Liberalism From 1789 to the Present*, Oxford, 1990, 87–110.

Bessel, R., *Political Violence and the Rise of Nazism. The Storm Troopers in Eastern Germany 1925–34*, London, 1984.

Bessel, R., 'The rise of the NSDAP and the Myth of Nazi Propaganda', *Wiener Library Bulletin*, (33) (1980), 20–29.

Blackbourn, D. and G. Eley, *The Peculiarities of German History: Bourgeois Society and Politics in Nineteenth-Century Germany*, Oxford, 1984.

Blaschke, K., 'Das Königreich Sachsen 1815–1918', in K. Schwabe, ed., *Die Regierungen der deutschen Mittel- und Kleinstaaten 1815–1933*, Boppard, 1983, 81–102.

Blaschke, K., 'Eigenarten und Leistungen sächsischer Landesgeschichte', *Jahrbuch für Regionalgeschichte*, 14 (1987), 33–54.

Blaschke, K., *Historisches Ortsverzeichnis von Sachsen*, Leipzig, 1957.

Böhnke, W., *Die NSDAP im Ruhrgebiet, 1920–1933*, Bonn-Bad Godesberg, 1974.

Bons, Joachim, 'Der Kampf um die Seele des deutschen Arbeiters. Zur Arbeiterpolitik der NSDAP 1920–1933', *Internationale Wissenschaftliche Korrespondenz*, 25 (1) (1989), 11–41.

Bracher, K.D., *The German Dictatorship*, Middlesex, 1985.

Bramke, W., 'Der erste Reichskriegertag in Leipzig 1925', in K. Keller, ed., *Feste und Feiern. Zum Wandel städtischer Festkultur in Leipzig*, Leipzig, 1995, 214–28.

Bramke, W., 'Der unbekannte Widerstand in Westsachsen 1933–1945', *Jahrbuch für Regionalgeschichte*, 13 (1986), 220–53.

Bramke, W., 'Die Industrieregion Sachsen. Ihre Herausbildung und Entwicklung bis zum Ende des Zweiten Weltkrieges', in R. Schulze, ed., *Industrieregion im Umbruch. Historische Voraussetzungen und Verlaufsmuster des regionalen Strukturwandels im europäischen Vergleich*, Essen, 1993, 291–317.

Bramke W. and U. Heß, eds., *Sachsen und Mitteldeutschland. Politische, wirtschaftliche und soziale Wandlungen im 20. Jahrhundert*, Weimar, 1995.

Bramke, W., 'Unter der faschistischen Diktatur', in K. Czok, ed., *Geschichte Sachsens*, Weimar, 1989, 480–517.

Bramke, W., 'Vom Freistaat zum Gau. Sachsen unter der faschistischen Diktatur 1933 bis 1939', *Zeitschrift für Geschichtswissenschaft*, 31 (1983), 1067–78.

Bramke W. and U. Heß, eds., *Wirtschaft und Gesellschaft in Sachsen im 20. Jahrhundert*, Leipzig, 1998.

Breuer, S., *Anatomie der Konservativen Revolution*, Darmstadt, 1993.

Brustein, W., *The Logic of Evil. The Social Origins of the Nazi Party, 1925–1933*, London, 1996.

Burleigh, M., *Death and Deliverance. 'Euthanasia' in Germany 1900–1945*, Cambridge, 1994,

Burleigh, M. and W. Wippermann, *The Racial State: Germany 1933–1945*, 2nd. repr., Cambridge, 1992.

Chickering, R., *We Men Who Feel Most German. A Cultural Study of the Pan-German League, 1886–1914*, London, 1984.

Childers, T., *The Nazi Voter: The Social Foundations of Fascism in Germany, 1919–1933*, London, 1983.

Childers, T., 'The Social Language of Politics in Germany: The Sociology of Political Discourse in the Weimar Republic', *American Historical Review*, 95 (2) (1990), 331–58.

Crew, D., ed., *Nazism and German Society 1933–1945*, London, 1994.

Czok, K., ed., *Geschichte Sachsens*, Weimar, 1989.

Dietrich, R., 'Zur industriellen Produktion, technischen Entwicklung und zum Unternehmertum in Mitteldeutschland, speziell in Sachsen im Zeitalter der Industrialisierung', *Jahrbuch für die Geschichte Mittel- und Ostdeutschlands*, 28 (1979), 221–72.

Dittmann, H., 'Zur Geschichte der Arbeiterbewegung in Auerbach', *Der Heimatfreund für den Kreis Stollberg/Erzgebirge*, (März-Juli) (1963), 57–59, 74f, 93f, 115–17, 133–35.

Dornheim, A., 'Emotionalisierung, Uniformierung und Militarisierung – nationalsozialistische Feiern in Leipzig', in K. Keller, ed., *Feste und Feiern. Zum Wandel städtischer Festkultur in Leipzig*, Leipzig, 1995, 283–99.

Dorpalen, A., *German History in Marxist Perspective. The East German Approach*, London, 1985.

Eichholtz, D., ed., *Brandenburg in der NS-Zeit. Studien und Dokumente*, Berlin, 1993.

Eley, G., 'Is there a History of the Kaiserreich?', in G. Eley, ed., *Society, Culture, and the State in Germany, 1870–1930*, Michigan, 1996, 1–42.

Eley, G., 'What produces fascism: pre-industrial traditions or a crisis of the capitalist state?', in G. Eley, *From Unification to Nazism. Reinterpreting the German Past*, London, 1992, 254–82.

Elliot, C.J., 'The Kriegervereine and the Weimar Republic', *Journal of Contemporary History*, 10 (1) (1975), 109–129.

Evans, R.J., 'Introduction: The Sociological Interpretation of German Labour History', in R.J. Evans, ed., *The German Working Class, 1888–1933: The Politics of Everyday Life*, London, 1982, 15–53.

Evans, R.J., *Rethinking German History: Nineteenth Century Germany and the Origins of the Third Reich*, London, 1987.

Fabian, W., 'Arbeiterführer und Arbeiterbildungswesen im Freistaat Sachsen. Ein Beitrag zur Führungsproblematik in der Arbeiter-bewegung der Weimarer Republik', *Herkunft und Mandat*, Frankfurt, (1976), 120–27.

Fäßler, P., 'Sozialhygiene – Rassenhygiene – Euthanasie: "Volksgesundheits-pflege" im Raum Dresden', in R. Pommerin, ed., *Dresden unterm Hakenkreuz*, Cologne, 1998, 193–207.

Falter, J.W. and D. Hänisch, 'Die Anfälligkeit von Arbeitern gegenüber der NSDAP bei den Reichstagswahlen 1928–1933', *Archiv für Sozial-geschichte*, 26 (1986), 179–216.

Falter, J.W., *Hitlers Wähler*, Munich, 1991.

Falter, J.W., 'How likely were Workers to Vote for the NSDAP?', in C.J. Fischer, ed., *The Rise of National Socialism and the Working Classes in Weimar Germany*, Oxford, 1996, 9–45.

Falter, J.W., 'The Young Membership of the NSDAP between 1925 and 1933. A Demographic and Social Profile', in C.J. Fischer, ed., *The Rise of National Socialism and the Working Classes in Weimar Germany*, Oxford, 1996, 79–98.

Falter, J.W., T. Lindenberger and S. Schumann, *Wahlen und Abstimmungen in der Weimarer Republik*, Munich, 1986.

Feldman, G., 'Saxony, the Reich and the Problem of Unemployment in the German Inflation', *Archiv für Sozialgeschichte*, 27 (1987), 103–44.

Fenske, H., 'Sachsen und Thüringen 1918–1933', in K. Schwabe, ed., *Die Regierungen der deutschen Mittel- und Kleinstaaten 1815–1933*, Boppard, 1980, 185–204.

Fischer, C.J., 'Gab es am Ende der Weimarer Republik einen marxistischen Wählerblock?', *Geschichte und Gesellschaft*, 21 (1) (1995), 63–76.

Fischer, C.J., *The German Communists and the Rise of Nazism*, London, 1991.

Fischer, C.J., ed., *The Rise of National Socialism and the Working Classes in Weimar Germany*, Oxford, 1996.

Fischer, C.J., *The Rise of the Nazis*, Manchester, 1996.

Förster, F., 'Das Wendenbild der NS-Wissenschaft', *Neues Archiv für sächsische Geschichte*, 64 (1993), 175–84.

Forberger, R., 'Sachsen als Pionierland der Industriellen Revolution in Deutschland im Spiegel der Fachliteratur', *Jahrbuch für Regionalgeschichte*, 14 (1987), 243–53.

Fritzsche, P., *Rehearsals for Fascism. Populism and Political Mobilization in Weimar Germany*, Oxford, 1990.

Fulbrook, M., *Germany 1918–1990: The Divided Nation*, London, 1991.

Fuchs-Materny, U., ' "Der Freiheitskampf" auf Kriegskurz. Dresdner Presse im Jahr 1939', *Dresdner Hefte*, 11 (35) (1993), 75–83.

Gebauer, H., 'Arbeiterbibliotheken in Leipzig', in R. Florsted, ed., *Leihbibliotheken, Arbeiterbibliotheken, Bücherhallen. Bibliothekarische Bemühungen um die Volksbildung vom Anfang des 19. Jahrhunderts bis 1933*, Leipzig, 1989, 31–44.

Gernert, D., *Schulvorschriften für den Geschichtsunterricht im 19./20. Jahrhundert. Dokumente aus Preußen, Bayern, Sachsen, Thüringen und Hamburg bis 1945*, Cologne, 1994.

Goldhagen, D., *Hitler's Willing Executioners, Ordinary Germans and the Holocaust*, London, 1996.

Graham H. and J. Labanyi, eds., *Spanish Cultural Studies. An Introduction. The Struggle for Modernity*, Oxford, 1995.

Grebing, H., H. Mommsen and K. Rudolph, eds., *Demokratie und Emanzipation zwischen Saale und Elbe. Beiträge zur Geschichte der sozialdemokratischen Arbeiterbewegung bis 1933*, Essen, 1993.

Grill, J.H., 'Local and regional studies on National Socialism: A Review', *Journal of Contemporary History*, 21 (2) (1986), 253–94.

Guttsman, W.L., Workers' *Culture in Weimar Germany. Between Tradition and Commitment*, Oxford, 1990.

Hänisch, D., and A. Elste, *Auf dem Weg zur Macht. Beiträge zur Geschichte der NSDAP in Kärnten von 1918 bis 1938*, Vienna, 1997.

Hänisch, D., *Die österreichischen NSDAP-Wähler: eine empirische Analyse ihrer politischen Herkunft und ihres Sozialprofils*, Vienna, 1998.

Hänisch, D., 'Inhalt und Struktur der Datenbank "Wahl- und Sozialdaten der Kreise und Gemeinden des Deutschen Reiches von 1920 bis 1933"', *Historical Social Research*, 14 (1989), 39–67.

Hänisch, D., *Sozialstrukturelle Bestimmungsgründe des Wahlverhaltens in der Weimarer Republik. Eine Aggredatdatenanalyse der Ergebnisse der Reichstagswahlen 1924 bis 1933*, Duisburg, 1983.

Hamilton, R.F., *Who voted for Hitler?*, Princeton, 1982.

Häupel, B. and M. Seidel, 'Der Konflikt der Weimarer Sozialdemokratie aus der sächsischen und thüringischen Perspektive', in W. Bramke and U. Heß, eds., *Sachsen und Mitteldeutschland. Politische, wirtschaftliche und soziale Wandlungen im 20. Jahrhundert, Weimar*, 1995, 415–34.

Harsch, D., *German Social Democracy and the Rise of Nazism*, London, 1993.

Hausmann, C., 'Die "Alte Sozialdemokratische Partei" 1926–1932. Ein gescheitertes Experiment zwischen den parteipolitischen Fronten', in H. Grebing, H. Mommsen and K. Rudolph, eds., *Demokratie und Emanzipation zwischen Saale und Elbe. Beiträge zur Geschichte der sozialdemokratischen Arbeiterbewegung bis 1933*, Essen, 1993, 273–94.

Hausmann, C. and K. Rudolph, 'Trotz allem: Sachsen, die rote Hochburg', *Politische Viertejahresschrift*, 34 (1) (1993), 92–97.

Heiber, H., *Goebbels*, New York, 1972.

Heidel, C.-P., 'Zwischen Naturheilkunde und Rassenhygiene – Dresdner Medizin im Nationalsozialismus', *Dresdner Hefte*, 11 (35) (1993), 39–50.

Heidel, G., 'Die Dresdner Internationale Hygiene-Ausstellung 1930/31', *Dresdner Hefte*, 9 (10) (1991), 35–44.

Heiden, D. and G. Mai, eds., *Nationalsozialismus* in *Thüringen*, Weimar, 1995.

Heidenreich, F., *Arbeiterkulturbewegung und Sozialdemokratie in Sachsen vor 1933*. Weimar, 1995.

Heidenreich, F., '"... Das Wichtigste Agitationsmittel für die Partei." Zur Geschichte der Sozialdemokratischen Presse in Sachsen vor 1933', *Internationale Wissenschaftliche Korrespondenz zur Geschichte der deutschen Arbeiterbewegung*, 27 (2) (1991), 139–71.

Heilbronner, O., 'Der verlassene Stammtisch. Vom Verfall der bürgerlichen Infrastruktur und dem Aufstieg der NSDAP am Beispiel der Region Schwarzwald', *Geschichte und Gesellschaft*, 19 (2) (1993), 178–201.

Heilbronner, O., 'Die NSDAP – ein bürgerlicher Verein?', *Tel Aviver Jahrbuch für deutsche Geschichte*, 23 (1994), 65–78.

Heilbronner, O., 'The Role of Nazi Antisemitism in the Nazi Party's Activity and Propaganda. A Regional Historiographical Study', *Leo Baeck Institute Yearbook 1990*, 397–439.

Heilbronner, O., 'Weimar Society: The Image of Soviet Russia', *Tel Aviver Jahrbuch für deutsche Geschichte*, 24 (1995), 179–92.

Hennig, E., '"Der Hunger naht" – "Mittelstand wehr Dich" – "Wir Bauern misten aus". Über angepaßtes und abweichendes Wahlverhalten in hessischen Agrarregionen', in E. Hennig, ed., *Hessen unterm Hakenkreuz. Studien zur Durchsetzung der NSDAP in Hessen*, Frankfurt, 1983, 379–432.

Heß, U., 'Rüstungs- und Kriegswirtschaft in Sachsen (1935–1945), in W. Bramke and U. Heß, eds., *Sachsen und Mitteldeutschland. Politische, wirtschaftliche und soziale Wandlungen im 20. Jahrhundert*, Weimar, 1995, 73–91.

Heß, U., 'Jubiläen Leipziger Firmen im 20. Jahrhundert – Zwischen Gründungsmythos und Traditionsbewußtsein', in K. Keller, ed., *Feste und Feiern. Zum Wandel städtischer Festkultur in Leipzig*, Leipzig, 1995, 266–82.

Hinze, S., '"Die ungewöhnlich geduldigen Deutschen". Arbeiterleben 1934–1936 im Spiegel ausgewählter Gestapodokumente (Regierungsbezirk Potsdam)', in D. Eichholtz, ed., *Brandenburg in der NS-Zeit. Studien und Dokumente*, Berlin, 1993, 32–62.

Hoffkes, K., *Hitlers Politische Generale*, Tübingen 1986.

Höppner, S., 'Leipziger Jugendliche im antifaschistischen Widerstand 1933/34 – die "Zelle Zentrum"', in H.-D. Schmid, ed., *Zwei Städte unter dem Hakenkreuz. Widerstand und Verweigerung in Hannover und Leipzig 1933–1945*, Leipzig, 1994, 119–43.

Hohmann, J.S., 'Die nationalsozialistische "Euthanasie" in sächsischen Anstalten und ihre strafrechtliche Ahndung in der SBZ', *Historical Social Research*, 20 (4) (1995), 31–60.

Huebner, T., 'Ethnicity denied: Nazi policy towards the Lusatian Sorbs', *German History*, 6 (1988), 250–77.

Hüttenberger, P., *Die Gauleiter. Studie zum Wandel des Machtgefüges in der NSDAP*, Stuttgart, 1969.

Jahn, M., 'Veränderungen wirtschaftlicher und sozialer Strukturen in Sachsen 1945 bis 1947 bei der Ansiedlung Vertriebener', in W. Bramke and U. Heß, eds., *Sachsen und Mitteldeutschland. Politische, wirtschaftliche und soziale Wandlungen im 20. Jahrhundert*, Weimar, 1995, 303–318.

James, H., 'Economic Reasons for the Collapse of the Weimar Republic', in I. Kershaw, ed., *Weimar: Why did German Democracy Fail?* London, 1990, 30–57.

Jochmann, W., *Nationalsozialismus und Revolution. Ursprung und Geschichte der NSDAP in Hamburg 1922–1933. Dokumente*, Frankfurt, 1960.

Jones, L.E., *German Liberalism and the Dissolution of the Weimar Party System, 1918–1933*, London, 1988.

Jones, L.E., 'Saxony, 1924–1930: A Study in the Dissolution of the Bourgeois Party System in Weimar Germany', in J. Retallack, ed., *Memory, Democracy, and the Mediated Nation. Political Cultures and Regional Identities in Germany, 1848–1998*, Conference Reader, Toronto, 1998.

Jones, L.E., 'The Dying Middle: Weimar Germany and the Fragmentation of Bourgeois Politics', *Central European History*, 5 (1972), 23–54.

Kaes, A., M. Jay and E. Dimendberg, eds., *The Weimar Republic Sourcebook*, London, 1994.

Kaiser, J.-C., K. Nowak and M. Schwartz, *Eugenik. Sterilisation, 'Euthanasie'. Politische Biologie in Deutschland 1895–1945. Eine Dokumentation*, Buchverlag Union.

Kater, M.H., 'Frauen in der NS-Bewegung', *Vierteljahreshefte für Zeitgeschichte*, 31 (1983), 202–241.

Kater, M.H., The Nazi Party. *A Social Profile of Members and Leaders, 1919–1945*, repr. 1985, Oxford.

Kater, M.H., 'Zur Soziographie der frühen NSDAP', *Vierteljahrshefte für Zeitgeschichte*, 19 (1971), 124–59.

Keller, J., 'Drei Jahrzehnte später – Aus dem Kampf der Bergarbeiter unter Führung der KPD gegen Krisenpolitik und Faschismus in Oelsnitz/Erzgebirge', *Der Heimatfreund für den Kreis Stollberg/Auerbach*, (1963: 90–2, 113–15, 131–33, 174; 1964: 9, 117–20, 138–40, 174–78).

Kershaw, I., *Hitler 1889–1936: Hubris*, London, 1998.

Kershaw, I., 'Ideology, Propaganda, and the Rise of the Nazi Party', in P.D. Stachura, ed., *The Nazi Machtergreifung*, London, 1983, 162–81.

Kershaw, I., *Popular Opinion and Political Dissent in the Third Reich. Bavaria 1933–1945*, Oxford, repr. 1991.

Kershaw, I., *The 'Hitler Myth'. Image and Reality in the Third Reich*, Oxford, 1987.

Kiesewetter, H., *Industrialisierung und Landwirtschaft. Sachsens Stellung im regionalen Industrialisierungsprozeß Deutschlands im 19. Jahrhundert*, Cologne, 1988.

Kirsch, G., 'Die Konstituierung der nationalsozialistischen Herrschaft in Sachsen 1933/34', *Sächsische Heimatblätter*, 41 (1) (1995), 23–27.

Klemperer, V., *Ich will Zeugnis ablegen bis zum letzten. Tagebücher 1933–1945*, 2 vols. Berlin, 1995.

Klenke, D., *Die SPD-Linke in der Weimarer Republik. Eine Untersuchung zu den regionalen organisatorischen Grundlagen und zur politischen Praxis und Theoriebildung des linken Flügels der SPD in den Jahren 1922–32*, 2 vols. Münster, 1983.

Klenke, D., 'Hermann Liebmann (1882–1935). Vom Architekten der "proletarischen Mehrheit" in Sachsen zum "Tolerierungs"-Politiker der

Ära Brüning', in P. Lösche et al., eds., *Vor dem Vergessen bewahren. Lebenswege Weimarer Sozialdemokraten*, Berlin, 1988, 193–222.

Kocka, J., 'Ursachen des Nationalsozialismus', *Aus Politik und Zeitgeschichte*, (25) (1980), 3–15.

Kolb, E., *The Weimar Republic*, London, 1988.

Koshar, R., *Social Life, Local Politics, and Nazism. Marburg, 1880–1935*, London, 1986.

Kratzenberg, V., *Arbeiter auf dem Weg zu Hitler? Die Nationalsozialistische Betriebszellen-Organisation. Ihre Entstehung, Ihre Programmatik, Ihr Scheitern 1927–1934*, Frankfurt/Main, 1989.

Krüger, R., 'Presse unter Druck. Differenzierte Berichterstattung trotz nationalsozialistischer Presselenkungsmaßnahmen. Die liberalen *Dresdner Neueste Nachrichten* und das NSDAP-Organ *Der Freiheitskampf* im Vergleich', in R. Pommerin, ed., Dresden unterm Hakenkreuz, Cologne, 1998, 43–66.

Kühnl, R., *Die nationalsozialistische Linke, 1925–30*, Meisenheim, 1966.

Kürschner, D., 'Leipzig im Frühling des Jahres 1945', *Sächsische Heimatblätter*, (4) (1995), 206–17.

Kuratorium Gedenkstätte Sonnenstein e. V. und Sächsische Landeszentrale für politische Bildung, eds., *Nationalsozialistische Euthanasie-Verbrechen in Sachsen. Beiträge zu ihrer Aufarbeitung*, 2nd. edn., Dresden, 1996.

Kurzweg, C., 'Unternehmeridentität und regionale Selbstthematisierung: Auseinandersetzungen um die maschinelle Herstellung von Zigarren im sächsischen Döbeln, *Comparativ*, 4 (1995), 127–45.

Lapp, B., 'A "National" Socialism: The Old Socialist Party of Saxony, 1926–32', *Journal of Contemporary History*, 30 (1995), 291–309.

Lapp, B., 'Der Aufstieg des Nationalsozialismus in Sachsen', in R. Pommerin, ed., *Dresden unterm Hakenkreuz, Cologne*, 1998, 1–24.

Lapp, B., *Revolution from the Right. Politics, Class, and the Rise of Nazism in Saxony, 1919–1933*, New Jersey, 1997.

Lässig, S., ' "Mit jeder Faser seines Lebens gehörte er zur Arbeiterbewegung". August Kaden (1850–1913)', in H. Grebing, H. Mommsen and K. Rudolph, eds., *Demokratie und Emanzipation zwischen Saale und Elbe. Beiträge zur Geschichte der sozialdemokratischen Arbeiterbewegung bis 1933*, Essen, 1993, 83–100.

Lässig, S., 'Nationalsozialistische "Judenpolitik" und jüdische Selbstbehauptung vor dem Novemberprogrom. Das Beispiel der Dresdner Bankiersfamilie Arnhold', in R. Pommerin, ed., *Dresden unterm Hakenkreuz*, Cologne, 1998, 129–91.

Lässig, S., 'Sozialdemokratisches Friedensengagement, Julikrise und der 4. August 1914 in Ostsachsen', in H. Grebing, H. Mommsen and K. Rudolph, eds., *Demokratie und Emanzipation zwischen Saale und Elbe. Beiträge zur Geschichte der sozialdemokratischen Arbeiterbewegung bis 1933*, Essen, *1993*, 147–170.

Lässig, S. and K.H. Pohl, eds., *Sachsen im Kaiserreich. Politik, Wirtschaft und Gesellschaft im Umbruch*, Weimar, 1997.

Lehnert, D. and K. Mengerle, eds., *Politische Identität und nationale Gedenktage. Zur politischen Kultur in der Weimarer Republik*, Opladen, 1989.

Lehnert, D. and K. Mengerle, eds., *Politische Teilkulturen zwischen Integration und Polarisierung. Zur politischen Kultur in der Weimarer Republik*, Opladen, 1990.

Lepsius, M.R., 'Parteiensystem und Sozialstruktur: Zum Problem der Demokratisierung der deutschen Gesellschaft', in G.A. Ritter, ed., *Die deutschen Parteien vor 1918*, Cologne, 1973, 56–80.

Levy, R.S., *The Downfall of the Anti-Semitic Political Parties in Imperial Germany*, London, 1975.

Liebsch, T., 'Dresdner Theaterkrise 1929–1933', *Dresdner Hefte*, 12 (39) (1994), 52–63.

Lienert, M., 'Der Einfluß des Nationalsozialismus auf die Technische Hochschule Dresden während der Weimarer Republik', *Neues Archiv für sächsische Geschichte*, 66 (1995), 273–91.

Lipset, S.M., ' "Fascism" – Left, Right, and Center', in S.M. Lipset, ed., *Political Man. The Social Bases of Politics*, New York, 1960, 127–79.

Lösche, P. and F. Walter, 'Zur Organisationskultur der sozialdemokratischen Arbeiterbewegung in der Weimarer Republik', *Geschichte und Gesellschaft*, 15 (4) (1989), 511–36.

Luebbert, G.M., *Liberalism, Fascism, or Social Democracy. Social Classes and the Political Origins of Regimes in Interwar Europe*, Oxford, 1991.

Lüdtke, A, 'The "Honor of Labor": Industrial Workers and the Power of Symbols under National Socialism', in D. Crew, ed., *Nazism and German Society 1933–1945*, London, 67–109.

Mai, G., 'Die Nationalsozialistische Betriebszellen-Organisation. Zum Verhältnis von Arbeiterschaft und Nationalsozialismus', *Vierteljahreshefte für Zeitgeschichte*, 31 (4) (1983), 573–613.

Mai, G., 'National Socialist Factory Cell Organisation and the German Labour Front: National Socialist Labour Policy and Organisations', in C.J. Fischer, ed., *The Rise of National Socialism and the Working Classes in Weimar Germany*, Oxford, 1996, 117–36.

Mai, G., ' "Verteidigungskrieg" und "Volksgemeinschaft". Staatliche Selbstbehauptung, nationale Solidarität und soziale Befreiung in Deutschland in der Zeit des Ersten Weltkrieges (1900–1925)', in W. Michalka, ed., *Der Erste Weltkrieg. Wirkung, Wahrnehmung, Analyse*, Munich, 1995, 583–602.

Mallmann, K.-M. and G. Paul, 'Omniscient, Omnipotent, Omnipresent? Gestapo, society and resistance', in D.F. Crew, ed., *Nazism and German Society 1933–1945*, London, 1994, 166–96.

Manstein, P., *Die Mitglieder und Wähler der NSDAP 1919–1933. Untersuchungen zu ihrer schichtmäßigen Zusammensetzung*, 3rd. edn., Frankfurt/Main, 1990.

Matschke, W., *Die industrielle Entwicklung in der Sowjetischen Besatzungszone Deutschlands (SBZ) von 1945 bis 1948*, Berlin, 1988.

Matthiesen, H., *Bürgertum und Nationalsozialismus in Thüringen. Das bürgerliche Gotha von 1918 bis 1930*, Jena, 1994.

Matzerath, H., *Nationalsozialismus und kommunale Selbstverwaltung*, Stuttgart, 1970.

Maurer, M., 'Feste und Feiern als Historischer Forschungsgegenstand', *Historische Zeitschrift*, (253) (1991), 101–130.

Möller, Horst, A. Wirsching and W. Ziegler, eds., *Nationalsozialismus in der Region*, Munich, 1996.

Moeller, R.G., 'The Kaiserreich Recast? Continuity and Change in Modern German Historiography', *Journal of Social History*, 17 (1984), 655–83.

Mohler, A., *Die konservative Revolution in Deutschland 1918–1932*, 2nd. edn., Darmstadt, 1972.

Mommsen, H., *The Rise and Fall of Weimar Democracy*, Chapel Hill, 1996.

Mommsen, H., 'The Decline of the Bürgertum in Late Nineteenth- and Early Twentieth-Century Germany', in H. Mommsen, *From Weimar To Auschwitz. Essays in German History*, Oxford, 1991, 11–27.

Morsch, G., *Arbeit und Brot. Studien zu Lage, Stimmung, Einstellung und Verhalten der deutschen Arbeiterschaft 1933–1936/37*, Frankfurt/Main, 1993.

Mosse, G.L., *The Nationalization of the Masses. Political Symbolism and Mass Movements in Germany from the Napoleonic Wars Through the Third Reich*, New York, 1975.

Mühlberger, D., 'A "Workers' Party" or a "Party Without Workers"? The Extent and Nature of the Working-Class Membership of the NSDAP, 1919–1933', in C.J. Fischer, ed., *The Rise of National Socialism and the Working Classes in Weimar Germany*, Oxford, 1996, 47–77.

Mühlberger, D., *Hitler's Followers. Studies in the Sociology of the Nazi Movement*, London, 1991.

Mühlberger, D., 'The Occupational and Social Structure of the NSDAP in the Border Province Posen-West Prussia in the early 1930s', *European History Quarterly*, 15, 1985, 281–311.

Mühlberger, D., *The Social Basis of European Fascist Movements*, London, 1987.

Naimark, N.M., *The Russians in Germany. A History of the Soviet Zone of Occupation*, 1945–1949, 2nd. print, London, 1996.

Neebe, R., *Großindustrie, Staat und NSDAP 1930–1933*, Göttingen, 1981.

Neocleous, M., *Fascism*, Bristol, 1997.

Nestler, G. and H. Ziegler, eds., *Die Pfalz Unterm Hakenkreuz. Eine Deutsche Provinz während der nationalsozialistischen Terrorherrschaft*, Landau, 1993.

Niekisch, Ernst, *Gewagtes Leben. Begegnungen und Begebnisse*, Cologne, 1958.

Noakes, J., *The Nazi Party in Lower Saxony 1921–1933*, London, 1971.

Noakes, J., and G. Pridham, *Nazism 1919–1945. Volume 2: State, Economy and Society 1933–1939*, Exeter, 1984.

Noakes, J., *Nazism 1919–1945. Volume 4: The German Home Front in World War II*, Exeter, 1998.

Nonn, C. 'Arbeiter, Bürger und "Agrarier": Stadt-Land-Gegensatz und Klassenkonflikt im Wilhelminischen Deutschland am Beispiel des Königreichs Sachsen', in H. Grebing, H. Mommsen and K. Rudolph, eds., *Demokratie und Emanzipation zwischen Saale und Elbe. Beiträge zur Geschichte der sozialdemokratischen Arbeiterbewegung bis 1933*, Essen, 1993, 101–113.

Ohr, D., 'Political Meetings of the National Socialists and the Increase of the NSDAP Vote. Analysing Conditions of Propaganda Effects with Aggregate Data', *Historical Social Research*, 22 (1) (1997), 29–58.

Ohr, D., 'War die NSDAP-Propaganda nur bei "Nationalistischen" Wählern erfolgreich? Eine Aggregatanalyse zur Wirkung der nationalsozialistischen Versammlungspropaganda', *Kölner Zeitschrift für Soziologie und Sozialpsychologie*, 46 (4) (1994), 646–67.

Orlow, D., *The History of the Nazi Party, Vol. I: 1919–1933*, Pittsburgh, 1969.

Orlow, D., *The History of the Nazi Party, Vol. II: 1933–1945*, Pittsburgh, 1973.

Osterloh, J., *Ein ganz normales Lager. Das Kriegsgefangenen-Mannschaftsstammlager 304 (IV H) Zeithain bei Riesa/Sa. 1941 bis* 1945, 2nd. edn., Leipzig, 1997.

Overy, R.J., *The Origins of the Second World War*, London, 1987.

Overy, R.J., *War and Economy in the Third Reich*, Oxford, 1994.

Paul, G., *Aufstand der Bilder. Die NS-Propaganda vor 1933*, Bonn, 1990.

Paul, G., *Die NSDAP des Saargebietes 1920–1935. Der Verspätete Aufstieg der NSDAP in der katholisch-proletarischen Provinz*, Saarbrücken, 1987.

Payne, S.G., *A History of Fascism 1914–45*, London, 1995.

Peukert, D.J.K., *Inside Nazi Germany, Conformity, Opposition and Racism in Everyday Life*, London, 1987.

Peukert, D.J.K., *The Weimar Republic. The Crisis of Classical Modernity*, London, 1991.

Pfalzer, S., 'Der "Butterkrawall" im Oktober 1915. Die erste größere Antikriegsbewegung in Chemnitz', in H. Grebing, H. Mommsen and K. Rudolph, eds., *Demokratie und Emanzipation zwischen Saale und*

Elbe. Beiträge zur Geschichte der sozialdemokratischen Arbeiterbewegung bis 1933, Essen, 1993, 196–201.

Pohl, K.H., ed., *Historiker in der DDR*, Göttingen, 1997.

Pohl, K.H., 'Wirtschaft und Wirtschaftsbürgertum im Königreich Sachsen im frühen 20. Jahrhundert', in W. Bramke and U. Heß, eds., *Sachsen und Mitteldeutschland. Politische, wirtschaftliche und soziale Wandlungen im 20. Jahrhundert*, Weimar, 1995, 319–36.

Pommerin, R., ed., *Dresden unterm Hakenkreuz*, Cologne, 1998.

Poste, B., *Schulreform in Sachsen, 1918–1923. Eine vergessene Tradition deutscher Schulgeschichte*, Frankfurt/Main, 1993.

Prater, G., *Kämpfer Wider Willen. Erinnerungen des Landesbischofs von Sachsen D. Hugo Hahn aus dem Kirchenkampf 1933–1945*, Metzingen, 1969.

Pridham, G., *Hitler's Rise to Power. The Nazi Movement in Bavaria*, London, 1973.

Pryce, D.B., 'The Reich Government versus Saxony, 1923: The Decision to Intervene', *Central European History*, 10 (2) (1977), 112–47.

Pyta, W., *Gegen Hitler und für die Republik. Die Auseinandersetzung der deutschen Sozialdemokratie mit der NSDAP in der Weimarer Republik*, Düsseldorf, 1989.

Rauh-Kühne, C., *Katholisches Milieu und Kleinstadtgesellschaft. Ettlingen 1918–1939*, Sigmaringen, 1991.

Reimus, K., '"Das Reich muß uns doch bleiben!" Die nationale Rechte', in D. Lehnert and K. Megerle, eds., *Politische Identität und nationale Gedenktage. Zur politischen Kultur in der Weimarer Republik*, Opladen, 1989, 231–51.

Reinhold, J., 'Die NSDAP und die Wahl zur Landwirtschaftskammer 1931 im Freistaat Sachsen', *Geschichte und Gegenwart*, 9 (3) (1990), 188–96.

Retallack, J., 'Antisocialism and Electoral Politics in Regional Perspective: The Kingdom of Saxony', in L.E. Jones and J. Retallack, eds., *Elections, Mass Politics, and Social Change in Modern Germany*, Cambridge, 1992, 49–91.

Retallack, J., ed., *Memory, Democracy, and the Mediated Nation. Political Cultures and Regional Identities in Germany, 1848–1998*, Conference Reader, Toronto, 1998. A revised version will appear as J. Retallack, ed., *Saxony in German History. Culture, Society, and Politics, 1830–1933*, Michigan, 2000.

Retallack, J., 'Society and Politics in Saxony, 1763–1990. Reflections on Recent Research', *Archiv für Sozialgeschichte*, 38 (1998) (in print).

Ritter, G.A., 'Wahlen und Wahlpolitik im Königreich Sachsen 1867–1914', in S. Lässig and K.H. Pohl, eds., *Sachsen im Kaiserreich. Politik, Wirtschaft und Gesellschaft im Umbruch*, Weimar, 1997, 29–86.

Rohe, K., 'German Elections and Party Systems in Historical and Regional Perspective: An Introduction', in K. Rohe, ed., *Elections, Parties and*

Political Traditions. Social Foundations of German Parties and Party Systems, 1867–1987, Oxford, 1990, 1–25.

Rohkrämer, T., *Der Militarismus der "kleinen Leute". Die Kriegervereine im Deutschen Kaiserreich 1871–1914*, Munich, 1990.

Roseman, Mark, ed., *Generations in Conflict. Youth revolt and generation formation in Germany 1770–1968*, Cambridge, 1995.

Roth, G., *The Social Democrats in Imperial Germany. A Study in Working-class Isolation and National Integration*, Totowa, 1963.

Rudloff, M., 'Die Sozialdemokratie in den Landtagen des Königreiches Sachsen (1877–1918), in M. Schmeitzner and M. Rudloff, *Geschichte der Sozialdemokratie im Sächsischen Landtag. Darstellung und Dokumentation 1877–1997, Dresden, 1997*, 11–55.

Rudloff, M., 'Die Strukturpolitik in den Debatten des sächsischen Landtags zur Zeit der Weltwirtschaftskrise', in W. Bramke and U. Heß, eds., *Sachsen und Mitteldeutschland. Politische, wirtschaftliche und soziale Wandlungen im 20. Jahrhundert*, Weimar, 1995, 241–60.

Rudloff, M., T. Adam and J. Schlimper, *Leipzig – Wiege der deutschen Sozialdemokratie*, Berlin, 1996.

Rudloff, M. and M. Schmeitzner, eds., *'Solche Schädlinge gibt es auch in Leipzig.' Sozialdemokraten und die SED*, Frankfurt, 1997.

Rudolph, K., 'Das Scheitern des Kommunismus im deutschen Oktober 1923', *Internationale Wissenschaftliche Korrespondenz zur Geschichte der Deutschen Arbeiterbewegung*, 32 (4) (1996), 484–519.

Rudolph, K., *Die sächsische Sozialdemokratie vom Kaiserreich zur Republik 1871–1923*, Weimar, 1995.

Sächsische Landeszentrale für politische Bildung, ed., *Unauslöschlich. Erinnerungen an das Kriegsende 1945. Ein Lesebuch*, Dresden, 1995.

Schildt, G., 'Die Arbeitsgemeinschaft Nord-West. Untersuchungen zur Geschichte der NSDAP 1925–26', Ph.D. diss., University of Freiburg, 1964.

Schmeitzner, M., 'Die sozialdemokratischen Landtagsfraktionen im Freistaat Sachsen (1919–1933)', in M. Schmeitzner and M. Rudloff, *Geschichte der Sozialdemokratie im Sächsischen Landtag. Darstellung und Dokumentation 1877–1997*, Dresden, 1997, 56–121.

Schmeitzner, M., 'Sozialdemokratische Landtagsabgeordnete in zwei Diktaturen (1933–1952/89)', in M. Schmeitzner and M. Rudloff, *Geschichte der Sozialdemokratie im Sächsischen Landtag. Darstellung und Dokumentation 1877–1997*, Dresden, 1997, 122–67.

Schmeitzner, M. and A. Thieme, 'Ausschnitte aus dem parlamentarischen Bild der sächsischen Linken am Vorabend und während der Weltwirtschaftskrise', *Dresdner Hefte*, 12 (39) (1994), 17–27.

Schmid, H.-D., 'Der organisierte Widerstand der Sozialdemokraten in Leipzig 1933–1935', in H.-D. Schmid, ed., *Zwei Städte unter dem Hakenkreuz. Widerstand und Verweigerung in Hannover und Leipzig 1933–1945*, Leipzig, 1994, 26–70.

Schmid, H.-D., 'Die Märzfeiern für die Opfer des Kapp–Putsches in Leipzig', in K. Keller, ed., *Feste und Feiern. Zum Wandel städtischer Festkultur in Leipzig*, Leipzig, 1995, 229–48.

Schmid, H.-D., *Gestapo Leipzig. Politische Abteilung des Polizeipräsidiums und Staatspolizeistelle Leipzig 1933–1945*, Leipzig, 1997.

Schmid, H.-D., 'Leipziger Sozialdemokratie und Nationalsozialismus', *Sächsische Heimatblätter*, 38 (5) (1992), 312–23.

Schröder, W., ' "... zu Grunde richten wird man uns nicht mehr." Sozialdemokratie und Wahlen im Königreich Sachsen 1867–1877', *Beiträge zur Geschichte der Arbeiterbewegung*, 17 (4) (1994), 3–18.

Schulz, F., 'Elitenwandel in der Leipziger Wirtschaftsregion 1945–1948. Von den Leipziger "sächsichen Industriefamilien" zu Kadern aus dem Leipziger Arbeitermilieu', *Comparativ*, 5 (4) (1995), 112–23.

Schulze, R., 'Region – Industrialisation – Structural Change: A Regional Approach to Problems of Socio-Economic Change', in R. Schulze, ed., *Industrieregion im Umbruch. Historische Voraussetzungen und Verlaufsmuster des regionalen Strukturwandels im europäischen Vergleich, Essen*, 1993, 40–63.

Schumann, H.-G., *Nationalsozialismus und Gewerkschaftsbewegung. Die Vernichtung der deutschen Gewerkschaften und der Aufbau der 'Deutschen Arbeitsfront'*, Hanover, 1958.

Schwarzbach, H., 'Die Differenzen zwischen dem Verband Sächsischer Industrieller und dem Reichsverband der Deutschen Industrie 1931', *Jahrbuch für Wirtschaftsgeschichte*, 12 (3) (1971), 75–93.

Seidel, J., 'Leipziger Maifeiern, Gewerkschafts- und Arbeitervereinsfeste im letzten Jahrzehnt des 19. Jahrhunderts', in K. Keller, ed., *Feste und Feiern. Zum Wandel städtischer Festkultur in Leipzig*, Leipzig, 1994, 179–95.

Siewert, H.-J., 'Zur Thematisierung des Vereinswesens in der deutschen Soziologie', in O. Dann, ed., *Vereinswesen und bürgerliche Gesellschaft in Deutschland, Historische Zeitschrift*, Beiheft 9, Munich, 1984, 151–80.

Sontheimer, K., *Antidemokratisches Denken in der Weimarer Republik. Die politischen Ideen des deutschen Nationalismus zwischen 1918 und 1933*, Munich, 1962.

Stachura, P.D., *Gregor Straßer and the Rise of Nazism*, London, 1983.

Stachura, P.D., *Nazi Youth in the Weimar Republic*, Oxford, 1975.

Staude, F., 'Sachsen im preußisch-deutschen Reich (1871–1917/18)', *Sächsische Heimatblätter*, 30 (1984), 123–37.

Stephenson, J., 'National Socialism and Women before 1933', in P. Stachura, ed., *The Nazi Machtergreifung*, London, 1982, 33–48.

Stephenson, J., *The Nazi Organisation of Women*, London, 1980.

Stiftung Sächsische Gedenkstätten zur Erinnerung an die Opfer politischer Gewaltherrschaft, ed., *Spuren Suchen und Erinnern. Gedenkstätten für die Opfer politischer Gewaltherrschaft in Sachsen*, Leipzig, 1996.

Stockhorst, E., *5000 Köpfe. Wer war was im Dritten Reich*, Bruchsal, 1967.

Szejnmann, C.-C.W., 'Review Article: The Missing Pieces are "Coming Home": Nazism in Central Germany', *German History*, 15 (3) (1997), 395–410.

Szejnmann, C.-C.W., 'Sächsische Unternehmer und die Weimarer Demokratie. Zur Rolle der sächsischen Unternehmer in der Zeit der Weltwirtschaftskrise und des Aufstiegs des Nationalsozialismus', in U. Hess and M. Schäfer, eds., *Unternehmer in Sachsen. Aufstieg – Krise – Untergang – Neubeginn*, Leipzig, 1998, 165–179.

Szejnmann, C.-C.W., 'The Rise of the Nazis in the Working-Class Milieu of Saxony', in C.J. Fischer, ed., *The Rise of National Socialism and the Working Classes in Weimar Germany*, Oxford, 1996, 189–216.

Tenfelde, K., 'Die Entfaltung des Vereinswesens während der Industriellen Revolution in Deutschland (1850–1873), in O. Dann, ed., *Vereinswesen und bürgerliche Gesellschaft in Deutschland, Historische Zeitschrift*, Beiheft 9, Munich, 1984, 55–114.

Theweleit, K., *Männer Phantasien. Band 1: Frauen, Fluten, Körper, Geschichte. Band 2: Männerkörper – Zur Psychoanalyse des weißen Terrors*, Frankfurt, 1977.

Thomsen, R.S., *Danish Elections 1920–1979. A Logit Approach to Ecological Analysis and Inference*, Arhus, 1987.

Tracey, D., 'Reform in the Early Weimar Republic: The Thuringian Example'. *Journal of Modern History*, 44 (2) (1972), 195–212.

Tracey, D.R., 'The Development of the National Socialist Party in Thuringia, 1924–1930', *Central European History*, 8 (1) (1975), 23–50.

Tyrell, A., *Führer befiehl ... Selbstzeugnisse aus der 'Kampfzeit' der NSDAP*, repr. Leipzig, 1991.

Ulbricht, J.H., 'Kulturrevolution von rechts. Das völkische Netzwerk 1900–1930', in D. Heiden and G. Mai, eds., *Nationalsozialismus in Thüringen*, Weimar, 1995, 29–48.

Unger, M., 'Die Leipziger Sondergerichtsakten 1940–1945 und der Volkswiderstand in Westsachsen', in H.-D. Schmid, ed., *Zwei Städte unter dem Hakenkreuz. Widerstand und Verweigerung in Hannover und Leipzig 1933–1945*, Leipzig, 1994, 178–97.

Usborne, C., *The Politics of the Body in Weimar Germany. Women's Reproductive Rights and Duties*, London, 1992.

Venus, E., *Amtshauptmann in Sachsen. Lebenserinnerungen des letzten Dresdener Amtshauptmanns und Landrats*, Reutlingen, 1970.

Walter, F., 'Analyse von regionalen Teilkulturen im Zerfall – das Beispiel Sachsen. Göttinger Antwort auf Bochumer Kritik, in PVS 34 (1993), S. 92–97', *Politische Vierteljahresschrift*, 34 (4) (1993), 674–80.

Walter, F., 'Freital: Das "Rote Wien Sachsens" ', in F. Walter, T. Dürr and K. Schmidke, eds., *Die SPD in Sachsen und Thüringen zwischen Hochburg und Diaspora*, Bonn, 1993, 39–181.

Walter, F., 'Sachsen – Ein Stammland der Sozialdemokratie', *Politische Vierteljahresschrift*, 32 (2) (1991), 207–231.

Walter, F. 'Sachsen und Thüringen: Von Mutterländern der Arbeiterbewegung zu Sorgenkindern der SPD. Einführung und Überblick', in F. Walter, T. Dürr and K. Schmidke, eds., *Die SPD in Sachsen und Thüringen zwischen Hochburg und Diaspora*, Bonn, 1993, 11–38.

Walter, F., 'Thüringen – Einst Hochburg der Sozialistischen Arbeiterbewegung?', *Internationale Wissenschaftliche Korrespondenz zur Geschichte der Arbeiterbewegung,* 28 (1) (1992), 21–39.

Weber, D., 'Erwerbstätigkeit von Frauen in der SBZ (1945–1949). Befunde aus Erfurt und Leipzig', in W. Bramke W. and U. Heß, eds., *Sachsen und Mitteldeutschland. Politische, wirtschaftliche und soziale Wandlungen im 20. Jahrhundert*, Weimar, 1995, 359–378.

Weindling, P., *Health, Race and German Politics between National Unification and Nazism 1870–1945*, Cambridge, 1989.

Willems, S., 'Widerstand aus Glauben. Lothar Kreyssig und die Euthanasieverbrechen', in D. Eichholtz, ed., *Brandenburg in der NS-Zeit*, Berlin, 1993, 383–410.

Winkler, H.A., *Der Weg in die Katastrophe. Arbeiter und Arbeiterbewegung in der Weimarer Republik 1930 bis 1933*, Bonn, 1990.

Winkler, H.A., *Mittelstand, Demokratie und Nationalsozialismus. Die politische Entwicklung von Handwerk und Kleinhandel in der Weimarer Republik*, Cologne, 1972.

Winkler, H.A., *Von der Revolution zur Stabilisierung. Arbeiter und Arbeiterbewegung in der Weimarer Republik 1918 bis 1924*, Berlin, 1985.

Woods, R., *The Conservative Revolution in the Weimar Republic*, London, 1996.

Index